Jason Brownlee

Clever Algorithms

Nature-Inspired Programming Recipes

Jason Brownlee, PhD

Jason Brownlee studied Applied Science at Swinburne University in Melbourne, Australia, going on to complete a Masters in Information Technology focusing on Niching Genetic Algorithms, and a PhD in the field of Artificial Immune Systems. Jason has worked for a number of years as a Consultant and Software Engineer for a range of Corporate and Government organizations. When not writing books, Jason likes to compete in Machine Learning competitions.

Cover Image

Clever Algorithms: Nature-Inspired Programming Recipes

First Edition. LuLu. January 2011
ISBN: 978-1-4467-8506-5

Webpage

Source code and additional resources can be downloaded from the books companion website online at http://www.CleverAlgorithms.com

Contents

Foreword

I am delighted to write this foreword. This book, a reference where one can look up the details of most any algorithm to find a clear unambiguous description, has long been needed and here it finally is. A concise reference that has taken many hours to write but which has the capacity to save vast amounts of time previously spent digging out original papers.

I have known the author for several years and have had experience of his amazing capacity for work and the sheer quality of his output, so this book comes as no surprise to me. But I hope it will be a surprise and delight to you, the reader for whom it has been written.

But useful as this book is, it is only a beginning. There are so many algorithms that no one author could hope to cover them all. So if you know of an algorithm that is not yet here, how about contributing it using the same clear and lucid style?

Professor Tim Hendtlass
Complex Intelligent Systems Laboratory
Faculty of Information and Communication Technologies
Swinburne University of Technology

Melbourne, Australia
2010

Preface

About the book

The need for this project was born of frustration while working towards my PhD. I was investigating optimization algorithms and was implementing a large number of them for a software platform called the Optimization Algorithm Toolkit (OAT)[1]. Each algorithm required considerable effort to locate the relevant source material (from books, papers, articles, and existing implementations), decipher and interpret the technique, and finally attempt to piece together a working implementation.

Taking a broader perspective, I realized that the communication of algorithmic techniques in the field of Artificial Intelligence was clearly a difficult and outstanding open problem. Generally, algorithm descriptions are:

- *Incomplete*: many techniques are ambiguously described, partially described, or not described at all.

- *Inconsistent*: a given technique may be described using a variety of formal and semi-formal methods that vary across different techniques, limiting the transferability of background skills an audience requires to read a technique (such as mathematics, pseudocode, program code, and narratives). An inconsistent representation for techniques means that the skills used to understand and internalize one technique may not be transferable to realizing different techniques or even extensions of the same technique.

- *Distributed*: the description of data structures, operations, and parameterization of a given technique may span a collection of papers, articles, books, and source code published over a number of years, the access to which may be restricted and difficult to obtain.

For the practitioner, a badly described algorithm may be simply frustrating, where the gaps in available information are filled with intuition and

---

[1] OAT located at http://optalgtoolkit.sourceforge.net

'best guess'. At the other end of the spectrum, a badly described algorithm may be an example of bad science and the failure of the scientific method, where the inability to understand and implement a technique may prevent the replication of results, the application, or the investigation and extension of a technique.

The software I produced provided a first step solution to this problem: a set of working algorithms implemented in a (somewhat) consistent way and downloaded from a single location (features likely provided by any library of artificial intelligence techniques). The next logical step needed to address this problem is to develop a methodology that anybody can follow. The strategy to address the open problem of poor algorithm communication is to present complete algorithm descriptions (rather than just implementations) in a consistent manner, and in a centralized location. This book is the outcome of developing such a strategy that not only provides a methodology for standardized algorithm descriptions, but provides a large corpus of complete and consistent algorithm descriptions in a single centralized location.

The algorithms described in this work are practical, interesting, and fun, and the goal of this project was to promote these features by making algorithms from the field more accessible, usable, and understandable. This project was developed over a number years through a lot of writing, discussion, and revision. This book has been released under a permissive license that encourages the reader to explore new and creative ways of further communicating its message and content.

I hope that this project has succeeded in some small way and that you too can enjoy applying, learning, and playing with Clever Algorithms.

Jason Brownlee

Melbourne, Australia
2011

Acknowledgments

This book could not have been completed without the commitment, passion, and hard work from a large group of editors and supporters.

A special thanks to Steve Dower for his incredible attention to detail in providing technical and copy edits for large portions of this book, and for his enthusiasm for the subject area. Also, a special thanks to Daniel Angus for the discussions around the genesis of the project, his continued support with the idea of an 'algorithms atlas' and for his attention to detail in providing technical and copy edits for key chapters.

In no particular order, thanks to: Juan Ojeda, Martin Goddard, David Howden, Sean Luke, David Zappia, Jeremy Wazny, and Andrew Murray.

Thanks to the hundreds of machine learning enthusiasts who voted on potential covers and helped shape what this book became. You know who you are!

Finally, I would like to thank my beautiful wife Ying Liu for her unrelenting support and patience throughout the project.

Part I

Background

Chapter 1

Introduction

Welcome to Clever Algorithms! This is a handbook of recipes for computational problem solving techniques from the fields of Computational Intelligence, Biologically Inspired Computation, and Metaheuristics. Clever Algorithms are interesting, practical, and fun to learn about and implement. Research scientists may be interested in browsing algorithm inspirations in search of an interesting system or process analogs to investigate. Developers and software engineers may compare various problem solving algorithms and technique-specific guidelines. Practitioners, students, and interested amateurs may implement state-of-the-art algorithms to address business or scientific needs, or simply play with the fascinating systems they represent.

This introductory chapter provides relevant background information on Artificial Intelligence and Algorithms. The core of the book provides a large corpus of algorithms presented in a complete and consistent manner. The final chapter covers some advanced topics to consider once a number of algorithms have been mastered. This book has been designed as a reference text, where specific techniques are looked up, or where the algorithms across whole fields of study can be browsed, rather than being read cover-to-cover. This book is an algorithm handbook and a technique guidebook, and I hope you find something useful.

1.1 What is AI

1.1.1 Artificial Intelligence

The field of classical *Artificial Intelligence* (AI) coalesced in the 1950s drawing on an understanding of the brain from neuroscience, the new mathematics of information theory, control theory referred to as cybernetics, and the dawn of the digital computer. AI is a cross-disciplinary field of research that is generally concerned with developing and investigating systems that operate or act intelligently. It is considered a discipline in the field of computer science given the strong focus on computation.

Russell and Norvig provide a perspective that defines Artificial Intelligence in four categories: 1) systems that think like humans, 2) systems that act like humans, 3) systems that think rationally, 4) systems that act rationally [43]. In their definition, acting like a human suggests that a system can do some specific things humans can do, this includes fields such as the Turing test, natural language processing, automated reasoning, knowledge representation, machine learning, computer vision, and robotics. Thinking like a human suggests systems that model the cognitive information processing properties of humans, for example a general problem solver and systems that build internal models of their world. Thinking rationally suggests laws of rationalism and structured thought, such as syllogisms and formal logic. Finally, acting rationally suggests systems that do rational things such as expected utility maximization and rational agents.

Luger and Stubblefield suggest that AI is a sub-field of computer science concerned with the automation of intelligence, and like other sub-fields of computer science has both theoretical concerns (*how and why do the systems work?*) and application concerns (*where and when can the systems be used?*) [34]. They suggest a strong empirical focus to research, because although there may be a strong desire for mathematical analysis, the systems themselves defy analysis given their complexity. The machines and software investigated in AI are not black boxes, rather analysis proceeds by observing the systems interactions with their environments, followed by an internal assessment of the system to relate its structure back to its behavior.

Artificial Intelligence is therefore concerned with investigating mechanisms that underlie intelligence and intelligence behavior. The traditional approach toward designing and investigating AI (the so-called 'good old fashioned' AI) has been to employ a symbolic basis for these mechanisms. A newer approach historically referred to as scruffy artificial intelligence or soft computing does not necessarily use a symbolic basis, instead patterning these mechanisms after biological or natural processes. This represents a modern paradigm shift in interest from symbolic knowledge representations, to inference strategies for adaptation and learning, and has been referred to as neat versus scruffy approaches to AI. The neat philosophy is concerned with formal symbolic models of intelligence that can explain *why* they work, whereas the scruffy philosophy is concerned with intelligent strategies that explain *how* they work [44].

Neat AI

The traditional stream of AI concerns a top down perspective of problem solving, generally involving symbolic representations and logic processes that most importantly can explain why the systems work. The successes of this prescriptive stream include a multitude of specialist approaches such as rule-based expert systems, automatic theorem provers, and operations research techniques that underly modern planning and scheduling software. Although traditional approaches have resulted in significant success they have their limits, most notably scalability. Increases in problem size result in an unmanageable increase in the complexity of such problems meaning that although traditional techniques can guarantee an optimal, precise, or true solution, the computational execution time or computing memory required can be intractable.

Scruffy AI

There have been a number of thrusts in the field of AI toward less crisp techniques that are able to locate approximate, imprecise, or partially-true solutions to problems with a reasonable cost of resources. Such approaches are typically *descriptive* rather than *prescriptive*, describing a process for achieving a solution (how), but not explaining why they work (like the neater approaches).

Scruffy AI approaches are defined as relatively simple procedures that result in complex emergent and self-organizing behavior that can defy traditional reductionist analyses, the effects of which can be exploited for quickly locating approximate solutions to intractable problems. A common characteristic of such techniques is the incorporation of randomness in their processes resulting in robust probabilistic and stochastic decision making contrasted to the sometimes more fragile determinism of the crisp approaches. Another important common attribute is the adoption of an inductive rather than deductive approach to problem solving, generalizing solutions or decisions from sets of specific observations made by the system.

1.1.2 Natural Computation

An important perspective on scruffy Artificial Intelligence is the motivation and inspiration for the core information processing strategy of a given technique. Computers can only do what they are instructed, therefore a consideration is to distill information processing from other fields of study, such as the physical world and biology. The study of biologically motivated computation is called Biologically Inspired Computing [16], and is one of three related fields of Natural Computing [22, 23, 39]. Natural Computing is an interdisciplinary field concerned with the relationship of computation and biology, which in addition to Biologically Inspired Computing is also comprised of Computationally Motivated Biology and Computing with Biology [36, 40].

Biologically Inspired Computation

Biologically Inspired Computation is computation inspired by biological metaphor, also referred to as *Biomimicry*, and *Biomemetics* in other engineering disciplines [6, 17]. The intent of this field is to devise mathematical and engineering tools to generate solutions to computation problems. The field involves using procedures for finding solutions abstracted from the natural world for addressing computationally phrased problems.

Computationally Motivated Biology

Computationally Motivated Biology involves investigating biology using computers. The intent of this area is to use information sciences and simulation to model biological systems in digital computers with the aim to replicate and better understand behaviors in biological systems. The field facilitates the ability to better understand life-as-it-is and investigate life-as-it-could-be. Typically, work in this sub-field is not concerned with the construction of mathematical and engineering tools, rather it is focused on simulating natural phenomena. Common examples include Artificial Life, Fractal Geometry (L-systems, Iterative Function Systems, Particle Systems, Brownian motion), and Cellular Automata. A related field is that of Computational Biology generally concerned with modeling biological systems and the application of statistical methods such as in the sub-field of Bioinformatics.

Computation with Biology

Computation with Biology is the investigation of substrates other than silicon in which to implement computation [1]. Common examples include molecular or DNA Computing and Quantum Computing.

1.1.3   Computational Intelligence

Computational Intelligence is a modern name for the sub-field of AI concerned with sub-symbolic (also called messy, scruffy, and soft) techniques. Computational Intelligence describes techniques that focus on *strategy* and *outcome*. The field broadly covers sub-disciplines that focus on adaptive and intelligence systems, not limited to: Evolutionary Computation, Swarm Intelligence (Particle Swarm and Ant Colony Optimization), Fuzzy Systems, Artificial Immune Systems, and Artificial Neural Networks [20, 41]. This section provides a brief summary of the each of the five primary areas of study.

Evolutionary Computation

A paradigm that is concerned with the investigation of systems inspired by the neo-Darwinian theory of evolution by means of natural selection (natural selection theory and an understanding of genetics). Popular evolutionary algorithms include the Genetic Algorithm, Evolution Strategy, Genetic and Evolutionary Programming, and Differential Evolution [4, 5]. The evolutionary process is considered an adaptive strategy and is typically applied to search and optimization domains [26, 28].

Swarm Intelligence

A paradigm that considers collective intelligence as a behavior that emerges through the interaction and cooperation of large numbers of lesser intelligent agents. The paradigm consists of two dominant sub-fields 1) Ant Colony Optimization that investigates probabilistic algorithms inspired by the foraging behavior of ants [10, 18], and 2) Particle Swarm Optimization that investigates probabilistic algorithms inspired by the flocking and foraging behavior of birds and fish [30]. Like evolutionary computation, swarm intelligence-based techniques are considered adaptive strategies and are typically applied to search and optimization domains.

Artificial Neural Networks

Neural Networks are a paradigm that is concerned with the investigation of architectures and learning strategies inspired by the modeling of neurons in the brain [8]. Learning strategies are typically divided into supervised and unsupervised which manage environmental feedback in different ways. Neural network learning processes are considered adaptive learning and are typically applied to function approximation and pattern recognition domains.

Fuzzy Intelligence

Fuzzy Intelligence is a paradigm that is concerned with the investigation of fuzzy logic, which is a form of logic that is not constrained to true and false determinations like propositional logic, but rather functions which define approximate truth, or degrees of truth [52]. Fuzzy logic and fuzzy systems are a logic system used as a reasoning strategy and are typically applied to expert system and control system domains.

Artificial Immune Systems

A collection of approaches inspired by the structure and function of the acquired immune system of vertebrates. Popular approaches include clonal selection, negative selection, the dendritic cell algorithm, and immune network algorithms. The immune-inspired adaptive processes vary in strategy and show similarities to the fields of Evolutionary Computation and Artificial Neural Networks, and are typically used for optimization and pattern recognition domains [15].

1.1.4   Metaheuristics

Another popular name for the strategy-outcome perspective of scruffy AI is *metaheuristics*. In this context, heuristic is an algorithm that locates 'good enough' solutions to a problem without concern for whether the solution can be proven to be correct or optimal [37]. Heuristic methods trade-off concerns such as precision, quality, and accuracy in favor of computational effort (space and time efficiency). The greedy search procedure that only takes cost-improving steps is an example of heuristic method.

Like heuristics, metaheuristics may be considered a general algorithmic framework that can be applied to different optimization problems with relative few modifications to adapt them to a specific problem [25, 46]. The difference is that metaheuristics are intended to extend the capabilities of heuristics by combining one or more heuristic methods (referred to as procedures) using a higher-level strategy (hence 'meta'). A procedure in a metaheuristic is considered black-box in that little (if any) prior knowledge is known about it by the metaheuristic, and as such it may be replaced with a different procedure. Procedures may be as simple as the manipulation of a representation, or as complex as another complete metaheuristic. Some examples of metaheuristics include iterated local search, tabu search, the genetic algorithm, ant colony optimization, and simulated annealing.

Blum and Roli outline nine properties of metaheuristics [9], as follows:

- Metaheuristics are strategies that "guide" the search process.

- The goal is to efficiently explore the search space in order to find (near-)optimal solutions.

- Techniques which constitute metaheuristic algorithms range from simple local search procedures to complex learning processes.

- Metaheuristic algorithms are approximate and usually non-deterministic.

- They may incorporate mechanisms to avoid getting trapped in confined areas of the search space.

- The basic concepts of metaheuristics permit an abstract level description.

- Metaheuristics are not problem-specific.

- Metaheuristics may make use of domain-specific knowledge in the form of heuristics that are controlled by the upper level strategy.

- Todays more advanced metaheuristics use search experience (embodied in some form of memory) to guide the search.

Hyperheuristics are yet another extension that focuses on heuristics that modify their parameters (online or offline) to improve the efficacy of solution, or the efficiency of the computation. Hyperheuristics provide high-level strategies that may employ machine learning and adapt their search behavior by modifying the application of the sub-procedures or even which procedures are used (operating on the space of heuristics which in turn operate within the problem domain) [12, 13].

1.1.5 Clever Algorithms

This book is concerned with 'clever algorithms', which are algorithms drawn from many sub-fields of artificial intelligence not limited to the scruffy fields of biologically inspired computation, computational intelligence and metaheuristics. The term *'clever algorithms'* is intended to unify a collection of interesting and useful computational tools under a consistent and accessible banner. An alternative name (*Inspired Algorithms*) was considered, although ultimately rejected given that not all of the algorithms to be described in the project have an inspiration (specifically a biological or physical inspiration) for their computational strategy. The set of algorithms described in this book may generally be referred to as 'unconventional optimization algorithms' (for example, see [14]), as optimization is the main form of computation provided by the listed approaches. A technically more appropriate name for these approaches is stochastic global optimization (for example, see [49] and [35]).

Algorithms were selected in order to provide a rich and interesting coverage of the fields of Biologically Inspired Computation, Metaheuristics and Computational Intelligence. Rather than a coverage of just the state-of-the-art and popular methods, the algorithms presented also include historic and newly described methods. The final selection was designed to provoke curiosity and encourage exploration and a wider view of the field.

1.2 Problem Domains

Algorithms from the fields of Computational Intelligence, Biologically Inspired Computing, and Metaheuristics are applied to difficult problems, to which more traditional approaches may not be suited. Michalewicz and Fogel propose five reasons why problems may be difficult [37] (page 11):

- The number of possible solutions in the search space is so large as to forbid an exhaustive search for the best answer.

- The problem is so complicated, that just to facilitate any answer at all, we have to use such simplified models of the problem that any result is essentially useless.

- The evaluation function that describes the quality of any proposed solution is noisy or varies with time, thereby requiring not just a single solution but an entire series of solutions.

- The possible solutions are so heavily constrained that constructing even one feasible answer is difficult, let alone searching for an optimal solution.

- The person solving the problem is inadequately prepared or imagines some psychological barrier that prevents them from discovering a solution.

This section introduces two problem formalisms that embody many of the most difficult problems faced by Artificial and Computational Intelligence. They are: Function Optimization and Function Approximation. Each class of problem is described in terms of its general properties, a formalism, and a set of specialized sub-problems. These problem classes provide a tangible framing of the algorithmic techniques described throughout the work.

1.2.1   Function Optimization

Real-world optimization problems and generalizations thereof can be drawn from most fields of science, engineering, and information technology (for a sample [2, 48]). Importantly, function optimization problems have had a long tradition in the fields of Artificial Intelligence in motivating basic research into new problem solving techniques, and for investigating and verifying systemic behavior against benchmark problem instances.

Problem Description

Mathematically, optimization is defined as the search for a combination of parameters commonly referred to as decision variables ($x = \{x_1, x_2, x_3, \ldots x_n\}$) which minimize or maximize some ordinal quantity (c) (typically a scalar called a score or cost) assigned by an objective function or cost function (f), under a set of constraints ($g = \{g_1, g_2, g_3, \ldots g_n\}$). For example, a general minimization case would be as follows: $f(x') \leq f(x), \forall x_i \in x$. Constraints may provide boundaries on decision variables (for example in a real-value hypercube $\Re^n$), or may generally define regions of feasibility and in-feasibility in the decision variable space. In applied mathematics the field may be referred to as Mathematical Programming. More generally the field may be referred to as Global or Function Optimization given the focus on the objective function. For more general information on optimization refer to Horst et al. [29].

Sub-Fields of Study

The study of optimization is comprised of many specialized sub-fields, based on an overlapping taxonomy that focuses on the principle concerns in the general formalism. For example, with regard to the decision variables, one may consider univariate and multivariate optimization problems. The type of decision variables promotes specialities for continuous, discrete, and permutations of variables. Dependencies between decision variables under a cost function define the fields of Linear Programming, Quadratic Programming, and Nonlinear Programming. A large class of optimization problems can be reduced to discrete sets and are considered in the field of Combinatorial Optimization, to which many theoretical properties are known, most importantly that many interesting and relevant problems cannot be solved by an approach with polynomial time complexity (so-called NP, for example see Papadimitriou and Steiglitz [38]).

THe evaluation of variables against a cost function, collectively may be considered a response surface. The shape of such a response surface may be convex, which is a class of functions to which many important theoretical findings have been made, not limited to the fact that location of the local optimal configuration also means the global optimal configuration of decision variables has been located [11]. Many interesting and real-world optimization problems produce cost surfaces that are non-convex or so called multi-modal[1] (rather than unimodal) suggesting that there are multiple peaks and valleys. Further, many real-world optimization problems with continuous decision variables cannot be differentiated given their complexity or limited information availability, meaning that derivative-based gradient decent methods (that are well understood) are not applicable, necessitating the use of so-called 'direct search' (sample or pattern-based) methods [33]. Real-world objective function evaluation may be noisy, discontinuous, and/or dynamic, and the constraints of real-world problem solving may require an approximate solution in limited time or using resources, motivating the need for heuristic approaches.

1.2.2 Function Approximation

Real-world Function Approximation problems are among the most computationally difficult considered in the broader field of Artificial Intelligence for reasons including: incomplete information, high-dimensionality, noise in the sample observations, and non-linearities in the target function. This section considers the Function Approximation formalism and related specialization's as a general motivating problem to contrast and compare with Function Optimization.

---

[1] Taken from statistics referring to the centers of mass in distributions, although in optimization it refers to 'regions of interest' in the search space, in particular valleys in minimization, and peaks in maximization cost surfaces.

Problem Description

Function Approximation is the problem of finding a function (f) that approximates a target function (g), where typically the approximated function is selected based on a sample of observations (x, also referred to as the training set) taken from the unknown target function. In machine learning, the function approximation formalism is used to describe general problem types commonly referred to as pattern recognition, such as classification, clustering, and curve fitting (called a decision or discrimination function). Such general problem types are described in terms of approximating an unknown Probability Density Function (PDF), which underlies the relationships in the problem space, and is represented in the sample data. This perspective of such problems is commonly referred to as statistical machine learning and/or density estimation [8, 24].

Sub-Fields of Study

The function approximation formalism can be used to phrase some of the hardest problems faced by Computer Science, and Artificial Intelligence in particular, such as natural language processing and computer vision. The general process focuses on 1) the collection and preparation of the observations from the target function, 2) the selection and/or preparation of a model of the target function, and 3) the application and ongoing refinement of the prepared model. Some important problem-based sub-fields include:

- *Feature Selection* where a feature is considered an aggregation of one-or-more attributes, where only those features that have meaning in the context of the target function are necessary to the modeling function [27, 32].

- *Classification* where observations are inherently organized into labelled groups (classes) and a supervised process models an underlying discrimination function to classify unobserved samples.

- *Clustering* where observations may be organized into groups based on underlying common features, although the groups are unlabeled requiring a process to model an underlying discrimination function without corrective feedback.

- *Curve or Surface Fitting* where a model is prepared that provides a 'best-fit' (called a regression) for a set of observations that may be used for interpolation over known observations and extrapolation for observations outside what has been modeled.

The field of Function Optimization is related to Function Approximation, as many-sub-problems of Function Approximation may be defined as optimization problems. Many of the technique paradigms used for function approximation are differentiated based on the representation and the optimization process used to minimize error or maximize effectiveness on a given approximation problem. The difficulty of Function Approximation problems centre around 1) the nature of the unknown relationships between attributes and features, 2) the number (dimensionality) of attributes and features, and 3) general concerns of noise in such relationships and the dynamic availability of samples from the target function. Additional difficulties include the incorporation of prior knowledge (such as imbalance in samples, incomplete information and the variable reliability of data), and problems of invariant features (such as transformation, translation, rotation, scaling, and skewing of features).

1.3 Unconventional Optimization

Not all algorithms described in this book are for optimization, although those that are may be referred to as 'unconventional' to differentiate them from the more traditional approaches. Examples of traditional approaches include (but are not not limited) mathematical optimization algorithms (such as Newton's method and Gradient Descent that use derivatives to locate a local minimum) and direct search methods (such as the Simplex method and the Nelder-Mead method that use a search pattern to locate optima). Unconventional optimization algorithms are designed for the more difficult problem instances, the attributes of which were introduced in Section 1.2.1. This section introduces some common attributes of this class of algorithm.

1.3.1 Black Box Algorithms

Black Box optimization algorithms are those that exploit little, if any, information from a problem domain in order to devise a solution. They are generalized problem solving procedures that may be applied to a range of problems with very little modification [19]. Domain specific knowledge refers to known relationships between solution representations and the objective cost function. Generally speaking, the less domain specific information incorporated into a technique, the more flexible the technique, although the less efficient it will be for a given problem. For example, 'random search' is the most general black box approach and is also the most flexible requiring only the generation of random solutions for a given problem. Random search allows resampling of the domain which gives it a worst case behavior that is worse than enumerating the entire search domain. In practice, the more prior knowledge available about a problem, the more information that can be exploited by a technique in order to efficiently locate a solution for the problem, heuristically or otherwise. Therefore, black box methods are those methods suitable for those problems where little information from the problem domain is available to be used by a problem solving approach.

1.3.2   No-Free-Lunch

The *No-Free-Lunch Theorem* of search and optimization by Wolpert and Macready proposes that all black box optimization algorithms are the same for searching for the extremum of a cost function when averaged over all possible functions [50, 51]. The theorem has caused a lot of pessimism and misunderstanding, particularly in relation to the evaluation and comparison of Metaheuristic and Computational Intelligence algorithms.

The implication of the theorem is that searching for the 'best' general-purpose black box optimization algorithm is irresponsible as no such procedure is theoretically possible. No-Free-Lunch applies to stochastic and deterministic optimization algorithms as well as to algorithms that learn and adjust their search strategy over time. It is independent of the performance measure used and the representation selected. Wolpert and Macready's original paper was produced at a time when grandiose generalizations were being made as to algorithm, representation, or configuration superiority. The practical impact of the theory is to encourage practitioners to bound claims of applicability for search and optimization algorithms. Wolpert and Macready encouraged effort be put into devising practical problem classes and into the matching of suitable algorithms to problem classes. Further, they compelled practitioners to exploit domain knowledge in optimization algorithm application, which is now an axiom in the field.

1.3.3   Stochastic Optimization

Stochastic optimization algorithms are those that use randomness to elicit non-deterministic behaviors, contrasted to purely deterministic procedures. Most algorithms from the fields of Computational Intelligence, Biologically Inspired Computation, and Metaheuristics may be considered to belong the field of Stochastic Optimization. Algorithms that exploit randomness are not random in behavior, rather they sample a problem space in a biased manner, focusing on areas of interest and neglecting less interesting areas [45]. A class of techniques that focus on the stochastic sampling of a domain, called Markov Chain Monte Carlo (MCMC) algorithms, provide good average performance, and generally offer a low chance of the worst case performance. Such approaches are suited to problems with many coupled degrees of freedom, for example large, high-dimensional spaces. MCMC approaches involve stochastically sampling from a target distribution function similar to Monte Carlo simulation methods using a process that resembles a biased Markov chain.

- *Monte Carlo* methods are used for selecting a statistical sample to approximate a given target probability density function and are traditionally used in statistical physics. Samples are drawn sequentially and the process may include criteria for rejecting samples and biasing the sampling locations within high-dimensional spaces.

- *Markov Chain* processes provide a probabilistic model for state transitions or moves within a discrete domain called a walk or a chain of steps. A Markov system is only dependent on the current position in the domain in order to probabilistically determine the next step in the walk.

MCMC techniques combine these two approaches to solve integration and optimization problems in large dimensional spaces by generating samples while exploring the space using a Markov chain process, rather than sequentially or independently [3]. The step generation is configured to bias sampling in more important regions of the domain. Three examples of MCMC techniques include the Metropolis-Hastings algorithm, Simulated Annealing for global optimization, and the Gibbs sampler which are commonly employed in the fields of physics, chemistry, statistics, and economics.

1.3.4 Inductive Learning

Many unconventional optimization algorithms employ a process that includes the iterative improvement of candidate solutions against an objective cost function. This process of adaptation is generally a method by which the process obtains characteristics that improve the system's (candidate solution) relative performance in an environment (cost function). This adaptive behavior is commonly achieved through a 'selectionist process' of repetition of the steps: generation, test, and selection. The use of non-deterministic processes mean that the sampling of the domain (the generation step) is typically non-parametric, although guided by past experience.

The method of acquiring information is called inductive learning or learning from example, where the approach uses the implicit assumption that specific examples are representative of the broader information content of the environment, specifically with regard to anticipated need. Many unconventional optimization approaches maintain a single candidate solution, a population of samples, or a compression thereof that provides both an instantaneous representation of all of the information acquired by the process, and the basis for generating and making future decisions.

This method of simultaneously acquiring and improving information from the domain and the optimization of decision making (where to direct future effort) is called the k-armed bandit (two-armed and multi-armed bandit) problem from the field of statistical decision making known as game theory [7, 42]. This formalism considers the capability of a strategy to allocate available resources proportional to the future payoff the strategy is expected to receive. The classic example is the 2-armed bandit problem used by Goldberg to describe the behavior of the genetic algorithm [26]. The example involves an agent that learns which one of the two slot machines provides more return by pulling the handle of each (sampling the domain) and biasing future handle pulls proportional to the expected utility, based on the probabilistic experience with the past distribution of the payoff. The formalism may also be used to understand the properties of inductive learning demonstrated by the adaptive behavior of most unconventional optimization algorithms.

The stochastic iterative process of generate and test can be computationally wasteful, potentially re-searching areas of the problem space already searched, and requiring many trials or samples in order to achieve a 'good enough' solution. The limited use of prior knowledge from the domain (black box) coupled with the stochastic sampling process mean that the adapted solutions are created without top-down insight or instruction can sometimes be interesting, innovative, and even competitive with decades of human expertise [31].

1.4   Book Organization

The remainder of this book is organized into two parts: *Algorithms* that describes a large number of techniques in a complete and a consistent manner presented in a rough algorithm groups, and *Extensions* that reviews more advanced topics suitable for when a number of algorithms have been mastered.

1.4.1   Algorithms

Algorithms are presented in six groups or kingdoms distilled from the broader fields of study each in their own chapter, as follows:

- *Stochastic Algorithms* that focuses on the introduction of randomness into heuristic methods (Chapter 2).

- *Evolutionary Algorithms* inspired by evolution by means of natural selection (Chapter 3).

- *Physical Algorithms* inspired by physical and social systems (Chapter 4).

- *Probabilistic Algorithms* that focuses on methods that build models and estimate distributions in search domains (Chapter 5).

- *Swarm Algorithms* that focuses on methods that exploit the properties of collective intelligence (Chapter 6).

- *Immune Algorithms* inspired by the adaptive immune system of vertebrates (Chapter 7).

- *Neural Algorithms* inspired by the plasticity and learning qualities of the human nervous system (Chapter 8).

A given algorithm is more than just a procedure or code listing, each approach is an island of research. The meta-information that define the context of a technique is just as important to understanding and application as abstract recipes and concrete implementations. A standardized algorithm description is adopted to provide a consistent presentation of algorithms with a mixture of softer narrative descriptions, programmatic descriptions both abstract and concrete, and most importantly useful sources for finding out more information about the technique.

The standardized algorithm description template covers the following subjects:

- *Name*: The algorithm name defines the canonical name used to refer to the technique, in addition to common aliases, abbreviations, and acronyms. The name is used as the heading of an algorithm description.

- *Taxonomy*: The algorithm taxonomy defines where a technique fits into the field, both the specific sub-fields of Computational Intelligence and Biologically Inspired Computation as well as the broader field of Artificial Intelligence. The taxonomy also provides a context for determining the relationships between algorithms.

- *Inspiration*: (where appropriate) The inspiration describes the specific system or process that provoked the inception of the algorithm. The inspiring system may non-exclusively be natural, biological, physical, or social. The description of the inspiring system may include relevant domain specific theory, observation, nomenclature, and those salient attributes of the system that are somehow abstractly or conceptually manifest in the technique.

- *Metaphor*: (where appropriate) The metaphor is a description of the technique in the context of the inspiring system or a different suitable system. The features of the technique are made apparent through an analogous description of the features of the inspiring system. The explanation through analogy is not expected to be literal, rather the method is used as an allegorical communication tool. The inspiring system is not explicitly described, this is the role of the 'inspiration' topic, which represents a loose dependency for this topic.

- *Strategy*: The strategy is an abstract description of the computational model. The strategy describes the information processing actions a technique shall take in order to achieve an objective, providing a logical separation between a computational realization (procedure) and an analogous system (mctaphor). A given problem solving strategy may be realized as one of a number of specific algorithms or problem solving systems.

- *Procedure*: The algorithmic procedure summarizes the specifics of realizing a strategy as a systemized and parameterized computation. It outlines how the algorithm is organized in terms of the computation, data structures, and representations.

- *Heuristics*: The heuristics section describes the commonsense, best practice, and demonstrated rules for applying and configuring a parameterized algorithm. The heuristics relate to the technical details of the technique's procedure and data structures for general classes of application (neither specific implementations nor specific problem instances).

- *Code Listing*: The code listing description provides a minimal but functional version of the technique implemented with a programming language. The code description can be typed into a computer and provide a working execution of the technique. The technique implementation also includes a minimal problem instance to which it is applied, and both the problem and algorithm implementations are complete enough to demonstrate the techniques procedure. The description is presented as a programming source code listing with a terse introductory summary.

- *References*: The references section includes a listing of both primary sources of information about the technique as well as useful introductory sources for novices to gain a deeper understanding of the theory and application of the technique. The description consists of hand-selected reference material including books, peer reviewed conference papers, and journal articles.

Source code examples are included in the algorithm descriptions, and the Ruby Programming Language was selected for use throughout the book. Ruby was selected because it supports the procedural programming paradigm, adopted to ensure that examples can be easily ported to object-oriented and other paradigms. Additionally, Ruby is an interpreted language, meaning the code can be directly executed without an introduced compilation step, and it is free to download and use from the Internet.[2] Ruby is concise, expressive, and supports meta-programming features that improve the readability of code examples.

The sample code provides a working version of a given technique for demonstration purposes. Having a tinker with a technique can really bring it to life and provide valuable insight into a method. The sample code is a minimum implementation, providing plenty of opportunity to

---

[2]Ruby can be downloaded for free from http://www.ruby-lang.org

explore, extend and optimize. All of the source code for the algorithms presented in this book is available from the companion website, online at `http://www.CleverAlgorithms.com`. All algorithm implementations were tested with Ruby 1.8.6, 1.8.7 and 1.9.

1.4.2 Extensions

There are some some advanced topics that cannot be meaningfully considered until one has a firm grasp of a number of algorithms, and these are discussed at the back of the book. The Advanced Topics chapter addresses topics such as: the use of alternative programming paradigms when implementing clever algorithms, methodologies used when devising entirely new approaches, strategies to consider when testing clever algorithms, visualizing the behavior and results of algorithms, and comparing algorithms based on the results they produce using statistical methods. Like the background information provided in this chapter, the extensions provide a gentle introduction and starting point into some advanced topics, and references for seeking a deeper understanding.

1.5 How to Read this Book

This book is a reference text that provides a large compendium of algorithm descriptions. It is a trusted handbook of practical computational recipes to be consulted when one is confronted with difficult function optimization and approximation problems. It is also an encompassing guidebook of modern heuristic methods that may be browsed for inspiration, exploration, and general interest.

The audience for this work may be interested in the fields of Computational Intelligence, Biologically Inspired Computation, and Metaheuristics and may count themselves as belonging to one of the following broader groups:

- *Scientists*: Research scientists concerned with theoretically or empirically investigating algorithms, addressing questions such as: *What is the motivating system and strategy for a given technique? What are some algorithms that may be used in a comparison within a given subfield or across subfields?*

- *Engineers*: Programmers and developers concerned with implementing, applying, or maintaining algorithms, addressing questions such as: *What is the procedure for a given technique? What are the best practice heuristics for employing a given technique?*

- *Students*: Undergraduate and graduate students interested in learning about techniques, addressing questions such as: *What are some interesting algorithms to study? How to implement a given approach?*

- *Amateurs*: Practitioners interested in knowing more about algorithms, addressing questions such as: *What classes of techniques exist and what algorithms do they provide? How to conceptualize the computation of a technique?*

1.6   Further Reading

This book is not an introduction to Artificial Intelligence or related sub-fields, nor is it a field guide for a specific class of algorithms. This section provides some pointers to selected books and articles for those readers seeking a deeper understanding of the fields of study to which the Clever Algorithms described in this book belong.

1.6.1   Artificial Intelligence

Artificial Intelligence is large field of study and many excellent texts have been written to introduce the subject. Russell and Novig's *"Artificial Intelligence: A Modern Approach"* is an excellent introductory text providing a broad and deep review of what the field has to offer and is useful for students and practitioners alike [43]. Luger and Stubblefield's *"Artificial Intelligence: Structures and Strategies for Complex Problem Solving"* is also an excellent reference text, providing a more empirical approach to the field [34].

1.6.2   Computational Intelligence

Introductory books for the field of Computational Intelligence generally focus on a handful of specific sub-fields and their techniques. Engelbrecht's *"Computational Intelligence: An Introduction"* provides a modern and detailed introduction to the field covering classic subjects such as Evolutionary Computation and Artificial Neural Networks, as well as more recent techniques such as Swarm Intelligence and Artificial Immune Systems [20]. Pedrycz's slightly more dated *"Computational Intelligence: An Introduction"* also provides a solid coverage of the core of the field with some deeper insights into fuzzy logic and fuzzy systems [41].

1.6.3   Biologically Inspired Computation

Computational methods inspired by natural and biologically systems represent a large portion of the algorithms described in this book. The collection of articles published in de Castro and Von Zuben's *"Recent Developments in Biologically Inspired Computing"* provides an overview of the state of the field, and the introductory chapter on need for such methods does an excellent job to motivate the field of study [17]. Forbes's *"Imitation of Life:*

How Biology Is Inspiring Computing" sets the scene for Natural Computing and the interrelated disciplines, of which Biologically Inspired Computing is but one useful example [22]. Finally, Benyus's *"Biomimicry: Innovation Inspired by Nature"* provides a good introduction into the broader related field of a new frontier in science and technology that involves building systems inspired by an understanding of the biological world [6].

1.6.4 Metaheuristics

The field of Metaheuristics was initially constrained to heuristics for applying classical optimization procedures, although has expanded to encompass a broader and diverse set of techniques. Michalewicz and Fogel's *"How to Solve It: Modern Heuristics"* provides a practical tour of heuristic methods with a consistent set of worked examples [37]. Glover and Kochenberger's *"Handbook of Metaheuristics"* provides a solid introduction into a broad collection of techniques and their capabilities [25].

1.6.5 The Ruby Programming Language

The Ruby Programming Language is a multi-paradigm dynamic language that appeared in approximately 1995. Its meta-programming capabilities coupled with concise and readable syntax have made it a popular language of choice for web development, scripting, and application development. The classic reference text for the language is Thomas, Fowler, and Hunt's *"Programming Ruby: The Pragmatic Programmers' Guide"* referred to as the 'pickaxe book' because of the picture of the pickaxe on the cover [47]. An updated edition is available that covers version 1.9 (compared to 1.8 in the cited version) that will work just as well for use as a reference for the examples in this book. Flanagan and Matsumoto's *"The Ruby Programming Language"* also provides a seminal reference text with contributions from Yukihiro Matsumoto, the author of the language [21]. For more information on the Ruby Programming Language, see the quick-start guide in Appendix A.

1.7 Bibliography

[1] S. Aaronson. NP-complete problems and physical reality. *ACM SIGACT News (COLUMN: Complexity theory)*, 36(1):30–52, 2005.

[2] M. M. Ali, C. Storey, and A Törn. Application of stochastic global optimization algorithms to practical problems. *Journal of Optimization Theory and Applications*, 95(3):545–563, 1997.

[3] C. Andrieu, N. de Freitas, A. Doucet, and M. I. Jordan. An introduction to MCMC for machine learning. *Machine Learning*, 50:5–43, 2003.

[4] T. Bäck, D. B. Fogel, and Z. Michalewicz, editors. *Evolutionary Computation 1: Basic Algorithms and Operators.* IoP, 2000.

[5] T. Bäck, D. B. Fogel, and Z. Michalewicz, editors. *Evolutionary Computation 2: Advanced Algorithms and Operations.* IoP, 2000.

[6] J. M. Benyus. *Biomimicry: Innovation Inspired by Nature.* Quill, 1998.

[7] D. Bergemann and J. Valimaki. Bandit problems. Cowles Foundation Discussion Papers 1551, Cowles Foundation, Yale University, January 2006.

[8] C. M. Bishop. *Neural Networks for Pattern Recognition.* Oxford University Press, 1995.

[9] C. Blum and A. Roli. Metaheuristics in combinatorial optimization: Overview and conceptual comparison. *ACM Computing Surveys (CSUR)*, 35(3):268–308, 2003.

[10] E. Bonabeau, M. Dorigo, and G. Theraulaz. *Swarm Intelligence: From Natural to Artificial Systems.* Oxford University Press US, 1999.

[11] S. Boyd and L. Vandenberghe. *Convex Optimization.* Cambridge University Press, 2004.

[12] E. K. Burke, E. Hart, G. Kendall, J. Newall, P. Ross, and S. Schulenburg. *Handbook of Metaheuristics*, chapter Hyper-heuristics: An emerging direction in modern search technology, pages 457–474. Kluwer, 2003.

[13] E. K. Burke, G. Kendall, and E. Soubeiga. A tabu-search hyper-heuristic for timetabling and rostering. *Journal of Heuristics*, 9(6):451–470, 2003.

[14] D. Corne, M. Dorigo, and F. Glover. *New Ideas in Optimization.* McGraw-Hill, 1999.

[15] L. N. de Castro and J. Timmis. *Artificial Immune Systems: A New Computational Intelligence Approach.* Springer, 2002.

[16] L. N. de Castro and F. J. Von Zuben. *Recent developments in biologically inspired computing*, chapter From biologically inspired computing to natural computing. Idea Group, 2005.

[17] L. N. de Castro and F. J. Von Zuben. *Recent developments in biologically inspired computing.* Idea Group Inc, 2005.

[18] M. Dorigo and T. Stützle. *Ant Colony Optimization.* MIT Press, 2004.

[19] S. Droste, T. Jansen, and I. Wegener. Upper and lower bounds for randomized search heuristics in black-box optimization. *Theory of Computing Systems*, 39(4):525–544, 2006.

[20] A. P. Engelbrecht. *Computational Intelligence: An Introduction*. John Wiley and Sons, second edition, 2007.

[21] D. Flanagan and Y. Matsumoto. *The Ruby Programming Language*. O'Reilly Media, 2008.

[22] N. Forbes. Biologically inspired computing. *Computing in Science and Engineering*, 2(6):83–87, 2000.

[23] N. Forbes. *Imitation of Life: How Biology Is Inspiring Computing*. The MIT Press, 2005.

[24] K. Fukunaga. *Introduction to Statistical Pattern Recognition*. Academic Press, 1990.

[25] F. Glover and G. A. Kochenberger. *Handbook of Metaheuristics*. Springer, 2003.

[26] D. E. Goldberg. *Genetic Algorithms in Search, Optimization, and Machine Learning*. Addison-Wesley, 1989.

[27] I. Guyon and A. Elisseeff. An introduction to variable and feature selection. *Journal of Machine Learning Research*, 3:1157–1182, 2003.

[28] J. H. Holland. *Adaptation in natural and artificial systems: An introductory analysis with applications to biology, control, and artificial intelligence*. University of Michigan Press, 1975.

[29] R. Horst, P. M. Pardalos, and N. V. Thoai. *Introduction to Global Optimization*. Kluwer Academic Publishers, 2nd edition, 2000.

[30] J. Kennedy, R. C. Eberhart, and Y. Shi. *Swarm Intelligence*. Morgan Kaufmann, 2001.

[31] J. R. Koza, M. A. Keane, M. J. Streeter, W. Mydlowec, J. Yu, and G. Lanza. *Genetic Programming IV: Routine Human-Competitive Machine Intelligence*. Springer, 2003.

[32] M. Kudo and J. Sklansky. Comparison of algorithms that select features for pattern classifiers. *Pattern Recognition*, 33:25–41, 2000.

[33] R. M. Lewis, V. T., and M. W. Trosset. Direct search methods: then and now. *Journal of Computational and Applied Mathematics*, 124:191–207, 2000.

[34] G. F. Luger and W. A. Stubblefield. *Artificial Intelligence: Structures and Strategies for Complex Problem Solving*. Benjamin/Cummings Pub. Co., second edition, 1993.

[35] S. Luke. *Essentials of Metaheuristics.* Lulu, 2010. available at http://cs.gmu.edu/~sean/book/metaheuristics/.

[36] P. Marrow. Nature-inspired computing technology and applications. *BT Technology Journal,* 18(4):13–23, 2000.

[37] Z. Michalewicz and D. B. Fogel. *How to Solve It: Modern Heuristics.* Springer, 2004.

[38] C. H. Papadimitriou and K. Steiglitz. *Combinatorial Optimization: Algorithms and Complexity.* Courier Dover Publications, 1998.

[39] R. Paton. *Computing With Biological Metaphors,* chapter Introduction to computing with biological metaphors, pages 1–8. Chapman & Hall, 1994.

[40] G. Paŭn. Bio-inspired computing paradigms (natural computing). *Unconventional Programming Paradigms,* 3566:155–160, 2005.

[41] W. Pedrycz. *Computational Intelligence: An Introduction.* CRC Press, 1997.

[42] H. Robbins. Some aspects of the sequential design of experiments. *Bull. Amer. Math. Soc.,* 58:527–535, 1952.

[43] S. Russell and P. Norvig. *Artificial Intelligence: A Modern Approach.* Prentice Hall, third edition, 2009.

[44] A. Sloman. *Evolving Knowledge in Natural Science and Artificial Intelligence,* chapter Must intelligent systems be scruffy? Pitman, 1990.

[45] J. C. Spall. *Introduction to stochastic search and optimization: estimation, simulation, and control.* John Wiley and Sons, 2003.

[46] E. G. Talbi. *Metaheuristics: From Design to Implementation.* John Wiley and Sons, 2009.

[47] D. Thomas, C. Fowler, and A. Hunt. *Programming Ruby: The Pragmatic Programmers' Guide.* Pragmatic Bookshelf, second edition, 2004.

[48] A. Törn, M. M. Ali, and S. Viitanen. Stochastic global optimization: Problem classes and solution techniques. *Journal of Global Optimization,* 14:437–447, 1999.

[49] T. Weise. *Global Optimization Algorithms - Theory and Application.* (Self Published), 2009-06-26 edition, 2007.

[50] D. H. Wolpert and W. G. Macready. No free lunch theorems for search. Technical report, Santa Fe Institute, Sante Fe, NM, USA, 1995.

[51] D. H. Wolpert and W. G. Macready. No free lunch theorems for optimization. *IEEE Transactions on Evolutionary Computation*, 1(67):67–82, 1997.

[52] L. A. Zadeh, G. J. Klir, and B. Yuan. *Fuzzy sets, fuzzy logic, and fuzzy systems: selected papers*. World Scientific, 1996.

Part II

Algorithms

Chapter 2

Stochastic Algorithms

2.1 Overview

This chapter describes Stochastic Algorithms.

2.1.1 Stochastic Optimization

The majority of the algorithms to be described in this book are comprised of probabilistic and stochastic processes. What differentiates the 'stochastic algorithms' in this chapter from the remaining algorithms is the specific lack of 1) an inspiring system, and 2) a metaphorical explanation. Both 'inspiration' and 'metaphor' refer to the descriptive elements in the standardized algorithm description.

These described algorithms are predominately global optimization algorithms and metaheuristics that manage the application of an embedded neighborhood exploring (local) search procedure. As such, with the exception of 'Stochastic Hill Climbing' and 'Random Search' the algorithms may be considered extensions of the multi-start search (also known as multi-restart search). This set of algorithms provide various different strategies by which 'better' and varied starting points can be generated and issued to a neighborhood searching technique for refinement, a process that is repeated with potentially improving or unexplored areas to search.

2.2   Random Search

Random Search, RS, Blind Random Search, Blind Search, Pure Random Search, PRS

2.2.1   Taxonomy

Random search belongs to the fields of Stochastic Optimization and Global Optimization. Random search is a direct search method as it does not require derivatives to search a continuous domain. This base approach is related to techniques that provide small improvements such as Directed Random Search, and Adaptive Random Search (Section 2.3).

2.2.2   Strategy

The strategy of Random Search is to sample solutions from across the entire search space using a uniform probability distribution. Each future sample is independent of the samples that come before it.

2.2.3   Procedure

Algorithm 2.2.1 provides a pseudocode listing of the Random Search Algorithm for minimizing a cost function.

Algorithm 2.2.1: Pseudocode for Random Search.

Input: NumIterations, ProblemSize, SearchSpace
Output: Best

1 Best $\leftarrow \emptyset$;
2 **foreach** $iter_i \in$ NumIterations **do**
3 $\quad$ $candidate_i \leftarrow$ RandomSolution(ProblemSize, SearchSpace);
4 $\quad$ **if** Cost($candidate_i$) < Cost(Best) **then**
5 $\quad\quad$ $\mid$ Best $\leftarrow candidate_i$;
6 $\quad$ **end**
7 **end**
8 **return** Best;

2.2.4   Heuristics

- Random search is minimal in that it only requires a candidate solution construction routine and a candidate solution evaluation routine, both of which may be calibrated using the approach.

- The worst case performance for Random Search for locating the optima is worse than an Enumeration of the search domain, given that Random Search has no memory and can blindly resample.

- Random Search can return a reasonable approximation of the optimal solution within a reasonable time under low problem dimensionality, although the approach does not scale well with problem size (such as the number of dimensions).

- Care must be taken with some problem domains to ensure that random candidate solution construction is unbiased

- The results of a Random Search can be used to seed another search technique, like a local search technique (such as the Hill Climbing algorithm) that can be used to locate the best solution in the neighborhood of the 'good' candidate solution.

2.2.5   Code Listing

Listing 2.1 provides an example of the Random Search Algorithm implemented in the Ruby Programming Language. In the example, the algorithm runs for a fixed number of iterations and returns the best candidate solution discovered. The example problem is an instance of a continuous function optimization that seeks $\min f(x)$ where $f = \sum_{i=1}^{n} x_i^2$, $-5.0 \leq x_i \leq 5.0$ and $n = 2$. The optimal solution for this basin function is $(v_0, \ldots, v_{n-1}) = 0.0$.

```ruby
def objective_function(vector)
  return vector.inject(0) {|sum, x| sum + (x ** 2.0)}
end

def random_vector(minmax)
  return Array.new(minmax.size) do |i|
    minmax[i][0] + ((minmax[i][1] - minmax[i][0]) * rand())
  end
end

def search(search_space, max_iter)
  best = nil
  max_iter.times do |iter|
    candidate = {}
    candidate[:vector] = random_vector(search_space)
    candidate[:cost] = objective_function(candidate[:vector])
    best = candidate if best.nil? or candidate[:cost] < best[:cost]
    puts " > iteration=#{(iter+1)}, best=#{best[:cost]}"
  end
  return best
end

if __FILE__ == $0
  # problem configuration
  problem_size = 2
  search_space = Array.new(problem_size) {|i| [-5, +5]}
```

```
27   # algorithm configuration
28   max_iter = 100
29   # execute the algorithm
30   best = search(search_space, max_iter)
31   puts "Done. Best Solution: c=#{best[:cost]}, v=#{best[:vector].inspect}"
32   end
```

Listing 2.1: Random Search in Ruby

2.2.6 References

Primary Sources

There is no seminal specification of the Random Search algorithm, rather there are discussions of the general approach and related random search methods from the 1950s through to the 1970s. This was around the time that pattern and direct search methods were actively researched. Brooks is credited with the so-called 'pure random search' [1]. Two seminal reviews of 'random search methods' of the time include: Karnopp [2] and prhaps Kul'chitskii [3].

Learn More

For overviews of Random Search Methods see Zhigljavsky [9], Solis and Wets [4], and also White [7] who provide an insightful review article. Spall provides a detailed overview of the field of Stochastic Optimization, including the Random Search method [5] (for example, see Chapter 2). For a shorter introduction by Spall, see [6] (specifically Section 6.2). Also see Zabinsky for another detailed review of the broader field [8].

2.2.7 Bibliography

[1] S. H. Brooks. A discussion of random methods for seeking maxima. *Operations Research*, 6(2):244–251, 1958.

[2] D. C. Karnopp. Random search techniques for optimization problems. *Automatica*, 1(2–3):111–121, 1963.

[3] O. Y. Kul'chitskii. Random-search algorithm for extrema in functional space under conditions of partial uncertainty. *Cybernetics and Systems Analysis*, 12(5):794–801, 1976.

[4] F. J. Solis and J. B. Wets. Minimization by random search techniques. *Mathematics of Operations Research*, 6:19–30, 1981.

[5] J. C. Spall. *Introduction to stochastic search and optimization: estimation, simulation, and control.* John Wiley and Sons, 2003.

[6] J. C. Spall. *Handbook of computational statistics: concepts and methods*, chapter 6. Stochastic Optimization, pages 169–198. Springer, 2004.

[7] R. C. White. A survey of random methods for parameter optimization. *Simulation*, 17(1):197–205, 1971.

[8] Z. B. Zabinsky. *Stochastic adaptive search for global optimization*. Kluwer Academic Publishers, 2003.

[9] A. A. Zhigljavsky. *Theory of Global Random Search*. Kluwer Academic, 1991.

2.3   Adaptive Random Search

Adaptive Random Search, ARS, Adaptive Step Size Random Search, ASSRS, Variable Step-Size Random Search.

2.3.1   Taxonomy

The Adaptive Random Search algorithm belongs to the general set of approaches known as Stochastic Optimization and Global Optimization. It is a direct search method in that it does not require derivatives to navigate the search space. Adaptive Random Search is an extension of the Random Search (Section 2.2) and Localized Random Search algorithms.

2.3.2   Strategy

The Adaptive Random Search algorithm was designed to address the limitations of the fixed step size in the Localized Random Search algorithm. The strategy for Adaptive Random Search is to continually approximate the optimal step size required to reach the global optimum in the search space. This is achieved by trialling and adopting smaller or larger step sizes only if they result in an improvement in the search performance.

The Strategy of the Adaptive Step Size Random Search algorithm (the specific technique reviewed) is to trial a larger step in each iteration and adopt the larger step if it results in an improved result. Very large step sizes are trialled in the same manner although with a much lower frequency. This strategy of preferring large moves is intended to allow the technique to escape local optima. Smaller step sizes are adopted if no improvement is made for an extended period.

2.3.3   Procedure

Algorithm 2.3.1 provides a pseudocode listing of the Adaptive Random Search Algorithm for minimizing a cost function based on the specification for 'Adaptive Step-Size Random Search' by Schummer and Steiglitz [6].

2.3.4   Heuristics

- Adaptive Random Search was designed for continuous function optimization problem domains.

- Candidates with equal cost should be considered improvements to allow the algorithm to make progress across plateaus in the response surface.

- Adaptive Random Search may adapt the search direction in addition to the step size.

Algorithm 2.3.1: Pseudocode for Adaptive Random Search.

Input: $Iter_{max}$, $Problem_{size}$, SearchSpace, $StepSize_{factor}^{init}$,
$StepSize_{factor}^{small}$, $StepSize_{factor}^{large}$, $StepSize_{factor}^{iter}$,
$NoChange_{max}$

Output: S

1   $NoChange_{count} \leftarrow 0$;
2   $StepSize_i \leftarrow$ InitializeStepSize(SearchSpace, $StepSize_{factor}^{init}$);
3   $S \leftarrow$ RandomSolution($Problem_{size}$, SearchSpace);
4   **for** $i = 0$ **to** $Iter_{max}$ **do**
5      $S_1 \leftarrow$ TakeStep(SearchSpace, S, $StepSize_i$);
6      $StepSize_i^{large} \leftarrow 0$;
7   **if** $i \bmod StepSize_{factor}^{iter}$ **then**
8         $StepSize_i^{large} \leftarrow StepSize_i \times StepSize_{factor}^{large}$;
9   **else**
10        $StepSize_i^{large} \leftarrow StepSize_i \times StepSize_{factor}^{small}$;
11   **end**
12      $S_2 \leftarrow$ TakeStep(SearchSpace, S, $StepSize_i^{large}$);
13   **if** Cost(S_1)$\leq$Cost(S) —— Cost(S_2)$\leq$Cost(S) **then**
14   **if** Cost(S_2)$<$Cost(S_1) **then**
15            $S \leftarrow S_2$;
16            $StepSize_i \leftarrow StepSize_i^{large}$;
17   **else**
18            $S \leftarrow S_1$;
19   **end**
20         $NoChange_{count} \leftarrow 0$;
21   **else**
22         $NoChange_{count} \leftarrow NoChange_{count} + 1$;
23   **if** $NoChange_{count} > NoChange_{max}$ **then**
24            $NoChange_{count} \leftarrow 0$;
25            $StepSize_i \leftarrow \dfrac{StepSize_i}{StepSize_{factor}^{small}}$;
26   **end**
27   **end**
28 **end**
29 **return** S;

- The step size may be adapted for all parameters, or for each parameter individually.

2.3.5   Code Listing

Listing 2.2 provides an example of the Adaptive Random Search Algorithm implemented in the Ruby Programming Language, based on the specification for 'Adaptive Step-Size Random Search' by Schummer and Steiglitz [6]. In the example, the algorithm runs for a fixed number of iterations and returns the best candidate solution discovered. The example problem is an instance of a continuous function optimization that seeks $\min f(x)$ where $f = \sum_{i=1}^{n} x_i^2$, $-5.0 < x_i < 5.0$ and $n = 2$. The optimal solution for this basin function is $(v_0, \ldots, v_{n-1}) = 0.0$.

```ruby
def objective_function(vector)
  return vector.inject(0) {|sum, x| sum + (x ** 2.0)}
end

def rand_in_bounds(min, max)
  return min + ((max-min) * rand())
end

def random_vector(minmax)
  return Array.new(minmax.size) do |i|
    rand_in_bounds(minmax[i][0], minmax[i][1])
  end
end

def take_step(minmax, current, step_size)
  position = Array.new(current.size)
  position.size.times do |i|
    min = [minmax[i][0], current[i]-step_size].max
    max = [minmax[i][1], current[i]+step_size].min
    position[i] = rand_in_bounds(min, max)
  end
  return position
end

def large_step_size(iter, step_size, s_factor, l_factor, iter_mult)
  return step_size * l_factor if iter>0 and iter.modulo(iter_mult) == 0
  return step_size * s_factor
end

def take_steps(bounds, current, step_size, big_stepsize)
  step, big_step = {}, {}
  step[:vector] = take_step(bounds, current[:vector], step_size)
  step[:cost] = objective_function(step[:vector])
  big_step[:vector] = take_step(bounds,current[:vector],big_stepsize)
  big_step[:cost] = objective_function(big_step[:vector])
  return step, big_step
end

def search(max_iter, bounds, init_factor, s_factor, l_factor, iter_mult,
    max_no_impr)
```

```
40    step_size = (bounds[0][1]-bounds[0][0]) * init_factor
41    current, count = {}, 0
42    current[:vector] = random_vector(bounds)
43    current[:cost] = objective_function(current[:vector])
44    max_iter.times do |iter|
45      big_stepsize = large_step_size(iter, step_size, s_factor, l_factor,
              iter_mult)
46      step, big_step = take_steps(bounds, current, step_size, big_stepsize)
47      if step[:cost] <= current[:cost] or big_step[:cost] <= current[:cost]
48        if big_step[:cost] <= step[:cost]
49          step_size, current = big_stepsize, big_step
50        else
51          current = step
52        end
53        count = 0
54      else
55        count += 1
56        count, stepSize = 0, (step_size/s_factor) if count >= max_no_impr
57      end
58      puts " > iteration #{(iter+1)}, best=#{current[:cost]}"
59    end
60    return current
61  end
62
63  if __FILE__ == $0
64    # problem configuration
65    problem_size = 2
66    bounds = Array.new(problem_size) {|i| [-5, +5]}
67    # algorithm configuration
68    max_iter = 1000
69    init_factor = 0.05
70    s_factor = 1.3
71    l_factor = 3.0
72    iter_mult = 10
73    max_no_impr = 30
74    # execute the algorithm
75    best = search(max_iter, bounds, init_factor, s_factor, l_factor,
            iter_mult, max_no_impr)
76    puts "Done. Best Solution: c=#{best[:cost]}, v=#{best[:vector].inspect}"
77  end
```

Listing 2.2: Adaptive Random Search in Ruby

2.3.6 References

Primary Sources

Many works in the 1960s and 1970s experimented with variable step sizes for Random Search methods. Schummer and Steiglitz are commonly credited the adaptive step size procedure, which they called 'Adaptive Step-Size Random Search' [6]. Their approach only modifies the step size based on an approximation of the optimal step size required to reach the global optima. Kregting and White review adaptive random search methods and propose an approach called 'Adaptive Directional Random Search' that modifies both the algorithms step size and direction in response to the cost function [2].

Learn More

White reviews extensions to Rastrigin's 'Creeping Random Search' [4] (fixed step size) that use probabilistic step sizes drawn stochastically from uniform and probabilistic distributions [7]. White also reviews works that propose dynamic control strategies for the step size, such as Karnopp [1] who proposes increases and decreases to the step size based on performance over very small numbers of trials. Schrack and Choit review random search methods that modify their step size in order to approximate optimal moves while searching, including the property of reversal [5]. Masri et al. describe an adaptive random search strategy that alternates between periods of fixed and variable step sizes [3].

2.3.7 Bibliography

[1] D. C. Karnopp. Random search techniques for optimization problems. *Automatica*, 1(2–3):111–121, 1963.

[2] J. Kregting and R. C. White. Adaptive random search. Technical Report TH-Report 71-E-24, Eindhoven University of Technology, Eindhoven, Netherlands, 1971.

[3] S. F. Masri, G. A. Bekey, and F. B. Safford. Global optimization algorithm using adaptive random search. *Applied Mathematics and Computation*, 7(4):353–376, 1980.

[4] L. A. Rastrigin. The convergence of the random search method in the extremal control of a many parameter system. *Automation and Remote Control*, 24:1337–1342, 1963.

[5] G. Schrack and M. Choit. Optimized relative step size random searches. *Mathematical Programming*, 10(1):230–244, 1976.

[6] M. Schumer and K. Steiglitz. Adaptive step size random search. *IEEE Transactions on Automatic Control*, 13(3):270–276, 1968.

[7] R. C. White. A survey of random methods for parameter optimization. *Simulation*, 17(1):197–205, 1971.

2.4 Stochastic Hill Climbing

Stochastic Hill Climbing, SHC, Random Hill Climbing, RHC, Random Mutation Hill Climbing, RMHC.

2.4.1 Taxonomy

The Stochastic Hill Climbing algorithm is a Stochastic Optimization algorithm and is a Local Optimization algorithm (contrasted to Global Optimization). It is a direct search technique, as it does not require derivatives of the search space. Stochastic Hill Climbing is an extension of deterministic hill climbing algorithms such as Simple Hill Climbing (first-best neighbor), Steepest-Ascent Hill Climbing (best neighbor), and a parent of approaches such as Parallel Hill Climbing and Random-Restart Hill Climbing.

2.4.2 Strategy

The strategy of the Stochastic Hill Climbing algorithm is iterate the process of randomly selecting a neighbor for a candidate solution and only accept it if it results in an improvement. The strategy was proposed to address the limitations of deterministic hill climbing techniques that were likely to get stuck in local optima due to their greedy acceptance of neighboring moves.

2.4.3 Procedure

Algorithm 2.4.1 provides a pseudocode listing of the Stochastic Hill Climbing algorithm for minimizing a cost function, specifically the Random Mutation Hill Climbing algorithm described by Forrest and Mitchell applied to a maximization optimization problem [3].

Algorithm 2.4.1: Pseudocode for Stochastic Hill Climbing.

    Input: $Iter_{max}$, ProblemSize
    Output: Current
1   Current ← RandomSolution(ProblemSize);
2   **foreach** $iter_i \in Iter_{max}$ **do**
3   Candidate ← RandomNeighbor(Current);
4   **if** Cost(Candidate) ≥ Cost(Current) **then**
5 | Current ← Candidate;
6   **end**
7   **end**
8   **return** Current;

2.4.4 Heuristics

- Stochastic Hill Climbing was designed to be used in discrete domains with explicit neighbors such as combinatorial optimization (compared to continuous function optimization).

- The algorithm's strategy may be applied to continuous domains by making use of a step-size to define candidate-solution neighbors (such as Localized Random Search and Fixed Step-Size Random Search).

- Stochastic Hill Climbing is a local search technique (compared to global search) and may be used to refine a result after the execution of a global search algorithm.

- Even though the technique uses a stochastic process, it can still get stuck in local optima.

- Neighbors with better or equal cost should be accepted, allowing the technique to navigate across plateaus in the response surface.

- The algorithm can be restarted and repeated a number of times after it converges to provide an improved result (called Multiple Restart Hill Climbing).

- The procedure can be applied to multiple candidate solutions concurrently, allowing multiple algorithm runs to be performed at the same time (called Parallel Hill Climbing).

2.4.5 Code Listing

Listing 2.3 provides an example of the Stochastic Hill Climbing algorithm implemented in the Ruby Programming Language, specifically the Random Mutation Hill Climbing algorithm described by Forrest and Mitchell [3]. The algorithm is executed for a fixed number of iterations and is applied to a binary string optimization problem called 'One Max'. The objective of this maximization problem is to prepare a string of all '1' bits, where the cost function only reports the number of bits in a given string.

```ruby
def onemax(vector)
  return vector.inject(0.0){|sum, v| sum + ((v=="1") ? 1 : 0)}
end

def random_bitstring(num_bits)
  return Array.new(num_bits){|i| (rand<0.5) ? "1" : "0"}
end

def random_neighbor(bitstring)
  mutant = Array.new(bitstring)
  pos = rand(bitstring.size)
  mutant[pos] = (mutant[pos]=='1') ? '0' : '1'
```

```
13    return mutant
14  end
15
16  def search(max_iterations, num_bits)
17    candidate = {}
18    candidate[:vector] = random_bitstring(num_bits)
19    candidate[:cost] = onemax(candidate[:vector])
20    max_iterations.times do |iter|
21      neighbor = {}
22      neighbor[:vector] = random_neighbor(candidate[:vector])
23      neighbor[:cost] = onemax(neighbor[:vector])
24      candidate = neighbor if neighbor[:cost] >= candidate[:cost]
25      puts " > iteration #{(iter+1)}, best=#{candidate[:cost]}"
26      break if candidate[:cost] == num_bits
27    end
28    return candidate
29  end
30
31  if __FILE__ == $0
32    # problem configuration
33    num_bits = 64
34    # algorithm configuration
35    max_iterations = 1000
36    # execute the algorithm
37    best = search(max_iterations, num_bits)
38    puts "Done. Best Solution: c=#{best[:cost]}, v=#{best[:vector].join}"
39  end
```

Listing 2.3: Stochastic Hill Climbing in Ruby

2.4.6   References

Primary Sources

Perhaps the most popular implementation of the Stochastic Hill Climbing algorithm is by Forrest and Mitchell, who proposed the Random Mutation Hill Climbing (RMHC) algorithm (with communication from Richard Palmer) in a study that investigated the behavior of the genetic algorithm on a deceptive class of (discrete) bit-string optimization problems called 'royal road' functions [3]. The RMHC was compared to two other hill climbing algorithms in addition to the genetic algorithm, specifically: the Steepest-Ascent Hill Climber, and the Next-Ascent Hill Climber. This study was then followed up by Mitchell and Holland [5].

Jules and Wattenberg were also early to consider stochastic hill climbing as an approach to compare to the genetic algorithm [4]. Skalak applied the RMHC algorithm to a single long bit-string that represented a number of prototype vectors for use in classification [8].

Learn More

The Stochastic Hill Climbing algorithm is related to the genetic algorithm without crossover. Simplified version's of the approach are investigated for bit-string based optimization problems with the population size of the genetic algorithm reduced to one. The general technique has been investigated under the names Iterated Hillclimbing [6], ES(1+1,m,hc) [7], Random Bit Climber [2], and (1+1)-Genetic Algorithm [1]. This main difference between RMHC and ES(1+1) is that the latter uses a fixed probability of a mutation for each discrete element of a solution (meaning the neighborhood size is probabilistic), whereas RMHC will only stochastically modify one element.

2.4.7   Bibliography

[1] T. Bäck. Optimal mutation rates in genetic search. In *Proceedings of the Fifth International Conference on Genetic Algorithms*, pages 2–9, 1993.

[2] L. Davis. Bit-climbing, representational bias, and test suite design. In *Proceedings of the fourth international conference on genetic algorithms*, pages 18–23, 1991.

[3] S. Forrest and M. Mitchell. Relative building-block fitness and the building-block hypothesis. In *Foundations of Genetic Algorithms 2*, pages 109–126. Morgan Kaufmann, 1993.

[4] A. Juels and M. Wattenberg. Stochastic hill climbing as a baseline method for evaluating genetic algorithms. Technical report, University of California, Berkeley, 1994.

[5] M. Mitchell and J. H. Holland. When will a genetic algorithm outperform hill climbing? In *Proceedings of the 5th International Conference on Genetic Algorithms*. Morgan Kaufmann Publishers Inc., 1993.

[6] H. Mühlenbein. Evolution in time and space - the parallel genetic algorithm. In *Foundations of Genetic Algorithms*, 1991.

[7] H. Mühlenbein. How genetic algorithms really work: I. mutation and hillclimbing. In *Parallel Problem Solving from Nature 2*, pages 15–26, 1992.

[8] D. B. Skalak. Prototype and feature selection by sampling and random mutation hill climbing algorithms. In *Proceedings of the eleventh international conference on machine learning*, pages 293–301. Morgan Kaufmann, 1994.

2.5 Iterated Local Search

Iterated Local Search, ILS.

2.5.1 Taxonomy

Iterated Local Search is a Metaheuristic and a Global Optimization technique. It is an extension of Mutli Start Search and may be considered a parent of many two-phase search approaches such as the Greedy Randomized Adaptive Search Procedure (Section 2.8) and Variable Neighborhood Search (Section 2.7).

2.5.2 Strategy

The objective of Iterated Local Search is to improve upon stochastic Mutli-Restart Search by sampling in the broader neighborhood of candidate solutions and using a Local Search technique to refine solutions to their local optima. Iterated Local Search explores a sequence of solutions created as perturbations of the current best solution, the result of which is refined using an embedded heuristic.

2.5.3 Procedure

Algorithm 2.5.1 provides a pseudocode listing of the Iterated Local Search algorithm for minimizing a cost function.

Algorithm 2.5.1: Pseudocode for Iterated Local Search.

    Input:
    Output: S_{best}
1 $S_{best} \leftarrow$ ConstructInitialSolution();
2 $S_{best} \leftarrow$ LocalSearch();
3 SearchHistory $\leftarrow S_{best}$;
4 **while** ¬ StopCondition() **do**
5     $S_{candidate} \leftarrow$ Perturbation(S_{best}, SearchHistory);
6     $S_{candidate} \leftarrow$ LocalSearch($S_{candidate}$);
7   SearchHistory $\leftarrow S_{candidate}$;
8   **if** AcceptanceCriterion(S_{best}, $S_{candidate}$, SearchHistory) **then**
9       $S_{best} \leftarrow S_{candidate}$;
10   **end**
11 **end**
12 **return** S_{best};

2.5.4   Heuristics

- Iterated Local Search was designed for and has been predominately applied to discrete domains, such as combinatorial optimization problems.

- The perturbation of the current best solution should be in a neighborhood beyond the reach of the embedded heuristic and should not be easily undone.

- Perturbations that are too small make the algorithm too greedy, perturbations that are too large make the algorithm too stochastic.

- The embedded heuristic is most commonly a problem-specific local search technique.

- The starting point for the search may be a randomly constructed candidate solution, or constructed using a problem-specific heuristic (such as nearest neighbor).

- Perturbations can be made deterministically, although stochastic and probabilistic (adaptive based on history) are the most common.

- The procedure may store as much or as little history as needed to be used during perturbation and acceptance criteria. No history represents a random walk in a larger neighborhood of the best solution and is the most common implementation of the approach.

- The simplest and most common acceptance criteria is an improvement in the cost of constructed candidate solutions.

2.5.5   Code Listing

Listing 2.4 provides an example of the Iterated Local Search algorithm implemented in the Ruby Programming Language. The algorithm is applied to the Berlin52 instance of the Traveling Salesman Problem (TSP), taken from the TSPLIB. The problem seeks a permutation of the order to visit cities (called a tour) that minimizes the total distance traveled. The optimal tour distance for Berlin52 instance is 7542 units.

The Iterated Local Search runs for a fixed number of iterations. The implementation is based on a common algorithm configuration for the TSP, where a 'double-bridge move' (4-opt) is used as the perturbation technique, and a stochastic 2-opt is used as the embedded Local Search heuristic. The double-bridge move involves partitioning a permutation into 4 pieces (a,b,c,d) and putting it back together in a specific and jumbled ordering (a,d,c,b).

```ruby
def euc_2d(c1, c2)
  Math.sqrt((c1[0] - c2[0])**2.0 + (c1[1] - c2[1])**2.0).round
end

def cost(permutation, cities)
  distance =0
  permutation.each_with_index do |c1, i|
    c2 = (i==permutation.size-1) ? permutation[0] : permutation[i+1]
    distance += euc_2d(cities[c1], cities[c2])
  end
  return distance
end

def random_permutation(cities)
  perm = Array.new(cities.size){|i| i}
  perm.each_index do |i|
    r = rand(perm.size-i) + i
    perm[r], perm[i] = perm[i], perm[r]
  end
  return perm
end

def stochastic_two_opt(permutation)
  perm = Array.new(permutation)
  c1, c2 = rand(perm.size), rand(perm.size)
  exclude = [c1]
  exclude << ((c1==0) ? perm.size-1 : c1-1)
  exclude << ((c1==perm.size-1) ? 0 : c1+1)
  c2 = rand(perm.size) while exclude.include?(c2)
  c1, c2 = c2, c1 if c2 < c1
  perm[c1...c2] = perm[c1...c2].reverse
  return perm
end

def local_search(best, cities, max_no_improv)
  count = 0
  begin
    candidate = {:vector=>stochastic_two_opt(best[:vector])}
    candidate[:cost] = cost(candidate[:vector], cities)
    count = (candidate[:cost] < best[:cost]) ? 0 : count+1
    best = candidate if candidate[:cost] < best[:cost]
  end until count >= max_no_improv
  return best
end

def double_bridge_move(perm)
  pos1 = 1 + rand(perm.size / 4)
  pos2 = pos1 + 1 + rand(perm.size / 4)
  pos3 = pos2 + 1 + rand(perm.size / 4)
  p1 = perm[0...pos1] + perm[pos3..perm.size]
  p2 = perm[pos2...pos3] + perm[pos1...pos2]
  return p1 + p2
end

def perturbation(cities, best)
```

```
56   candidate = {}
57   candidate[:vector] = double_bridge_move(best[:vector])
58   candidate[:cost] = cost(candidate[:vector], cities)
59   return candidate
60  end
61
62  def search(cities, max_iterations, max_no_improv)
63    best = {}
64    best[:vector] = random_permutation(cities)
65    best[:cost] = cost(best[:vector], cities)
66    best = local_search(best, cities, max_no_improv)
67    max_iterations.times do |iter|
68      candidate = perturbation(cities, best)
69      candidate = local_search(candidate, cities, max_no_improv)
70      best = candidate if candidate[:cost] < best[:cost]
71      puts " > iteration #{(iter+1)}, best=#{best[:cost]}"
72    end
73    return best
74  end
75
76  if __FILE__ == $0
77    # problem configuration
78    berlin52 = [[565,575],[25,185],[345,750],[945,685],[845,655],
79      [880,660],[25,230],[525,1000],[580,1175],[650,1130],[1605,620],
80      [1220,580],[1465,200],[1530,5],[845,680],[725,370],[145,665],
81      [415,635],[510,875],[560,365],[300,465],[520,585],[480,415],
82      [835,625],[975,580],[1215,245],[1320,315],[1250,400],[660,180],
83      [410,250],[420,555],[575,665],[1150,1160],[700,580],[685,595],
84      [685,610],[770,610],[795,645],[720,635],[760,650],[475,960],
85      [95,260],[875,920],[700,500],[555,815],[830,485],[1170,65],
86      [830,610],[605,625],[595,360],[1340,725],[1740,245]]
87    # algorithm configuration
88    max_iterations = 100
89    max_no_improv = 50
90    # execute the algorithm
91    best = search(berlin52, max_iterations, max_no_improv)
92    puts "Done. Best Solution: c=#{best[:cost]}, v=#{best[:vector].inspect}"
93  end
```

Listing 2.4: Iterated Local Search in Ruby

2.5.6   References

Primary Sources

The definition and framework for Iterated Local Search was described by
Stützle in his PhD dissertation [12]. Specifically he proposed constrains on
what constitutes an Iterated Local Search algorithm as 1) a single chain of
candidate solutions, and 2) the method used to improve candidate solutions
occurs within a reduced space by a black-box heuristic. Stützle does not take
credit for the approach, instead highlighting specific instances of Iterated
Local Search from the literature, such as 'iterated descent' [1], 'large-step
Markov chains' [7], 'iterated Lin-Kernighan' [3], 'chained local optimization'

[6], as well as [2] that introduces the principle, and [4] that summarized it (list taken from [8]).

Learn More

Two early technical reports by Stützle that present applications of Iterated Local Search include a report on the Quadratic Assignment Problem [10], and another on the permutation flow shop problem [9]. Stützle and Hoos also published an early paper studying Iterated Local Search for to the TSP [11]. Lourenco, Martin, and Stützle provide a concise presentation of the technique, related techniques and the framework, much as it is presented in Stützle's dissertation [5]. The same author's also preset an authoritative summary of the approach and its applications as a book chapter [8].

2.5.7 Bibliography

[1] E. B. Baum. Towards practical "neural" computation for combinatorial optimization problems. In *AIP conference proceedings: Neural Networks for Computing*, pages 53–64, 1986.

[2] J. Baxter. Local optima avoidance in depot location. *Journal of the Operational Research Society*, 32:815–819, 1981.

[3] D. S. Johnson. Local optimization and the travelling salesman problem. In *Proceedings of the 17th Colloquium on Automata, Languages, and Programming*, pages 446–461, 1990.

[4] D. S. Johnson and L. A. McGeoch. *Local Search in Combinatorial Optimization*, chapter The travelling salesman problem: A case study in local optimization, pages 215–310. John Wiley & Sons, 1997.

[5] H. R. Lourenco, O. Martin, and T. Stützle. A beginners introduction to iterated local search. In *Proceedings 4th Metaheuristics International Conference (MIC2001)*, 2001.

[6] O. Martin and S. W. Otto. Combining simulated annealing with local search heuristics. *Annals of Operations Research*, 63:57–75, 1996.

[7] O. Martin, S. W. Otto, and E. W. Felten. Large-step markov chains for the traveling salesman problems. *Complex Systems*, 5(3):299–326, 1991.

[8] H. Ramalhinho-Lourenco, O. C. Martin, and T. Stützle. *Handbook of Metaheuristics*, chapter Iterated Local Search, pages 320–353. Springer, 2003.

[9] T. Stützle. Applying iterated local search to the permutation flow shop problem. Technical Report AIDA9804, FG Intellektik, TU Darmstadt, 1998.

[10] T. Stützle. Iterated local search for the quadratic assignment problem. Technical Report AIDA-99-03, FG Intellektik, FB Informatik, TU Darmstadt, 1999.

[11] T. Stützle and H. H. Hoos. Analyzing the run-time behaviour of iterated local search for the TSP. In *Proceedings III Metaheuristics International Conference*, 1999.

[12] T. G. Stützle. *Local Search Algorithms for Combinatorial Problems: Analysis, Improvements, and New Applications*. PhD thesis, Darmstadt University of Technology, Department of Computer Science, 1998.

2.6 Guided Local Search

Guided Local Search, GLS.

2.6.1 Taxonomy

The Guided Local Search algorithm is a Metaheuristic and a Global Optimization algorithm that makes use of an embedded Local Search algorithm. It is an extension to Local Search algorithms such as Hill Climbing (Section 2.4) and is similar in strategy to the Tabu Search algorithm (Section 2.10) and the Iterated Local Search algorithm (Section 2.5).

2.6.2 Strategy

The strategy for the Guided Local Search algorithm is to use penalties to encourage a Local Search technique to escape local optima and discover the global optima. A Local Search algorithm is run until it gets stuck in a local optima. The features from the local optima are evaluated and penalized, the results of which are used in an augmented cost function employed by the Local Search procedure. The Local Search is repeated a number of times using the last local optima discovered and the augmented cost function that guides exploration away from solutions with features present in discovered local optima.

2.6.3 Procedure

Algorithm 2.6.1 provides a pseudocode listing of the Guided Local Search algorithm for minimization. The Local Search algorithm used by the Guided Local Search algorithm uses an augmented cost function in the form $h(s) = g(s) + \lambda \cdot \sum_{i=1}^{M} f_i$, where $h(s)$ is the augmented cost function, $g(s)$ is the problem cost function, λ is the 'regularization parameter' (a coefficient for scaling the penalties), s is a locally optimal solution of M features, and f_i is the i'th feature in locally optimal solution. The augmented cost function is only used by the local search procedure, the Guided Local Search algorithm uses the problem specific cost function without augmentation.

Penalties are only updated for those features in a locally optimal solution that maximize utility, updated by adding 1 to the penalty for the future (a counter). The utility for a feature is calculated as $U_{feature} = \frac{C_{feature}}{1+P_{feature}}$, where $U_{feature}$ is the utility for penalizing a feature (maximizing), $C_{feature}$ is the cost of the feature, and $P_{feature}$ is the current penalty for the feature.

2.6.4 Heuristics

- The Guided Local Search procedure is independent of the Local Search procedure embedded within it. A suitable domain-specific

---

Algorithm 2.6.1: Pseudocode for Guided Local Search.

   Input: $Iter_{max}$, λ
   Output: S_{best}

1 $f_{penalties} \leftarrow \emptyset$;
2 $S_{best} \leftarrow$ RandomSolution();
3 **foreach** $Iter_i \in Iter_{max}$ **do**
4     $S_{curr} \leftarrow$ LocalSearch(S_{best}, λ, $f_{penalties}$);
5     $f_{utilities} \leftarrow$ CalculateFeatureUtilities(S_{curr}, $f_{penalties}$);
6     $f_{penalties} \leftarrow$ UpdateFeaturePenalties(S_{curr}, $f_{penalties}$, $f_{utilities}$);
7   **if** Cost(S_{curr}) $\leq$ Cost(S_{best}) **then**
8 | $S_{best} \leftarrow S_{curr}$;
9   **end**
10 **end**
11 **return** S_{best};

---

search procedure should be identified and employed.

- The Guided Local Search procedure may need to be executed for thousands to hundreds-of-thousands of iterations, each iteration of which assumes a run of a Local Search algorithm to convergence.

- The algorithm was designed for discrete optimization problems where a solution is comprised of independently assessable 'features' such as Combinatorial Optimization, although it has been applied to continuous function optimization modeled as binary strings.

- The λ parameter is a scaling factor for feature penalization that must be in the same proportion to the candidate solution costs from the specific problem instance to which the algorithm is being applied. As such, the value for λ must be meaningful when used within the augmented cost function (such as when it is added to a candidate solution cost in minimization and subtracted from a cost in the case of a maximization problem).

2.6.5   Code Listing

Listing 2.5 provides an example of the Guided Local Search algorithm implemented in the Ruby Programming Language. The algorithm is applied to the Berlin52 instance of the Traveling Salesman Problem (TSP), taken from the TSPLIB. The problem seeks a permutation of the order to visit cities (called a tour) that minimizes the total distance traveled. The optimal tour distance for Berlin52 instance is 7542 units.

The implementation of the algorithm for the TSP was based on the configuration specified by Voudouris in [7]. A TSP-specific local search algorithm is used called 2-opt that selects two points in a permutation and reconnects the tour, potentially untwisting the tour at the selected points. The stopping condition for 2-opt was configured to be a fixed number of non-improving moves.

The equation for setting λ for TSP instances is $\lambda = \alpha \cdot \frac{cost(optima)}{N}$, where N is the number of cities, $cost(optima)$ is the cost of a local optimum found by a local search, and $\alpha \in (0, 1]$ (around 0.3 for TSP and 2-opt). The cost of a local optima was fixed to the approximated value of 15000 for the Berlin52 instance. The utility function for features (edges) in the TSP is $U_{edge} = \frac{D_{edge}}{1 + P_{edge}}$, where U_{edge} is the utility for penalizing an edge (maximizing), D_{edge} is the cost of the edge (distance between cities) and P_{edge} is the current penalty for the edge.

```ruby
def euc_2d(c1, c2)
  Math.sqrt((c1[0] - c2[0])**2.0 + (c1[1] - c2[1])**2.0).round
end

def random_permutation(cities)
  perm = Array.new(cities.size){|i| i}
  perm.each_index do |i|
    r = rand(perm.size-i) + i
    perm[r], perm[i] = perm[i], perm[r]
  end
  return perm
end

def stochastic_two_opt(permutation)
  perm = Array.new(permutation)
  c1, c2 = rand(perm.size), rand(perm.size)
  exclude = [c1]
  exclude << ((c1==0) ? perm.size-1 : c1-1)
  exclude << ((c1==perm.size-1) ? 0 : c1+1)
  c2 = rand(perm.size) while exclude.include?(c2)
  c1, c2 = c2, c1 if c2 < c1
  perm[c1...c2] = perm[c1...c2].reverse
  return perm
end

def augmented_cost(permutation, penalties, cities, lambda)
  distance, augmented = 0, 0
  permutation.each_with_index do |c1, i|
    c2 = (i==permutation.size-1) ? permutation[0] : permutation[i+1]
    c1, c2 = c2, c1 if c2 < c1
    d = euc_2d(cities[c1], cities[c2])
    distance += d
    augmented += d + (lambda * (penalties[c1][c2]))
  end
  return [distance, augmented]
end

def cost(cand, penalties, cities, lambda)
```

```
39    cost, acost = augmented_cost(cand[:vector], penalties, cities, lambda)
40    cand[:cost], cand[:aug_cost] = cost, acost
41  end
42
43  def local_search(current, cities, penalties, max_no_improv, lambda)
44    cost(current, penalties, cities, lambda)
45    count = 0
46    begin
47      candidate = {:vector=> stochastic_two_opt(current[:vector])}
48      cost(candidate, penalties, cities, lambda)
49      count = (candidate[:aug_cost] < current[:aug_cost]) ? 0 : count+1
50      current = candidate if candidate[:aug_cost] < current[:aug_cost]
51    end until count >= max_no_improv
52    return current
53  end
54
55  def calculate_feature_utilities(penal, cities, permutation)
56    utilities = Array.new(permutation.size,0)
57    permutation.each_with_index do |c1, i|
58      c2 = (i==permutation.size-1) ? permutation[0] : permutation[i+1]
59      c1, c2 = c2, c1 if c2 < c1
60      utilities[i] = euc_2d(cities[c1], cities[c2]) / (1.0 + penal[c1][c2])
61    end
62    return utilities
63  end
64
65  def update_penalties!(penalties, cities, permutation, utilities)
66    max = utilities.max()
67    permutation.each_with_index do |c1, i|
68      c2 = (i==permutation.size-1) ? permutation[0] : permutation[i+1]
69      c1, c2 = c2, c1 if c2 < c1
70      penalties[c1][c2] += 1 if utilities[i] == max
71    end
72    return penalties
73  end
74
75  def search(max_iterations, cities, max_no_improv, lambda)
76    current = {:vector=>random_permutation(cities)}
77    best = nil
78    penalties = Array.new(cities.size){ Array.new(cities.size, 0) }
79    max_iterations.times do |iter|
80      current=local_search(current, cities, penalties, max_no_improv, lambda)
81      utilities=calculate_feature_utilities(penalties,cities,current[:vector])
82      update_penalties!(penalties, cities, current[:vector], utilities)
83      best = current if best.nil? or current[:cost] < best[:cost]
84      puts " > iter=#{(iter+1)}, best=#{best[:cost]}, aug=#{best[:aug_cost]}"
85    end
86    return best
87  end
88
89  if __FILE__ == $0
90    # problem configuration
91    berlin52 = [[565,575],[25,185],[345,750],[945,685],[845,655],
92      [880,660],[25,230],[525,1000],[580,1175],[650,1130],[1605,620],
93      [1220,580],[1465,200],[1530,5],[845,680],[725,370],[145,665],
94      [415,635],[510,875],[560,365],[300,465],[520,585],[480,415],
```

```
95    [835,625],[975,580],[1215,245],[1320,315],[1250,400],[660,180],
96    [410,250],[420,555],[575,665],[1150,1160],[700,580],[685,595],
97    [685,610],[770,610],[795,645],[720,635],[760,650],[475,960],
98    [95,260],[875,920],[700,500],[555,815],[830,485],[1170,65],
99    [830,610],[605,625],[595,360],[1340,725],[1740,245]]
100   # algorithm configuration
101   max_iterations = 150
102   max_no_improv = 20
103   alpha = 0.3
104   local_search_optima = 12000.0
105   lambda = alpha * (local_search_optima/berlin52.size.to_f)
106   # execute the algorithm
107   best = search(max_iterations, berlin52, max_no_improv, lambda)
108   puts "Done. Best Solution: c=#{best[:cost]}, v=#{best[:vector].inspect}"
109   end
```

Listing 2.5: Guided Local Search in Ruby

2.6.6 References

Primary Sources

Guided Local Search emerged from an approach called GENET, which is a connectionist approach to constraint satisfaction [6, 13]. Guided Local Search was presented by Voudouris and Tsang in a series of technical reports (that were later published) that described the technique and provided example applications of it to constraint satisfaction [8], combinatorial optimization [5, 10], and function optimization [9]. The seminal work on the technique was Voudouris' PhD dissertation [7].

Learn More

Voudouris and Tsang provide a high-level introduction to the technique [11], and a contemporary summary of the approach in Glover and Kochenberger's 'Handbook of metaheuristics' [12] that includes a review of the technique, application areas, and demonstration applications on a diverse set of problem instances. Mills et al. elaborated on the approach, devising an 'Extended Guided Local Search' (EGLS) technique that added 'aspiration criteria' and random moves to the procedure [4], work which culminated in Mills' PhD dissertation [3]. Lau and Tsang further extended the approach by integrating it with a Genetic Algorithm, called the 'Guided Genetic Algorithm' (GGA) [2], that also culminated in a PhD dissertation by Lau [1].

2.6.7 Bibliography

[1] L. T. Lau. *Guided Genetic Algorithm*. PhD thesis, Department of Computer Science, University of Essex, 1999.

[2] T. L. Lau and E. P. K. Tsang. The guided genetic algorithm and its application to the general assignment problems. In *IEEE 10th International Conference on Tools with Artificial Intelligence (ICTAI'98)*, 1998.

[3] P. Mills. *Extensions to Guided Local Search*. PhD thesis, Department of Computer Science, University of Essex, 2002.

[4] P. Mills, E. Tsang, and J. Ford. Applying an extended guided local search on the quadratic assignment problem. *Annals of Operations Research*, 118:121–135, 2003.

[5] E. Tsang and C. Voudouris. Fast local search and guided local search and their application to british telecom's workforce scheduling problem. Technical Report CSM-246, Department of Computer Science University of Essex Colchester CO4 3SQ, 1995.

[6] E. P. K. Tsang and C. J. Wang. A generic neural network approach for constraint satisfaction problems. In Taylor G, editor, *Neural network applications*, pages 12–22, 1992.

[7] C. Voudouris. *Guided local search for combinatorial optimisation problems*. PhD thesis, Department of Computer Science, University of Essex, Colchester, UK, July 1997.

[8] C. Voudouris and E. Tsang. The tunneling algorithm for partial csps and combinatorial optimization problems. Technical Report CSM-213, Department of Computer Science, University of Essex, Colchester, C04 3SQ, UK, 1994.

[9] C. Voudouris and E. Tsang. Function optimization using guided local search. Technical Report CSM-249, Department of Computer Science University of Essex Colchester, CO4 3SQ, UK, 1995.

[10] C. Voudouris and E. Tsang. Guided local search. Technical Report CSM-247, Department of Computer Science, University of Essex, Colchester, C04 3SQ, UK, 1995.

[11] C. Voudouris and E. P. K. Tsang. Guided local search joins the elite in discrete optimisation. In *Proceedings, DIMACS Workshop on Constraint Programming and Large Scale Discrete Optimisation*, 1998.

[12] C. Voudouris and E. P. K. Tsang. *Handbook of Metaheuristics*, chapter 7: Guided Local Search, pages 185–218. Springer, 2003.

[13] C. J. Wang and E. P. K. Tsang. Solving constraint satisfaction problems using neural networks. In *Proceedings Second International Conference on Artificial Neural Networks*, pages 295–299, 1991.

2.7 Variable Neighborhood Search

Variable Neighborhood Search, VNS.

2.7.1 Taxonomy

Variable Neighborhood Search is a Metaheuristic and a Global Optimization technique that manages a Local Search technique. It is related to the Iterative Local Search algorithm (Section 2.5).

2.7.2 Strategy

The strategy for the Variable Neighborhood Search involves iterative exploration of larger and larger neighborhoods for a given local optima until an improvement is located after which time the search across expanding neighborhoods is repeated. The strategy is motivated by three principles: 1) a local minimum for one neighborhood structure may not be a local minimum for a different neighborhood structure, 2) a global minimum is a local minimum for all possible neighborhood structures, and 3) local minima are relatively close to global minima for many problem classes.

2.7.3 Procedure

Algorithm 2.7.1 provides a pseudocode listing of the Variable Neighborhood Search algorithm for minimizing a cost function. The Pseudocode shows that the systematic search of expanding neighborhoods for a local optimum is abandoned when a global improvement is achieved (shown with the `Break` jump).

2.7.4 Heuristics

- Approximation methods (such as stochastic hill climbing) are suggested for use as the Local Search procedure for large problem instances in order to reduce the running time.

- Variable Neighborhood Search has been applied to a very wide array of combinatorial optimization problems as well as clustering and continuous function optimization problems.

- The embedded Local Search technique should be specialized to the problem type and instance to which the technique is being applied.

- The Variable Neighborhood Descent (VND) can be embedded in the Variable Neighborhood Search as a the Local Search procedure and has been shown to be most effective.

Algorithm 2.7.1: Pseudocode for VNS.

Input: Neighborhoods
Output: S_{best}

1 $S_{best} \leftarrow$ RandomSolution();
2 **while** $\neg$ StopCondition() **do**
3   **foreach** $Neighborhood_i \in$ Neighborhoods **do**
4          $Neighborhood_{curr} \leftarrow$ CalculateNeighborhood(S_{best}, $Neighborhood_i$);
5          $S_{candidate} \leftarrow$ RandomSolutionInNeighborhood($Neighborhood_{curr}$);
6          $S_{candidate} \leftarrow$ LocalSearch($S_{candidate}$);
7   **if** Cost($S_{candidate}$) < Cost(S_{best}) **then**
8              $S_{best} \leftarrow S_{candidate}$;
9   Break;
10   **end**
11   **end**
12 **end**
13 **return** S_{best};

2.7.5   Code Listing

Listing 2.6 provides an example of the Variable Neighborhood Search algorithm implemented in the Ruby Programming Language. The algorithm is applied to the Berlin52 instance of the Traveling Salesman Problem (TSP), taken from the TSPLIB. The problem seeks a permutation of the order to visit cities (called a tour) that minimizes the total distance traveled. The optimal tour distance for Berlin52 instance is 7542 units.

The Variable Neighborhood Search uses a stochastic 2-opt procedure as the embedded local search. The procedure deletes two edges and reverses the sequence in-between the deleted edges, potentially removing 'twists' in the tour. The neighborhood structure used in the search is the number of times the 2-opt procedure is performed on a permutation, between 1 and 20 times. The stopping condition for the local search procedure is a maximum number of iterations without improvement. The same stop condition is employed by the higher-order Variable Neighborhood Search procedure, although with a lower boundary on the number of non-improving iterations.

```ruby
def euc_2d(c1, c2)
  Math.sqrt((c1[0] - c2[0])**2.0 + (c1[1] - c2[1])**2.0).round
end

def cost(perm, cities)
  distance =0
  perm.each_with_index do |c1, i|
    c2 = (i==perm.size-1) ? perm[0] : perm[i+1]
```

```
 9      distance += euc_2d(cities[c1], cities[c2])
10    end
11    return distance
12  end
13
14  def random_permutation(cities)
15    perm = Array.new(cities.size){|i| i}
16    perm.each_index do |i|
17      r = rand(perm.size-i) + i
18      perm[r], perm[i] = perm[i], perm[r]
19    end
20    return perm
21  end
22
23  def stochastic_two_opt!(perm)
24    c1, c2 = rand(perm.size), rand(perm.size)
25    exclude = [c1]
26    exclude << ((c1==0) ? perm.size-1 : c1-1)
27    exclude << ((c1==perm.size-1) ? 0 : c1+1)
28    c2 = rand(perm.size) while exclude.include?(c2)
29    c1, c2 = c2, c1 if c2 < c1
30    perm[c1...c2] = perm[c1...c2].reverse
31    return perm
32  end
33
34  def local_search(best, cities, max_no_improv, neighborhood)
35    count = 0
36    begin
37      candidate = {}
38      candidate[:vector] = Array.new(best[:vector])
39      neighborhood.times{stochastic_two_opt!(candidate[:vector])}
40      candidate[:cost] = cost(candidate[:vector], cities)
41      if candidate[:cost] < best[:cost]
42        count, best = 0, candidate
43      else
44        count += 1
45      end
46    end until count >= max_no_improv
47    return best
48  end
49
50  def search(cities, neighborhoods, max_no_improv, max_no_improv_ls)
51    best = {}
52    best[:vector] = random_permutation(cities)
53    best[:cost] = cost(best[:vector], cities)
54    iter, count = 0, 0
55    begin
56      neighborhoods.each do |neigh|
57        candidate = {}
58        candidate[:vector] = Array.new(best[:vector])
59        neigh.times{stochastic_two_opt!(candidate[:vector])}
60        candidate[:cost] = cost(candidate[:vector], cities)
61        candidate = local_search(candidate, cities, max_no_improv_ls, neigh)
62        puts " > iteration #{(iter+1)}, neigh=#{neigh}, best=#{best[:cost]}"
63        iter += 1
64        if(candidate[:cost] < best[:cost])
```

```
65        best, count = candidate, 0
66        puts "New best, restarting neighborhood search."
67        break
68      else
69        count += 1
70      end
71    end
72  end until count >= max_no_improv
73  return best
74 end
75
76 if __FILE__ == $0
77   # problem configuration
78   berlin52 = [[565,575],[25,185],[345,750],[945,685],[845,655],
79     [880,660],[25,230],[525,1000],[580,1175],[650,1130],[1605,620],
80     [1220,580],[1465,200],[1530,5],[845,680],[725,370],[145,665],
81     [415,635],[510,875],[560,365],[300,465],[520,585],[480,415],
82     [835,625],[975,580],[1215,245],[1320,315],[1250,400],[660,180],
83     [410,250],[420,555],[575,665],[1150,1160],[700,580],[685,595],
84     [685,610],[770,610],[795,645],[720,635],[760,650],[475,960],
85     [95,260],[875,920],[700,500],[555,815],[830,485],[1170,65],
86     [830,610],[605,625],[595,360],[1340,725],[1740,245]]
87   # algorithm configuration
88   max_no_improv = 50
89   max_no_improv_ls = 70
90   neighborhoods = 1...20
91   # execute the algorithm
92   best = search(berlin52, neighborhoods, max_no_improv, max_no_improv_ls)
93   puts "Done. Best Solution: c=#{best[:cost]}, v=#{best[:vector].inspect}"
94 end
```

Listing 2.6: Variable Neighborhood Search in Ruby

2.7.6   References

Primary Sources

The seminal paper for describing Variable Neighborhood Search was by Mladenovic and Hansen in 1997 [7], although an early abstract by Mladenovic is sometimes cited [6]. The approach is explained in terms of three different variations on the general theme. Variable Neighborhood Descent (VND) refers to the use of a Local Search procedure and the deterministic (as opposed to stochastic or probabilistic) change of neighborhood size. Reduced Variable Neighborhood Search (RVNS) involves performing a stochastic random search within a neighborhood and no refinement via a local search technique. Basic Variable Neighborhood Search is the canonical approach described by Mladenovic and Hansen in the seminal paper.

Learn More

There are a large number of papers published on Variable Neighborhood Search, its applications and variations. Hansen and Mladenovic provide an overview of the approach that includes its recent history, extensions and a detailed review of the numerous areas of application [4]. For some additional useful overviews of the technique, its principles, and applications, see [1–3]. There are many extensions to Variable Neighborhood Search. Some popular examples include: Variable Neighborhood Decomposition Search (VNDS) that involves embedding a second heuristic or metaheuristic approach in VNS to replace the Local Search procedure [5], Skewed Variable Neighborhood Search (SVNS) that encourages exploration of neighborhoods far away from discovered local optima, and Parallel Variable Neighborhood Search (PVNS) that either parallelizes the local search of a neighborhood or parallelizes the searching of the neighborhoods themselves.

2.7.7 Bibliography

[1] P. Hansen and N. Mladenović. *Meta-heuristics, Advances and trends in local search paradigms for optimization*, chapter An introduction to Variable neighborhood search, pages 433–458. Kluwer Academic Publishers, 1998.

[2] P. Hansen and N. Mladenović. Variable neighborhood search: Principles and applications. *European Journal of Operational Research*, 130(3):449–467, 2001.

[3] P. Hansen and N. Mladenović. *Handbook of Applied Optimization*, chapter Variable neighbourhood search, pages 221–234. Oxford University Press, 2002.

[4] P. Hansen and N. Mladenović. *Handbook of Metaheuristics*, chapter 6: Variable Neighborhood Search, pages 145–184. Springer, 2003.

[5] P. Hansen, N. Mladenović, and D. Perez-Britos. Variable neighborhood decomposition search. *Journal of Heuristics*, 7(4):1381–1231, 2001.

[6] N. Mladenović. A variable neighborhood algorithm - a new metaheuristic for combinatorial optimization. In *Abstracts of papers presented at Optimization Days*, 1995.

[7] N. Mladenović and P. Hansen. Variable neighborhood search. *Computers & Operations Research*, 24(11):1097–1100, 1997.

2.8   Greedy Randomized Adaptive Search

Greedy Randomized Adaptive Search Procedure, GRASP.

2.8.1   Taxonomy

The Greedy Randomized Adaptive Search Procedure is a Metaheuristic and Global Optimization algorithm, originally proposed for the Operations Research practitioners. The iterative application of an embedded Local Search technique relate the approach to Iterative Local Search (Section 2.5) and Multi-Start techniques.

2.8.2   Strategy

The objective of the Greedy Randomized Adaptive Search Procedure is to repeatedly sample stochastically greedy solutions, and then use a local search procedure to refine them to a local optima. The strategy of the procedure is centered on the stochastic and greedy step-wise construction mechanism that constrains the selection and order-of-inclusion of the components of a solution based on the value they are expected to provide.

2.8.3   Procedure

Algorithm 2.8.1 provides a pseudocode listing of the Greedy Randomized Adaptive Search Procedure for minimizing a cost function.

Algorithm 2.8.1: Pseudocode for the GRASP.

Input: α
Output: S_{best}
1 $S_{best} \leftarrow$ ConstructRandomSolution();
2 **while** $\neg$ StopCondition() **do**
3     $S_{candidate} \leftarrow$ GreedyRandomizedConstruction(α);
4     $S_{candidate} \leftarrow$ LocalSearch($S_{candidate}$);
5   **if** Cost($S_{candidate}$) $<$ Cost(S_{best}) **then**
6 | $S_{best} \leftarrow S_{candidate}$;
7   **end**
8 **end**
9 **return** S_{best};

Algorithm 2.8.2 provides the pseudocode the Greedy Randomized Construction function. The function involves the step-wise construction of a candidate solution using a stochastically greedy construction process. The function works by building a Restricted Candidate List (RCL) that constraints the components of a solution (features) that may be selected from each cycle. The RCL may be constrained by an explicit size, or by using a threshold ($\alpha \in [0,1]$) on the cost of adding each feature to the current candidate solution.

Algorithm 2.8.2: Pseudocode the `GreedyRandomizedConstruction` function.

    Input: α
    Output: $S_{candidate}$
1 $S_{candidate} \leftarrow \emptyset$;
2 **while** $S_{candidate} \neq$ ProblemSize **do**
3     $Feature_{costs} \leftarrow \emptyset$;
4   **for** $Feature_i \notin S_{candidate}$ **do**
5       $Feature_{costs} \leftarrow$
        `CostOfAddingFeatureToSolution`($S_{candidate}$, $Feature_i$);
6   **end**
7   RCL $\leftarrow \emptyset$;
8     $Fcost_{min} \leftarrow$ `MinCost`($Feature_{costs}$);
9     $Fcost_{max} \leftarrow$ `MaxCost`($Feature_{costs}$);
10   **for** $F_i cost \in Feature_{costs}$ **do**
11   **if** $F_i cost \leq Fcost_{min} + \alpha \cdot (Fcost_{max} - Fcost_{min})$ **then**
12   RCL $\leftarrow Feature_i$;
13   **end**
14   **end**
15    $S_{candidate} \leftarrow$ `SelectRandomFeature`(RCL);
16 **end**
17 **return** $S_{candidate}$;

2.8.4 Heuristics

- The α threshold defines the amount of greediness of the construction mechanism, where values close to 0 may be too greedy, and values close to 1 may be too generalized.

- As an alternative to using the α threshold, the RCL can be constrained to the top $n\%$ of candidate features that may be selected from each construction cycle.

- The technique was designed for discrete problem classes such as combinatorial optimization problems.

2.8.5 Code Listing

Listing 2.7 provides an example of the Greedy Randomized Adaptive Search Procedure implemented in the Ruby Programming Language. The algorithm is applied to the Berlin52 instance of the Traveling Salesman Problem (TSP), taken from the TSPLIB. The problem seeks a permutation of the order to visit cities (called a tour) that minimizes the total distance traveled. The optimal tour distance for Berlin52 instance is 7542 units.

The stochastic and greedy step-wise construction of a tour involves evaluating candidate cities by the the cost they contribute as being the next city in the tour. The algorithm uses a stochastic 2-opt procedure for the Local Search with a fixed number of non-improving iterations as the stopping condition.

```ruby
def euc_2d(c1, c2)
  Math.sqrt((c1[0] - c2[0])**2.0 + (c1[1] - c2[1])**2.0).round
end

def cost(perm, cities)
  distance =0
  perm.each_with_index do |c1, i|
    c2 = (i==perm.size-1) ? perm[0] : perm[i+1]
    distance += euc_2d(cities[c1], cities[c2])
  end
  return distance
end

def stochastic_two_opt(permutation)
  perm = Array.new(permutation)
  c1, c2 = rand(perm.size), rand(perm.size)
  exclude = [c1]
  exclude << ((c1==0) ? perm.size-1 : c1-1)
  exclude << ((c1==perm.size-1) ? 0 : c1+1)
  c2 = rand(perm.size) while exclude.include?(c2)
  c1, c2 = c2, c1 if c2 < c1
  perm[c1...c2] = perm[c1...c2].reverse
  return perm
end

def local_search(best, cities, max_no_improv)
  count = 0
  begin
    candidate = {:vector=>stochastic_two_opt(best[:vector])}
    candidate[:cost] = cost(candidate[:vector], cities)
    count = (candidate[:cost] < best[:cost]) ? 0 : count+1
    best = candidate if candidate[:cost] < best[:cost]
  end until count >= max_no_improv
  return best
end

def construct_randomized_greedy_solution(cities, alpha)
  candidate = {}
  candidate[:vector] = [rand(cities.size)]
  allCities = Array.new(cities.size) {|i| i}
  while candidate[:vector].size < cities.size
    candidates = allCities - candidate[:vector]
    costs = Array.new(candidates.size) do |i|
      euc_2d(cities[candidate[:vector].last], cities[i])
```

```
45    end
46    rcl, max, min = [], costs.max, costs.min
47    costs.each_with_index do |c,i|
48      rcl << candidates[i] if c <= (min + alpha*(max-min))
49    end
50    candidate[:vector] << rcl[rand(rcl.size)]
51  end
52  candidate[:cost] = cost(candidate[:vector], cities)
53  return candidate
54 end
55
56 def search(cities, max_iter, max_no_improv, alpha)
57  best = nil
58  max_iter.times do |iter|
59    candidate = construct_randomized_greedy_solution(cities, alpha);
60    candidate = local_search(candidate, cities, max_no_improv)
61    best = candidate if best.nil? or candidate[:cost] < best[:cost]
62    puts " > iteration #{(iter+1)}, best=#{best[:cost]}"
63  end
64  return best
65 end
66
67 if __FILE__ == $0
68  # problem configuration
69  berlin52 = [[565,575],[25,185],[345,750],[945,685],[845,655],
70    [880,660],[25,230],[525,1000],[580,1175],[650,1130],[1605,620],
71    [1220,580],[1465,200],[1530,5],[845,680],[725,370],[145,665],
72    [415,635],[510,875],[560,365],[300,465],[520,585],[480,415],
73    [835,625],[975,580],[1215,245],[1320,315],[1250,400],[660,180],
74    [410,250],[420,555],[575,665],[1150,1160],[700,580],[685,595],
75    [685,610],[770,610],[795,645],[720,635],[760,650],[475,960],
76    [95,260],[875,920],[700,500],[555,815],[830,485],[1170,65],
77    [830,610],[605,625],[595,360],[1340,725],[1740,245]]
78  # algorithm configuration
79  max_iter = 50
80  max_no_improv = 50
81  greediness_factor = 0.3
82  # execute the algorithm
83  best = search(berlin52, max_iter, max_no_improv, greediness_factor)
84  puts "Done. Best Solution: c=#{best[:cost]}, v=#{best[:vector].inspect}"
85 end
```

Listing 2.7: Greedy Randomized Adaptive Search Procedure in Ruby

2.8.6   References

Primary Sources

The seminal paper that introduces the general approach of stochastic and greedy step-wise construction of candidate solutions is by Feo and Resende [3]. The general approach was inspired by greedy heuristics by Hart and Shogan [9]. The seminal review paper that is cited with the preliminary paper is by Feo and Resende [4], and provides a coherent description of the GRASP technique, an example, and review of early applications. An early application was by Feo, Venkatraman and Bard for a machine scheduling problem [7]. Other early applications to scheduling problems include technical reports [2] (later published as [1]) and [5] (also later published as [6]).

Learn More

There are a vast number of review, application, and extension papers for GRASP. Pitsoulis and Resende provide an extensive contemporary overview of the field as a review chapter [11], as does Resende and Ribeiro that includes a clear presentation of the use of the α threshold parameter instead of a fixed size for the RCL [13]. Festa and Resende provide an annotated bibliography as a review chapter that provides some needed insight into large amount of study that has gone into the approach [8]. There are numerous extensions to GRASP, not limited to the popular Reactive GRASP for adapting α [12], the use of long term memory to allow the technique to learn from candidate solutions discovered in previous iterations, and parallel implementations of the procedure such as 'Parallel GRASP' [10].

2.8.7 Bibliography

[1] J. F. Bard, T. A. Feo, and S. Holland. A GRASP for scheduling printed wiring board assembly. *I.I.E. Trans.*, 28:155–165, 1996.

[2] T. A. Feo, J. Bard, and S. Holland. A GRASP for scheduling printed wiring board assembly. Technical Report TX 78712-1063, Operations Research Group, Department of Mechanical Engineering, The University of Texas at Austin, 1993.

[3] T. A. Feo and M. G. C. Resende. A probabilistic heuristic for a computationally difficult set covering problem. *Operations Research Letters*, 8:67–71, 1989.

[4] T. A. Feo and M. G. C. Resende. Greedy randomized adaptive search procedures. *Journal of Global Optimization*, 6:109–133, 1995.

[5] T. A. Feo, K. Sarathy, and J. McGahan. A GRASP for single machine scheduling with sequence dependent setup costs and linear delay penalties. Technical Report TX 78712-1063, Operations Research Group, Department of Mechanical Engineering, The University of Texas at Austin, 1994.

[6] T. A. Feo, K. Sarathy, and J. McGahan. A grasp for single machine scheduling with sequence dependent setup costs and linear delay penalties. *Computers & Operations Research*, 23(9):881–895, 1996.

[7] T. A. Feo, K. Venkatraman, and J. F. Bard. A GRASP for a difficult single machine scheduling problem. *Computers & Operations Research*, 18:635–643, 1991.

[8] P. Festa and M. G. C. Resende. *Essays and Surveys on Metaheuristics*, chapter GRASP: An annotated bibliography, pages 325–367. Kluwer Academic Publishers, 2002.

[9] J. P. Hart and A. W. Shogan. Semi–greedy heuristics: An empirical study. *Operations Research Letters*, 6:107–114, 1987.

[10] P. M. Pardalos, L. S. Pitsoulis, and M. G. C. Resende. A parallel GRASP implementation for the quadratic assignment problems. In *Parallel Algorithms for Irregularly Structured Problems (Irregular94)*, pages 111–130. Kluwer Academic Publishers, 1995.

[11] L. Pitsoulis and M. G. C. Resende. *Handbook of Applied Optimization*, chapter Greedy randomized adaptive search procedures, pages 168–181. Oxford University Press, 2002.

[12] M. Prais and C. C. Ribeiro. Reactive GRASP: An application to a matrix decomposition problem in TDMA traffic assignment. *INFORMS Journal on Computing*, 12:164–176, 2000.

[13] M. G. C. Resende and C. C. Ribeiro. *Handbook of Metaheuristics*, chapter Greedy randomized adaptive search procedures, pages 219–249. Kluwer Academic Publishers, 2003.

2.9 Scatter Search

Scatter Search, SS.

2.9.1 Taxonomy

Scatter search is a Metaheuristic and a Global Optimization algorithm. It is also sometimes associated with the field of Evolutionary Computation given the use of a population and recombination in the structure of the technique. Scatter Search is a sibling of Tabu Search (Section 2.10), developed by the same author and based on similar origins.

2.9.2 Strategy

The objective of Scatter Search is to maintain a set of diverse and high-quality candidate solutions. The principle of the approach is that useful information about the global optima is stored in a diverse and elite set of solutions (the reference set) and that recombining samples from the set can exploit this information. The strategy involves an iterative process, where a population of diverse and high-quality candidate solutions that are partitioned into subsets and linearly recombined to create weighted centroids of sample-based neighborhoods. The results of recombination are refined using an embedded heuristic and assessed in the context of the reference set as to whether or not they are retained.

2.9.3 Procedure

Algorithm 2.9.1 provides a pseudocode listing of the Scatter Search algorithm for minimizing a cost function. The procedure is based on the abstract form presented by Glover as a template for the general class of technique [3], with influences from an application of the technique to function optimization by Glover [3].

2.9.4 Heuristics

- Scatter search is suitable for both discrete domains such as combinatorial optimization as well as continuous domains such as non-linear programming (continuous function optimization).

- Small set sizes are preferred for the `ReferenceSet`, such as 10 or 20 members.

- Subset sizes can be 2, 3, 4 or more members that are all recombined to produce viable candidate solutions within the neighborhood of the members of the subset.

Algorithm 2.9.1: Pseudocode for Scatter Search.

Input: $DiverseSet_{size}$, $ReferenceSet_{size}$
Output: ReferenceSet

1 InitialSet $\leftarrow$ ConstructInitialSolution($DiverseSet_{size}$);
2 RefinedSet $\leftarrow \emptyset$;
3 **for** $S_i \in$ InitialSet **do**
4 | RefinedSet $\leftarrow$ LocalSearch(S_i);
5 **end**
6 ReferenceSet $\leftarrow$ SelectInitialReferenceSet($ReferenceSet_{size}$);
7 **while** $\neg$ StopCondition() **do**
8 | Subsets $\leftarrow$ SelectSubset(ReferenceSet);
9 | CandidateSet $\leftarrow \emptyset$;
10 | **for** $Subset_i \in$ Subsets **do**
11 | RecombinedCandidates $\leftarrow$ RecombineMembers($Subset_i$);
12 | **for** $S_i \in$ RecombinedCandidates **do**
13 | CandidateSet $\leftarrow$ LocalSearch(S_i);
14 | **end**
15 | **end**
16 | ReferenceSet $\leftarrow$ Select(ReferenceSet, CandidateSet, $ReferenceSet_{size}$);
17 **end**
18 **return** ReferenceSet;

- Each subset should comprise at least one member added to the set in the previous algorithm iteration.

- The Local Search procedure should be a problem-specific improvement heuristic.

- The selection of members for the ReferenceSet at the end of each iteration favors solutions with higher quality and may also promote diversity.

- The ReferenceSet may be updated at the end of an iteration, or dynamically as candidates are created (a so-called steady-state population in some evolutionary computation literature).

- A lack of changes to the ReferenceSet may be used as a signal to stop the current search, and potentially restart the search with a newly initialized ReferenceSet.

2.9.5 Code Listing

Listing 2.8 provides an example of the Scatter Search algorithm implemented in the Ruby Programming Language. The example problem is an instance of a continuous function optimization that seeks $\min f(x)$ where $f = \sum_{i=1}^{n} x_i^2$, $-5.0 \leq x_i \leq 5.0$ and $n = 3$. The optimal solution for this basin function is $(v_1, \ldots, v_n) = 0.0$.

The algorithm is an implementation of Scatter Search as described in an application of the technique to unconstrained non-linear optimization by Glover [6]. The seeds for initial solutions are generated as random vectors, as opposed to stratified samples. The example was further simplified by not including a restart strategy, and the exclusion of diversity maintenance in the `ReferenceSet`. A stochastic local search algorithm is used as the embedded heuristic that uses a stochastic step size in the range of half a percent of the search space.

```ruby
def objective_function(vector)
  return vector.inject(0) {|sum, x| sum + (x ** 2.0)}
end

def rand_in_bounds(min, max)
  return min + ((max-min) * rand())
end

def random_vector(minmax)
  return Array.new(minmax.size) do |i|
    rand_in_bounds(minmax[i][0], minmax[i][1])
  end
end

def take_step(minmax, current, step_size)
  position = Array.new(current.size)
  position.size.times do |i|
    min = [minmax[i][0], current[i]-step_size].max
    max = [minmax[i][1], current[i]+step_size].min
    position[i] = rand_in_bounds(min, max)
  end
  return position
end

def local_search(best, bounds, max_no_improv, step_size)
  count = 0
  begin
    candidate = {:vector=>take_step(bounds, best[:vector], step_size)}
    candidate[:cost] = objective_function(candidate[:vector])
    count = (candidate[:cost] < best[:cost]) ? 0 : count+1
    best = candidate if candidate[:cost] < best[:cost]
  end until count >= max_no_improv
  return best
end

def construct_initial_set(bounds, set_size, max_no_improv, step_size)
  diverse_set = []
  begin
    cand = {:vector=>random_vector(bounds)}
    cand[:cost] = objective_function(cand[:vector])
    cand = local_search(cand, bounds, max_no_improv, step_size)
    diverse_set << cand if !diverse_set.any? {|x| x[:vector]==cand[:vector]}
```

```
43    end until diverse_set.size == set_size
44    return diverse_set
45  end
46
47  def euclidean_distance(c1, c2)
48    sum = 0.0
49    c1.each_index {|i| sum += (c1[i]-c2[i])**2.0}
50    return Math.sqrt(sum)
51  end
52
53  def distance(v, set)
54    return set.inject(0){|s,x| s + euclidean_distance(v, x[:vector])}
55  end
56
57  def diversify(diverse_set, num_elite, ref_set_size)
58    diverse_set.sort!{|x,y| x[:cost] <=> y[:cost]}
59    ref_set = Array.new(num_elite){|i| diverse_set[i]}
60    remainder = diverse_set - ref_set
61    remainder.each{|c| c[:dist] = distance(c[:vector], ref_set)}
62    remainder.sort!{|x,y| y[:dist]<=>x[:dist]}
63    ref_set = ref_set + remainder.first(ref_set_size-ref_set.size)
64    return [ref_set, ref_set[0]]
65  end
66
67  def select_subsets(ref_set)
68    additions = ref_set.select{|c| c[:new]}
69    remainder = ref_set - additions
70    remainder = additions if remainder.nil? or remainder.empty?
71    subsets = []
72    additions.each do |a|
73      remainder.each{|r| subsets << [a,r] if a!=r && !subsets.include?([r,a])}
74    end
75    return subsets
76  end
77
78  def recombine(subset, minmax)
79    a, b = subset
80    d = rand(euclidean_distance(a[:vector], b[:vector]))/2.0
81    children = []
82    subset.each do |p|
83      step = (rand<0.5) ? +d : -d
84      child = {:vector=>Array.new(minmax.size)}
85      child[:vector].each_index do |i|
86        child[:vector][i] = p[:vector][i] + step
87        child[:vector][i]=minmax[i][0] if child[:vector][i]<minmax[i][0]
88        child[:vector][i]=minmax[i][1] if child[:vector][i]>minmax[i][1]
89      end
90      child[:cost] = objective_function(child[:vector])
91      children << child
92    end
93    return children
94  end
95
96  def explore_subsets(bounds, ref_set, max_no_improv, step_size)
97    was_change = false
98    subsets = select_subsets(ref_set)
```

```
 99    ref_set.each{|c| c[:new] = false}
100    subsets.each do |subset|
101      candidates = recombine(subset, bounds)
102      improved = Array.new(candidates.size) do |i|
103        local_search(candidates[i], bounds, max_no_improv, step_size)
104      end
105      improved.each do |c|
106        if !ref_set.any? {|x| x[:vector]==c[:vector]}
107          c[:new] = true
108          ref_set.sort!{|x,y| x[:cost] <=> y[:cost]}
109          if c[:cost] < ref_set.last[:cost]
110            ref_set.delete(ref_set.last)
111            ref_set << c
112            puts " >> added, cost=#{c[:cost]}"
113            was_change = true
114          end
115        end
116      end
117    end
118    return was_change
119  end
120
121  def search(bounds, max_iter, ref_set_size, div_set_size, max_no_improv,
               step_size, max_elite)
122    diverse_set = construct_initial_set(bounds, div_set_size, max_no_improv,
                  step_size)
123    ref_set, best = diversify(diverse_set, max_elite, ref_set_size)
124    ref_set.each{|c| c[:new] = true}
125    max_iter.times do |iter|
126      was_change = explore_subsets(bounds, ref_set, max_no_improv, step_size)
127      ref_set.sort!{|x,y| x[:cost] <=> y[:cost]}
128      best = ref_set.first if ref_set.first[:cost] < best[:cost]
129      puts " > iter=#{(iter+1)}, best=#{best[:cost]}"
130      break if !was_change
131    end
132    return best
133  end
134
135  if __FILE__ == $0
136    # problem configuration
137    problem_size = 3
138    bounds = Array.new(problem_size) {|i| [-5, +5]}
139    # algorithm configuration
140    max_iter = 100
141    step_size = (bounds[0][1]-bounds[0][0])*0.005
142    max_no_improv = 30
143    ref_set_size = 10
144    diverse_set_size = 20
145    no_elite = 5
146    # execute the algorithm
147    best = search(bounds, max_iter, ref_set_size, diverse_set_size,
                 max_no_improv, step_size, no_elite)
148    puts "Done. Best Solution: c=#{best[:cost]}, v=#{best[:vector].inspect}"
149  end
```

Listing 2.8: Scatter Search in Ruby

2.9.6 References

Primary Sources

A form of the Scatter Search algorithm was proposed by Glover for integer programming [1], based on Glover's earlier work on surrogate constraints. The approach remained idle until it was revisited by Glover and combined with Tabu Search [2]. The modern canonical reference of the approach was proposed by Glover who provides an abstract template of the procedure that may be specialized for a given application domain [3].

Learn More

The primary reference for the approach is the book by Laguna and Martí that reviews the principles of the approach in detail and presents tutorials on applications of the approach on standard problems using the C programming language [7]. There are many review articles and chapters on Scatter Search that may be used to supplement an understanding of the approach, such as a detailed review chapter by Glover [4], a review of the fundamentals of the approach and its relationship to an abstraction called 'path linking' by Glover, Laguna, and Martí [5], and a modern overview of the technique by Martí, Laguna, and Glover [8].

2.9.7 Bibliography

[1] F. Glover. Heuristics for integer programming using surrogate constraints. *Decision Sciences*, 8(1):156–166, 1977.

[2] F. Glover. Tabu search for nonlinear and parametric optimization (with links to genetic algorithms). *Discrete Applied Mathematics*, 49:231–255, 1994.

[3] F. Glover. *Artificial Evolution*, chapter A Template For Scatter Search And Path Relinking, page 13. Sprinter, 1998.

[4] F. Glover. *New Ideas in Optimization*, chapter Scatter search and path relinking, pages 297–316. McGraw-Hill Ltd., 1999.

[5] F. Glover, M. Laguna, and R. Martí. Fundamentals of scatter search and path relinking. *Control and Cybernetics*, 39(3):653–684, 2000.

[6] F. Glover, M. Laguna, and R. Martí. *Advances in Evolutionary Computation: Theory and Applications*, chapter Scatter Search, pages 519–537. Springer-Verlag, 2003.

[7] M. Laguna and R. Martí. *Scatter search: methodology and implementations in C*. Kluwer Academic Publishers, 2003.

[8] R. Martí, M. Laguna, and F. Glover. Principles of scatter search. *European Journal of Operational Research*, 169(1):359–372, 2006.

2.10 Tabu Search

Tabu Search, TS, Taboo Search.

2.10.1 Taxonomy

Tabu Search is a Global Optimization algorithm and a Metaheuristic or Meta-strategy for controlling an embedded heuristic technique. Tabu Search is a parent for a large family of derivative approaches that introduce memory structures in Metaheuristics, such as Reactive Tabu Search (Section 2.11) and Parallel Tabu Search.

2.10.2 Strategy

The objective for the Tabu Search algorithm is to constrain an embedded heuristic from returning to recently visited areas of the search space, referred to as cycling. The strategy of the approach is to maintain a short term memory of the specific changes of recent moves within the search space and preventing future moves from undoing those changes. Additional intermediate-term memory structures may be introduced to bias moves toward promising areas of the search space, as well as longer-term memory structures that promote a general diversity in the search across the search space.

2.10.3 Procedure

Algorithm 2.10.1 provides a pseudocode listing of the Tabu Search algorithm for minimizing a cost function. The listing shows the simple Tabu Search algorithm with short term memory, without intermediate and long term memory management.

2.10.4 Heuristics

- Tabu search was designed to manage an embedded hill climbing heuristic, although may be adapted to manage any neighborhood exploration heuristic.

- Tabu search was designed for, and has predominately been applied to discrete domains such as combinatorial optimization problems.

- Candidates for neighboring moves can be generated deterministically for the entire neighborhood or the neighborhood can be stochastically sampled to a fixed size, trading off efficiency for accuracy.

- Intermediate-term memory structures can be introduced (complementing the short-term memory) to focus the search on promising areas of the search space (intensification), called aspiration criteria.

Algorithm 2.10.1: Pseudocode for Tabu Search.

Input: $TabuList_{size}$
Output: S_{best}

1 $S_{best} \leftarrow$ ConstructInitialSolution();
2 TabuList $\leftarrow \emptyset$;
3 **while** $\neg$ StopCondition() **do**
4   CandidateList $\leftarrow \emptyset$;
5   **for** $S_{candidate} \in Sbest_{neighborhood}$ **do**
6   **if** $\neg$ ContainsAnyFeatures($S_{candidate}$, TabuList) **then**
7   CandidateList $\leftarrow S_{candidate}$;
8   **end**
9   **end**
10      $S_{candidate} \leftarrow$ LocateBestCandidate(CandidateList);
11   **if** Cost($S_{candidate}$) $\leq$ Cost(S_{best}) **then**
12          $S_{best} \leftarrow S_{candidate}$;
13   TabuList $\leftarrow$ FeatureDifferences($S_{candidate}$, S_{best});
14   **while** TabuList $> TabuList_{size}$ **do**
15   DeleteFeature(TabuList);
16   **end**
17   **end**
18 **end**
19 **return** S_{best};

- Long-term memory structures can be introduced (complementing the short-term memory) to encourage useful exploration of the broader search space, called diversification. Strategies may include generating solutions with rarely used components and biasing the generation away from the most commonly used solution components.

2.10.5   Code Listing

Listing 2.9 provides an example of the Tabu Search algorithm implemented in the Ruby Programming Language. The algorithm is applied to the Berlin52 instance of the Traveling Salesman Problem (TSP), taken from the TSPLIB. The problem seeks a permutation of the order to visit cities (called a tour) that minimizes the total distance traveled. The optimal tour distance for Berli52 instance is 7542 units.

The algorithm is an implementation of the simple Tabu Search with a short term memory structure that executes for a fixed number of iterations. The starting point for the search is prepared using a random permutation that is refined using a stochastic 2-opt Local Search procedure. The stochastic 2-opt procedure is used as the embedded hill climbing heuristic with a fixed sized candidate list. The two edges that are deleted in each 2-opt move are stored on the tabu list. This general approach is similar to that used by Knox in his work on Tabu Search for symmetrical TSP [12] and Fiechter for the Parallel Tabu Search for the TSP [2].

```ruby
def euc_2d(c1, c2)
  Math.sqrt((c1[0] - c2[0])**2.0 + (c1[1] - c2[1])**2.0).round
end

def cost(perm, cities)
  distance = 0
  perm.each_with_index do |c1, i|
    c2 = (i==perm.size-1) ? perm[0] : perm[i+1]
    distance += euc_2d(cities[c1], cities[c2])
  end
  return distance
end

def random_permutation(cities)
  perm = Array.new(cities.size){|i| i}
  perm.each_index do |i|
    r = rand(perm.size-i) + i
    perm[r], perm[i] = perm[i], perm[r]
  end
  return perm
end

def stochastic_two_opt(parent)
  perm = Array.new(parent)
  c1, c2 = rand(perm.size), rand(perm.size)
  exclude = [c1]
  exclude << ((c1==0) ? perm.size-1 : c1-1)
  exclude << ((c1==perm.size-1) ? 0 : c1+1)
  c2 = rand(perm.size) while exclude.include?(c2)
  c1, c2 = c2, c1 if c2 < c1
  perm[c1...c2] = perm[c1...c2].reverse
  return perm, [[parent[c1-1], parent[c1]], [parent[c2-1], parent[c2]]]
end

def is_tabu?(permutation, tabu_list)
  permutation.each_with_index do |c1, i|
    c2 = (i==permutation.size-1) ? permutation[0] : permutation[i+1]
    tabu_list.each do |forbidden_edge|
      return true if forbidden_edge == [c1, c2]
    end
  end
  return false
end

def generate_candidate(best, tabu_list, cities)
  perm, edges = nil, nil
  begin
    perm, edges = stochastic_two_opt(best[:vector])
  end while is_tabu?(perm, tabu_list)
  candidate = {:vector=>perm}
  candidate[:cost] = cost(candidate[:vector], cities)
  return candidate, edges
```

```
53   end
54
55   def search(cities, tabu_list_size, candidate_list_size, max_iter)
56     current = {:vector=>random_permutation(cities)}
57     current[:cost] = cost(current[:vector], cities)
58     best = current
59     tabu_list = Array.new(tabu_list_size)
60     max_iter.times do |iter|
61       candidates = Array.new(candidate_list_size) do |i|
62         generate_candidate(current, tabu_list, cities)
63       end
64       candidates.sort! {|x,y| x.first[:cost] <=> y.first[:cost]}
65       best_candidate = candidates.first[0]
66       best_candidate_edges = candidates.first[1]
67       if best_candidate[:cost] < current[:cost]
68         current = best_candidate
69         best = best_candidate if best_candidate[:cost] < best[:cost]
70         best_candidate_edges.each {|edge| tabu_list.push(edge)}
71         tabu_list.pop while tabu_list.size > tabu_list_size
72       end
73       puts " > iteration #{(iter+1)}, best=#{best[:cost]}"
74     end
75     return best
76   end
77
78   if __FILE__ == $0
79     # problem configuration
80     berlin52 = [[565,575],[25,185],[345,750],[945,685],[845,655],
81       [880,660],[25,230],[525,1000],[580,1175],[650,1130],[1605,620],
82       [1220,580],[1465,200],[1530,5],[845,680],[725,370],[145,665],
83       [415,635],[510,875],[560,365],[300,465],[520,585],[480,415],
84       [835,625],[975,580],[1215,245],[1320,315],[1250,400],[660,180],
85       [410,250],[420,555],[575,665],[1150,1160],[700,580],[685,595],
86       [685,610],[770,610],[795,645],[720,635],[760,650],[475,960],
87       [95,260],[875,920],[700,500],[555,815],[830,485],[1170,65],
88       [830,610],[605,625],[595,360],[1340,725],[1740,245]]
89     # algorithm configuration
90     max_iter = 100
91     tabu_list_size = 15
92     max_candidates = 50
93     # execute the algorithm
94     best = search(berlin52, tabu_list_size, max_candidates, max_iter)
95     puts "Done. Best Solution: c=#{best[:cost]}, v=#{best[:vector].inspect}"
96   end
```

Listing 2.9: Tabu Search in Ruby

2.10.6   References

Primary Sources

Tabu Search was introduced by Glover applied to scheduling employees to
duty rosters [9] and a more general overview in the context of the TSP [5],
based on his previous work on surrogate constraints on integer programming

problems [4]. Glover provided a seminal overview of the algorithm in a two-part journal article, the first part of which introduced the algorithm and reviewed then-recent applications [6], and the second which focused on advanced topics and open areas of research [7].

Learn More

Glover provides a high-level introduction to Tabu Search in the form of a practical tutorial [8], as does Glover and Taillard in a user guide format [10]. The best source of information for Tabu Search is the book dedicated to the approach by Glover and Laguna that covers the principles of the technique in detail as well as an in-depth review of applications [11]. The approach appeared in Science, that considered a modification for its application to continuous function optimization problems [1]. Finally, Gendreau provides an excellent contemporary review of the algorithm, highlighting best practices and application heuristics collected from across the field of study [3].

2.10.7 Bibliography

[1] D. Cvijovic and J. Klinowski. Taboo search: An approach to the multiple minima problem. *Science*, 267:664–666, 1995.

[2] C-N. Fiechter. A parallel tabu search algorithm for large traveling salesman problems. *Discrete Applied Mathematics*, 3(6):243–267, 1994.

[3] M. Gendreau. *Handbook of Metaheuristics*, chapter 2: An Introduction to Tabu Search, pages 37–54. Springer, 2003.

[4] F. Glover. Heuristics for integer programming using surrogate constraints. *Decision Sciences*, 8(1):156–166, 1977.

[5] F. Glover. Future paths for integer programming and links to artificial intelligence. *Computers and Operations Research*, 13(5):533–549, 1986.

[6] F. Glover. Tabu search – Part I. *ORSA Journal on Computing*, 1(3):190–206, 1989.

[7] F. Glover. Tabu search – Part II. *ORSA Journal on Computing*, 2(1):4–32, 1990.

[8] F. Glover. Tabu search: A tutorial. *Interfaces*, 4:74–94, 1990.

[9] F. Glover and C. McMillan. The general employee scheduling problem: an integration of MS and AI. *Computers and Operations Research*, 13(5):536–573, 1986.

[10] F. Glover and E. Taillard. A user's guide to tabu search. *Annals of Operations Research*, 41(1):1–28, 1993.

[11] F. W. Glover and M. Laguna. *Tabu Search*. Springer, 1998.

[12] J. Knox. Tabu search performance on the symmetric traveling salesman problem. *Computers & Operations Research*, 21(8):867–876, 1994.

2.11   Reactive Tabu Search

Reactive Tabu Search, RTS, R-TABU, Reactive Taboo Search.

2.11.1   Taxonomy

Reactive Tabu Search is a Metaheuristic and a Global Optimization algorithm. It is an extension of Tabu Search (Section 2.10) and the basis for a field of reactive techniques called Reactive Local Search and more broadly the field of Reactive Search Optimization.

2.11.2   Strategy

The objective of Tabu Search is to avoid cycles while applying a local search technique. The Reactive Tabu Search addresses this objective by explicitly monitoring the search and reacting to the occurrence of cycles and their repetition by adapting the tabu tenure (tabu list size). The strategy of the broader field of Reactive Search Optimization is to automate the process by which a practitioner configures a search procedure by monitoring its online behavior and to use machine learning techniques to adapt a techniques configuration.

2.11.3   Procedure

Algorithm 2.11.1 provides a pseudocode listing of the Reactive Tabu Search algorithm for minimizing a cost function. The Pseudocode is based on the version of the Reactive Tabu Search described by Battiti and Tecchiolli in [9] with supplements like the IsTabu function from [7]. The procedure has been modified for brevity to exude the diversification procedure (escape move). Algorithm 2.11.2 describes the memory based reaction that manipulates the size of the ProhibitionPeriod in response to identified cycles in the ongoing search. Algorithm 2.11.3 describes the selection of the best move from a list of candidate moves in the neighborhood of a given solution. The function permits prohibited moves in the case where a prohibited move is better than the best know solution and the selected admissible move (called aspiration). Algorithm 2.11.4 determines whether a given neighborhood move is tabu based on the current ProhibitionPeriod, and is employed by sub-functions of the Algorithm 2.11.3 function.

2.11.4   Heuristics

- Reactive Tabu Search is an extension of Tabu Search and as such should exploit the best practices used for the parent algorithm.

Algorithm 2.11.1: Pseudocode for Reactive Tabu Search.

Input: $Iteration_{max}$, Increase, Decrease, ProblemSize
Output: S_{best}
1   $S_{curr} \leftarrow$ ConstructInitialSolution();
2   $S_{best} \leftarrow S_{curr}$;
3   TabuList $\leftarrow \emptyset$;
4   ProhibitionPeriod $\leftarrow 1$;
5   **foreach** $Iteration_i \in Iteration_{max}$ **do**
6   MemoryBasedReaction(Increase, Decrease, ProblemSize);
7   CandidateList $\leftarrow$ GenerateCandidateNeighborhood(S_{curr});
8      $S_{curr} \leftarrow$ BestMove(CandidateList);
9   TabuList $\leftarrow Scurr_{feature}$;
10   **if** Cost(S_{curr}) $\leq$ Cost(S_{best}) **then**
11       $S_{best} \leftarrow S_{curr}$;
12   **end**
13 **end**
14 **return** S_{best};

Algorithm 2.11.2: Pseudocode for the MemoryBasedReaction function.

Input: Increase, Decrease, ProblemSize
Output:
1   **if** HaveVisitedSolutionBefore(S_{curr}, VisitedSolutions) **then**
2      $Scurr_t \leftarrow$ RetrieveLastTimeVisited(VisitedSolutions, S_{curr});
3   RepetitionInterval $\leftarrow Iteration_i - Scurr_t$;
4      $Scurr_t \leftarrow Iteration_i$;
5   **if** RepetitionInterval $< 2 \times$ ProblemSize **then**
6        $RepetitionInterval_{avg} \leftarrow 0.1 \times$ RepetitionInterval $+ 0.9 \times$ $RepetitionInterval_{avg}$;
7   ProhibitionPeriod $\leftarrow$ ProhibitionPeriod $\times$ Increase;
8        $ProhibitionPeriod_t \leftarrow Iteration_i$;
9   **end**
10 **else**
11   VisitedSolutions $\leftarrow S_{curr}$;
12     $Scurr_t \leftarrow Iteration_i$;
13 **end**
14 **if** $Iteration_i - ProhibitionPeriod_t > RepetitionInterval_{avg}$ **then**
15   ProhibitionPeriod $\leftarrow$ Max(1, ProhibitionPeriod $\times$ Decrease);
16     $ProhibitionPeriod_t \leftarrow Iteration_i$;
17 **end**

Algorithm 2.11.3: Pseudocode for the `BestMove` function.

Input: ProblemSize
Output: S_{curr}

1 $CandidateList_{admissible} \leftarrow$ `GetAdmissibleMoves`(CandidateList);
2 $CandidateList_{tabu} \leftarrow$ CandidateList $- CandidateList_{admissible}$;
3 **if** `Size`($CandidateList_{admissible}$) < 2 **then**
4 $\quad$ ProhibitionPeriod $\leftarrow$ ProblemSize $- 2$;
5 $\quad$ $ProhibitionPeriod_t \leftarrow Iteration_i$;
6 **end**
7 $S_{curr} \leftarrow$ `GetBest`($CandidateList_{admissible}$);
8 $Sbest_{tabu} \leftarrow$ `GetBest`($CandidateList_{tabu}$);
9 **if** `Cost`($Sbest_{tabu}$) $<$ `Cost`(S_{best}) $\wedge$ `Cost`($Sbest_{tabu}$) $<$ `Cost`(S_{curr})
   then
10 $\quad$ $S_{curr} \leftarrow Sbest_{tabu}$;
11 **end**
12 **return** S_{curr};

Algorithm 2.11.4: Pseudocode for the `IsTabu` function.

Input:
Output: Tabu

1 Tabu $\leftarrow$ FALSE;
2 $Scurr^t_{feature} \leftarrow$ `RetrieveTimeFeatureLastUsed`($Scurr_{feature}$);
3 **if** $Scurr^t_{feature} \geq Iteration_{curr} -$ ProhibitionPeriod **then**
4 $\quad$ Tabu $\leftarrow$ TRUE;
5 **end**
6 **return** Tabu;

- Reactive Tabu Search was designed for discrete domains such as combinatorial optimization, although has been applied to continuous function optimization.

- Reactive Tabu Search was proposed to use efficient memory data structures such as hash tables.

- Reactive Tabu Search was proposed to use an long-term memory to diversify the search after a threshold of cycle repetitions has been reached.

- The `increase` parameter should be greater than one (such as 1.1 or 1.3) and the `decrease` parameter should be less than one (such as 0.9 or 0.8).

2.11.5   Code Listing

Listing 2.10 provides an example of the Reactive Tabu Search algorithm implemented in the Ruby Programming Language. The algorithm is applied to the Berlin52 instance of the Traveling Salesman Problem (TSP), taken from the TSPLIB. The problem seeks a permutation of the order to visit cities (called a tour) that minimizes the total distance traveled. The optimal tour distance for Berlin52 instance is 7542 units.

The procedure is based on the code listing described by Battiti and Tecchiolli in [9] with supplements like the `IsTabu` function from [7]. The implementation does not use efficient memory data structures such as hash tables. The algorithm is initialized with a stochastic 2-opt local search, and the neighborhood is generated as a fixed candidate list of stochastic 2-opt moves. The edges selected for changing in the 2-opt move are stored as features in the tabu list. The example does not implement the escape procedure for search diversification.

```
1   def euc_2d(c1, c2)
2     Math.sqrt((c1[0] - c2[0])**2.0 + (c1[1] - c2[1])**2.0).round
3   end
4
5   def cost(perm, cities)
6     distance = 0
7     perm.each_with_index do |c1, i|
8       c2 = (i==perm.size-1) ? perm[0] : perm[i+1]
9       distance += euc_2d(cities[c1], cities[c2])
10    end
11    return distance
12  end
13
14  def random_permutation(cities)
15    perm = Array.new(cities.size){|i| i}
16    perm.each_index do |i|
17      r = rand(perm.size-i) + i
18      perm[r], perm[i] = perm[i], perm[r]
19    end
20    return perm
21  end
22
23  def stochastic_two_opt(parent)
24    perm = Array.new(parent)
25    c1, c2 = rand(perm.size), rand(perm.size)
26    exclude = [c1]
27    exclude << ((c1==0) ? perm.size-1 : c1-1)
28    exclude << ((c1==perm.size-1) ? 0 : c1+1)
29    c2 = rand(perm.size) while exclude.include?(c2)
30    c1, c2 = c2, c1 if c2 < c1
31    perm[c1...c2] = perm[c1...c2].reverse
32    return perm, [[parent[c1-1], parent[c1]], [parent[c2-1], parent[c2]]]
33  end
34
35  def is_tabu?(edge, tabu_list, iter, prohib_period)
36    tabu_list.each do |entry|
```

```
37        if entry[:edge] == edge
38          return true if entry[:iter] >= iter-prohib_period
39          return false
40        end
41      end
42      return false
43    end
44
45    def make_tabu(tabu_list, edge, iter)
46      tabu_list.each do |entry|
47        if entry[:edge] == edge
48          entry[:iter] = iter
49          return entry
50        end
51      end
52      entry = {:edge=>edge, :iter=>iter}
53      tabu_list.push(entry)
54      return entry
55    end
56
57    def to_edge_list(perm)
58      list = []
59      perm.each_with_index do |c1, i|
60        c2 = (i==perm.size-1) ? perm[0] : perm[i+1]
61        c1, c2 = c2, c1 if c1 > c2
62        list << [c1, c2]
63      end
64      return list
65    end
66
67    def equivalent?(el1, el2)
68      el1.each {|e| return false if !el2.include?(e) }
69      return true
70    end
71
72    def generate_candidate(best, cities)
73      candidate = {}
74      candidate[:vector], edges = stochastic_two_opt(best[:vector])
75      candidate[:cost] = cost(candidate[:vector], cities)
76      return candidate, edges
77    end
78
79    def get_candidate_entry(visited_list, permutation)
80      edgeList = to_edge_list(permutation)
81      visited_list.each do |entry|
82        return entry if equivalent?(edgeList, entry[:edgelist])
83      end
84      return nil
85    end
86
87    def store_permutation(visited_list, permutation, iteration)
88      entry = {}
89      entry[:edgelist] = to_edge_list(permutation)
90      entry[:iter] = iteration
91      entry[:visits] = 1
92      visited_list.push(entry)
```

```ruby
 93    return entry
 94  end
 95
 96  def sort_neighborhood(candidates, tabu_list, prohib_period, iteration)
 97    tabu, admissable = [], []
 98    candidates.each do |a|
 99      if is_tabu?(a[1][0], tabu_list, iteration, prohib_period) or
100         is_tabu?(a[1][1], tabu_list, iteration, prohib_period)
101        tabu << a
102      else
103        admissable << a
104      end
105    end
106    return [tabu, admissable]
107  end
108
109  def search(cities, max_cand, max_iter, increase, decrease)
110    current = {:vector=>random_permutation(cities)}
111    current[:cost] = cost(current[:vector], cities)
112    best = current
113    tabu_list, prohib_period = [], 1
114    visited_list, avg_size, last_change = [], 1, 0
115    max_iter.times do |iter|
116      candidate_entry = get_candidate_entry(visited_list, current[:vector])
117      if !candidate_entry.nil?
118        repetition_interval = iter - candidate_entry[:iter]
119        candidate_entry[:iter] = iter
120        candidate_entry[:visits] += 1
121        if repetition_interval < 2*(cities.size-1)
122          avg_size = 0.1*(iter-candidate_entry[:iter]) + 0.9*avg_size
123          prohib_period = (prohib_period.to_f * increase)
124          last_change = iter
125        end
126      else
127        store_permutation(visited_list, current[:vector], iter)
128      end
129      if iter-last_change > avg_size
130        prohib_period = [prohib_period*decrease,1].max
131        last_change = iter
132      end
133      candidates = Array.new(max_cand) do |i|
134        generate_candidate(current, cities)
135      end
136      candidates.sort! {|x,y| x.first[:cost] <=> y.first[:cost]}
137      tabu,admis = sort_neighborhood(candidates,tabu_list,prohib_period,iter)
138      if admis.size < 2
139        prohib_period = cities.size-2
140        last_change = iter
141      end
142      current,best_move_edges = (admis.empty?) ? tabu.first : admis.first
143      if !tabu.empty?
144        tf = tabu.first[0]
145        if tf[:cost]<best[:cost] and tf[:cost]<current[:cost]
146          current, best_move_edges = tabu.first
147        end
148      end
```

```
149    best_move_edges.each {|edge| make_tabu(tabu_list, edge, iter)}
150    best = candidates.first[0] if candidates.first[0][:cost] < best[:cost]
151    puts " > it=#{iter}, tenure=#{prohib_period.round}, best=#{best[:cost]}"
152  end
153  return best
154 end
155
156 if __FILE__ == $0
157  # problem configuration
158  berlin52 = [[565,575],[25,185],[345,750],[945,685],[845,655],
159    [880,660],[25,230],[525,1000],[580,1175],[650,1130],[1605,620],
160    [1220,580],[1465,200],[1530,5],[845,680],[725,370],[145,665],
161    [415,635],[510,875],[560,365],[300,465],[520,585],[480,415],
162    [835,625],[975,580],[1215,245],[1320,315],[1250,400],[660,180],
163    [410,250],[420,555],[575,665],[1150,1160],[700,580],[685,595],
164    [685,610],[770,610],[795,645],[720,635],[760,650],[475,960],
165    [95,260],[875,920],[700,500],[555,815],[830,485],[1170,65],
166    [830,610],[605,625],[595,360],[1340,725],[1740,245]]
167  # algorithm configuration
168  max_iter = 100
169  max_candidates = 50
170  increase = 1.3
171  decrease = 0.9
172  # execute the algorithm
173  best = search(berlin52, max_candidates, max_iter, increase, decrease)
174  puts "Done. Best Solution: c=#{best[:cost]}, v=#{best[:vector].inspect}"
175 end
```

Listing 2.10: Reactive Tabu Search in Ruby

2.11.6   References

Primary Sources

Reactive Tabu Search was proposed by Battiti and Tecchiolli as an extension to Tabu Search that included an adaptive tabu list size in addition to a diversification mechanism [7]. The technique also used efficient memory structures that were based on an earlier work by Battiti and Tecchiolli that considered a parallel tabu search [6]. Some early application papers by Battiti and Tecchiolli include a comparison to Simulated Annealing applied to the Quadratic Assignment Problem [8], benchmarked on instances of the knapsack problem and N-K models and compared with Repeated Local Minima Search, Simulated Annealing, and Genetic Algorithms [9], and training neural networks on an array of problem instances [10].

Learn More

Reactive Tabu Search was abstracted to a form called Reactive Local Search that considers adaptive methods that learn suitable parameters for heuristics that manage an embedded local search technique [4, 5]. Under this abstraction, the Reactive Tabu Search algorithm is a single example

of the Reactive Local Search principle applied to the Tabu Search. This
framework was further extended to the use of any adaptive machine learning
techniques to adapt the parameters of an algorithm by reacting to algorithm
outcomes online while solving a problem, called Reactive Search [1]. The
best reference for this general framework is the book on Reactive Search
Optimization by Battiti, Brunato, and Mascia [3]. Additionally, the review
chapter by Battiti and Brunato provides a contemporary description [2].

2.11.7   Bibliography

[1] R. Battiti. Machine learning methods for parameter tuning in heuristics.
    In *5th DIMACS Challenge Workshop: Experimental Methodology Day*,
    1996.

[2] R. Battiti and M. Brunato. *Handbook of Metaheuristics*, chapter
    Reactive Search Optimization: Learning while Optimizing. Springer
    Verlag, 2nd edition, 2009.

[3] R. Battiti, M. Brunato, and F. Mascia. *Reactive Search and Intelligent
    Optimization*. Springer, 2008.

[4] R. Battiti and M. Protasi. Reactive local search for the maximum
    clique problem. Technical Report TR-95-052, International Computer
    Science Institute, Berkeley, CA, 1995.

[5] R. Battiti and M. Protasi. Reactive local search for the maximum
    clique problem. *Algorithmica*, 29(4):610–637, 2001.

[6] R. Battiti and G. Tecchiolli. Parallel biased search for combinato-
    rial optimization: genetic algorithms and tabu. *Microprocessors and
    Microsystems*, 16(7):351–367, 1992.

[7] R. Battiti and G. Tecchiolli. The reactive tabu search. *ORSA Journal
    on Computing*, 6(2):126–140, 1994.

[8] R. Battiti and G. Tecchiolli. Simulated annealing and tabu search in
    the long run: a comparison on qap tasks. *Computer and Mathematics
    with Applications*, 28(6):1–8, 1994.

[9] R. Battiti and G. Tecchiolli. Local search with memory: Benchmarking
    RTS. *Operations Research Spektrum*, 17(2/3):67–86, 1995.

[10] R. Battiti and G. Tecchiolli. Training neural nets with the reactive
    tabu search. *IEEE Transactions on Neural Networks*, 6(5):1185–1200,
    1995.

Chapter 3

Evolutionary Algorithms

3.1 Overview

This chapter describes Evolutionary Algorithms.

3.1.1 Evolution

Evolutionary Algorithms belong to the Evolutionary Computation field of study concerned with computational methods inspired by the process and mechanisms of biological evolution. The process of evolution by means of natural selection (descent with modification) was proposed by Darwin to account for the variety of life and its suitability (adaptive fit) for its environment. The mechanisms of evolution describe how evolution actually takes place through the modification and propagation of genetic material (proteins). Evolutionary Algorithms are concerned with investigating computational systems that resemble simplified versions of the processes and mechanisms of evolution toward achieving the effects of these processes and mechanisms, namely the development of adaptive systems. Additional subject areas that fall within the realm of Evolutionary Computation are algorithms that seek to exploit the properties from the related fields of Population Genetics, Population Ecology, Coevolutionary Biology, and Developmental Biology.

3.1.2 References

Evolutionary Algorithms share properties of adaptation through an iterative process that accumulates and amplifies beneficial variation through trial and error. Candidate solutions represent members of a virtual population striving to survive in an environment defined by a problem specific objective function. In each case, the evolutionary process refines the adaptive fit of the population of candidate solutions in the environment, typically using surrogates for the mechanisms of evolution such as genetic recombination and mutation.

There are many excellent texts on the theory of evolution, although Darwin's original source can be an interesting and surprisingly enjoyable read [5]. Huxley's book defined the modern synthesis in evolutionary biology that combined Darwin's natural selection with Mendel's genetic mechanisms [25], although any good textbook on evolution will suffice (such as Futuyma's "*Evolution*" [13]). Popular science books on evolution are an easy place to start, such as Dawkins' "*The Selfish Gene*" that presents a gene-centric perspective on evolution [6], and Dennett's "*Darwin's Dangerous Idea*" that considers the algorithmic properties of the process [8].

Goldberg's classic text is still a valuable resource for the Genetic Algorithm [14], and Holland's text is interesting for those looking to learn about the research into adaptive systems that became the Genetic Algorithm [23]. Additionally, the seminal work by Koza should be considered for those interested in Genetic Programming [30], and Schwefel's seminal work should be considered for those with an interest in Evolution Strategies [34]. For an in-depth review of the history of research into the use of simulated evolutionary processed for problem solving, see Fogel [12] For a rounded and modern review of the field of Evolutionary Computation, Bäck, Fogel, and Michalewicz's two volumes of "*Evolutionary Computation*" are an excellent resource covering the major techniques, theory, and application specific concerns [2, 3]. For some additional modern books on the unified field of Evolutionary Computation and Evolutionary Algorithms, see De Jong [26], a recent edition of Fogel [11], and Eiben and Smith [9].

3.1.3   Extensions

There are many other algorithms and classes of algorithm that were not described from the field of Evolutionary Computation, not limited to:

- **Distributed Evolutionary Computation**: that are designed to partition a population across computer networks or computational units such as the Distributed or 'Island Population' Genetic Algorithm [4, 35] and Diffusion Genetic Algorithms (also known as Cellular Genetic Algorithms) [1].

- **Niching Genetic Algorithms**: that form groups or sub-populations automatically within a population such as the Deterministic Crowding Genetic Algorithm [31, 32], Restricted Tournament Selection [20, 21], and Fitness Sharing Genetic Algorithm [7, 19].

- **Evolutionary Multiple Objective Optimization Algorithms**: such as Vector-Evaluated Genetic Algorithm (VEGA) [33], Pareto Archived Evolution Strategy (PAES) [28, 29], and the Niched Pareto Genetic Algorithm (NPGA) [24].

- **Classical Techniques**: such as GENITOR [36], and the CHC Genetic Algorithm [10].

- **Competent Genetic Algorithms**: (so-called [15]) such as the Messy Genetic Algorithm [17, 18], Fast Messy Genetic Algorithm [16], Gene Expression Messy Genetic Algorithm [27], and the Linkage-Learning Genetic Algorithm [22].

3.1.4 Bibliography

[1] E. Alba and B. Dorronsoro. *Cellular Genetic Algorithms*. Springer, 2008.

[2] T. Bäck, D. B. Fogel, and Z. Michalewicz, editors. *Evolutionary Computation 1: Basic Algorithms and Operators*. IoP, 2000.

[3] T. Bäck, D. B. Fogel, and Z. Michalewicz, editors. *Evolutionary Computation 2: Advanced Algorithms and Operations*. IoP, 2000.

[4] E. Cantú-Paz. *Efficient and Accurate Parallel Genetic Algorithms*. Kluwer Academic Publishers (Springer), 2000.

[5] C. Darwin. *On the Origin of Species by Means of Natural Selection, or the Preservation of Favoured Races in the Struggle for Life*. John Murray, 1859.

[6] R. Dawkins. *The selfish gene*. Oxford University Press, 1976.

[7] K. Deb and D. E. Goldberg. An investigation of niche and species formation in genetic function optimization. In *Proceedings of the Second International Conference on Genetic Algorithms*, 1989.

[8] D. C. Dennett. *Darwin's Dangerous Idea*. Simon & Schuster, 1995.

[9] A. E. Eiben and J. E. Smith. *Introduction to evolutionary computing*. Springer, 2003.

[10] L. J. Eshelman. The CHC adaptive search algorithm: How to do safe search when engaging in nontraditional genetic recombination. In *Proceedings Foundations of Genetic Algorithms Conf.*, pages 265–283, 1991.

[11] D. B. Fogel. *Evolutionary computation: Toward a new philosophy of machine intelligence*. IEEE Press, 1995.

[12] D. B. Fogel. *Evolutionary Computation: The Fossil Record*. Wiley-IEEE Press, 1998.

[13] D. Futuyma. *Evolution*. Sinauer Associates Inc., 2nd edition, 2009.

[14] D. E. Goldberg. *Genetic Algorithms in Search, Optimization, and Machine Learning.* Addison-Wesley, 1989.

[15] D. E. Goldberg. *The design of innovation: Lessons from and for competent genetic algorithms.* Springer, 2002.

[16] D. E. Goldberg, K. Deb, H. Kargupta, and G. Harik. Rapid, accurate optimization of difficult problems using fast messy genetic algorithms. In *Proceedings of the Fifth International Conference on Genetic Algorithms*, 1993.

[17] D. E. Goldberg, K. Deb, and B. Korb. Messy genetic algorithms revisited: studies in mixed size and scale. *Complex Systems*, 4:415–444, 1990.

[18] D. E. Goldberg, B. Korb, and K. Deb. Messy genetic algorithms: Motivation, analysis, and first results. *Complex Systems*, 3:493–530, 1989.

[19] D. E. Goldberg and J. Richardson. Genetic algorithms with sharing for multimodal function optimization. In *Proceedings of the 2nd Internaltional Conference on Genetic Algorithms*, 1987.

[20] G. Harik. Finding multiple solutions in problems of bounded difficulty. Technical Report IlliGAL Report No. 94002, University of Illinois at Urbana–Champaign, 1994.

[21] G. Harik. Finding multimodal solutions using restricted tournament selection. In *Proceedings of the Sixth International Conference on Genetic Algorithms*, pages 24–31, 1995.

[22] G. R. Harik and D. E. Goldberg. Learning linkage. In *Foundations of Genetic Algorithms 4*, pages 247–262, 1996.

[23] J. H. Holland. *Adaptation in natural and artificial systems: An introductory analysis with applications to biology, control, and artificial intelligence.* University of Michigan Press, 1975.

[24] J. Horn, N. Nafpliotis, and D. E. Goldberg. A niched pareto genetic algorithm for multiobjective optimization. In *Proceedings of the First IEEE Conference on Evolutionary Computation, IEEE World Congress on Computational Intelligence*, volume 1, pages 82–87, 1994.

[25] J. Huxley. *Evolution: The Modern Synthesis.* Allen & Unwin, 1942.

[26] K. A. De Jong. *Evolutionary computation: A unified approach.* MIT Press, 2006.

[27] H. Kargupta. The gene expression messy genetic algorithm. In *Proceedings of the IEEE International Conference on Evolutionary Computation*, pages 814–819, 1996.

[28] J. D. Knowles and D. W. Corne. Local search, multiobjective optimization and the pareto archived evolution strategy. In *Proceedings of the Third Australia–Japan Joint Workshop on Intelligent and Evolutionary Systems*, pages 209–216, 1999.

[29] J. D. Knowles and D. W. Corne. The pareto archived evolution strategy : A new baseline algorithm for pareto multiobjective optimisation. In *Proceedings of the 1999 Congress on Evolutionary Computation*, pages 98–105, 1999.

[30] J. R. Koza. *Genetic programming: On the programming of computers by means of natural selection.* MIT Press, 1992.

[31] S. W. Mahfoud. Crowding and preselection revised. In *Parallel Problem Solving from Nature 2*, pages 27–36, 1992.

[32] S. W. Mahfoud. *Niching Methods for Genetic Algorithms.* PhD thesis, University of Illinois at Urbana–Champaign, 1995.

[33] D. J. Schaffer. *Some experiments in machine learning using vector evaluated genetic algorithms.* PhD thesis, Vanderbilt University, Tennessee, 1984.

[34] H-P. Schwefel. *Numerical Optimization of Computer Models.* John Wiley & Sons, 1981.

[35] R. Tanese. Distributed genetic algorithms. In *Proceedings of the third international conference on Genetic algorithms*, pages 434–439. Morgan Kaufmann Publishers Inc., 1989.

[36] D. Whitley. The GENITOR algorithm and selective pressure: Why rank-based allocation of reproductive trials is best. In D. Schaffer, editor, *Proceedings of the 3rd International Conference on Genetic Algorithms*, pages 116–121. Morgan Kaufmann, 1989.

3.2   Genetic Algorithm

Genetic Algorithm, GA, Simple Genetic Algorithm, SGA, Canonical Genetic Algorithm, CGA.

3.2.1   Taxonomy

The Genetic Algorithm is an Adaptive Strategy and a Global Optimization technique. It is an Evolutionary Algorithm and belongs to the broader study of Evolutionary Computation. The Genetic Algorithm is a sibling of other Evolutionary Algorithms such as Genetic Programming (Section 3.3), Evolution Strategies (Section 3.4), Evolutionary Programming (Section 3.6), and Learning Classifier Systems (Section 3.9). The Genetic Algorithm is a parent of a large number of variant techniques and sub-fields too numerous to list.

3.2.2   Inspiration

The Genetic Algorithm is inspired by population genetics (including heredity and gene frequencies), and evolution at the population level, as well as the Mendelian understanding of the structure (such as chromosomes, genes, alleles) and mechanisms (such as recombination and mutation). This is the so-called new or modern synthesis of evolutionary biology.

3.2.3   Metaphor

Individuals of a population contribute their genetic material (called the genotype) proportional to their suitability of their expressed genome (called their phenotype) to their environment, in the form of offspring. The next generation is created through a process of mating that involves recombination of two individuals genomes in the population with the introduction of random copying errors (called mutation). This iterative process may result in an improved adaptive-fit between the phenotypes of individuals in a population and the environment.

3.2.4   Strategy

The objective of the Genetic Algorithm is to maximize the payoff of candidate solutions in the population against a cost function from the problem domain. The strategy for the Genetic Algorithm is to repeatedly employ surrogates for the recombination and mutation genetic mechanisms on the population of candidate solutions, where the cost function (also known as objective or fitness function) applied to a decoded representation of a candidate governs the probabilistic contributions a given candidate solution can make to the subsequent generation of candidate solutions.

3.2.5 Procedure

Algorithm 3.2.1 provides a pseudocode listing of the Genetic Algorithm for minimizing a cost function.

Algorithm 3.2.1: Pseudocode for the Genetic Algorithm.

Input: $Population_{size}$, $Problem_{size}$, $P_{crossover}$, $P_{mutation}$
Output: S_{best}
1 Population ← InitializePopulation($Population_{size}$, $Problem_{size}$);
2 EvaluatePopulation(Population);
3 S_{best} ← GetBestSolution(Population);
4 **while** ¬StopCondition() **do**
5   Parents ← SelectParents(Population, $Population_{size}$);
6   Children ← ∅;
7   **foreach** $Parent_1$, $Parent_2$ ∈ Parents **do**
8       $Child_1$, $Child_2$ ← Crossover($Parent_1$, $Parent_2$, $P_{crossover}$);
9   Children ← Mutate($Child_1$, $P_{mutation}$);
10   Children ← Mutate($Child_2$, $P_{mutation}$);
11   **end**
12   EvaluatePopulation(Children);
13   S_{best} ← GetBestSolution(Children);
14   Population ← Replace(Population, Children);
15 **end**
16 **return** S_{best};

3.2.6 Heuristics

- Binary strings (referred to as 'bitstrings') are the classical representation as they can be decoded to almost any desired representation. Real-valued and integer variables can be decoded using the binary coded decimal method, one's or two's complement methods, or the gray code method, the latter of which is generally preferred.

- Problem specific representations and customized genetic operators should be adopted, incorporating as much prior information about the problem domain as possible.

- The size of the population must be large enough to provide sufficient coverage of the domain and mixing of the useful sub-components of the solution [7].

- The Genetic Algorithm is classically configured with a high probability of recombination (such as 95%-99% of the selected population) and a low probability of mutation (such as $\frac{1}{L}$ where L is the number of components in a solution) [1, 18].

- The fitness-proportionate selection of candidate solutions to contribute to the next generation should be neither too greedy (to avoid the takeover of fitter candidate solutions) nor too random.

3.2.7   Code Listing

Listing 3.1 provides an example of the Genetic Algorithm implemented in the Ruby Programming Language. The demonstration problem is a maximizing binary optimization problem called OneMax that seeks a binary string of unity (all '1' bits). The objective function provides only an indication of the number of correct bits in a candidate string, not the positions of the correct bits.

The Genetic Algorithm is implemented with a conservative configuration including binary tournament selection for the selection operator, one-point crossover for the recombination operator, and point mutations for the mutation operator.

```ruby
def onemax(bitstring)
  sum = 0
  bitstring.size.times {|i| sum+=1 if bitstring[i].chr=='1'}
  return sum
end

def random_bitstring(num_bits)
  return (0...num_bits).inject(""){|s,i| s<<((rand<0.5) ? "1" : "0")}
end

def binary_tournament(pop)
  i, j = rand(pop.size), rand(pop.size)
  j = rand(pop.size) while j==i
  return (pop[i][:fitness] > pop[j][:fitness]) ? pop[i] : pop[j]
end

def point_mutation(bitstring, rate=1.0/bitstring.size)
  child = ""
  bitstring.size.times do |i|
    bit = bitstring[i].chr
    child << ((rand()<rate) ? ((bit=='1') ? "0" : "1") : bit)
  end
  return child
end

def crossover(parent1, parent2, rate)
  return ""+parent1 if rand()>=rate
  point = 1 + rand(parent1.size-2)
  return parent1[0...point]+parent2[point...(parent1.size)]
end

def reproduce(selected, pop_size, p_cross, p_mutation)
```

```ruby
33    children = []
34    selected.each_with_index do |p1, i|
35      p2 = (i.modulo(2)==0) ? selected[i+1] : selected[i-1]
36      p2 = selected[0] if i == selected.size-1
37      child = {}
38      child[:bitstring] = crossover(p1[:bitstring], p2[:bitstring], p_cross)
39      child[:bitstring] = point_mutation(child[:bitstring], p_mutation)
40      children << child
41      break if children.size >= pop_size
42    end
43    return children
44  end
45
46  def search(max_gens, num_bits, pop_size, p_crossover, p_mutation)
47    population = Array.new(pop_size) do |i|
48      {:bitstring=>random_bitstring(num_bits)}
49    end
50    population.each{|c| c[:fitness] = onemax(c[:bitstring])}
51    best = population.sort{|x,y| y[:fitness] <=> x[:fitness]}.first
52    max_gens.times do |gen|
53      selected = Array.new(pop_size){|i| binary_tournament(population)}
54      children = reproduce(selected, pop_size, p_crossover, p_mutation)
55      children.each{|c| c[:fitness] = onemax(c[:bitstring])}
56      children.sort!{|x,y| y[:fitness] <=> x[:fitness]}
57      best = children.first if children.first[:fitness] >= best[:fitness]
58      population = children
59      puts " > gen #{gen}, best: #{best[:fitness]}, #{best[:bitstring]}"
60      break if best[:fitness] == num_bits
61    end
62    return best
63  end
64
65  if __FILE__ == $0
66    # problem configuration
67    num_bits = 64
68    # algorithm configuration
69    max_gens = 100
70    pop_size = 100
71    p_crossover = 0.98
72    p_mutation = 1.0/num_bits
73    # execute the algorithm
74    best = search(max_gens, num_bits, pop_size, p_crossover, p_mutation)
75    puts "done! Solution: f=#{best[:fitness]}, s=#{best[:bitstring]}"
76  end
```

Listing 3.1: Genetic Algorithm in Ruby

3.2.8 References

Primary Sources

Holland is the grandfather of the field that became Genetic Algorithms. Holland investigated adaptive systems in the late 1960s proposing an adaptive system formalism and adaptive strategies referred to as 'adaptive plans'

[8–10]. Holland's theoretical framework was investigated and elaborated by his Ph.D. students at the University of Michigan. Rosenberg investigated a chemical and molecular model of a biological inspired adaptive plan [19]. Bagley investigated meta-environments and a genetic adaptive plan referred to as a genetic algorithm applied to a simple game called hexapawn [2]. Cavicchio further elaborated the genetic adaptive plan by proposing numerous variations, referring to some as 'reproductive plans' [15].

Other important contributions were made by Frantz who investigated what were referred to as genetic algorithms for search [3], and Hollstien who investigated genetic plans for adaptive control and function optimization [12]. De Jong performed a seminal investigation of the genetic adaptive model (genetic plans) applied to continuous function optimization and his suite of test problems adopted are still commonly used [13]. Holland wrote the the seminal book on his research focusing on the proposed adaptive systems formalism, the reproductive and genetic adaptive plans, and provided a theoretical framework for the mechanisms used and explanation for the capabilities of what would become genetic algorithms [11].

Learn More

The field of genetic algorithms is very large, resulting in large numbers of variations on the canonical technique. Goldberg provides a classical overview of the field in a review article [5], as does Mitchell [16]. Whitley describes a classical tutorial for the Genetic Algorithm covering both practical and theoretical concerns [20].

The algorithm is highly-modular and a sub-field exists to study each sub-process, specifically: selection, recombination, mutation, and representation. The Genetic Algorithm is most commonly used as an optimization technique, although it should also be considered a general adaptive strategy [14]. The schema theorem is a classical explanation for the power of the Genetic Algorithm proposed by Holland [11], and investigated by Goldberg under the name of the building block hypothesis [4].

The classical book on genetic algorithms as an optimization and machine learning technique was written by Goldberg and provides an in-depth review and practical study of the approach [4]. Mitchell provides a contemporary reference text introducing the technique and the field [17]. Finally, Goldberg provides a modern study of the field, the lessons learned, and reviews the broader toolset of optimization algorithms that the field has produced [6].

3.2.9 Bibliography

[1] T. Bäck. Optimal mutation rates in genetic search. In *Proceedings of the Fifth International Conference on Genetic Algorithms*, pages 2–9, 1993.

[2] J. D. Bagley. *The behavior of adaptive systems which employ genetic and correlation algorithms*. PhD thesis, University of Michigan, 1967.

[3] D. R. Frantz. *Non-linearities in genetic adaptive search*. PhD thesis, University of Michigan, 1972.

[4] D. E. Goldberg. *Genetic Algorithms in Search, Optimization, and Machine Learning*. Addison-Wesley, 1989.

[5] D. E. Goldberg. Genetic and evolutionary algorithms come of age. *Communications of the ACM*, 37(3):113–119, 1994.

[6] D. E. Goldberg. *The design of innovation: Lessons from and for competent genetic algorithms*. Springer, 2002.

[7] D. E. Goldberg, K. Deb, and J. H. Clark. Genetic algorithms, noise, and the sizing of populations. *Complex Systems*, 6:333–362, 1992.

[8] J. H. Holland. Information processing in adaptive systems. In *Processing of Information in the Nervous System*, pages 330–338, 1962.

[9] J. H. Holland. Outline for a logical theory of adaptive systems. *Journal of the ACM (JACM)*, 9(3):297–314, 1962.

[10] J. H. Holland. Adaptive plans optimal for payoff-only environments. In *Proceedings of the Second Hawaii Conference on Systems Sciences*, 1969.

[11] J. H. Holland. *Adaptation in natural and artificial systems: An introductory analysis with applications to biology, control, and artificial intelligence*. University of Michigan Press, 1975.

[12] R. B. Hollstien. *Artificial genetic adaptation in computer control systems*. PhD thesis, The University of Michigan, 1971.

[13] K. A. De Jong. *An analysis of the behavior of a class of genetic adaptive systems*. PhD thesis, University of Michigan Ann Arbor, MI, USA, 1975.

[14] K. A. De Jong. Genetic algorithms are NOT function optimizers. In *Proceedings of the Second Workshop on Foundations of Genetic Algorithms*, pages 5–17. Morgan Kaufmann, 1992.

[15] D. J. Cavicchio Jr. *Adaptive Search Using Simulated Evolution*. PhD thesis, The University of Michigan, 1970.

[16] M. Mitchell. Genetic algorithms: An overview. *Complexity*, 1(1):31–39, 1995.

[17] M. Mitchell. *An Introduction to Genetic Algorithms*. MIT Press, 1998.

[18] H. Mühlenbein. How genetic algorithms really work: I. mutation and hillclimbing. In *Parallel Problem Solving from Nature 2*, pages 15–26, 1992.

[19] R. Rosenberg. *Simulation of genetic populations with biochemical properties*. PhD thesis, University of Michigan, 1967.

[20] D. Whitley. A genetic algorithm tutorial. *Statistics and Computing*, 4:65–85, 1994.

3.3   Genetic Programming

Genetic Programming, GP.

3.3.1   Taxonomy

The Genetic Programming algorithm is an example of an Evolutionary Algorithm and belongs to the field of Evolutionary Computation and more broadly Computational Intelligence and Biologically Inspired Computation. The Genetic Programming algorithm is a sibling to other Evolutionary Algorithms such as the Genetic Algorithm (Section 3.2), Evolution Strategies (Section 3.4), Evolutionary Programming (Section 3.6), and Learning Classifier Systems (Section 3.9). Technically, the Genetic Programming algorithm is an extension of the Genetic Algorithm. The Genetic Algorithm is a parent to a host of variations and extensions.

3.3.2   Inspiration

The Genetic Programming algorithm is inspired by population genetics (including heredity and gene frequencies), and evolution at the population level, as well as the Mendelian understanding of the structure (such as chromosomes, genes, alleles) and mechanisms (such as recombination and mutation). This is the so-called new or modern synthesis of evolutionary biology.

3.3.3   Metaphor

Individuals of a population contribute their genetic material (called the genotype) proportional to their suitability of their expressed genome (called their phenotype) to their environment. The next generation is created through a process of mating that involves genetic operators such as recombination of two individuals genomes in the population and the introduction of random copying errors (called mutation). This iterative process may result in an improved adaptive-fit between the phenotypes of individuals in a population and the environment.

Programs may be evolved and used in a secondary adaptive process, where an assessment of candidates at the end of that secondary adaptive process is used for differential reproductive success in the first evolutionary process. This system may be understood as the inter-dependencies experienced in evolutionary development where evolution operates upon an embryo that in turn develops into an individual in an environment that eventually may reproduce.

3.3.4   Strategy

The objective of the Genetic Programming algorithm is to use induction to devise a computer program. This is achieved by using evolutionary operators on candidate programs with a tree structure to improve the adaptive fit between the population of candidate programs and an objective function. An assessment of a candidate solution involves its execution.

3.3.5   Procedure

Algorithm 3.3.1 provides a pseudocode listing of the Genetic Programming algorithm for minimizing a cost function, based on Koza and Poli's tutorial [9].

The Genetic Program uses LISP-like symbolic expressions called S-expressions that represent the graph of a program with function nodes and terminal nodes. While the algorithm is running, the programs are treated like data, and when they are evaluated they are executed. The traversal of a program graph is always depth first, and functions must always return a value.

3.3.6   Heuristics

- The Genetic Programming algorithm was designed for inductive automatic programming and is well suited to symbolic regression, controller design, and machine learning tasks under the broader name of function approximation.

- Traditionally Lisp symbolic expressions are evolved and evaluated in a virtual machine, although the approach has been applied with compiled programming languages.

- The evaluation (fitness assignment) of a candidate solution typically takes the structure of the program into account, rewarding parsimony.

- The selection process should be balanced between random selection and greedy selection to bias the search towards fitter candidate solutions (exploitation), whilst promoting useful diversity into the population (exploration).

- A program may respond to zero or more input values and may produce one or more outputs.

- All functions used in the function node set must return a usable result. For example, the division function must return a sensible value (such as zero or one) when a division by zero occurs.

- All genetic operations ensure (or should ensure) that syntactically valid and executable programs are produced as a result of their application.

Algorithm 3.3.1: Pseudocode for Genetic Programming.

Input: $Population_{size}$, $nodes_{func}$, $nodes_{term}$, $P_{crossover}$, $P_{mutation}$, $P_{reproduction}$, $P_{alteration}$

Output: S_{best}

1   Population $\leftarrow$ InitializePopulation($Population_{size}$, $nodes_{func}$, $nodes_{term}$);

2   EvaluatePopulation(Population);

3   $S_{best} \leftarrow$ GetBestSolution(Population);

4   **while** ¬StopCondition() **do**

5   Children $\leftarrow \emptyset$;

6   **while** Size(Children) $< Population_{size}$ **do**

7   Operator $\leftarrow$ SelectGeneticOperator($P_{crossover}$, $P_{mutation}$, $P_{reproduction}$, $P_{alteration}$);

8   **if** Operator $\equiv$ CrossoverOperator **then**

9            $Parent_1$, $Parent_2 \leftarrow$ SelectParents(Population, $Population_{size}$);

10            $Child_1$, $Child_2 \leftarrow$ Crossover($Parent_1$, $Parent_2$);

11   Children $\leftarrow Child_1$;

12   Children $\leftarrow Child_2$;

13   **else if** Operator $\equiv$ MutationOperator **then**

14            $Parent_1 \leftarrow$ SelectParents(Population, $Population_{size}$);

15            $Child_1 \leftarrow$ Mutate($Parent_1$);

16   Children $\leftarrow Child_1$;

17   **else if** Operator $\equiv$ ReproductionOperator **then**

18            $Parent_1 \leftarrow$ SelectParents(Population, $Population_{size}$);

19            $Child_1 \leftarrow$ Reproduce($Parent_1$);

20   Children $\leftarrow Child_1$;

21   **else if** Operator $\equiv$ AlterationOperator **then**

22            $Parent_1 \leftarrow$ SelectParents(Population, $Population_{size}$);

23            $Child_1 \leftarrow$ AlterArchitecture($Parent_1$);

24   Children $\leftarrow Child_1$;

25   **end**

26   **end**

27   EvaluatePopulation(Children);

28      $S_{best} \leftarrow$ GetBestSolution(Children, S_{best});

29   Population $\leftarrow$ Children;

30   **end**

31   **return** S_{best};

- The Genetic Programming algorithm is commonly configured with a high-probability of crossover ($\geq 90\%$) and a low-probability of mutation ($\leq 1\%$). Other operators such as reproduction and architecture alterations are used with moderate-level probabilities and fill in the probabilistic gap.

- Architecture altering operations are not limited to the duplication and deletion of sub-structures of a given program.

- The crossover genetic operator in the algorithm is commonly configured to select a function as a the cross-point with a high-probability ($\geq 90\%$) and low-probability of selecting a terminal as a cross-point ($\leq 10\%$).

- The function set may also include control structures such as conditional statements and loop constructs.

- The Genetic Programing algorithm can be realized as a stack-based virtual machine as opposed to a call graph [11].

- The Genetic Programming algorithm can make use of Automatically Defined Functions (ADFs) that are sub-graphs and are promoted to the status of functions for reuse and are co-evolved with the programs.

- The genetic operators employed during reproduction in the algorithm may be considered transformation programs for candidate solutions and may themselves be co-evolved in the algorithm [1].

3.3.7   Code Listing

Listing 3.2 provides an example of the Genetic Programming algorithm implemented in the Ruby Programming Language based on Koza and Poli's tutorial [9].

The demonstration problem is an instance of a symbolic regression, where a function must be devised to match a set of observations. In this case the target function is a quadratic polynomial $x^2 + x + 1$ where $x \in [-1, 1]$. The observations are generated directly from the target function without noise for the purposes of this example. In practical problems, if one knew and had access to the target function then the genetic program would not be required.

The algorithm is configured to search for a program with the function set $\{+, -, \times, \div\}$ and the terminal set $\{X, R\}$, where X is the input value, and R is a static random variable generated for a program $X \in [-5, 5]$. A division by zero returns a value of one. The fitness of a candidate solution is calculated by evaluating the program on range of random input values and calculating the Root Mean Squared Error (RMSE). The algorithm is configured with a 90% probability of crossover, 8% probability of reproduction (copying), and a 2% probability of mutation. For brevity, the algorithm does not implement the architecture altering genetic operation and does not bias crossover points towards functions over terminals.

```ruby
def rand_in_bounds(min, max)
  return min + (max-min)*rand()
end

def print_program(node)
  return node if !node.kind_of?(Array)
  return "(#{node[0]} #{print_program(node[1])} #{print_program(node[2])})"
end

def eval_program(node, map)
  if !node.kind_of?(Array)
    return map[node].to_f if !map[node].nil?
    return node.to_f
  end
  arg1, arg2 = eval_program(node[1], map), eval_program(node[2], map)
  return 0 if node[0] === :/ and arg2 == 0.0
  return arg1.__send__(node[0], arg2)
end

def generate_random_program(max, funcs, terms, depth=0)
  if depth==max-1 or (depth>1 and rand()<0.1)
    t = terms[rand(terms.size)]
    return ((t=='R') ? rand_in_bounds(-5.0, +5.0) : t)
  end
  depth += 1
  arg1 = generate_random_program(max, funcs, terms, depth)
  arg2 = generate_random_program(max, funcs, terms, depth)
  return [funcs[rand(funcs.size)], arg1, arg2]
end

def count_nodes(node)
  return 1 if !node.kind_of?(Array)
  a1 = count_nodes(node[1])
  a2 = count_nodes(node[2])
  return a1+a2+1
end

def target_function(input)
  return input**2 + input + 1
end

def fitness(program, num_trials=20)
  sum_error = 0.0
  num_trials.times do |i|
    input = rand_in_bounds(-1.0, 1.0)
    error = eval_program(program, {'X'=>input}) - target_function(input)
    sum_error += error.abs
  end
  return sum_error / num_trials.to_f
end

def tournament_selection(pop, bouts)
  selected = Array.new(bouts){pop[rand(pop.size)]}
```

```ruby
54    selected.sort!{|x,y| x[:fitness]<=>y[:fitness]}
55    return selected.first
56  end
57
58  def replace_node(node, replacement, node_num, cur_node=0)
59    return [replacement,(cur_node+1)] if cur_node == node_num
60    cur_node += 1
61    return [node,cur_node] if !node.kind_of?(Array)
62    a1, cur_node = replace_node(node[1], replacement, node_num, cur_node)
63    a2, cur_node = replace_node(node[2], replacement, node_num, cur_node)
64    return [[node[0], a1, a2], cur_node]
65  end
66
67  def copy_program(node)
68    return node if !node.kind_of?(Array)
69    return [node[0], copy_program(node[1]), copy_program(node[2])]
70  end
71
72  def get_node(node, node_num, current_node=0)
73    return node,(current_node+1) if current_node == node_num
74    current_node += 1
75    return nil,current_node if !node.kind_of?(Array)
76    a1, current_node = get_node(node[1], node_num, current_node)
77    return a1,current_node if !a1.nil?
78    a2, current_node = get_node(node[2], node_num, current_node)
79    return a2,current_node if !a2.nil?
80    return nil,current_node
81  end
82
83  def prune(node, max_depth, terms, depth=0)
84    if depth == max_depth-1
85      t = terms[rand(terms.size)]
86      return ((t=='R') ? rand_in_bounds(-5.0, +5.0) : t)
87    end
88    depth += 1
89    return node if !node.kind_of?(Array)
90    a1 = prune(node[1], max_depth, terms, depth)
91    a2 = prune(node[2], max_depth, terms, depth)
92    return [node[0], a1, a2]
93  end
94
95  def crossover(parent1, parent2, max_depth, terms)
96    pt1, pt2 = rand(count_nodes(parent1)-2)+1, rand(count_nodes(parent2)-2)+1
97    tree1, c1 = get_node(parent1, pt1)
98    tree2, c2 = get_node(parent2, pt2)
99    child1, c1 = replace_node(parent1, copy_program(tree2), pt1)
100   child1 = prune(child1, max_depth, terms)
101   child2, c2 = replace_node(parent2, copy_program(tree1), pt2)
102   child2 = prune(child2, max_depth, terms)
103   return [child1, child2]
104 end
105
106 def mutation(parent, max_depth, functs, terms)
107   random_tree = generate_random_program(max_depth/2, functs, terms)
108   point = rand(count_nodes(parent))
109   child, count = replace_node(parent, random_tree, point)
```

```
110    child = prune(child, max_depth, terms)
111    return child
112  end
113
114  def search(max_gens, pop_size, max_depth, bouts, p_repro, p_cross, p_mut,
          functs, terms)
115    population = Array.new(pop_size) do |i|
116      {:prog=>generate_random_program(max_depth, functs, terms)}
117    end
118    population.each{|c| c[:fitness] = fitness(c[:prog])}
119    best = population.sort{|x,y| x[:fitness] <=> y[:fitness]}.first
120    max_gens.times do |gen|
121      children = []
122      while children.size < pop_size
123        operation = rand()
124        p1 = tournament_selection(population, bouts)
125        c1 = {}
126        if operation < p_repro
127          c1[:prog] = copy_program(p1[:prog])
128        elsif operation < p_repro+p_cross
129          p2 = tournament_selection(population, bouts)
130          c2 = {}
131          c1[:prog],c2[:prog] = crossover(p1[:prog], p2[:prog], max_depth,
              terms)
132          children << c2
133        elsif operation < p_repro+p_cross+p_mut
134          c1[:prog] = mutation(p1[:prog], max_depth, functs, terms)
135        end
136        children << c1 if children.size < pop_size
137      end
138      children.each{|c| c[:fitness] = fitness(c[:prog])}
139      population = children
140      population.sort!{|x,y| x[:fitness] <=> y[:fitness]}
141      best = population.first if population.first[:fitness] <= best[:fitness]
142      puts " > gen #{gen}, fitness=#{best[:fitness]}"
143      break if best[:fitness] == 0
144    end
145    return best
146  end
147
148  if __FILE__ == $0
149    # problem configuration
150    terms = ['X', 'R']
151    functs = [:+, :-, :*, :/]
152    # algorithm configuration
153    max_gens = 100
154    max_depth = 7
155    pop_size = 100
156    bouts = 5
157    p_repro = 0.08
158    p_cross = 0.90
159    p_mut = 0.02
160    # execute the algorithm
161    best = search(max_gens, pop_size, max_depth, bouts, p_repro, p_cross,
          p_mut, functs, terms)
162    puts "done! Solution: f=#{best[:fitness]}, #{print_program(best[:prog])}"
```

end

Listing 3.2: Genetic Programming in Ruby

3.3.8   References

Primary Sources

An early work by Cramer involved the study of a Genetic Algorithm using an expression tree structure for representing computer programs for primitive mathematical operations [3]. Koza is credited with the development of the field of Genetic Programming. An early paper by Koza referred to his hierarchical genetic algorithms as an extension to the simple genetic algorithm that use symbolic expressions (S-expressions) as a representation and were applied to a range of induction-style problems [4]. The seminal reference for the field is Koza's 1992 book on Genetic Programming [5].

Learn More

The field of Genetic Programming is vast, including many books, dedicated conferences and thousands of publications. Koza is generally credited with the development and popularizing of the field, publishing a large number of books and papers himself. Koza provides a practical introduction to the field as a tutorial and provides recent overview of the broader field and usage of the technique [9].

In addition his the seminal 1992 book, Koza has released three more volumes in the series including volume II on Automatically Defined Functions (ADFs) [6], volume III that considered the Genetic Programming Problem Solver (GPPS) for automatically defining the function set and program structure for a given problem [7], and volume IV that focuses on the human competitive results the technique is able to achieve in a routine manner [8]. All books are rich with targeted and practical demonstration problem instances.

Some additional excellent books include a text by Banzhaf et al. that provides an introduction to the field [2], Langdon and Poli's detailed look at the technique [10], and Poli, Langdon, and McPhee's contemporary and practical field guide to Genetic Programming [12].

3.3.9   Bibliography

[1] P. J. Angeline. Two self-adaptive crossover operators for genetic programming. In Peter J. Angeline and K. E. Kinnear, Jr., editors, *Advances in Genetic Programming 2*, pages 89–110. MIT Press, 1996.

[2] W. Banzhaf, P. Nordin, R. E. Keller, and F. D. Francone. *Genetic Programming – An Introduction; On the Automatic Evolution of Computer Programs and its Applications.* Morgan Kaufmann, 1998.

[3] N. L. Cramer. A representation for the adaptive generation of simple sequential programs. In J. J. Grefenstette, editor, *Proceedings of the 1st International Conference on Genetic Algorithms*, pages 183–187, 1985.

[4] J. R. Koza. Hierarchical genetic algorithms operating on populations of computer programs. In N. S. Sridharan, editor, *Proceedings of the Eleventh International Joint Conference on Artificial Intelligence IJCAI-89*, volume 1, pages 768–774, 1989.

[5] J. R. Koza. *Genetic programming: On the programming of computers by means of natural selection.* MIT Press, 1992.

[6] J. R. Koza. *Genetic programming II: Automatic discovery of reusable programs.* MIT Press, 1994.

[7] J. R. Koza, F. H. Bennett III, D. Andre, and M. A. Keane. *Genetic programming III: Darwinian invention and problem solving.* Morgan Kaufmann, 1999.

[8] J. R. Koza, M. A. Keane, M. J. Streeter, W. Mydlowec, J. Yu, and G. Lanza. *Genetic Programming IV: Routine Human-Competitive Machine Intelligence.* Springer, 2003.

[9] J. R. Koza and R. Poli. *Search methodologies: Introductory tutorials in optimization and decision support techniques*, chapter 5: Genetic Programming, pages 127–164. Springer, 2005.

[10] W. B. Langdon and R. Poli. *Foundations of Genetic Programming.* Springer-Verlag, 2002.

[11] T. Perkis. Stack-based genetic programming. In *Proc IEEE Congress on Computational Intelligence*, 1994.

[12] R. Poli, W. B. Langdon, and N. F. McPhee. *A Field Programmers Guide to Genetic Programming.* Lulu Enterprises, 2008.

3.4   Evolution Strategies

Evolution Strategies, Evolution Strategy, Evolutionary Strategies, ES.

3.4.1   Taxonomy

Evolution Strategies is a global optimization algorithm and is an instance of an Evolutionary Algorithm from the field of Evolutionary Computation. Evolution Strategies is a sibling technique to other Evolutionary Algorithms such as Genetic Algorithms (Section 3.2), Genetic Programming (Section 3.3), Learning Classifier Systems (Section 3.9), and Evolutionary Programming (Section 3.6). A popular descendant of the Evolution Strategies algorithm is the Covariance Matrix Adaptation Evolution Strategies (CMA-ES).

3.4.2   Inspiration

Evolution Strategies is inspired by the theory of evolution by means of natural selection. Specifically, the technique is inspired by macro-level or the species-level process of evolution (phenotype, hereditary, variation) and is not concerned with the genetic mechanisms of evolution (genome, chromosomes, genes, alleles).

3.4.3   Strategy

The objective of the Evolution Strategies algorithm is to maximize the suitability of collection of candidate solutions in the context of an objective function from a domain. The objective was classically achieved through the adoption of dynamic variation, a surrogate for descent with modification, where the amount of variation was adapted dynamically with performance-based heuristics. Contemporary approaches co-adapt parameters that control the amount and bias of variation with the candidate solutions.

3.4.4   Procedure

Instances of Evolution Strategies algorithms may be concisely described with a custom terminology in the form $(\mu, \lambda) - ES$, where μ is number of candidate solutions in the parent generation, and λ is the number of candidate solutions generated from the parent generation. In this configuration, the best μ are kept if $\lambda > \mu$, where λ must be great or equal to μ. In addition to the so-called comma-selection Evolution Strategies algorithm, a plus-selection variation may be defined $(\mu + \lambda) - ES$, where the best members of the union of the μ and λ generations compete based on objective fitness for a position in the next generation. The simplest configuration is the $(1 + 1) - ES$, which is a type of greedy hill climbing algorithm. Algorithm 3.4.1 provides a pseudocode listing of the $(\mu, \lambda) - ES$ algorithm for minimizing a cost function. The algorithm shows the adaptation of candidate solutions that co-adapt their own strategy parameters that influence the amount of mutation applied to a candidate solutions descendants.

Algorithm 3.4.1: Pseudocode for (μ, λ) Evolution Strategies.

Input: μ, λ, ProblemSize
Output: S_{best}
1 Population $\leftarrow$ InitializePopulation(μ, ProblemSize);
2 EvaluatePopulation(Population);
3 $S_{best} \leftarrow$ GetBest(Population, 1);
4 **while** ¬StopCondition() **do**
5 | Children $\leftarrow \emptyset$;
6 | **for** $i = 0$ to λ **do**
7 | | $Parent_i \leftarrow$ GetParent(Population, i);
8 | | $S_i \leftarrow \emptyset$;
9 | | $Si_{problem} \leftarrow$ Mutate($Pi_{problem}$, $Pi_{strategy}$);
10 | | $Si_{strategy} \leftarrow$ Mutate($Pi_{strategy}$);
11 | | Children $\leftarrow S_i$;
12 | **end**
13 | EvaluatePopulation(Children);
14 | $S_{best} \leftarrow$ GetBest(Children + S_{best}, 1);
15 | Population $\leftarrow$ SelectBest(Population, Children, μ);
16 **end**
17 **return** S_{best};

3.4.5 Heuristics

- Evolution Strategies uses problem specific representations, such as real values for continuous function optimization.

- The algorithm is commonly configured such that $1 \leq \mu \leq \lambda$.

- The ratio of μ to λ influences the amount of selection pressure (greediness) exerted by the algorithm.

- A contemporary update to the algorithms notation includes a ρ as $(\mu/\rho, \lambda) - ES$ that specifies the number of parents that will contribute to each new candidate solution using a recombination operator.

- A classical rule used to govern the amount of mutation (standard deviation used in mutation for continuous function optimization) was the $\frac{1}{5}$-rule, where the ratio of successful mutations should be $\frac{1}{5}$ of all mutations. If it is greater the variance is increased, otherwise if the ratio is is less, the variance is decreased.

- The comma-selection variation of the algorithm can be good for dynamic problem instances given its capability for continued exploration of the search space, whereas the plus-selection variation can be good for refinement and convergence.

3.4.6   Code Listing

Listing 3.3 provides an example of the Evolution Strategies algorithm implemented in the Ruby Programming Language. The demonstration problem is an instance of a continuous function optimization that seeks $\min f(x)$ where $f = \sum_{i=1}^{n} x_i^2$, $-5.0 \leq x_i \leq 5.0$ and $n = 2$. The optimal solution for this basin function is $(v_0, \ldots, v_{n-1}) = 0.0$. The algorithm is a implementation of Evolution Strategies based on simple version described by Bäck and Schwefel [2], which was also used as the basis of a detailed empirical study [11]. The algorithm is an $(30+20)-ES$ that adapts both the problem and strategy (standard deviations) variables. More contemporary implementations may modify the strategy variables differently, and include an additional set of adapted strategy parameters to influence the direction of mutation (see [7] for a concise description).

```ruby
def objective_function(vector)
  return vector.inject(0.0) {|sum, x| sum + (x ** 2.0)}
end

def random_vector(minmax)
  return Array.new(minmax.size) do |i|
    minmax[i][0] + ((minmax[i][1] - minmax[i][0]) * rand())
  end
end

def random_gaussian(mean=0.0, stdev=1.0)
  u1 = u2 = w = 0
  begin
    u1 = 2 * rand() - 1
    u2 = 2 * rand() - 1
    w = u1 * u1 + u2 * u2
  end while w >= 1
  w = Math.sqrt((-2.0 * Math.log(w)) / w)
  return mean + (u2 * w) * stdev
end

def mutate_problem(vector, stdevs, search_space)
  child = Array(vector.size)
  vector.each_with_index do |v, i|
    child[i] = v + stdevs[i] * random_gaussian()
    child[i] = search_space[i][0] if child[i] < search_space[i][0]
    child[i] = search_space[i][1] if child[i] > search_space[i][1]
  end
  return child
```

```ruby
30  end
31
32  def mutate_strategy(stdevs)
33    tau = Math.sqrt(2.0*stdevs.size.to_f)**-1.0
34    tau_p = Math.sqrt(2.0*Math.sqrt(stdevs.size.to_f))**-1.0
35    child = Array.new(stdevs.size) do |i|
36      stdevs[i] * Math.exp(tau_p*random_gaussian() + tau*random_gaussian())
37    end
38    return child
39  end
40
41  def mutate(par, minmax)
42    child = {}
43    child[:vector] = mutate_problem(par[:vector], par[:strategy], minmax)
44    child[:strategy] = mutate_strategy(par[:strategy])
45    return child
46  end
47
48  def init_population(minmax, pop_size)
49    strategy = Array.new(minmax.size) do |i|
50      [0, (minmax[i][1]-minmax[i][0]) * 0.05]
51    end
52    pop = Array.new(pop_size, {})
53    pop.each_index do |i|
54      pop[i][:vector] = random_vector(minmax)
55      pop[i][:strategy] = random_vector(strategy)
56    end
57    pop.each{|c| c[:fitness] = objective_function(c[:vector])}
58    return pop
59  end
60
61  def search(max_gens, search_space, pop_size, num_children)
62    population = init_population(search_space, pop_size)
63    best = population.sort{|x,y| x[:fitness] <=> y[:fitness]}.first
64    max_gens.times do |gen|
65      children = Array.new(num_children) do |i|
66        mutate(population[i], search_space)
67      end
68      children.each{|c| c[:fitness] = objective_function(c[:vector])}
69      union = children+population
70      union.sort!{|x,y| x[:fitness] <=> y[:fitness]}
71      best = union.first if union.first[:fitness] < best[:fitness]
72      population = union.first(pop_size)
73      puts " > gen #{gen}, fitness=#{best[:fitness]}"
74    end
75    return best
76  end
77
78  if __FILE__ == $0
79    # problem configuration
80    problem_size = 2
81    search_space = Array.new(problem_size) {|i| [-5, +5]}
82    # algorithm configuration
83    max_gens = 100
84    pop_size = 30
85    num_children = 20
```

```
86   # execute the algorithm
87   best = search(max_gens, search_space, pop_size, num_children)
88   puts "done! Solution: f=#{best[:fitness]}, s=#{best[:vector].inspect}"
89 end
```

Listing 3.3: Evolution Strategies in Ruby

3.4.7   References

Primary Sources

Evolution Strategies was developed by three students (Bienert, Rechenberg, Schwefel) at the Technical University in Berlin in 1964 in an effort to robotically optimize an aerodynamics design problem. The seminal work in Evolution Strategies was Rechenberg's PhD thesis [5] that was later published as a book [6], both in German. Many technical reports and papers were published by Schwefel and Rechenberg, although the seminal paper published in English was by Klockgether and Schwefel on the two–phase nozzle design problem [4].

Learn More

Schwefel published his PhD dissertation [8] not long after Rechenberg, which was also published as a book [9], both in German. Schwefel's book was later translated into English and represents a classical reference for the technique [10]. Bäck et al. provide a classical introduction to the technique, covering the history, development of the algorithm, and the steps that lead it to where it was in 1991 [1]. Beyer and Schwefel provide a contemporary introduction to the field that includes a detailed history of the approach, the developments and improvements since its inception, and an overview of the theoretical findings that have been made [3].

3.4.8   Bibliography

[1] T. Bäck, F. Hoffmeister, and H-P. Schwefel. A survey of evolution strategies. In *Proceedings of the Fourth International Conference on Genetic Algorithms*, pages 2–9, 1991.

[2] T. Bäck and H-P. Schwefel. An overview of evolutionary algorithms for parameter optimization. *Evolutionary Computation*, 1(1):1–23, 1993.

[3] H-G. Beyer and H-P. Schwefel. Evolution strategies: A comprehensive introduction. *Natural Computing: an international journal*, 1(1):3–52, 2002.

[4] J. Klockgether and H-P. Schwefel. Two–phase nozzle and hollow core jet experiments. In *Proceedings of the Eleventh Symp. Engineering*

Aspects of Magnetohydrodynamics, pages 141–148. California Institute of Technology, 1970.

[5] I. Rechenberg. *Evolutionsstrategie: Optimierung technischer Systeme nach Prinzipien der biologischen Evolution.* PhD thesis, Technical University of Berlin, Department of Process Engineering, 1971.

[6] I. Rechenberg. *Evolutionsstrategie: Optimierung technischer Systeme nach Prinzipien der biologischen Evolution.* Frommann-Holzboog Verlag, 1973.

[7] G. Rudolph. *Evolutionary Computation 1: Basic Algorithms and Operations*, chapter 9: Evolution Strategies, pages 81–88. IoP Press, 2000.

[8] H-P. Schwefel. *Evolutionsstrategie und numerische Optimierung.* PhD thesis, Technical University of Berlin, Department of Process Engineering, 1975.

[9] H-P. Schwefel. *Numerische Optimierung von Computer – Modellen mittels der Evolutionsstrategie.* Birkhaeuser, 1977.

[10] H-P. Schwefel. *Numerical Optimization of Computer Models.* John Wiley & Sons, 1981.

[11] X. Yao and Y. Liu. Fast evolution strategies. In *Proceedings of the 6th International Conference on Evolutionary Programming VI*, pages 151–162, 1997.

3.5   Differential Evolution

Differential Evolution, DE.

3.5.1   Taxonomy

Differential Evolution is a Stochastic Direct Search and Global Optimization algorithm, and is an instance of an Evolutionary Algorithm from the field of Evolutionary Computation. It is related to sibling Evolutionary Algorithms such as the Genetic Algorithm (Section 3.2), Evolutionary Programming (Section 3.6), and Evolution Strategies (Section 3.4), and has some similarities with Particle Swarm Optimization (Section 6.2).

3.5.2   Strategy

The Differential Evolution algorithm involves maintaining a population of candidate solutions subjected to iterations of recombination, evaluation, and selection. The recombination approach involves the creation of new candidate solution components based on the weighted difference between two randomly selected population members added to a third population member. This perturbs population members relative to the spread of the broader population. In conjunction with selection, the perturbation effect self-organizes the sampling of the problem space, bounding it to known areas of interest.

3.5.3   Procedure

Differential Evolution has a specialized nomenclature that describes the adopted configuration. This takes the form of $DE/x/y/z$, where x represents the solution to be perturbed (such a random or best). The y signifies the number of difference vectors used in the perturbation of x, where a difference vectors is the difference between two randomly selected although distinct members of the population. Finally, z signifies the recombination operator performed such as `bin` for binomial and `exp` for exponential.

Algorithm 3.5.1 provides a pseudocode listing of the Differential Evolution algorithm for minimizing a cost function, specifically a DE/rand/-1/bin configuration. Algorithm 3.5.2 provides a pseudocode listing of the `NewSample` function from the Differential Evolution algorithm.

3.5.4   Heuristics

- Differential evolution was designed for nonlinear, non-differentiable continuous function optimization.

- The weighting factor $F \in [0, 2]$ controls the amplification of differential variation, a value of 0.8 is suggested.

Algorithm 3.5.1: Pseudocode for Differential Evolution.

Input: $Population_{size}$, $Problem_{size}$, $Weighting_{factor}$, $Crossover_{rate}$

Output: S_{best}

1   Population $\leftarrow$ InitializePopulation($Population_{size}$, $Problem_{size}$);

2   EvaluatePopulation(Population);

3   S_{best} $\leftarrow$ GetBestSolution(Population);

4   **while** $\neg$ StopCondition() **do**

5   NewPopulation $\leftarrow \emptyset$;

6   **foreach** $P_i \in$ Population **do**

7         $S_i \leftarrow$ NewSample(P_i, Population, $Problem_{size}$, $Weighting_{factor}$, $Crossover_{rate}$);

8   **if** Cost(S_i) $\leq$ Cost(P_i) **then**

9   NewPopulation $\leftarrow S_i$;

10   **else**

11   NewPopulation $\leftarrow P_i$;

12   **end**

13   **end**

14   Population $\leftarrow$ NewPopulation;

15   EvaluatePopulation(Population);

16   S_{best} $\leftarrow$ GetBestSolution(Population);

17   **end**

18   **return** S_{best};

- the crossover weight $CR \in [0, 1]$ probabilistically controls the amount of recombination, a value of 0.9 is suggested.

- The initial population of candidate solutions should be randomly generated from within the space of valid solutions.

- The popular configurations are DE/rand/1/* and DE/best/2/*.

3.5.5 Code Listing

Listing 3.4 provides an example of the Differential Evolution algorithm implemented in the Ruby Programming Language. The demonstration problem is an instance of a continuous function optimization that seeks $\min f(x)$ where $f = \sum_{i=1}^{n} x_i^2$, $-5.0 \leq x_i \leq 5.0$ and $n = 3$. The optimal solution for this basin function is $(v_0, \ldots, v_{n-1}) = 0.0$. The algorithm is an implementation of Differential Evolution with the DE/rand/1/bin configuration proposed by Storn and Price [9].

Algorithm 3.5.2: Pseudocode for the `NewSample` function.

Input: P_0, Population, NP, F, CR
Output: S

1 **repeat**
2 | $P_1 \leftarrow$ RandomMember(Population);
3 **until** $P_1 \neq P_0$;
4 **repeat**
5 | $P_2 \leftarrow$ RandomMember(Population);
6 **until** $P_2 \neq P_0 \vee P_2 \neq P_1$;
7 **repeat**
8 | $P_3 \leftarrow$ RandomMember(Population);
9 **until** $P_3 \neq P_0 \vee P_3 \neq P_1 \vee P_3 \neq P_2$;
10 CutPoint $\leftarrow$ RandomPosition(NP);
11 $S \leftarrow 0$;
12 **for** i **to** NP **do**
13 | **if** $i \equiv$ CutPoint $\wedge$ Rand() $<$ CR **then**
14 | | $S_i \leftarrow P_{3_i} +$ F $\times (P_{1_i}$- $P_{2_i})$;
15 | **else**
16 | | $S_i \leftarrow P_{0_i}$;
17 | **end**
18 **end**
19 **return** S;

```ruby
def objective_function(vector)
  return vector.inject(0.0) {|sum, x| sum + (x ** 2.0)}
end

def random_vector(minmax)
  return Array.new(minmax.size) do |i|
    minmax[i][0] + ((minmax[i][1] - minmax[i][0]) * rand())
  end
end

def de_rand_1_bin(p0, p1, p2, p3, f, cr, search_space)
  sample = {:vector=>Array.new(p0[:vector].size)}
  cut = rand(sample[:vector].size-1) + 1
  sample[:vector].each_index do |i|
    sample[:vector][i] = p0[:vector][i]
    if (i==cut or rand() < cr)
      v = p3[:vector][i] + f * (p1[:vector][i] - p2[:vector][i])
      v = search_space[i][0] if v < search_space[i][0]
      v = search_space[i][1] if v > search_space[i][1]
      sample[:vector][i] = v
    end
  end
  return sample
end
```

```ruby
25
26  def select_parents(pop, current)
27    p1, p2, p3 = rand(pop.size), rand(pop.size), rand(pop.size)
28    p1 = rand(pop.size) until p1 != current
29    p2 = rand(pop.size) until p2 != current and p2 != p1
30    p3 = rand(pop.size) until p3 != current and p3 != p1 and p3 != p2
31    return [p1,p2,p3]
32  end
33
34  def create_children(pop, minmax, f, cr)
35    children = []
36    pop.each_with_index do |p0, i|
37      p1, p2, p3 = select_parents(pop, i)
38      children << de_rand_1_bin(p0, pop[p1], pop[p2], pop[p3], f, cr, minmax)
39    end
40    return children
41  end
42
43  def select_population(parents, children)
44    return Array.new(parents.size) do |i|
45      (children[i][:cost]<=parents[i][:cost]) ? children[i] : parents[i]
46    end
47  end
48
49  def search(max_gens, search_space, pop_size, f, cr)
50    pop = Array.new(pop_size) {|i| {:vector=>random_vector(search_space)}}
51    pop.each{|c| c[:cost] = objective_function(c[:vector])}
52    best = pop.sort{|x,y| x[:cost] <=> y[:cost]}.first
53    max_gens.times do |gen|
54      children = create_children(pop, search_space, f, cr)
55      children.each{|c| c[:cost] = objective_function(c[:vector])}
56      pop = select_population(pop, children)
57      pop.sort!{|x,y| x[:cost] <=> y[:cost]}
58      best = pop.first if pop.first[:cost] < best[:cost]
59      puts " > gen #{gen+1}, fitness=#{best[:cost]}"
60    end
61    return best
62  end
63
64  if __FILE__ == $0
65    # problem configuration
66    problem_size = 3
67    search_space = Array.new(problem_size) {|i| [-5, +5]}
68    # algorithm configuration
69    max_gens = 200
70    pop_size = 10*problem_size
71    weightf = 0.8
72    crossf = 0.9
73    # execute the algorithm
74    best = search(max_gens, search_space, pop_size, weightf, crossf)
75    puts "done! Solution: f=#{best[:cost]}, s=#{best[:vector].inspect}"
76  end
```

Listing 3.4: Differential Evolution in Ruby

3.5.6   References

Primary Sources

The Differential Evolution algorithm was presented by Storn and Price in a technical report that considered DE1 and DE2 variants of the approach applied to a suite of continuous function optimization problems [7]. An early paper by Storn applied the approach to the optimization of an IIR-filter (Infinite Impulse Response) [5]. A second early paper applied the approach to a second suite of benchmark problem instances, adopting the contemporary nomenclature for describing the approach, including the DE/rand/1/* and DE/best/2/* variations [8]. The early work including technical reports and conference papers by Storn and Price culminated in a seminal journal article [9].

Learn More

A classical overview of Differential Evolution was presented by Price and Storn [2], and terse introduction to the approach for function optimization is presented by Storn [6]. A seminal extended description of the algorithm with sample applications was presented by Storn and Price as a book chapter [3]. Price, Storn, and Lampinen released a contemporary book dedicated to Differential Evolution including theory, benchmarks, sample code, and numerous application demonstrations [4]. Chakraborty also released a book considering extensions to address complexities such as rotation invariance and stopping criteria [1].

3.5.7   Bibliography

[1] U. K. Chakraborty. *Advances in Differential Evolution*. Springer, 2008.

[2] K. Price and R. Storn. Differential evolution: Numerical optimization made easy. *Dr. Dobb's Journal*, 78:18–24, 1997.

[3] K. V. Price. *New Ideas in Optimization*, chapter An introduction to differential evolution, pages 79–108. McGraw-Hill Ltd., UK, 1999.

[4] K. V. Price, R. M. Storn, and J. A. Lampinen. *Differential evolution: A practical approach to global optimization*. Springer, 2005.

[5] R. Storn. Differential evolution design of an IIR-filter. In *Proceedings IEEE Conference Evolutionary Computation*, pages 268–273. IEEE, 1996.

[6] R. Storn. On the usage of differential evolution for function optimization. In *Proceedings Fuzzy Information Processing Society, 1996 Biennial Conference of the North American*, pages 519–523, 1996.

[7] R. Storn and K. Price. Differential evolution: A simple and efficient adaptive scheme for global optimization over continuous spaces. Technical Report TR-95-012, International Computer Science Institute, Berkeley, CA, 1995.

[8] R. Storn and K. Price. Minimizing the real functions of the ICEC'96 contest by differential evolution. In *Proceedings of IEEE International Conference on Evolutionary Computation*, pages 842–844. IEEE, 1996.

[9] R. Storn and K. Price. Differential evolution: A simple and efficient heuristic for global optimization over continuous spaces. *Journal of Global Optimization*, 11:341–359, 1997.

3.6   Evolutionary Programming

Evolutionary Programming, EP.

3.6.1   Taxonomy

Evolutionary Programming is a Global Optimization algorithm and is
an instance of an Evolutionary Algorithm from the field of Evolutionary
Computation. The approach is a sibling of other Evolutionary Algorithms
such as the Genetic Algorithm (Section 3.2), and Learning Classifier Systems
(Section 3.9). It is sometimes confused with Genetic Programming given
the similarity in name (Section 3.3), and more recently it shows a strong
functional similarity to Evolution Strategies (Section 3.4).

3.6.2   Inspiration

Evolutionary Programming is inspired by the theory of evolution by means
of natural selection. Specifically, the technique is inspired by macro-level
or the species-level process of evolution (phenotype, hereditary, variation)
and is not concerned with the genetic mechanisms of evolution (genome,
chromosomes, genes, alleles).

3.6.3   Metaphor

A population of a species reproduce, creating progeny with small pheno-
typical variation. The progeny and the parents compete based on their
suitability to the environment, where the generally more fit members constitute the subsequent generation and are provided with the opportunity
to reproduce themselves. This process repeats, improving the adaptive fit
between the species and the environment.

3.6.4   Strategy

The objective of the Evolutionary Programming algorithm is to maximize the
suitability of a collection of candidate solutions in the context of an objective
function from the domain. This objective is pursued by using an adaptive
model with surrogates for the processes of evolution, specifically hereditary
(reproduction with variation) under competition. The representation used
for candidate solutions is directly assessable by a cost or objective function
from the domain.

3.6.5   Procedure

Algorithm 3.6.1 provides a pseudocode listing of the Evolutionary Programming algorithm for minimizing a cost function.

Algorithm 3.6.1: Pseudocode for Evolutionary Programming.

Input: $Population_{size}$, ProblemSize, BoutSize
Output: S_{best}
1 Population ← InitializePopulation($Population_{size}$, ProblemSize);
2 EvaluatePopulation(Population);
3 S_{best} ← GetBestSolution(Population);
4 **while** ¬StopCondition() **do**
5   Children ← ∅;
6   **foreach** $Parent_i$ ∈ Population **do**
7         $Child_i$ ← Mutate($Parent_i$);
8   Children ← $Child_i$;
9   **end**
10   EvaluatePopulation(Children);
11   S_{best} ← GetBestSolution(Children, S_{best});
12   Union ← Population + Children;
13   **foreach** S_i ∈ Union **do**
14   **for** 1 to BoutSize **do**
15   S_j ← RandomSelection(Union);
16   **if** Cost(S_i) < Cost(S_j) **then**
17   Si_{wins} ← Si_{wins} + 1;
18   **end**
19   **end**
20   **end**
21   Population ← SelectBestByWins(Union, $Population_{size}$);
22 **end**
23 **return** S_{best};

3.6.6 Heuristics

- The representation for candidate solutions should be domain specific, such as real numbers for continuous function optimization.

- The sample size (bout size) for tournament selection during competition is commonly between 5% and 10% of the population size.

- Evolutionary Programming traditionally only uses the mutation operator to create new candidate solutions from existing candidate solutions. The crossover operator that is used in some other Evolutionary Algorithms is not employed in Evolutionary Programming.

- Evolutionary Programming is concerned with the linkage between parent and child candidate solutions and is not concerned with surrogates for genetic mechanisms.

- Continuous function optimization is a popular application for the approach, where real-valued representations are used with a Gaussian-based mutation operator.

- The mutation-specific parameters used in the application of the algorithm to continuous function optimization can be adapted in concert with the candidate solutions [4].

3.6.7   Code Listing

Listing 3.5 provides an example of the Evolutionary Programming algorithm implemented in the Ruby Programming Language. The demonstration problem is an instance of a continuous function optimization that seeks $\min f(x)$ where $f = \sum_{i=1}^{n} x_i^2$, $-5.0 \leq x_i \leq 5.0$ and $n = 2$. The optimal solution for this basin function is $(v_0, \ldots, v_{n-1}) = 0.0$. The algorithm is an implementation of Evolutionary Programming based on the classical implementation for continuous function optimization by Fogel et al. [4] with per-variable adaptive variance based on Fogel's description for a self-adaptive variation on page 160 of his 1995 book [3].

```ruby
def objective_function(vector)
  return vector.inject(0.0) {|sum, x| sum + (x ** 2.0)}
end

def random_vector(minmax)
  return Array.new(minmax.size) do |i|
    minmax[i][0] + ((minmax[i][1] - minmax[i][0]) * rand())
  end
end

def random_gaussian(mean=0.0, stdev=1.0)
  u1 = u2 = w = 0
  begin
    u1 = 2 * rand() - 1
    u2 = 2 * rand() - 1
    w = u1 * u1 + u2 * u2
  end while w >= 1
  w = Math.sqrt((-2.0 * Math.log(w)) / w)
  return mean + (u2 * w) * stdev
end

def mutate(candidate, search_space)
  child = {:vector=>[], :strategy=>[]}
  candidate[:vector].each_with_index do |v_old, i|
    s_old = candidate[:strategy][i]
    v = v_old + s_old * random_gaussian()
    v = search_space[i][0] if v < search_space[i][0]
    v = search_space[i][1] if v > search_space[i][1]
    child[:vector] << v
    child[:strategy] << s_old + random_gaussian() * s_old.abs**0.5
  end
  return child
```

```ruby
33   end
34
35   def tournament(candidate, population, bout_size)
36     candidate[:wins] = 0
37     bout_size.times do |i|
38       other = population[rand(population.size)]
39       candidate[:wins] += 1 if candidate[:fitness] < other[:fitness]
40     end
41   end
42
43   def init_population(minmax, pop_size)
44     strategy = Array.new(minmax.size) do |i|
45       [0, (minmax[i][1]-minmax[i][0]) * 0.05]
46     end
47     pop = Array.new(pop_size, {})
48     pop.each_index do |i|
49       pop[i][:vector] = random_vector(minmax)
50       pop[i][:strategy] = random_vector(strategy)
51     end
52     pop.each{|c| c[:fitness] = objective_function(c[:vector])}
53     return pop
54   end
55
56   def search(max_gens, search_space, pop_size, bout_size)
57     population = init_population(search_space, pop_size)
58     population.each{|c| c[:fitness] = objective_function(c[:vector])}
59     best = population.sort{|x,y| x[:fitness] <=> y[:fitness]}.first
60     max_gens.times do |gen|
61       children = Array.new(pop_size) {|i| mutate(population[i], search_space)}
62       children.each{|c| c[:fitness] = objective_function(c[:vector])}
63       children.sort!{|x,y| x[:fitness] <=> y[:fitness]}
64       best = children.first if children.first[:fitness] < best[:fitness]
65       union = children+population
66       union.each{|c| tournament(c, union, bout_size)}
67       union.sort!{|x,y| y[:wins] <=> x[:wins]}
68       population = union.first(pop_size)
69       puts " > gen #{gen}, fitness=#{best[:fitness]}"
70     end
71     return best
72   end
73
74   if __FILE__ == $0
75     # problem configuration
76     problem_size = 2
77     search_space = Array.new(problem_size) {|i| [-5, +5]}
78     # algorithm configuration
79     max_gens = 200
80     pop_size = 100
81     bout_size = 5
82     # execute the algorithm
83     best = search(max_gens, search_space, pop_size, bout_size)
84     puts "done! Solution: f=#{best[:fitness]}, s=#{best[:vector].inspect}"
85   end
```

Listing 3.5: Evolutionary Programming in Ruby

3.6.8   References

Primary Sources

Evolutionary Programming was developed by Lawrence Fogel, outlined in early papers (such as [5]) and later became the focus of his PhD dissertation [6]. Fogel focused on the use of an evolutionary process for the development of control systems using Finite State Machine (FSM) representations. Fogel's early work on Evolutionary Programming culminated in a book (co-authored with Owens and Walsh) that elaborated the approach, focusing on the evolution of state machines for the prediction of symbols in time series data [9].

Learn More

The field of Evolutionary Programming lay relatively dormant for 30 years until it was revived by Fogel's son, David. Early works considered the application of Evolutionary Programming to control systems [11], and later function optimization (system identification) culminating in a book on the approach [1], and David Fogel's PhD dissertation [2]. Lawrence Fogel collaborated in the revival of the technique, including reviews [7, 8] and extensions on what became the focus of the approach on function optimization [4].

Yao et al. provide a seminal study of Evolutionary Programming proposing an extension and racing it against the classical approach on a large number of test problems [12]. Finally, Porto provides an excellent contemporary overview of the field and the technique [10].

3.6.9   Bibliography

[1] D. B. Fogel. *System Identification Through Simulated Evolution: A Machine Learning Approach to Modeling*. Needham Heights, 1991.

[2] D. B. Fogel. *Evolving artificial intelligence*. PhD thesis, University of California, San Diego, CA, USA, 1992.

[3] D. B. Fogel. *Evolutionary computation: Toward a new philosophy of machine intelligence*. IEEE Press, 1995.

[4] D. B. Fogel, L. J. Fogel, and J. W. Atmar. Meta-evolutionary programming. In *Proceedings 25th Asilomar Conf. Signals, Systems, and Computers*, pages 540–545, 1991.

[5] L. J. Fogel. Autonomous automata. *Industrial Research*, 4:14–19, 1962.

[6] L. J. Fogel. *On the Organization of Intellect*. PhD thesis, UCLA, 1964.

[7] L. J. Fogel. The future of evolutionary programming. In *Proceedings of the Conference on Signals, Systems and Computers*, 1990.

[8] L. J. Fogel. *Computational Intelligence: Imitating Life*, chapter Evolutionary Programming in Perspective: the Top-down View, pages 135–146. IEEE Press, 1994.

[9] L. J. Fogel, A. J. Owens, and M. J. Walsh. *Artificial Intelligence Through Simulated Evolution*. Wiley, 1966.

[10] V. W. Porto. *Evolutionary Computation 1: Basic Algorithms and Operations*, chapter 10: Evolutionary Programming, pages 89–102. IoP Press, 2000.

[11] A. V. Sebald and D. B. Fogel. Design of SLAYR neural networks using evolutionary programming. In *Proceedings of the 24th Asilomar Conference on Signals, Systems and Computers*, pages 1020–1024, 1990.

[12] X. Yao, Y. Liu, and G. Lin. Evolutionary programming made faster. *IEEE Transactions on Evolutionary Computation*, 3(2):82–102, 1999.

3.7   Grammatical Evolution

Grammatical Evolution, GE.

3.7.1   Taxonomy

Grammatical Evolution is a Global Optimization technique and an instance of an Evolutionary Algorithm from the field of Evolutionary Computation. It may also be considered an algorithm for Automatic Programming. Grammatical Evolution is related to other Evolutionary Algorithms for evolving programs such as Genetic Programming (Section 3.3) and Gene Expression Programming (Section 3.8), as well as the classical Genetic Algorithm that uses binary strings (Section 3.2).

3.7.2   Inspiration

The Grammatical Evolution algorithm is inspired by the biological process used for generating a protein from genetic material as well as the broader genetic evolutionary process. The genome is comprised of DNA as a string of building blocks that are transcribed to RNA. RNA codons are in turn translated into sequences of amino acids and used in the protein. The resulting protein in its environment is the phenotype.

3.7.3   Metaphor

The phenotype is a computer program that is created from a binary string-based genome. The genome is decoded into a sequence of integers that are in turn mapped onto pre-defined rules that makeup the program. The mapping from genotype to the phenotype is a one-to-many process that uses a wrapping feature. This is like the biological process observed in many bacteria, viruses, and mitochondria, where the same genetic material is used in the expression of different genes. The mapping adds robustness to the process both in the ability to adopt structure-agnostic genetic operators used during the evolutionary process on the sub-symbolic representation and the transcription of well-formed executable programs from the representation.

3.7.4   Strategy

The objective of Grammatical Evolution is to adapt an executable program to a problem specific objective function. This is achieved through an iterative process with surrogates of evolutionary mechanisms such as descent with variation, genetic mutation and recombination, and genetic transcription and gene expression. A population of programs are evolved in a sub-symbolic form as variable length binary strings and mapped to a symbolic and well-structured form as a context free grammar for execution.

3.7.5 Procedure

A grammar is defined in Backus Normal Form (BNF), which is a context free grammar expressed as a series of production rules comprised of terminals and non-terminals. A variable-length binary string representation is used for the optimization process. Bits are read from the a candidate solutions genome in blocks of 8 called a codon, and decoded to an integer (in the range between 0 and $2^8 - 1$). If the end of the binary string is reached when reading integers, the reading process loops back to the start of the string, effectively creating a circular genome. The integers are mapped to expressions from the BNF until a complete syntactically correct expression is formed. This may not use a solutions entire genome, or use the decoded genome more than once given it's circular nature. Algorithm 3.7.1 provides a pseudocode listing of the Grammatical Evolution algorithm for minimizing a cost function.

3.7.6 Heuristics

- Grammatical Evolution was designed to optimize programs (such as mathematical equations) to specific cost functions.

- Classical genetic operators used by the Genetic Algorithm may be used in the Grammatical Evolution algorithm, such as point mutations and one-point crossover.

- Codons (groups of bits mapped to an integer) are commonly fixed at 8 bits, proving a range of integers $\in [0, 2^8 - 1]$ that is scaled to the range of rules using a modulo function.

- Additional genetic operators may be used with variable-length representations such as codon segments, duplication (add to the end), number of codons selected at random, and deletion.

3.7.7 Code Listing

Listing 3.6 provides an example of the Grammatical Evolution algorithm implemented in the Ruby Programming Language based on the version described by O'Neill and Ryan [5]. The demonstration problem is an instance of symbolic regression $f(x) = x^4 + x^3 + x^2 + x$, where $x \in [1, 10]$. The grammar used in this problem is:

- Non-terminals: $N = \{expr, op, pre\_op\}$

- Terminals: $T = \{+, -, \div, \times, x, 1.0\}$

- Expression (program): $S = $ `<expr>`

The production rules for the grammar in BNF are:

Algorithm 3.7.1: Pseudocode for Grammatical Evolution.

Input: Grammar, $Codon_{numbits}$, $Population_{size}$, $P_{crossover}$, $P_{mutation}$, P_{delete}, $P_{duplicate}$

Output: S_{best}

1 Population $\leftarrow$ InitializePopulation($Population_{size}$, $Codon_{numbits}$);
2 **foreach** $S_i \in$ Population **do**
3     $Si_{integers} \leftarrow$ Decode($Si_{bitstring}$, $Codon_{numbits}$);
4     $Si_{program} \leftarrow$ Map($Si_{integers}$, Grammar);
5     $Si_{cost} \leftarrow$ Execute($Si_{program}$);
6 **end**
7 $S_{best} \leftarrow$ GetBestSolution(Population);
8 **while** $\neg$StopCondition() **do**
9   Parents $\leftarrow$ SelectParents(Population, $Population_{size}$);
10   Children $\leftarrow \emptyset$;
11   **foreach** $Parent_i$, $Parent_j \in$ Parents **do**
12       $S_i \leftarrow$ Crossover($Parent_i$, $Parent_j$, $P_{crossover}$);
13       $Si_{bitstring} \leftarrow$ CodonDeletion($Si_{bitstring}$, P_{delete});
14       $Si_{bitstring} \leftarrow$ CodonDuplication($Si_{bitstring}$, $P_{duplicate}$);
15       $Si_{bitstring} \leftarrow$ Mutate($Si_{bitstring}$, $P_{mutation}$);
16   Children $\leftarrow S_i$;
17   **end**
18   **foreach** $S_i \in$ Children **do**
19       $Si_{integers} \leftarrow$ Decode($Si_{bitstring}$, $Codon_{numbits}$);
20       $Si_{program} \leftarrow$ Map($Si_{integers}$, Grammar);
21       $Si_{cost} \leftarrow$ Execute($Si_{program}$);
22   **end**
23    $S_{best} \leftarrow$ GetBestSolution(Children);
24   Population $\leftarrow$ Replace(Population, Children);
25 **end**
26 **return** S_{best};

- `<expr> ::= <expr><op><expr>` , `(<expr><op><expr>)`, `<pre_op>(<expr>)`, `<var>`

- `<op> ::=` $+, -, \div, \times$

- `<var> ::=` x, 1.0

The algorithm uses point mutation and a codon-respecting one-point crossover operator. Binary tournament selection is used to determine the parent population's contribution to the subsequent generation. Binary strings are decoded to integers using an unsigned binary. Candidate solutions are then mapped directly into executable Ruby code and executed. A given candidate solution is evaluated by comparing its output against the target function and taking the sum of the absolute errors over a number of trials. The probabilities of point mutation, codon deletion, and codon duplication are hard coded as relative probabilities to each solution, although should be parameters of the algorithm. In this case they are heuristically defined as $\frac{1.0}{L}$, $\frac{0.5}{NC}$ and $\frac{1.0}{NC}$ respectively, where L is the total number of bits, and NC is the number of codons in a given candidate solution.

Solutions are evaluated by generating a number of random samples from the domain and calculating the mean error of the program to the expected outcome. Programs that contain a single term or those that return an invalid (NaN) or infinite result are penalized with an enormous error value. The implementation uses a maximum depth in the expression tree, whereas traditionally such deep expression trees are marked as invalid. Programs that resolve to a single expression that returns the output are penalized.

```ruby
def binary_tournament(pop)
  i, j = rand(pop.size), rand(pop.size)
  j = rand(pop.size) while j==i
  return (pop[i][:fitness] < pop[j][:fitness]) ? pop[i] : pop[j]
end

def point_mutation(bitstring, rate=1.0/bitstring.size.to_f)
  child = ""
  bitstring.size.times do |i|
    bit = bitstring[i].chr
    child << ((rand()<rate) ? ((bit=='1') ? "0" : "1") : bit)
  end
  return child
end

def one_point_crossover(parent1, parent2, codon_bits, p_cross=0.30)
  return ""+parent1[:bitstring] if rand()>=p_cross
  cut = rand([parent1.size, parent2.size].min/codon_bits)
  cut *= codon_bits
  p2size = parent2[:bitstring].size
  return parent1[:bitstring][0...cut]+parent2[:bitstring][cut...p2size]
end

def codon_duplication(bitstring, codon_bits, rate=1.0/codon_bits.to_f)
  return bitstring if rand() >= rate
  codons = bitstring.size/codon_bits
  return bitstring + bitstring[rand(codons)*codon_bits, codon_bits]
end

def codon_deletion(bitstring, codon_bits, rate=0.5/codon_bits.to_f)
  return bitstring if rand() >= rate
  codons = bitstring.size/codon_bits
  off = rand(codons)*codon_bits
  return bitstring[0...off] + bitstring[off+codon_bits...bitstring.size]
end

def reproduce(selected, pop_size, p_cross, codon_bits)
  children = []
```

```ruby
39    selected.each_with_index do |p1, i|
40      p2 = (i.modulo(2)==0) ? selected[i+1] : selected[i-1]
41      p2 = selected[0] if i == selected.size-1
42      child = {}
43      child[:bitstring] = one_point_crossover(p1, p2, codon_bits, p_cross)
44      child[:bitstring] = codon_deletion(child[:bitstring], codon_bits)
45      child[:bitstring] = codon_duplication(child[:bitstring], codon_bits)
46      child[:bitstring] = point_mutation(child[:bitstring])
47      children << child
48      break if children.size == pop_size
49    end
50    return children
51  end
52
53  def random_bitstring(num_bits)
54    return (0...num_bits).inject(""){|s,i| s<<((rand<0.5) ? "1" : "0")}
55  end
56
57  def decode_integers(bitstring, codon_bits)
58    ints = []
59    (bitstring.size/codon_bits).times do |off|
60      codon = bitstring[off*codon_bits, codon_bits]
61      sum = 0
62      codon.size.times do |i|
63        sum += ((codon[i].chr=='1') ? 1 : 0) * (2 ** i);
64      end
65      ints << sum
66    end
67    return ints
68  end
69
70  def map(grammar, integers, max_depth)
71    done, offset, depth = false, 0, 0
72    symbolic_string = grammar["S"]
73    begin
74      done = true
75      grammar.keys.each do |key|
76        symbolic_string = symbolic_string.gsub(key) do |k|
77          done = false
78          set = (k=="EXP" && depth>=max_depth-1) ? grammar["VAR"] : grammar[k]
79          integer = integers[offset].modulo(set.size)
80          offset = (offset==integers.size-1) ? 0 : offset+1
81          set[integer]
82        end
83      end
84      depth += 1
85    end until done
86    return symbolic_string
87  end
88
89  def target_function(x)
90    return x**4.0 + x**3.0 + x**2.0 + x
91  end
92
93  def sample_from_bounds(bounds)
94    return bounds[0] + ((bounds[1] - bounds[0]) * rand())
```

```
95    end
96
97    def cost(program, bounds, num_trials=30)
98      return 9999999 if program.strip == "INPUT"
99      sum_error = 0.0
100     num_trials.times do
101       x = sample_from_bounds(bounds)
102       expression = program.gsub("INPUT", x.to_s)
103       begin score = eval(expression) rescue score = 0.0/0.0 end
104       return 9999999 if score.nan? or score.infinite?
105       sum_error += (score - target_function(x)).abs
106     end
107     return sum_error / num_trials.to_f
108   end
109
110   def evaluate(candidate, codon_bits, grammar, max_depth, bounds)
111     candidate[:integers] = decode_integers(candidate[:bitstring], codon_bits)
112     candidate[:program] = map(grammar, candidate[:integers], max_depth)
113     candidate[:fitness] = cost(candidate[:program], bounds)
114   end
115
116   def search(max_gens, pop_size, codon_bits, num_bits, p_cross, grammar,
              max_depth, bounds)
117     pop = Array.new(pop_size) {|i| {:bitstring=>random_bitstring(num_bits)}}
118     pop.each{|c| evaluate(c,codon_bits, grammar, max_depth, bounds)}
119     best = pop.sort{|x,y| x[:fitness] <=> y[:fitness]}.first
120     max_gens.times do |gen|
121       selected = Array.new(pop_size){|i| binary_tournament(pop)}
122       children = reproduce(selected, pop_size, p_cross,codon_bits)
123       children.each{|c| evaluate(c, codon_bits, grammar, max_depth, bounds)}
124       children.sort!{|x,y| x[:fitness] <=> y[:fitness]}
125       best = children.first if children.first[:fitness] <= best[:fitness]
126       pop=(children+pop).sort{|x,y| x[:fitness]<=>y[:fitness]}.first(pop_size)
127       puts " > gen=#{gen}, f=#{best[:fitness]}, s=#{best[:bitstring]}"
128       break if best[:fitness] == 0.0
129     end
130     return best
131   end
132
133   if __FILE__ == $0
134     # problem configuration
135     grammar = {"S"=>"EXP",
136       "EXP"=>[" EXP BINARY EXP ", " (EXP BINARY EXP) ", " VAR "],
137       "BINARY"=>["+", "-", "/", "*" ],
138       "VAR"=>["INPUT", "1.0"]}
139     bounds = [1, 10]
140     # algorithm configuration
141     max_depth = 7
142     max_gens = 50
143     pop_size = 100
144     codon_bits = 4
145     num_bits = 10*codon_bits
146     p_cross = 0.30
147     # execute the algorithm
148     best = search(max_gens, pop_size, codon_bits, num_bits, p_cross, grammar,
              max_depth, bounds)
```

```
149    puts "done! Solution: f=#{best[:fitness]}, s=#{best[:program]}"
150    end
```

Listing 3.6: Grammatical Evolution in Ruby

3.7.8 References

Primary Sources

Grammatical Evolution was proposed by Ryan, Collins and O'Neill in a seminal conference paper that applied the approach to a symbolic regression problem [7]. The approach was born out of the desire for syntax preservation while evolving programs using the Genetic Programming algorithm. This seminal work was followed by application papers for a symbolic integration problem [2, 3] and solving trigonometric identities [8].

Learn More

O'Neill and Ryan provide a high-level introduction to Grammatical Evolution and early demonstration applications [4]. The same authors provide a thorough introduction to the technique and overview of the state of the field [5]. O'Neill and Ryan present a seminal reference for Grammatical Evolution in their book [6]. A second more recent book considers extensions to the approach improving its capability on dynamic problems [1].

3.7.9 Bibliography

[1] I. Dempsey, M. O'Neill, and A. Brabazon. *Foundations in Grammatical Evolution for Dynamic Environments.* Springer, 2009.

[2] M. O'Neill and C. Ryan. Grammatical evolution: A steady state approach. In *Proceedings of the Second International Workshop on Frontiers in Evolutionary Algorithms*, pages 419–423, 1998.

[3] M. O'Neill and C. Ryan. Grammatical evolution: A steady state approach. In *Late Breaking Papers at the Genetic Programming 1998 Conference*, 1998.

[4] M. O'Neill and C. Ryan. Under the hood of grammatical evolution. In *Proceedings of the Genetic and Evolutionary Computation Conference*, 1999.

[5] M. O'Neill and C. Ryan. Grammatical evolution. *IEEE Transactions on Evolutionary Computation*, 5(4):349–358, 2001.

[6] M. O'Neill and C. Ryan. *Grammatical Evolution: Evolutionary Automatic Programming in an Arbitrary Language.* Springer, 2003.

[7] C. Ryan, J. J. Collins, and M. O'Neill. Grammatical evolution: Evolving programs for an arbitrary language. In *Lecture Notes in Computer Science 1391. First European Workshop on Genetic Programming*, 1998.

[8] C. Ryan, J. J. Collins, and M. O'Neill. Grammatical evolution: Solving trigonometric identities. In *Proceedings of Mendel 1998: 4th International Mendel Conference on Genetic Algorithms, Optimisation Problems, Fuzzy Logic, Neural Networks, Rough Sets.*, pages 111–119, 1998.

3.8   Gene Expression Programming

Gene Expression Programming, GEP.

3.8.1   Taxonomy

Gene Expression Programming is a Global Optimization algorithm and an Automatic Programming technique, and it is an instance of an Evolutionary Algorithm from the field of Evolutionary Computation. It is a sibling of other Evolutionary Algorithms such as a the Genetic Algorithm (Section 3.2) as well as other Evolutionary Automatic Programming techniques such as Genetic Programming (Section 3.3) and Grammatical Evolution (Section 3.7).

3.8.2   Inspiration

Gene Expression Programming is inspired by the replication and expression of the DNA molecule, specifically at the gene level. The expression of a gene involves the transcription of its DNA to RNA which in turn forms amino acids that make up proteins in the phenotype of an organism. The DNA building blocks are subjected to mechanisms of variation (mutations such as coping errors) as well as recombination during sexual reproduction.

3.8.3   Metaphor

Gene Expression Programming uses a linear genome as the basis for genetic operators such as mutation, recombination, inversion, and transposition. The genome is comprised of chromosomes and each chromosome is comprised of genes that are translated into an expression tree to solve a given problem. The robust gene definition means that genetic operators can be applied to the sub-symbolic representation without concern for the structure of the resultant gene expression, providing separation of genotype and phenotype.

3.8.4   Strategy

The objective of the Gene Expression Programming algorithm is to improve the adaptive fit of an expressed program in the context of a problem specific cost function. This is achieved through the use of an evolutionary process that operates on a sub-symbolic representation of candidate solutions using surrogates for the processes (descent with modification) and mechanisms (genetic recombination, mutation, inversion, transposition, and gene expression) of evolution.

3.8.5 Procedure

A candidate solution is represented as a linear string of symbols called Karva notation or a K-expression, where each symbol maps to a function or terminal node. The linear representation is mapped to an expression tree in a breadth-first manner. A K-expression has fixed length and is comprised of one or more sub-expressions (genes), which are also defined with a fixed length. A gene is comprised of two sections, a head which may contain any function or terminal symbols, and a tail section that may only contain terminal symbols. Each gene will always translate to a syntactically correct expression tree, where the tail portion of the gene provides a genetic buffer which ensures closure of the expression.

Algorithm 3.8.1 provides a pseudocode listing of the Gene Expression Programming algorithm for minimizing a cost function.

Algorithm 3.8.1: Pseudocode for GEP.

Input: Grammar, $Population_{size}$, $Head_{length}$, $Tail_{length}$, $P_{crossover}$, $P_{mutation}$

Output: S_{best}

1 Population $\leftarrow$ InitializePopulation($Population_{size}$, Grammar, $Head_{length}$, $Tail_{length}$);
2 **foreach** $S_i \in$ Population **do**
3      $Si_{program} \leftarrow$ DecodeBreadthFirst(Si_{genome}, Grammar);
4      $Si_{cost} \leftarrow$ Execute($Si_{program}$);
5 **end**
6 $S_{best} \leftarrow$ GetBestSolution(Population);
7 **while** ¬StopCondition() **do**
8   Parents $\leftarrow$ SelectParents(Population, $Population_{size}$);
9   Children $\leftarrow \emptyset$;
10   **foreach** $Parent_1$, $Parent_2 \in$ Parents **do**
11          $Si_{genome} \leftarrow$ Crossover($Parent_1$, $Parent_2$, $P_{crossover}$);
12          $Si_{genome} \leftarrow$ Mutate(Si_{genome}, $P_{mutation}$);
13   Children $\leftarrow S_i$;
14   **end**
15   **foreach** $S_i \in$ Children **do**
16          $Si_{program} \leftarrow$ DecodeBreadthFirst(Si_{genome}, Grammar);
17          $Si_{cost} \leftarrow$ Execute($Si_{program}$);
18   **end**
19   Population $\leftarrow$ Replace(Population, Children);
20      $S_{best} \leftarrow$ GetBestSolution(Children);
21 **end**
22 **return** S_{best};

3.8.6   Heuristics

- The length of a chromosome is defined by the number of genes, where a gene length is defined by $h + t$. The h is a user defined parameter (such as 10), and t is defined as $t = h(n-1)+1$, where the n represents the maximum arity of functional nodes in the expression (such as 2 if the arithmetic functions $\times, \div, -, +$ are used).

- The mutation operator substitutes expressions along the genome, although must respect the gene rules such that function and terminal nodes are mutated in the head of genes, whereas only terminal nodes are substituted in the tail of genes.

- Crossover occurs between two selected parents from the population and can occur based on a one-point cross, two point cross, or a gene-based approach where genes are selected from the parents with uniform probability.

- An inversion operator may be used with a low probability that reverses a small sequence of symbols (1-3) within a section of a gene (tail or head).

- A transposition operator may be used that has a number of different modes, including: duplicate a small sequences (1-3) from somewhere on a gene to the head, small sequences on a gene to the root of the gene, and moving of entire genes in the chromosome. In the case of intra-gene transpositions, the sequence in the head of the gene is moved down to accommodate the copied sequence and the length of the head is truncated to maintain consistent gene sizes.

- A '?' may be included in the terminal set that represents a numeric constant from an array that is evolved on the end of the genome. The constants are read from the end of the genome and are substituted for '?' as the expression tree is created (in breadth first order). Finally the numeric constants are used as array indices in yet another chromosome of numerical values which are substituted into the expression tree.

- Mutation is low (such as $\frac{1}{L}$), selection can be any of the classical approaches (such as roulette wheel or tournament), and crossover rates are typically high (0.7 of offspring)

- Use multiple sub-expressions linked together on hard problems when one gene is not sufficient to address the problem. The sub-expressions are linked using link expressions which are function nodes that are either statically defined (such as a conjunction) or evolved on the genome with the genes.

3.8.7 Code Listing

Listing 3.7 provides an example of the Gene Expression Programming algorithm implemented in the Ruby Programming Language based on the seminal version proposed by Ferreira [1]. The demonstration problem is an instance of symbolic regression $f(x) = x^4 + x^3 + x^2 + x$, where $x \in [1, 10]$. The grammar used in this problem is: Functions: $F = \{+, -, \div, \times, \}$ and Terminals: $T = \{x\}$.

The algorithm uses binary tournament selection, uniform crossover and point mutations. The K-expression is decoded to an expression tree in a breadth-first manner, which is then parsed depth first as a Ruby expression string for display and direct evaluation. Solutions are evaluated by generating a number of random samples from the domain and calculating the mean error of the program to the expected outcome. Programs that contain a single term or those that return an invalid (NaN) or infinite result are penalized with an enormous error value.

```ruby
def binary_tournament(pop)
  i, j = rand(pop.size), rand(pop.size)
  return (pop[i][:fitness] < pop[j][:fitness]) ? pop[i] : pop[j]
end

def point_mutation(grammar, genome, head_length, rate=1.0/genome.size.to_f)
  child =""
  genome.size.times do |i|
    bit = genome[i].chr
    if rand() < rate
      if i < head_length
        selection = (rand() < 0.5) ? grammar["FUNC"]: grammar["TERM"]
        bit = selection[rand(selection.size)]
      else
        bit = grammar["TERM"][rand(grammar["TERM"].size)]
      end
    end
    child << bit
  end
  return child
end

def crossover(parent1, parent2, rate)
  return ""+parent1 if rand()>=rate
  child = ""
  parent1.size.times do |i|
    child << ((rand()<0.5) ? parent1[i] : parent2[i])
  end
  return child
end

def reproduce(grammar, selected, pop_size, p_crossover, head_length)
  children = []
  selected.each_with_index do |p1, i|
    p2 = (i.modulo(2)==0) ? selected[i+1] : selected[i-1]
    p2 = selected[0] if i == selected.size-1
```

```
37        child = {}
38        child[:genome] = crossover(p1[:genome], p2[:genome], p_crossover)
39        child[:genome] = point_mutation(grammar, child[:genome], head_length)
40        children << child
41      end
42      return children
43    end
44
45    def random_genome(grammar, head_length, tail_length)
46      s = ""
47      head_length.times do
48        selection = (rand() < 0.5) ? grammar["FUNC"]: grammar["TERM"]
49        s << selection[rand(selection.size)]
50      end
51      tail_length.times { s << grammar["TERM"][rand(grammar["TERM"].size)]}
52      return s
53    end
54
55    def target_function(x)
56      return x**4.0 + x**3.0 + x**2.0 + x
57    end
58
59    def sample_from_bounds(bounds)
60      return bounds[0] + ((bounds[1] - bounds[0]) * rand())
61    end
62
63    def cost(program, bounds, num_trials=30)
64      errors = 0.0
65      num_trials.times do
66        x = sample_from_bounds(bounds)
67        expression, score = program.gsub("x", x.to_s), 0.0
68        begin score = eval(expression) rescue score = 0.0/0.0 end
69        return 9999999 if score.nan? or score.infinite?
70        errors += (score - target_function(x)).abs
71      end
72      return errors / num_trials.to_f
73    end
74
75    def mapping(genome, grammar)
76      off, queue = 0, []
77      root = {}
78      root[:node] = genome[off].chr; off+=1
79      queue.push(root)
80      while !queue.empty? do
81        current = queue.shift
82        if grammar["FUNC"].include?(current[:node])
83          current[:left] = {}
84          current[:left][:node] = genome[off].chr; off+=1
85          queue.push(current[:left])
86          current[:right] = {}
87          current[:right][:node] = genome[off].chr; off+=1
88          queue.push(current[:right])
89        end
90      end
91      return root
92    end
```

```
93
94  def tree_to_string(exp)
95    return exp[:node] if (exp[:left].nil? or exp[:right].nil?)
96    left = tree_to_string(exp[:left])
97    right = tree_to_string(exp[:right])
98    return "(#{left} #{exp[:node]} #{right})"
99  end
100
101 def evaluate(candidate, grammar, bounds)
102   candidate[:expression] = mapping(candidate[:genome], grammar)
103   candidate[:program] = tree_to_string(candidate[:expression])
104   candidate[:fitness] = cost(candidate[:program], bounds)
105 end
106
107 def search(grammar, bounds, h_length, t_length, max_gens, pop_size, p_cross)
108   pop = Array.new(pop_size) do
109     {:genome=>random_genome(grammar, h_length, t_length)}
110   end
111   pop.each{|c| evaluate(c, grammar, bounds)}
112   best = pop.sort{|x,y| x[:fitness] <=> y[:fitness]}.first
113   max_gens.times do |gen|
114     selected = Array.new(pop){|i| binary_tournament(pop)}
115     children = reproduce(grammar, selected, pop_size, p_cross, h_length)
116     children.each{|c| evaluate(c, grammar, bounds)}
117     children.sort!{|x,y| x[:fitness] <=> y[:fitness]}
118     best = children.first if children.first[:fitness] <= best[:fitness]
119     pop = (children+pop).first(pop_size)
120     puts " > gen=#{gen}, f=#{best[:fitness]}, g=#{best[:genome]}"
121   end
122   return best
123 end
124
125 if __FILE__ == $0
126   # problem configuration
127   grammar = {"FUNC"=>["+","-","*","/"], "TERM"=>["x"]}
128   bounds = [1.0, 10.0]
129   # algorithm configuration
130   h_length = 20
131   t_length = h_length * (2-1) + 1
132   max_gens = 150
133   pop_size = 80
134   p_cross = 0.85
135   # execute the algorithm
136   best = search(grammar, bounds, h_length, t_length, max_gens, pop_size,
            p_cross)
137   puts "done! Solution: f=#{best[:fitness]}, program=#{best[:program]}"
138 end
```

Listing 3.7: Gene Expression Programming in Ruby

3.8.8 References

Primary Sources

The Gene Expression Programming algorithm was proposed by Ferreira in a paper that detailed the approach, provided a careful walkthrough of the process and operators, and demonstrated the the algorithm on a number of benchmark problem instances including symbolic regression [1].

Learn More

Ferreira provided an early and detailed introduction and overview of the approach as book chapter, providing a step-by-step walkthrough of the procedure and sample applications [2]. A more contemporary and detailed introduction is provided in a later book chapter [3]. Ferreira published a book on the approach in 2002 covering background, the algorithm, and demonstration applications which is now in its second edition [4].

3.8.9 Bibliography

[1] C. Ferreira. Gene expression programming: A new adaptive algorithm for solving problems. *Complex Systems*, 13(2):87–129, 2001.

[2] C. Ferreira. *Soft Computing and Industry: Recent Applications*, chapter Gene Expression Programming in Problem Solving, pages 635–654. Springer-Verlag, 2002.

[3] C. Ferreira. *Recent Developments in Biologically Inspired Computing*, chapter Gene Expression Programming and the Evolution of computer programs, pages 82–103. Idea Group Publishing, 2005.

[4] C. Ferreira. *Gene expression programming: Mathematical modeling by an artificial intelligence*. Springer-Verlag, second edition, 2006.

3.9 Learning Classifier System

Learning Classifier System, LCS.

3.9.1 Taxonomy

The Learning Classifier System algorithm is both an instance of an Evolutionary Algorithm from the field of Evolutionary Computation and an instance of a Reinforcement Learning algorithm from Machine Learning. Internally, Learning Classifier Systems make use of a Genetic Algorithm (Section 3.2). The Learning Classifier System is a theoretical system with a number of implementations. The two main approaches to implementing and investigating the system empirically are the Pittsburgh-style that seeks to optimize the whole classifier, and the Michigan-style that optimize responsive rulesets. The Michigan-style Learning Classifier is the most common and is comprised of two versions: the ZCS (zeroth-level classifier system) and the XCS (accuracy-based classifier system).

3.9.2 Strategy

The objective of the Learning Classifier System algorithm is to optimize payoff based on exposure to stimuli from a problem-specific environment. This is achieved by managing credit assignment for those rules that prove useful and searching for new rules and new variations on existing rules using an evolutionary process.

3.9.3 Procedure

The actors of the system include detectors, messages, effectors, feedback, and classifiers. Detectors are used by the system to perceive the state of the environment. Messages are the discrete information packets passed from the detectors into the system. The system performs information processing on messages, and messages may directly result in actions in the environment. Effectors control the actions of the system on and within the environment. In addition to the system actively perceiving via its detections, it may also receive directed feedback from the environment (payoff). Classifiers are condition-action rules that provide a filter for messages. If a message satisfies the conditional part of the classifier, the action of the classifier triggers. Rules act as message processors. Message a fixed length bitstring. A classifier is defined as a ternary string with an alphabet $\in \{1, 0, \#\}$, where the $\#$ represents do not care (matching either 1 or 0).

The processing loop for the Learning Classifier system is as follows:

1. Messages from the environment are placed on the message list.

2. The conditions of each classifier are checked to see if they are satisfied by at least one message in the message list.

3. All classifiers that are satisfied participate in a competition, those that win post their action to the message list.

4. All messages directed to the effectors are executed (causing actions in the environment).

5. All messages on the message list from the previous cycle are deleted (messages persist for a single cycle).

The algorithm may be described in terms of the main processing loop and two sub-algorithms: a reinforcement learning algorithm such as the bucket brigade algorithm or Q-learning, and a genetic algorithm for optimization of the system. Algorithm 3.9.1 provides a pseudocode listing of the high-level processing loop of the Learning Classifier System, specifically the XCS as described by Butz and Wilson [3].

3.9.4 Heuristics

The majority of the heuristics in this section are specific to the XCS Learning Classifier System as described by Butz and Wilson [3].

- Learning Classifier Systems are suited for problems with the following characteristics: perpetually novel events with significant noise, continual real-time requirements for action, implicitly or inexactly defined goals, and sparse payoff or reinforcement obtainable only through long sequences of tasks.

- The learning rate β for a classifier's expected payoff, error, and fitness are typically in the range $[0.1, 0.2]$.

- The frequency of running the genetic algorithm θ_{GA} should be in the range $[25, 50]$.

- The discount factor used in multi-step programs γ are typically in the around 0.71.

- The minimum error whereby classifiers are considered to have equal accuracy ϵ_0 is typically 10% of the maximum reward.

- The probability of crossover in the genetic algorithm χ is typically in the range $[0.5, 1.0]$.

- The probability of mutating a single position in a classifier in the genetic algorithm μ is typically in the range $[0.01, 0.05]$.

Algorithm 3.9.1: Pseudocode for the LCS.

Input: EnvironmentDetails
Output: Population

1 env ← InitializeEnvironment(EnvironmentDetails);
2 Population ← InitializePopulation();
3 $ActionSet_{t-1} \leftarrow \emptyset$;
4 $Input_{t-1} \leftarrow \emptyset$;
5 $Reward_{t-1} \leftarrow \emptyset$;
6 **while** ¬StopCondition() **do**
7      $Input_t \leftarrow$ env;
8   Matchset ← GenerateMatchSet(Population, $Input_t$);
9   Prediction ← GeneratePrediction(Matchset);
10   Action ← SelectionAction(Prediction);
11     $ActionSet_t \leftarrow$ GenerateActionSet(Action, Matchset);
12     $Reward_t \leftarrow$ ExecuteAction(Action, env);
13   **if** $ActionSet_{t-1} \neq \emptyset$ **then**
14         $Payoff_t \leftarrow$ CalculatePayoff($Reward_{t-1}$, Prediction);
15   PerformLearning($ActionSet_{t-1}$, $Payoff_t$, Population);
16   RunGeneticAlgorithm($ActionSet_{t-1}$, $Input_{t-1}$, Population);
17   **end**
18   **if** LastStepOfTask(env, Action) **then**
19         $Payoff_t \leftarrow Reward_t$;
20   PerformLearning($ActionSet_t$, $Payoff_t$, Population);
21   RunGeneticAlgorithm($ActionSet_t$, $Input_t$, Population);
22         $ActionSet_{t-1} \leftarrow \emptyset$;
23   **else**
24         $ActionSet_{t-1} \leftarrow ActionSet_t$;
25         $Input_{t-1} \leftarrow Input_t$;
26         $Reward_{t-1} \leftarrow Reward_t$;
27   **end**
28 **end**

- The experience threshold during classifier deletion θ_{del} is typically about 20.

- The experience threshold for a classifier during subsumption θ_{sub} is typically around 20.

- The initial values for a classifier's expected payoff p_1, error ϵ_1, and fitness f_1 are typically small and close to zero.

- The probability of selecting a random action for the purposes of exploration p_{exp} is typically close to 0.5.

- The minimum number of different actions that must be specified in a match set θ_{mna} is usually the total number of possible actions in the environment for the input.

- Subsumption should be used on problem domains that are known contain well defined rules for mapping inputs to outputs.

3.9.5 Code Listing

Listing 3.8 provides an example of the Learning Classifier System algorithm implemented in the Ruby Programming Language. The problem is an instance of a Boolean multiplexer called the 6-multiplexer. It can be described as a classification problem, where each of the 2^6 patterns of bits is associated with a boolean class $\in \{1,0\}$. For this problem instance, the first two bits may be decoded as an address into the remaining four bits that specify the class (for example in 100011, '10' decode to the index of '2' in the remaining 4 bits making the class '1'). In propositional logic this problem instance may be described as $F = (\neg x_0)(\neg x_1)x_2 + (\neg x_0)x_1x_3 + x_0(\neg x_1)x_4 + x_0x_1x_5$. The algorithm is an instance of XCS based on the description provided by Butz and Wilson [3] with the parameters based on the application of XCS to Boolean multiplexer problems by Wilson [14, 15]. The population is grown as needed, and subsumption which would be appropriate for the Boolean multiplexer problem was not used for brevity. The multiplexer problem is a single step problem, so the complexities of delayed payoff are not required. A number of parameters were hard coded to recommended values, specifically: $\alpha = 0.1$, $v = -0.5$, $\delta = 0.1$ and $P_{\#} = \frac{1}{3}$.

```ruby
def neg(bit)
  return (bit==1) ? 0 : 1
end

def target_function(s)
  ints = Array.new(6){|i| s[i].chr.to_i}
  x0,x1,x2,x3,x4,x5 = ints
  return neg(x0)*neg(x1)*x2 + neg(x0)*x1*x3 + x0*neg(x1)*x4 + x0*x1*x5
end

def new_classifier(condition, action, gen, p1=10.0, e1=0.0, f1=10.0)
  other = {}
  other[:condition],other[:action],other[:lasttime] = condition, action, gen
  other[:pred], other[:error], other[:fitness] = p1, e1, f1
  other[:exp], other[:setsize], other[:num] = 0.0, 1.0, 1.0
  return other
end

def copy_classifier(parent)
  copy = {}
  parent.keys.each do |k|
    copy[k] = (parent[k].kind_of? String) ? ""+parent[k] : parent[k]
  end
```

```ruby
24      copy[:num],copy[:exp] = 1.0, 0.0
25      return copy
26    end
27
28    def random_bitstring(size=6)
29      return (0...size).inject(""){|s,i| s+((rand<0.5) ? "1" : "0")}
30    end
31
32    def calculate_deletion_vote(classifier, pop, del_thresh, f_thresh=0.1)
33      vote = classifier[:setsize] * classifier[:num]
34      total = pop.inject(0.0){|s,c| s+c[:num]}
35      avg_fitness = pop.inject(0.0){|s,c| s + (c[:fitness]/total)}
36      derated = classifier[:fitness] / classifier[:num].to_f
37      if classifier[:exp]>del_thresh and derated<(f_thresh*avg_fitness)
38        return vote * (avg_fitness / derated)
39      end
40      return vote
41    end
42
43    def delete_from_pop(pop, pop_size, del_thresh=20.0)
44      total = pop.inject(0) {|s,c| s+c[:num]}
45      return if total <= pop_size
46      pop.each {|c| c[:dvote] = calculate_deletion_vote(c, pop, del_thresh)}
47      vote_sum = pop.inject(0.0) {|s,c| s+c[:dvote]}
48      point = rand() * vote_sum
49      vote_sum, index = 0.0, 0
50      pop.each_with_index do |c,i|
51        vote_sum += c[:dvote]
52        if vote_sum >= point
53          index = i
54          break
55        end
56      end
57      if pop[index][:num] > 1
58        pop[index][:num] -= 1
59      else
60        pop.delete_at(index)
61      end
62    end
63
64    def generate_random_classifier(input, actions, gen, rate=1.0/3.0)
65      condition = ""
66      input.size.times {|i| condition << ((rand<rate) ? '#' : input[i].chr)}
67      action = actions[rand(actions.size)]
68      return new_classifier(condition, action, gen)
69    end
70
71    def does_match?(input, condition)
72      input.size.times do |i|
73        return false if condition[i].chr!='#' and input[i].chr!=condition[i].chr
74      end
75      return true
76    end
77
78    def get_actions(pop)
79      actions = []
```

```ruby
80    pop.each do |c|
81      actions << c[:action] if !actions.include?(c[:action])
82    end
83    return actions
84  end
85
86  def generate_match_set(input, pop, all_actions, gen, pop_size)
87    match_set = pop.select{|c| does_match?(input, c[:condition])}
88    actions = get_actions(match_set)
89    while actions.size < all_actions.size do
90      remaining = all_actions - actions
91      classifier = generate_random_classifier(input, remaining, gen)
92      pop << classifier
93      match_set << classifier
94      delete_from_pop(pop, pop_size)
95      actions << classifier[:action]
96    end
97    return match_set
98  end
99
100 def generate_prediction(match_set)
101   pred = {}
102   match_set.each do |classifier|
103     key = classifier[:action]
104     pred[key] = {:sum=>0.0,:count=>0.0,:weight=>0.0} if pred[key].nil?
105     pred[key][:sum] += classifier[:pred]*classifier[:fitness]
106     pred[key][:count] += classifier[:fitness]
107   end
108   pred.keys.each do |key|
109     pred[key][:weight] = 0.0
110     if pred[key][:count] > 0
111       pred[key][:weight] = pred[key][:sum]/pred[key][:count]
112     end
113   end
114   return pred
115 end
116
117 def select_action(predictions, p_explore=false)
118   keys = Array.new(predictions.keys)
119   return keys[rand(keys.size)] if p_explore
120   keys.sort!{|x,y| predictions[y][:weight]<=>predictions[x][:weight]}
121   return keys.first
122 end
123
124 def update_set(action_set, reward, beta=0.2)
125   sum = action_set.inject(0.0) {|s,other| s+other[:num]}
126   action_set.each do |c|
127     c[:exp] += 1.0
128     if c[:exp] < 1.0/beta
129       c[:error] = (c[:error]*(c[:exp]-1.0)+(reward-c[:pred]).abs)/c[:exp]
130       c[:pred] = (c[:pred] * (c[:exp]-1.0) + reward) / c[:exp]
131       c[:setsize] = (c[:setsize]*(c[:exp]-1.0)+sum) / c[:exp]
132     else
133       c[:error] += beta * ((reward-c[:pred]).abs - c[:error])
134       c[:pred] += beta * (reward-c[:pred])
135       c[:setsize] += beta * (sum - c[:setsize])
```

```
136        end
137      end
138    end
139
140    def update_fitness(action_set, min_error=10, l_rate=0.2, alpha=0.1, v=-5.0)
141      sum = 0.0
142      acc = Array.new(action_set.size)
143      action_set.each_with_index do |c,i|
144        acc[i] = (c[:error]<min_error) ? 1.0 : alpha*(c[:error]/min_error)**v
145        sum += acc[i] * c[:num].to_f
146      end
147      action_set.each_with_index do |c,i|
148        c[:fitness] += l_rate * ((acc[i] * c[:num].to_f) / sum - c[:fitness])
149      end
150    end
151
152    def can_run_genetic_algorithm(action_set, gen, ga_freq)
153      return false if action_set.size <= 2
154      total = action_set.inject(0.0) {|s,c| s+c[:lasttime]*c[:num]}
155      sum = action_set.inject(0.0) {|s,c| s+c[:num]}
156      return true if gen - (total/sum) > ga_freq
157      return false
158    end
159
160    def binary_tournament(pop)
161      i, j = rand(pop.size), rand(pop.size)
162      j = rand(pop.size) while j==i
163      return (pop[i][:fitness] > pop[j][:fitness]) ? pop[i] : pop[j]
164    end
165
166    def mutation(cl, action_set, input, rate=0.04)
167      cl[:condition].size.times do |i|
168        if rand() < rate
169          cl[:condition][i] = (cl[:condition][i].chr=='#') ? input[i] : '#'
170        end
171      end
172      if rand() < rate
173        subset = action_set - [cl[:action]]
174        cl[:action] = subset[rand(subset.size)]
175      end
176    end
177
178    def uniform_crossover(parent1, parent2)
179      child = ""
180      parent1.size.times do |i|
181        child << ((rand()<0.5) ? parent1[i].chr : parent2[i].chr)
182      end
183      return child
184    end
185
186    def insert_in_pop(cla, pop)
187      pop.each do |c|
188        if cla[:condition]==c[:condition] and cla[:action]==c[:action]
189          c[:num] += 1
190          return
191        end
```

```
192      end
193      pop << cla
194    end
195
196    def crossover(c1, c2, p1, p2)
197      c1[:condition] = uniform_crossover(p1[:condition], p2[:condition])
198      c2[:condition] = uniform_crossover(p1[:condition], p2[:condition])
199      c2[:pred] = c1[:pred] = (p1[:pred]+p2[:pred])/2.0
200      c2[:error] = c1[:error] = 0.25*(p1[:error]+p2[:error])/2.0
201      c2[:fitness] = c1[:fitness] = 0.1*(p1[:fitness]+p2[:fitness])/2.0
202    end
203
204    def run_ga(actions, pop, action_set, input, gen, pop_size, crate=0.8)
205      p1, p2 = binary_tournament(action_set), binary_tournament(action_set)
206      c1, c2 = copy_classifier(p1), copy_classifier(p2)
207      crossover(c1, c2, p1, p2) if rand() < crate
208      [c1,c2].each do |c|
209        mutation(c, actions, input)
210        insert_in_pop(c, pop)
211      end
212      while pop.inject(0) {|s,c| s+c[:num]} > pop_size
213        delete_from_pop(pop, pop_size)
214      end
215    end
216
217    def train_model(pop_size, max_gens, actions, ga_freq)
218      pop, perf = [], []
219      max_gens.times do |gen|
220        explore = gen.modulo(2)==0
221        input = random_bitstring()
222        match_set = generate_match_set(input, pop, actions, gen, pop_size)
223        pred_array = generate_prediction(match_set)
224        action = select_action(pred_array, explore)
225        reward = (target_function(input)==action.to_i) ? 1000.0 : 0.0
226        if explore
227          action_set = match_set.select{|c| c[:action]==action}
228          update_set(action_set, reward)
229          update_fitness(action_set)
230          if can_run_genetic_algorithm(action_set, gen, ga_freq)
231            action_set.each {|c| c[:lasttime] = gen}
232            run_ga(actions, pop, action_set, input, gen, pop_size)
233          end
234        else
235          e,a = (pred_array[action][:weight]-reward).abs, ((reward==1000.0)?1:0)
236          perf << {:error=>e,:correct=>a}
237          if perf.size >= 50
238            err = (perf.inject(0){|s,x|s+x[:error]}/perf.size).round
239            acc = perf.inject(0.0){|s,x|s+x[:correct]}/perf.size
240            puts " >iter=#{gen+1} size=#{pop.size}, error=#{err}, acc=#{acc}"
241            perf = []
242          end
243        end
244      end
245      return pop
246    end
247
```

```
248  def test_model(system, num_trials=50)
249    correct = 0
250    num_trials.times do
251      input = random_bitstring()
252      match_set = system.select{|c| does_match?(input, c[:condition])}
253      pred_array = generate_prediction(match_set)
254      action = select_action(pred_array, false)
255      correct += 1 if target_function(input) == action.to_i
256    end
257    puts "Done! classified correctly=#{correct}/#{num_trials}"
258    return correct
259  end
260
261  def execute(pop_size, max_gens, actions, ga_freq)
262    system = train_model(pop_size, max_gens, actions, ga_freq)
263    test_model(system)
264    return system
265  end
266
267  if __FILE__ == $0
268    # problem configuration
269    all_actions = ['0', '1']
270    # algorithm configuration
271    max_gens, pop_size = 5000, 200
272    ga_freq = 25
273    # execute the algorithm
274    execute(pop_size, max_gens, all_actions, ga_freq)
275  end
```

Listing 3.8: Learning Classifier System in Ruby

3.9.6 References

Primary Sources

Early ideas on the theory of Learning Classifier Systems were proposed by Holland [4, 7], culminating in a standardized presentation a few years later [5]. A number of implementations of the theoretical system were investigated, although a taxonomy of the two main streams was proposed by De Jong [9]: 1) Pittsburgh-style proposed by Smith [11, 12] and 2) Holland-style or Michigan-style Learning classifiers that are further comprised of the Zeroth-level classifier (ZCS) [13] and the accuracy-based classifier (XCS) [14].

Learn More

Booker, Goldberg, and Holland provide a classical introduction to Learning Classifier Systems including an overview of the state of the field and the algorithm in detail [1]. Wilson and Goldberg also provide an introduction and review of the approach, taking a more critical stance [16]. Holmes et al. provide a contemporary review of the field focusing both on a description of the method and application areas to which the approach has been demonstrated successfully [8]. Lanzi, Stolzmann, and Wilson provide a seminal book in the field as a collection of papers covering the basics, advanced topics, and demonstration applications; a particular highlight from this book is the first section that provides a concise description of Learning Classifier Systems by many leaders and major contributors to the field [6], providing rare insight. Another paper from Lanzi and Riolo's book provides a detailed review of the development of the approach as it matured throughout the 1990s [10]. Bull and Kovacs provide a second book introductory book to the field focusing on the theory of the approach and its practical application [2].

3.9.7   Bibliography

[1] L. B. Booker, D. E. Goldberg, and J. H. Holland. Classifier systems and genetic algorithms. *Artificial Intelligence*, 40:235–282, 1989.

[2] L. Bull and T. Kovacs. *Foundations of learning classifier systems.* Springer, 2005.

[3] M. V. Butz and S. W. Wilson. An algorithmic description of XCS. *Journal of Soft Computing*, 6(3–4):144–153, 2002.

[4] J. H. Holland. *Progress in Theoretical Biology IV*, chapter Adaptation, pages 263–293. Academic Press, 1976.

[5] J. H. Holland. Adaptive algorithms for discovering and using general patterns in growing knowledge-bases. *International Journal of Policy Analysis and Information Systems*, 4:217–240, 1980.

[6] J. H. Holland, L. B. Booker, M. Colombetti, M. Dorigo, D. E. Goldberg, S. Forrest, R. L. Riolo, R. E. Smith, P. L. Lanzi, W. Stolzmann, and S. W. Wilson. *Learning classifier systems: from foundations to applications*, chapter What is a learning classifier system?, pages 3–32. Springer, 2000.

[7] J. H. Holland and J. S. Reitman. Cognitive systems based on adaptive algorithms. *ACM SIGART Bulletin*, 63:49, 1977.

[8] J. H. Holmes, P. L. Lanzi, W. Stolzmann, and S. W. Wilson. Learning classifier systems: New models, successful applications. *Information Processing Letters*, 82:23–30, 2002.

[9] K. De Jong. Learning with genetic algorithms: An overview. *Machine Learning*, 3:121–138, 1988.

[10] P. L. Lanzi and R. L. Riolo. *Learning classifier systems: from foundations to applications*, chapter A Roadmap to the Last Decade of Learning Classifier System Research, pages 33–62. Springer, 2000.

[11] S. Smith. Flexible learning of problem solving heuristics through adaptive search. In *Proceedings 8th International Joint Conference on Artificial Intelligence*, pages 422–425, 1983.

[12] S. F. Smith. *A learning system based on genetic adaptive algorithms.* PhD thesis, Department of Computer Science, University of Pittsburgh, 1980.

[13] S. W. Wilson. ZCS: A zeroth level classifier systems. *Evolutionary Computation*, 2:1–18, 1994.

[14] S. W. Wilson. Classifier fitness based on accuracy. *Evolutionary Computation*, 3:149–175, 1995.

[15] S. W. Wilson. Generalization in the XCS classifier systems. In *Genetic Programming 1998: Proceedings of the Third Annual Conference*, pages 665–674. Morgan Kaufmann, 1998.

[16] S. W. Wilson and D. E. Goldberg. A critical review of classifier systems. In *Proceedings of the third international conference on Genetic algorithms*, pages 244–255, 1989.

3.10   Non-dominated Sorting Genetic Algorithm

Non-dominated Sorting Genetic Algorithm, Nondominated Sorting Genetic Algorithm, Fast Elitist Non-dominated Sorting Genetic Algorithm, NSGA, NSGA-II, NSGAII.

3.10.1   Taxonomy

The Non-dominated Sorting Genetic Algorithm is a Multiple Objective Optimization (MOO) algorithm and is an instance of an Evolutionary Algorithm from the field of Evolutionary Computation. Refer to Section 9.5.3 for more information and references on Multiple Objective Optimization. NSGA is an extension of the Genetic Algorithm for multiple objective function optimization (Section 3.2). It is related to other Evolutionary Multiple Objective Optimization Algorithms (EMOO) (or Multiple Objective Evolutionary Algorithms MOEA) such as the Vector-Evaluated Genetic Algorithm (VEGA), Strength Pareto Evolutionary Algorithm (SPEA) (Section 3.11), and Pareto Archived Evolution Strategy (PAES). There are two versions of the algorithm, the classical NSGA and the updated and currently canonical form NSGA-II.

3.10.2   Strategy

The objective of the NSGA algorithm is to improve the adaptive fit of a population of candidate solutions to a Pareto front constrained by a set of objective functions. The algorithm uses an evolutionary process with surrogates for evolutionary operators including selection, genetic crossover, and genetic mutation. The population is sorted into a hierarchy of sub-populations based on the ordering of Pareto dominance. Similarity between members of each sub-group is evaluated on the Pareto front, and the resulting groups and similarity measures are used to promote a diverse front of non-dominated solutions.

3.10.3   Procedure

Algorithm 3.10.1 provides a pseudocode listing of the Non-dominated Sorting Genetic Algorithm II (NSGA-II) for minimizing a cost function. The `SortByRankAndDistance` function orders the population into a hierarchy of non-dominated Pareto fronts. The `CrowdingDistanceAssignment` calculates the average distance between members of each front on the front itself. Refer to Deb et al. for a clear presentation of the Pseudocode and explanation of these functions [4]. The `CrossoverAndMutation` function performs the classical crossover and mutation genetic operators of the Genetic Algorithm. Both the `SelectParentsByRankAndDistance` and

SortByRankAndDistance functions discriminate members of the population first by rank (order of dominated precedence of the front to which the solution belongs) and then distance within the front (calculated by CrowdingDistanceAssignment).

Algorithm 3.10.1: Pseudocode for NSGAII.

Input: $Population_{size}$, ProblemSize, $P_{crossover}$, $P_{mutation}$
Output: Children
1 Population $\leftarrow$ InitializePopulation($Population_{size}$, ProblemSize);
2 EvaluateAgainstObjectiveFunctions(Population);
3 FastNondominatedSort(Population);
4 Selected $\leftarrow$ SelectParentsByRank(Population, $Population_{size}$);
5 Children $\leftarrow$ CrossoverAndMutation(Selected, $P_{crossover}$, $P_{mutation}$);
6 **while** ¬StopCondition() **do**
7   EvaluateAgainstObjectiveFunctions(Children);
8   Union $\leftarrow$ Merge(Population, Children);
9   Fronts $\leftarrow$ FastNondominatedSort(Union);
10   Parents $\leftarrow \emptyset$;
11     $Front_L \leftarrow \emptyset$;
12   **foreach** $Front_i \in$ Fronts **do**
13   CrowdingDistanceAssignment($Front_i$);
14   **if** Size(Parents)+Size($Front_i$) $> Population_{size}$ **then**
15             $Front_L \leftarrow i$;
16   Break();
17   **else**
18   Parents $\leftarrow$ Merge(Parents, $Front_i$);
19   **end**
20   **end**
21   **if** Size(Parents)$< Population_{size}$ **then**
22         $Front_L \leftarrow$ SortByRankAndDistance($Front_L$);
23   **for** P_1 to $P_{Population_{size}-Size(Front_L)}$ **do**
24   Parents $\leftarrow Pi$;
25   **end**
26   **end**
27   Selected $\leftarrow$ SelectParentsByRankAndDistance(Parents, $Population_{size}$);
28   Population $\leftarrow$ Children;
29   Children $\leftarrow$ CrossoverAndMutation(Selected, $P_{crossover}$, $P_{mutation}$);
30 **end**
31 **return** Children;

3.10.4   Heuristics

- NSGA was designed for and is suited to continuous function multiple objective optimization problem instances.

- A binary representation can be used in conjunction with classical genetic operators such as one-point crossover and point mutation.

- A real-valued representation is recommended for continuous function optimization problems, in turn requiring representation specific genetic operators such as Simulated Binary Crossover (SBX) and polynomial mutation [2].

3.10.5   Code Listing

Listing 3.9 provides an example of the Non-dominated Sorting Genetic Algorithm II (NSGA-II) implemented in the Ruby Programming Language. The demonstration problem is an instance of continuous multiple objective function optimization called SCH (problem one in [4]). The problem seeks the minimum of two functions: $f1 = \sum_{i=1}^{n} x_i^2$ and $f2 = \sum_{i=1}^{n}(x_i - 2)^2$, $-10 \leq x_i \leq 10$ and $n = 1$. The optimal solution for this function are $x \in [0, 2]$. The algorithm is an implementation of NSGA-II based on the presentation by Deb et al. [4]. The algorithm uses a binary string representation (16 bits per objective function parameter) that is decoded and rescaled to the function domain. The implementation uses a uniform crossover operator and point mutations with a fixed mutation rate of $\frac{1}{L}$, where L is the number of bits in a solution's binary string.

```ruby
def objective1(vector)
  return vector.inject(0.0) {|sum, x| sum + (x**2.0)}
end

def objective2(vector)
  return vector.inject(0.0) {|sum, x| sum + ((x-2.0)**2.0)}
end

def decode(bitstring, search_space, bits_per_param)
  vector = []
  search_space.each_with_index do |bounds, i|
    off, sum = i*bits_per_param, 0.0
    param = bitstring[off...(off+bits_per_param)].reverse
    param.size.times do |j|
      sum += ((param[j].chr=='1') ? 1.0 : 0.0) * (2.0 ** j.to_f)
    end
    min, max = bounds
    vector << min + ((max-min)/((2.0**bits_per_param.to_f)-1.0)) * sum
  end
  return vector
end

def random_bitstring(num_bits)
```

```
24    return (0...num_bits).inject(""){|s,i| s<<((rand<0.5) ? "1" : "0")}
25  end
26
27  def point_mutation(bitstring, rate=1.0/bitstring.size)
28    child = ""
29     bitstring.size.times do |i|
30       bit = bitstring[i].chr
31       child << ((rand()<rate) ? ((bit=='1') ? "0" : "1") : bit)
32     end
33    return child
34  end
35
36  def crossover(parent1, parent2, rate)
37    return ""+parent1 if rand()>=rate
38    child = ""
39    parent1.size.times do |i|
40       child << ((rand()<0.5) ? parent1[i].chr : parent2[i].chr)
41    end
42    return child
43  end
44
45  def reproduce(selected, pop_size, p_cross)
46    children = []
47    selected.each_with_index do |p1, i|
48       p2 = (i.modulo(2)==0) ? selected[i+1] : selected[i-1]
49       p2 = selected[0] if i == selected.size-1
50       child = {}
51       child[:bitstring] = crossover(p1[:bitstring], p2[:bitstring], p_cross)
52       child[:bitstring] = point_mutation(child[:bitstring])
53       children << child
54       break if children.size >= pop_size
55    end
56    return children
57  end
58
59  def calculate_objectives(pop, search_space, bits_per_param)
60    pop.each do |p|
61       p[:vector] = decode(p[:bitstring], search_space, bits_per_param)
62       p[:objectives] = [objective1(p[:vector]), objective2(p[:vector])]
63    end
64  end
65
66  def dominates(p1, p2)
67    p1[:objectives].each_index do |i|
68       return false if p1[:objectives][i] > p2[:objectives][i]
69    end
70    return true
71  end
72
73  def fast_nondominated_sort(pop)
74    fronts = Array.new(1){[]}
75    pop.each do |p1|
76       p1[:dom_count], p1[:dom_set] = 0, []
77       pop.each do |p2|
78         if dominates(p1, p2)
79           p1[:dom_set] << p2
```

```ruby
80        elsif dominates(p2, p1)
81          p1[:dom_count] += 1
82        end
83      end
84      if p1[:dom_count] == 0
85        p1[:rank] = 0
86        fronts.first << p1
87      end
88    end
89    curr = 0
90    begin
91      next_front = []
92      fronts[curr].each do |p1|
93        p1[:dom_set].each do |p2|
94          p2[:dom_count] -= 1
95          if p2[:dom_count] == 0
96            p2[:rank] = (curr+1)
97            next_front << p2
98          end
99        end
100     end
101     curr += 1
102     fronts << next_front if !next_front.empty?
103   end while curr < fronts.size
104   return fronts
105 end
106
107 def calculate_crowding_distance(pop)
108   pop.each {|p| p[:dist] = 0.0}
109   num_obs = pop.first[:objectives].size
110   num_obs.times do |i|
111     min = pop.min{|x,y| x[:objectives][i]<=>y[:objectives][i]}
112     max = pop.max{|x,y| x[:objectives][i]<=>y[:objectives][i]}
113     rge = max[:objectives][i] - min[:objectives][i]
114     pop.first[:dist], pop.last[:dist] = 1.0/0.0, 1.0/0.0
115     next if rge == 0.0
116     (1...(pop.size-1)).each do |j|
117       pop[j][:dist]+=(pop[j+1][:objectives][i]-pop[j-1][:objectives][i])/rge
118     end
119   end
120 end
121
122 def crowded_comparison_operator(x,y)
123   return y[:dist]<=>x[:dist] if x[:rank] == y[:rank]
124   return x[:rank]<=>y[:rank]
125 end
126
127 def better(x,y)
128   if !x[:dist].nil? and x[:rank] == y[:rank]
129     return (x[:dist]>y[:dist]) ? x : y
130   end
131   return (x[:rank]<y[:rank]) ? x : y
132 end
133
134 def select_parents(fronts, pop_size)
135   fronts.each {|f| calculate_crowding_distance(f)}
```

```
136    offspring, last_front = [], 0
137    fronts.each do |front|
138      break if (offspring.size+front.size) > pop_size
139      front.each {|p| offspring << p}
140      last_front += 1
141    end
142    if (remaining = pop_size-offspring.size) > 0
143      fronts[last_front].sort! {|x,y| crowded_comparison_operator(x,y)}
144      offspring += fronts[last_front][0...remaining]
145    end
146    return offspring
147  end
148
149  def weighted_sum(x)
150    return x[:objectives].inject(0.0) {|sum, x| sum+x}
151  end
152
153  def search(search_space, max_gens, pop_size, p_cross, bits_per_param=16)
154    pop = Array.new(pop_size) do |i|
155      {:bitstring=>random_bitstring(search_space.size*bits_per_param)}
156    end
157    calculate_objectives(pop, search_space, bits_per_param)
158    fast_nondominated_sort(pop)
159    selected = Array.new(pop_size) do
160      better(pop[rand(pop_size)], pop[rand(pop_size)])
161    end
162    children = reproduce(selected, pop_size, p_cross)
163    calculate_objectives(children, search_space, bits_per_param)
164    max_gens.times do |gen|
165      union = pop + children
166      fronts = fast_nondominated_sort(union)
167      parents = select_parents(fronts, pop_size)
168      selected = Array.new(pop_size) do
169        better(parents[rand(pop_size)], parents[rand(pop_size)])
170      end
171      pop = children
172      children = reproduce(selected, pop_size, p_cross)
173      calculate_objectives(children, search_space, bits_per_param)
174      best = parents.sort!{|x,y| weighted_sum(x)<=>weighted_sum(y)}.first
175      best_s = "[x=#{best[:vector]}, objs=#{best[:objectives].join(', ')}]"
176      puts " > gen=#{gen+1}, fronts=#{fronts.size}, best=#{best_s}"
177    end
178    union = pop + children
179    fronts = fast_nondominated_sort(union)
180    parents = select_parents(fronts, pop_size)
181    return parents
182  end
183
184  if __FILE__ == $0
185    # problem configuration
186    problem_size = 1
187    search_space = Array.new(problem_size) {|i| [-10, 10]}
188    # algorithm configuration
189    max_gens = 50
190    pop_size = 100
191    p_cross = 0.98
```

```
192    # execute the algorithm
193    pop = search(search_space, max_gens, pop_size, p_cross)
194    puts "done!"
195    end
```

Listing 3.9: NSGA-II in Ruby

3.10.6 References

Primary Sources

Srinivas and Deb proposed the NSGA inspired by Goldberg's notion of a non-dominated sorting procedure [6]. Goldberg proposed a non-dominated sorting procedure in his book in considering the biases in the Pareto optimal solutions provided by VEGA [5]. Srinivas and Deb's NSGA used the sorting procedure as a ranking selection method, and a fitness sharing niching method to maintain stable sub-populations across the Pareto front. Deb et al. later extended NSGA to address three criticism of the approach: the $O(mN^3)$ time complexity, the lack of elitism, and the need for a sharing parameter for the fitness sharing niching method [3, 4].

Learn More

Deb provides in depth coverage of Evolutionary Multiple Objective Optimization algorithms in his book, including a detailed description of the NSGA in Chapter 5 [1].

3.10.7 Bibliography

[1] K. Deb. *Multi-Objective Optimization Using Evolutionary Algorithms.* John Wiley and Sons, 2001.

[2] K. Deb and R. B. Agrawal. Simulated binary crossover for continuous search space. *Complex Systems*, 9:115–148, 1995.

[3] K. Deb, S. Agrawal, A. Pratap, and T. Meyarivan. A fast elitist non–dominated sorting genetic algorithm for multi–objective optimization: NSGA–II. *Parallel Problem Solving from Nature PPSN VI*, 1917:849–858, 2000.

[4] K. Deb, A. Pratap, S. Agarwal, and T. Meyarivan. A fast and elitist multiobjective genetic algorithm: NSGA–II. *IEEE Transactions on Evolutionary Computation*, 6(2):182–197, 2002.

[5] D. E. Goldberg. *Genetic Algorithms in Search, Optimization, and Machine Learning.* Addison-Wesley, 1989.

[6] N. Srinivas and K. Deb. Muiltiobjective optimization using nondominated sorting in genetic algorithms. *Evolutionary Computation*, 2(3):221–248, 1994.

3.11   Strength Pareto Evolutionary Algorithm

Strength Pareto Evolutionary Algorithm, SPEA, SPEA2.

3.11.1   Taxonomy

Strength Pareto Evolutionary Algorithm is a Multiple Objective Optimization (MOO) algorithm and an Evolutionary Algorithm from the field of Evolutionary Computation. It belongs to the field of Evolutionary Multiple Objective (EMO) algorithms. Refer to Section 9.5.3 for more information and references on Multiple Objective Optimization. Strength Pareto Evolutionary Algorithm is an extension of the Genetic Algorithm for multiple objective optimization problems (Section 3.2). It is related to sibling Evolutionary Algorithms such as Non-dominated Sorting Genetic Algorithm (NSGA) (Section 3.10), Vector-Evaluated Genetic Algorithm (VEGA), and Pareto Archived Evolution Strategy (PAES). There are two versions of SPEA, the original SPEA algorithm and the extension SPEA2. Additional extensions include SPEA+ and iSPEA.

3.11.2   Strategy

The objective of the algorithm is to locate and and maintain a front of non-dominated solutions, ideally a set of Pareto optimal solutions. This is achieved by using an evolutionary process (with surrogate procedures for genetic recombination and mutation) to explore the search space, and a selection process that uses a combination of the degree to which a candidate solution is dominated (strength) and an estimation of density of the Pareto front as an assigned fitness. An archive of the non-dominated set is maintained separate from the population of candidate solutions used in the evolutionary process, providing a form of elitism.

3.11.3   Procedure

Algorithm 3.11.1 provides a pseudocode listing of the Strength Pareto Evolutionary Algorithm 2 (SPEA2) for minimizing a cost function. The `CalculateRawFitness` function calculates the raw fitness as the sum of the strength values of the solutions that dominate a given candidate, where strength is the number of solutions that a give solution dominate. The `CandidateDensity` function estimates the density of an area of the Pareto front as $\frac{1.0}{\sigma^k+2}$ where σ^k is the Euclidean distance of the objective values between a given solution the kth nearest neighbor of the solution, and k is the square root of the size of the population and archive combined. The `PopulateWithRemainingBest` function iteratively fills the archive with the remaining candidate solutions in order of fitness. The `RemoveMostSimilar` function truncates the archive population removing those members with the smallest σ^k values as calculated against the archive. The `SelectParents` function selects parents from a population using a Genetic Algorithm selection method such as binary tournament selection. The `CrossoverAndMutation` function performs the crossover and mutation genetic operators from the Genetic Algorithm.

Algorithm 3.11.1: Pseudocode for SPEA2.

Input: $Population_{size}$, $Archive_{size}$, ProblemSize, $P_{crossover}$, $P_{mutation}$

Output: Archive

1   Population $\leftarrow$ InitializePopulation($Population_{size}$, ProblemSize);
2   Archive $\leftarrow \emptyset$;
3   **while** $\neg$StopCondition() **do**
4   **for** $S_i \in$ Population **do**
5         $Si_{objectives} \leftarrow$ CalculateObjectives(S_i);
6   **end**
7   Union $\leftarrow$ Population + Archive;
8   **for** $S_i \in$ Union **do**
9         $Si_{raw} \leftarrow$ CalculateRawFitness(S_i, Union);
10        $Si_{density} \leftarrow$ CalculateSolutionDensity(S_i, Union);
11        $Si_{fitness} \leftarrow Si_{raw} + Si_{density}$;
12   **end**
13   Archive $\leftarrow$ GetNonDominated(Union);
14   **if** Size(Archive) $< Archive_{size}$ **then**
15   PopulateWithRemainingBest(Union, Archive, $Archive_{size}$);
16   **else if** Size(Archive) $> Archive_{size}$ **then**
17   RemoveMostSimilar(Archive, $Archive_{size}$);
18   **end**
19   Selected $\leftarrow$ SelectParents(Archive, $Population_{size}$);
20   Population $\leftarrow$ CrossoverAndMutation(Selected, $P_{crossover}$, $P_{mutation}$);
21   **end**
22   **return** $GetNonDominated$Archive;

3.11.4   Heuristics

- SPEA was designed for and is suited to combinatorial and continuous function multiple objective optimization problem instances.

- A binary representation can be used for continuous function optimization problems in conjunction with classical genetic operators such as one-point crossover and point mutation.

- A k value of 1 may be used for efficiency whilst still providing useful results.

- The size of the archive is commonly smaller than the size of the population.

- There is a lot of room for implementation optimization in density and Pareto dominance calculations.

3.11.5   Code Listing

Listing 3.10 provides an example of the Strength Pareto Evolutionary Algorithm 2 (SPEA2) implemented in the Ruby Programming Language. The demonstration problem is an instance of continuous multiple objective function optimization called SCH (problem one in [1]). The problem seeks the minimum of two functions: $f1 = \sum_{i=1}^{n} x_i^2$ and $f2 = \sum_{i=1}^{n}(x_i - 2)^2$, $-10 \leq x_i \leq 10$ and $n = 1$. The optimal solutions for this function are $x \in [0, 2]$. The algorithm is an implementation of SPEA2 based on the presentation by Zitzler, Laumanns, and Thiele [5]. The algorithm uses a binary string representation (16 bits per objective function parameter) that is decoded and rescaled to the function domain. The implementation uses a uniform crossover operator and point mutations with a fixed mutation rate of $\frac{1}{L}$, where L is the number of bits in a solution's binary string.

```ruby
def objective1(vector)
  return vector.inject(0.0) {|sum, x| sum + (x**2.0)}
end

def objective2(vector)
  return vector.inject(0.0) {|sum, x| sum + ((x-2.0)**2.0)}
end

def decode(bitstring, search_space, bits_per_param)
  vector = []
  search_space.each_with_index do |bounds, i|
    off, sum = i*bits_per_param, 0.0
    param = bitstring[off...(off+bits_per_param)].reverse
    param.size.times do |j|
      sum += ((param[j].chr=='1') ? 1.0 : 0.0) * (2.0 ** j.to_f)
    end
    min, max = bounds
    vector << min + ((max-min)/((2.0**bits_per_param.to_f)-1.0)) * sum
  end
  return vector
end

def point_mutation(bitstring, rate=1.0/bitstring.size)
  child = ""
  bitstring.size.times do |i|
    bit = bitstring[i].chr
    child << ((rand()<rate) ? ((bit=='1') ? "0" : "1") : bit)
  end
```

```
29    return child
30  end
31
32  def binary_tournament(pop)
33    i, j = rand(pop.size), rand(pop.size)
34    j = rand(pop.size) while j==i
35    return (pop[i][:fitness] < pop[j][:fitness]) ? pop[i] : pop[j]
36  end
37
38  def crossover(parent1, parent2, rate)
39    return ""+parent1 if rand()>=rate
40    child = ""
41    parent1.size.times do |i|
42      child << ((rand()<0.5) ? parent1[i].chr : parent2[i].chr)
43    end
44    return child
45  end
46
47  def reproduce(selected, pop_size, p_cross)
48    children = []
49    selected.each_with_index do |p1, i|
50      p2 = (i.modulo(2)==0) ? selected[i+1] : selected[i-1]
51      p2 = selected[0] if i == selected.size-1
52      child = {}
53      child[:bitstring] = crossover(p1[:bitstring], p2[:bitstring], p_cross)
54      child[:bitstring] = point_mutation(child[:bitstring])
55      children << child
56      break if children.size >= pop_size
57    end
58    return children
59  end
60
61  def random_bitstring(num_bits)
62    return (0...num_bits).inject(""){|s,i| s<<((rand<0.5) ? "1" : "0")}
63  end
64
65  def calculate_objectives(pop, search_space, bits_per_param)
66    pop.each do |p|
67      p[:vector] = decode(p[:bitstring], search_space, bits_per_param)
68      p[:objectives] = []
69      p[:objectives] << objective1(p[:vector])
70      p[:objectives] << objective2(p[:vector])
71    end
72  end
73
74  def dominates?(p1, p2)
75    p1[:objectives].each_index do |i|
76      return false if p1[:objectives][i] > p2[:objectives][i]
77    end
78    return true
79  end
80
81  def weighted_sum(x)
82    return x[:objectives].inject(0.0) {|sum, x| sum+x}
83  end
84
```

```ruby
85   def euclidean_distance(c1, c2)
86     sum = 0.0
87     c1.each_index {|i| sum += (c1[i]-c2[i])**2.0}
88     return Math.sqrt(sum)
89   end
90
91   def calculate_dominated(pop)
92     pop.each do |p1|
93       p1[:dom_set] = pop.select {|p2| p1!=p2 and dominates?(p1, p2) }
94     end
95   end
96
97   def calculate_raw_fitness(p1, pop)
98     return pop.inject(0.0) do |sum, p2|
99       (dominates?(p2, p1)) ? sum + p2[:dom_set].size.to_f : sum
100    end
101  end
102
103  def calculate_density(p1, pop)
104    pop.each do |p2|
105      p2[:dist] = euclidean_distance(p1[:objectives], p2[:objectives])
106    end
107    list = pop.sort{|x,y| x[:dist]<=>y[:dist]}
108    k = Math.sqrt(pop.size).to_i
109    return 1.0 / (list[k][:dist] + 2.0)
110  end
111
112  def calculate_fitness(pop, archive, search_space, bits_per_param)
113    calculate_objectives(pop, search_space, bits_per_param)
114    union = archive + pop
115    calculate_dominated(union)
116    union.each do |p|
117      p[:raw_fitness] = calculate_raw_fitness(p, union)
118      p[:density] = calculate_density(p, union)
119      p[:fitness] = p[:raw_fitness] + p[:density]
120    end
121  end
122
123  def environmental_selection(pop, archive, archive_size)
124    union = archive + pop
125    environment = union.select {|p| p[:fitness]<1.0}
126    if environment.size < archive_size
127      union.sort!{|x,y| x[:fitness]<=>y[:fitness]}
128      union.each do |p|
129        environment << p if p[:fitness] >= 1.0
130        break if environment.size >= archive_size
131      end
132    elsif environment.size > archive_size
133      begin
134        k = Math.sqrt(environment.size).to_i
135        environment.each do |p1|
136          environment.each do |p2|
137            p2[:dist] = euclidean_distance(p1[:objectives], p2[:objectives])
138          end
139          list = environment.sort{|x,y| x[:dist]<=>y[:dist]}
140          p1[:density] = list[k][:dist]
```

```
141      end
142      environment.sort!{|x,y| x[:density]<=>y[:density]}
143      environment.shift
144    end until environment.size <= archive_size
145   end
146   return environment
147 end
148
149 def search(search_space, max_gens, pop_size, archive_size, p_cross,
        bits_per_param=16)
150   pop = Array.new(pop_size) do |i|
151     {:bitstring=>random_bitstring(search_space.size*bits_per_param)}
152   end
153   gen, archive = 0, []
154   begin
155     calculate_fitness(pop, archive, search_space, bits_per_param)
156     archive = environmental_selection(pop, archive, archive_size)
157     best = archive.sort{|x,y| weighted_sum(x)<=>weighted_sum(y)}.first
158     puts ">gen=#{gen}, objs=#{best[:objectives].join(', ')}"
159     break if gen >= max_gens
160     selected = Array.new(pop_size){binary_tournament(archive)}
161     pop = reproduce(selected, pop_size, p_cross)
162     gen += 1
163   end while true
164   return archive
165 end
166
167 if __FILE__ == $0
168   # problem configuration
169   problem_size = 1
170   search_space = Array.new(problem_size) {|i| [-10, 10]}
171   # algorithm configuration
172   max_gens = 50
173   pop_size = 80
174   archive_size = 40
175   p_cross = 0.90
176   # execute the algorithm
177   pop = search(search_space, max_gens, pop_size, archive_size, p_cross)
178   puts "done!"
179 end
```

Listing 3.10: SPEA2 in Ruby

3.11.6   References

Primary Sources

Zitzler and Thiele introduced the Strength Pareto Evolutionary Algorithm as a technical report on a multiple objective optimization algorithm with elitism and clustering along the Pareto front [6]. The technical report was later published [7]. The Strength Pareto Evolutionary Algorithm was developed as a part of Zitzler's PhD thesis [2]. Zitzler, Laumanns, and Thiele later extended SPEA to address some inefficiencies of the approach, the algorithm was called SPEA2 and was released as a technical report [4] and later published [5]. SPEA2 provides fine-grained fitness assignment, density estimation of the Pareto front, and an archive truncation operator.

Learn More

Zitzler, Laumanns, and Bleuler provide a tutorial on SPEA2 as a book chapter that considers the basics of multiple objective optimization, and the differences from SPEA and the other related Multiple Objective Evolutionary Algorithms [3].

3.11.7   Bibliography

[1] K. Deb, A. Pratap, S. Agarwal, and T. Meyarivan. A fast and elitist multiobjective genetic algorithm: NSGA–II. *IEEE Transactions on Evolutionary Computation*, 6(2):182–197, 2002.

[2] E. Zitzler. *Evolutionary Algorithms for Multiobjective Optimization: Methods and Applications*. PhD thesis, Shaker Verlag, Aachen, Germany, 1999.

[3] E. Zitzler, M. Laumanns, and S. Bleuler. *Metaheuristics for Multiobjective Optimisation*, chapter A Tutorial on Evolutionary Multiobjective Optimization, pages 3–37. Springer, 2004.

[4] E. Zitzler, M. Laumanns, and L. Thiele. SPEA2: Improving the strength pareto evolutionary algorithm. Technical Report 103, Computer Engineering and Networks Laboratory (TIK), Swiss Federal Institute of Technology (ETH) Zurich, Gloriastrasse 35, CH-8092 Zurich, Switzerland, May 2001.

[5] E. Zitzler, M. Laumanns, and L. Thiele. SPEA2: Improving the strength pareto evolutionary algorithm for multiobjective optimization. In *Evolutionary Methods for Design, Optimisation and Control with Application to Industrial Problems (EUROGEN 2001)*, pages 95–100, 2002.

[6] E. Zitzler and L. Thiele. An evolutionary algorithm for multiobjective optimization: The strength pareto approach. Technical Report 43, Computer Engineering and Networks Laboratory (TIK), Swiss Federal Institute of Technology (ETH) Zurich, Gloriastrasse 35, CH-8092 Zurich, Switzerland, May 1998.

[7] E. Zitzler and L. Thiele. Multiobjective evolutionary algorithms: A comparative case study and the strength pareto approach. *IEEE Transactions on Evolutionary Computation*, 3(4):257–271, 1999.

Chapter 4

Physical Algorithms

4.1 Overview

This chapter describes Physical Algorithms.

4.1.1 Physical Properties

Physical algorithms are those algorithms inspired by a physical process. The described physical algorithm generally belong to the fields of Metaheustics and Computational Intelligence, although do not fit neatly into the existing categories of the biological inspired techniques (such as Swarm, Immune, Neural, and Evolution). In this vein, they could just as easily be referred to as nature inspired algorithms.

The inspiring physical systems range from metallurgy, music, the interplay between culture and evolution, and complex dynamic systems such as avalanches. They are generally stochastic optimization algorithms with a mixtures of local (neighborhood-based) and global search techniques.

4.1.2 Extensions

There are many other algorithms and classes of algorithm that were not described inspired by natural systems, not limited to:

- **More Annealing**: Extensions to the classical Simulated Annealing algorithm, such as Adaptive Simulated Annealing (formally Very Fast Simulated Re-annealing) [3, 4], and Quantum Annealing [1, 2].

- **Stochastic tunneling**: based on the physical idea of a particle tunneling through structures [5].

4.1.3 Bibliography

[1] B. Apolloni, C. Caravalho, and D. De Falco. Quantum stochastic optimization. *Stochastic Processes and their Applications*, 33:233–244, 1989.

[2] A. Das and B. K. Chakrabarti. *Quantum annealing and related optimization methods*. Springer, 2005.

[3] L. Ingber. Very fast simulated re-annealing. *Mathematical and Computer Modelling*, 12(8):967–973, 1989.

[4] L. Ingber. Adaptive simulated annealing (ASA): Lessons learned. *Control and Cybernetics*, 25(1):33–54, 1996.

[5] W. Wenzel and K. Hamacher. A stochastic tunneling approach for global minimization of complex potential energy landscapes. *Phys. Rev. Lett.*, 82(15):3003–3007, 1999.

4.2 Simulated Annealing

Simulated Annealing, SA.

4.2.1 Taxonomy

Simulated Annealing is a global optimization algorithm that belongs to the field of Stochastic Optimization and Metaheuristics. Simulated Annealing is an adaptation of the Metropolis-Hastings Monte Carlo algorithm and is used in function optimization. Like the Genetic Algorithm (Section 3.2), it provides a basis for a large variety of extensions and specialization's of the general method not limited to Parallel Simulated Annealing, Fast Simulated Annealing, and Adaptive Simulated Annealing.

4.2.2 Inspiration

Simulated Annealing is inspired by the process of annealing in metallurgy. In this natural process a material is heated and slowly cooled under controlled conditions to increase the size of the crystals in the material and reduce their defects. This has the effect of improving the strength and durability of the material. The heat increases the energy of the atoms allowing them to move freely, and the slow cooling schedule allows a new low-energy configuration to be discovered and exploited.

4.2.3 Metaphor

Each configuration of a solution in the search space represents a different internal energy of the system. Heating the system results in a relaxation of the acceptance criteria of the samples taken from the search space. As the system is cooled, the acceptance criteria of samples is narrowed to focus on improving movements. Once the system has cooled, the configuration will represent a sample at or close to a global optimum.

4.2.4 Strategy

The information processing objective of the technique is to locate the minimum cost configuration in the search space. The algorithms plan of action is to probabilistically re-sample the problem space where the acceptance of new samples into the currently held sample is managed by a probabilistic function that becomes more discerning of the cost of samples it accepts over the execution time of the algorithm. This probabilistic decision is based on the Metropolis-Hastings algorithm for simulating samples from a thermodynamic system.

4.2.5   Procedure

Algorithm 4.2.1 provides a pseudocode listing of the main Simulated Annealing algorithm for minimizing a cost function.

Algorithm 4.2.1: Pseudocode for Simulated Annealing.

Input: ProblemSize, $iterations_{max}$, $temp_{max}$
Output: S_{best}

1 $S_{current} \leftarrow$ CreateInitialSolution(ProblemSize);
2 $S_{best} \leftarrow S_{current}$;
3 **for** $i = 1$ **to** $iterations_{max}$ **do**
4 $\quad$ $S_i \leftarrow$ CreateNeighborSolution($S_{current}$);
5 $\quad$ $temp_{curr} \leftarrow$ CalculateTemperature(i, $temp_{max}$);
6 $\quad$ **if** Cost(S_i) $\leq$ Cost($S_{current}$) **then**
7 $\quad\quad$ $S_{current} \leftarrow S_i$;
8 $\quad\quad$ **if** Cost(S_i) $\leq$ Cost(S_{best}) **then**
9 $\quad\quad\quad$ $S_{best} \leftarrow S_i$;
10 $\quad\quad$ **end**
11 $\quad$ **else if** Exp($\frac{Cost(S_{current}) - Cost(S_i)}{temp_{curr}}$) $>$ Rand() **then**
12 $\quad\quad$ $S_{current} \leftarrow S_i$;
13 $\quad$ **end**
14 **end**
15 **return** S_{best};

4.2.6   Heuristics

- Simulated Annealing was designed for use with combinatorial optimization problems, although it has been adapted for continuous function optimization problems.

- The convergence proof suggests that with a long enough cooling period, the system will always converge to the global optimum. The downside of this theoretical finding is that the number of samples taken for optimum convergence to occur on some problems may be more than a complete enumeration of the search space.

- Performance improvements can be given with the selection of a candidate move generation scheme (neighborhood) that is less likely to generate candidates of significantly higher cost.

- Restarting the cooling schedule using the best found solution so far can lead to an improved outcome on some problems.

- A common acceptance method is to always accept improving solutions and accept worse solutions with a probability of $P(accept) \leftarrow$

$\exp(\frac{e-e'}{T})$, where T is the current temperature, e is the energy (or cost) of the current solution and e' is the energy of a candidate solution being considered.

- The size of the neighborhood considered in generating candidate solutions may also change over time or be influenced by the temperature, starting initially broad and narrowing with the execution of the algorithm.

- A problem specific heuristic method can be used to provide the starting point for the search.

4.2.7 Code Listing

Listing 4.1 provides an example of the Simulated Annealing algorithm implemented in the Ruby Programming Language. The algorithm is applied to the Berlin52 instance of the Traveling Salesman Problem (TSP), taken from the TSPLIB. The problem seeks a permutation of the order to visit cities (called a tour) that minimizes the total distance traveled. The optimal tour distance for Berlin52 instance is 7542 units.

The algorithm implementation uses a two-opt procedure for the neighborhood function and the classical $P(accept) \leftarrow \exp(\frac{e-e'}{T})$ as the acceptance function. A simple linear cooling regime is used with a large initial temperature which is decreased each iteration.

```ruby
def euc_2d(c1, c2)
  Math.sqrt((c1[0] - c2[0])**2.0 + (c1[1] - c2[1])**2.0).round
end

def cost(permutation, cities)
  distance =0
  permutation.each_with_index do |c1, i|
    c2 = (i==permutation.size-1) ? permutation[0] : permutation[i+1]
    distance += euc_2d(cities[c1], cities[c2])
  end
  return distance
end

def random_permutation(cities)
  perm = Array.new(cities.size){|i| i}
  perm.each_index do |i|
    r = rand(perm.size-i) + i
    perm[r], perm[i] = perm[i], perm[r]
  end
  return perm
end

def stochastic_two_opt!(perm)
  c1, c2 = rand(perm.size), rand(perm.size)
  exclude = [c1]
  exclude << ((c1==0) ? perm.size-1 : c1-1)
```

```ruby
27      exclude << ((c1==perm.size-1) ? 0 : c1+1)
28      c2 = rand(perm.size) while exclude.include?(c2)
29      c1, c2 = c2, c1 if c2 < c1
30      perm[c1...c2] = perm[c1...c2].reverse
31      return perm
32    end
33
34    def create_neighbor(current, cities)
35      candidate = {}
36      candidate[:vector] = Array.new(current[:vector])
37      stochastic_two_opt!(candidate[:vector])
38      candidate[:cost] = cost(candidate[:vector], cities)
39      return candidate
40    end
41
42    def should_accept?(candidate, current, temp)
43      return true if candidate[:cost] <= current[:cost]
44      return Math.exp((current[:cost] - candidate[:cost]) / temp) > rand()
45    end
46
47    def search(cities, max_iter, max_temp, temp_change)
48      current = {:vector=>random_permutation(cities)}
49      current[:cost] = cost(current[:vector], cities)
50      temp, best = max_temp, current
51      max_iter.times do |iter|
52        candidate = create_neighbor(current, cities)
53        temp = temp * temp_change
54        current = candidate if should_accept?(candidate, current, temp)
55        best = candidate if candidate[:cost] < best[:cost]
56        if (iter+1).modulo(10) == 0
57          puts " > iteration #{(iter+1)}, temp=#{temp}, best=#{best[:cost]}"
58        end
59      end
60      return best
61    end
62
63    if __FILE__ == $0
64      # problem configuration
65      berlin52 = [[565,575],[25,185],[345,750],[945,685],[845,655],
66        [880,660],[25,230],[525,1000],[580,1175],[650,1130],[1605,620],
67        [1220,580],[1465,200],[1530,5],[845,680],[725,370],[145,665],
68        [415,635],[510,875],[560,365],[300,465],[520,585],[480,415],
69        [835,625],[975,580],[1215,245],[1320,315],[1250,400],[660,180],
70        [410,250],[420,555],[575,665],[1150,1160],[700,580],[685,595],
71        [685,610],[770,610],[795,645],[720,635],[760,650],[475,960],
72        [95,260],[875,920],[700,500],[555,815],[830,485],[1170,65],
73        [830,610],[605,625],[595,360],[1340,725],[1740,245]]
74      # algorithm configuration
75      max_iterations = 2000
76      max_temp = 100000.0
77      temp_change = 0.98
78      # execute the algorithm
79      best = search(berlin52, max_iterations, max_temp, temp_change)
80      puts "Done. Best Solution: c=#{best[:cost]}, v=#{best[:vector].inspect}"
81    end
```

Listing 4.1: Simulated Annealing in Ruby

4.2.8 References

Primary Sources

Simulated Annealing is credited to Kirkpatrick, Gelatt, and Vecchi in 1983
[5]. Granville, Krivanek, and Rasson provided the proof for convergence
for Simulated Annealing in 1994 [2]. There were a number of early studies
and application papers such as Kirkpatrick's investigation into the TSP
and minimum cut problems [4], and a study by Vecchi and Kirkpatrick on
Simulated Annealing applied to the global wiring problem [7].

Learn More

There are many excellent reviews of Simulated Annealing, not limited to
the review by Ingber that describes improved methods such as Adaptive
Simulated Annealing, Simulated Quenching, and hybrid methods [3]. There
are books dedicated to Simulated Annealing, applications and variations.
Two examples of good texts include "Simulated Annealing: Theory and
Applications" by Laarhoven and Aarts [6] that provides an introduction
to the technique and applications, and "Simulated Annealing: Parallelization Techniques" by Robert Azencott [1] that focuses on the theory and
applications of parallel methods for Simulated Annealing.

4.2.9 Bibliography

[1] R. Azencott. *Simulated annealing: parallelization techniques.* Wiley,
     1992.

[2] V. Granville, M. Krivanek, and J-P. Rasson. Simulated annealing: A
     proof of convergence. *IEEE Transactions on Pattern Analysis and
     Machine Intelligence*, 16(6):652–656, 1994.

[3] L. Ingber. Simulated annealing: Practice versus theory. *Math. Comput.
     Modelling*, 18:29–57, 1993.

[4] S. Kirkpatrick. Optimization by simulated annealing: Quantitative
     studies. *Journal of Statistical Physics*, 34:975–986, 1983.

[5] S. Kirkpatrick, C. D. Gelatt, and M. P. Vecchi. Optimization by simu-
     lated annealing. *Science*, 220(4598):671–680, 1983.

[6] P. J. M. van Laarhoven and E. H. L. Aarts. *Simulated Annealing: Theory
     and Applications.* Springer, 1988.

[7] M. P. Vecchi and S. Kirkpatrick. Global wiring by simulated annealing. *IEEE Transactions on Computer-Aided Design of Integrated Circuits and Systems*, 2(4):215–222, 1983.

4.3 Extremal Optimization

Extremal Optimization, EO.

4.3.1 Taxonomy

Extremal Optimization is a stochastic search technique that has the properties of being a local and global search method. It is generally related to hill-climbing algorithms and provides the basis for extensions such as Generalized Extremal Optimization.

4.3.2 Inspiration

Extremal Optimization is inspired by the Bak-Sneppen self-organized criticality model of co-evolution from the field of statistical physics. The self-organized criticality model suggests that some dynamical systems have a critical point as an attractor, whereby the systems exhibit periods of slow movement or accumulation followed by short periods of avalanche or instability. Examples of such systems include land formation, earthquakes, and the dynamics of sand piles. The Bak-Sneppen model considers these dynamics in co-evolutionary systems and in the punctuated equilibrium model, which is described as long periods of status followed by short periods of extinction and large evolutionary change.

4.3.3 Metaphor

The dynamics of the system result in the steady improvement of a candidate solution with sudden and large crashes in the quality of the candidate solution. These dynamics allow two main phases of activity in the system: 1) to exploit higher quality solutions in a local search like manner, and 2) escape possible local optima with a population crash and explore the search space for a new area of high quality solutions.

4.3.4 Strategy

The objective of the information processing strategy is to iteratively identify the worst performing components of a given solution and replace or swap them with other components. This is achieved through the allocation of cost to the components of the solution based on their contribution to the overall cost of the solution in the problem domain. Once components are assessed they can be ranked and the weaker components replaced or switched with a randomly selected component.

4.3.5 Procedure

Algorithm 4.3.1 provides a pseudocode listing of the Extremal Optimization algorithm for minimizing a cost function. The deterministic selection of the worst component in the SelectWeakComponent function and replacement in the SelectReplacementComponent function is classical EO. If these decisions are probabilistic making use of τ parameter, this is referred to as τ-Extremal Optimization.

Algorithm 4.3.1: Pseudocode for Extremal Optimization.

Input: ProblemSize, $iterations_{max}$, τ
Output: S_{best}

1   $S_{current} \leftarrow$ CreateInitialSolution(ProblemSize);
2   $S_{best} \leftarrow S_{current}$;
3   **for** $i = 1$ **to** $iterations_{max}$ **do**
4   **foreach** $Component_i \in S_{current}$ **do**
5       $Component_i^{cost} \leftarrow$ Cost($Component_i$, $S_{current}$);
6   **end**
7   RankedComponents $\leftarrow$ Rank($Si_{components}$)
8     $Component_i \leftarrow$ SelectWeakComponent(RankedComponents, $Component_i$, τ);
9     $Component_j \leftarrow$ SelectReplacementComponent(RankedComponents, τ);
10    $S_{candidate} \leftarrow$ Replace($S_{current}$, $Component_i$, $Component_j$);
11   **if** Cost($S_{candidate}$) $\leq$ Cost(S_{best}) **then**
12     $S_{best} \leftarrow S_{candidate}$;
13   **end**
14 **end**
15 **return** S_{best};

4.3.6 Heuristics

- Extremal Optimization was designed for combinatorial optimization problems, although variations have been applied to continuous function optimization.

- The selection of the worst component and the replacement component each iteration can be deterministic or probabilistic, the latter of which is referred to as τ-Extremal Optimization given the use of a τ parameter.

- The selection of an appropriate scoring function of the components of a solution is the most difficult part in the application of the technique.

- For τ-Extremal Optimization, low τ values are used (such as $\tau \in [1.2, 1.6]$) have been found to be effective for the TSP.

4.3.7 Code Listing

Listing 4.2 provides an example of the Extremal Optimization algorithm implemented in the Ruby Programming Language. The algorithm is applied to the Berlin52 instance of the Traveling Salesman Problem (TSP), taken from the TSPLIB. The problem seeks a permutation of the order to visit cities (called a tour) that minimizes the total distance traveled. The optimal tour distance for Berlin52 instance is 7542 units.

The algorithm implementation is based on the seminal work by Boettcher and Percus [5]. A solution is comprised of a permutation of city components. Each city can potentially form a connection to any other city, and the connections to other cities ordered by distance may be considered its neighborhood. For a given candidate solution, the city components of a solution are scored based on the neighborhood rank of the cities to which they are connected: $fitness_k \leftarrow \frac{3}{r_i + r_j}$, where r_i and r_j are the neighborhood ranks of cities i and j against city k. A city is selected for modification probabilistically where the probability of selecting a given city is proportional to $n_i^{-\tau}$, where n is the rank of city i. The longest connection is broken, and the city is connected with another neighboring city that is also probabilistically selected.

```ruby
def euc_2d(c1, c2)
  Math.sqrt((c1[0] - c2[0])**2.0 + (c1[1] - c2[1])**2.0).round
end

def cost(permutation, cities)
  distance =0
  permutation.each_with_index do |c1, i|
    c2 = (i==permutation.size-1) ? permutation[0] : permutation[i+1]
    distance += euc_2d(cities[c1], cities[c2])
  end
  return distance
end

def random_permutation(cities)
  perm = Array.new(cities.size){|i| i}
  perm.each_index do |i|
    r = rand(perm.size-i) + i
    perm[r], perm[i] = perm[i], perm[r]
  end
  return perm
end

def calculate_neighbor_rank(city_number, cities, ignore=[])
  neighbors = []
  cities.each_with_index do |city, i|
    next if i==city_number or ignore.include?(i)
    neighbor = {:number=>i}
```

```ruby
28        neighbor[:distance] = euc_2d(cities[city_number], city)
29        neighbors << neighbor
30      end
31      return neighbors.sort!{|x,y| x[:distance] <=> y[:distance]}
32    end
33
34    def get_edges_for_city(city_number, permutation)
35      c1, c2 = nil, nil
36      permutation.each_with_index do |c, i|
37        if c == city_number
38          c1 = (i==0) ? permutation.last : permutation[i-1]
39          c2 = (i==permutation.size-1) ? permutation.first : permutation[i+1]
40          break
41        end
42      end
43      return [c1, c2]
44    end
45
46    def calculate_city_fitness(permutation, city_number, cities)
47      c1, c2 = get_edges_for_city(city_number, permutation)
48      neighbors = calculate_neighbor_rank(city_number, cities)
49      n1, n2 = -1, -1
50      neighbors.each_with_index do |neighbor,i|
51        n1 = i+1 if neighbor[:number] == c1
52        n2 = i+1 if neighbor[:number] == c2
53        break if n1!=-1 and n2!=-1
54      end
55      return 3.0 / (n1.to_f + n2.to_f)
56    end
57
58    def calculate_city_fitnesses(cities, permutation)
59      city_fitnesses = []
60      cities.each_with_index do |city, i|
61        city_fitness = {:number=>i}
62        city_fitness[:fitness] = calculate_city_fitness(permutation, i, cities)
63        city_fitnesses << city_fitness
64      end
65      return city_fitnesses.sort!{|x,y| y[:fitness] <=> x[:fitness]}
66    end
67
68    def calculate_component_probabilities(ordered_components, tau)
69      sum = 0.0
70      ordered_components.each_with_index do |component, i|
71        component[:prob] = (i+1.0)**(-tau)
72        sum += component[:prob]
73      end
74      return sum
75    end
76
77    def make_selection(components, sum_probability)
78      selection = rand()
79      components.each_with_index do |component, i|
80        selection -= (component[:prob] / sum_probability)
81        return component[:number] if selection <= 0.0
82      end
83      return components.last[:number]
```

```ruby
84    end
85
86    def probabilistic_selection(ordered_components, tau, exclude=[])
87      sum = calculate_component_probabilities(ordered_components, tau)
88      selected_city = nil
89      begin
90        selected_city = make_selection(ordered_components, sum)
91      end while exclude.include?(selected_city)
92      return selected_city
93    end
94
95    def vary_permutation(permutation, selected, new, long_edge)
96      perm = Array.new(permutation)
97      c1, c2 = perm.rindex(selected), perm.rindex(new)
98      p1,p2 = (c1<c2) ? [c1,c2] : [c2,c1]
99      right = (c1==perm.size-1) ? 0 : c1+1
100     if perm[right] == long_edge
101       perm[p1+1..p2] = perm[p1+1..p2].reverse
102     else
103       perm[p1...p2] = perm[p1...p2].reverse
104     end
105     return perm
106   end
107
108   def get_long_edge(edges, neighbor_distances)
109     n1 = neighbor_distances.find {|x| x[:number]==edges[0]}
110     n2 = neighbor_distances.find {|x| x[:number]==edges[1]}
111     return (n1[:distance] > n2[:distance]) ? n1[:number] : n2[:number]
112   end
113
114   def create_new_perm(cities, tau, perm)
115     city_fitnesses = calculate_city_fitnesses(cities, perm)
116     selected_city = probabilistic_selection(city_fitnesses.reverse, tau)
117     edges = get_edges_for_city(selected_city, perm)
118     neighbors = calculate_neighbor_rank(selected_city, cities)
119     new_neighbor = probabilistic_selection(neighbors, tau, edges)
120     long_edge = get_long_edge(edges, neighbors)
121     return vary_permutation(perm, selected_city, new_neighbor, long_edge)
122   end
123
124   def search(cities, max_iterations, tau)
125     current = {:vector=>random_permutation(cities)}
126     current[:cost] = cost(current[:vector], cities)
127     best = current
128     max_iterations.times do |iter|
129       candidate = {}
130       candidate[:vector] = create_new_perm(cities, tau, current[:vector])
131       candidate[:cost] = cost(candidate[:vector], cities)
132       current = candidate
133       best = candidate if candidate[:cost] < best[:cost]
134       puts " > iter #{(iter+1)}, curr=#{current[:cost]}, best=#{best[:cost]}"
135     end
136     return best
137   end
138
139   if __FILE__ == $0
```

```
140   # problem configuration
141   berlin52 = [[565,575],[25,185],[345,750],[945,685],[845,655],
142     [880,660],[25,230],[525,1000],[580,1175],[650,1130],[1605,620],
143     [1220,580],[1465,200],[1530,5],[845,680],[725,370],[145,665],
144     [415,635],[510,875],[560,365],[300,465],[520,585],[480,415],
145     [835,625],[975,580],[1215,245],[1320,315],[1250,400],[660,180],
146     [410,250],[420,555],[575,665],[1150,1160],[700,580],[685,595],
147     [685,610],[770,610],[795,645],[720,635],[760,650],[475,960],
148     [95,260],[875,920],[700,500],[555,815],[830,485],[1170,65],
149     [830,610],[605,625],[595,360],[1340,725],[1740,245]]
150   # algorithm configuration
151   max_iterations = 250
152   tau = 1.8
153   # execute the algorithm
154   best = search(berlin52, max_iterations, tau)
155   puts "Done. Best Solution: c=#{best[:cost]}, v=#{best[:vector].inspect}"
156   end
```

Listing 4.2: Extremal Optimization in Ruby

4.3.8   References

Primary Sources

Extremal Optimization was proposed as an optimization heuristic by Boettcher and Percus applied to graph partitioning and the Traveling Salesman Problem [5]. The approach was inspired by the Bak-Sneppen self-organized criticality model of co-evolution [1, 2].

Learn More

A number of detailed reviews of Extremal Optimization have been presented, including a review and studies by Boettcher and Percus [4], an accessible review by Boettcher [3], and a focused study on the Spin Glass problem by Boettcher and Percus [6].

4.3.9   Bibliography

[1] P. Bak and K. Sneppen. Punctuated equilibrium and criticality in a simple model of evolution. *Physical Review Letters*, 71:4083–4086, 1993.

[2] P. Bak, C. Tang, and K. Wiesenfeld. Self-organized criticality: An explanation of the 1/f noise. *Physical Review Letters*, 59:381–384, 1987.

[3] S. Boettcher. Extremal optimization: heuristics via coevolutionary avalanches. *Computing in Science & Engineering*, 2(6):75–82, 2000.

[4] S. Boettcher and A. Percus. Natures way of optimizing. *Artificial Intelligence*, 119(1-2):275–286, 2000.

[5] S. Boettcher and A. G. Percus. Extremal optimization: Methods derived from co-evolution. In *Proceedings of the Genetic and Evolutionary Computation Conference*, 1999.

[6] S. Boettcher and A. G. Percus. Optimization with extremal dynamics. *Phys. Rev. Lett.*, 86:5211–5214, 2001.

4.4   Harmony Search

Harmony Search, HS.

4.4.1   Taxonomy

Harmony Search belongs to the fields of Computational Intelligence and Metaheuristics.

4.4.2   Inspiration

Harmony Search was inspired by the improvisation of Jazz musicians. Specifically, the process by which the musicians (who may have never played together before) rapidly refine their individual improvisation through variation resulting in an aesthetic harmony.

4.4.3   Metaphor

Each musician corresponds to an attribute in a candidate solution from a problem domain, and each instrument's pitch and range corresponds to the bounds and constraints on the decision variable. The harmony between the musicians is taken as a complete candidate solution at a given time, and the audiences aesthetic appreciation of the harmony represent the problem specific cost function. The musicians seek harmony over time through small variations and improvisations, which results in an improvement against the cost function.

4.4.4   Strategy

The information processing objective of the technique is to use good candidate solutions already discovered to influence the creation of new candidate solutions toward locating the problems optima. This is achieved by stochastically creating candidate solutions in a step-wise manner, where each component is either drawn randomly from a memory of high-quality solutions, adjusted from the memory of high-quality solutions, or assigned randomly within the bounds of the problem. The memory of candidate solutions is initially random, and a greedy acceptance criteria is used to admit new candidate solutions only if they have an improved objective value, replacing an existing member.

4.4.5   Procedure

Algorithm 4.4.1 provides a pseudocode listing of the Harmony Search algorithm for minimizing a cost function. The adjustment of a pitch selected from the harmony memory is typically linear, for example for continuous function optimization:

$$x' \leftarrow x + range \times \epsilon \qquad (4.1)$$

where $range$ is a the user parameter (pitch bandwidth) to control the size of the changes, and ϵ is a uniformly random number $\in [-1, 1]$.

Algorithm 4.4.1: Pseudocode for Harmony Search.

Input: $Pitch_{num}$, $Pitch_{bounds}$, $Memory_{size}$, $Consolidation_{rate}$, $PitchAdjust_{rate}$, $Improvisation_{max}$
Output: $Harmony_{best}$

1   Harmonies ← InitializeHarmonyMemory($Pitch_{num}$, $Pitch_{bounds}$, $Memory_{size}$);
2   EvaluateHarmonies(Harmonies);
3   **for** i to $Improvisation_{max}$ **do**
4     $Harmony \leftarrow \emptyset$;
5   **foreach** $Pitch_i \in Pitch_{num}$ **do**
6   **if** Rand() $\leq Consolidation_{rate}$ **then**
7         $RandomHarmony^i_{pitch} \leftarrow$ SelectRandomHarmonyPitch(Harmonies, $Pitch_i$);
8   **if** Rand() $\leq PitchAdjust_{rate}$ **then**
9           $Harmony^i_{pitch} \leftarrow$ AdjustPitch($RandomHarmony^i_{pitch}$);
10   **else**
11           $Harmony^i_{pitch} \leftarrow RandomHarmony^i_{pitch}$;
12   **end**
13   **else**
14         $Harmony^i_{pitch} \leftarrow$ RandomPitch($Pitch_{bounds}$);
15   **end**
16   **end**
17   EvaluateHarmonies($Harmony$);
18   **if** Cost($Harmony$) $\leq$ Cost(Worst(Harmonies)) **then**
19   Worst(Harmonies) ← $Harmony$;
20   **end**
21 **end**
22 **return** $Harmony_{best}$;

4.4.6   Heuristics

- Harmony Search was designed as a generalized optimization method for continuous, discrete, and constrained optimization and has been applied to numerous types of optimization problems.

- The harmony memory considering rate (HMCR) $\in [0, 1]$ controls the use of information from the harmony memory or the generation of a random pitch. As such, it controls the rate of convergence of the algorithm and is typically configured $\in [0.7, 0.95]$.

- The pitch adjustment rate (PAR) $\in [0, 1]$ controls the frequency of adjustment of pitches selected from harmony memory, typically configured $\in [0.1, 0.5]$. High values can result in the premature convergence of the search.

- The pitch adjustment rate and the adjustment method (amount of adjustment or fret width) are typically fixed, having a linear effect through time. Non-linear methods have been considered, for example refer to Geem [4].

- When creating a new harmony, aggregations of pitches can be taken from across musicians in the harmony memory.

- The harmony memory update is typically a greedy process, although other considerations such as diversity may be used where the most similar harmony is replaced.

4.4.7   Code Listing

Listing 4.3 provides an example of the Harmony Search algorithm implemented in the Ruby Programming Language. The demonstration problem is an instance of a continuous function optimization that seeks $minf(x)$ where $f = \sum_{i=1}^{n} x_i^2$, $-5.0 \leq x_i \leq 5.0$ and $n = 3$. The optimal solution for this basin function is $(v_0, \dots, v_{n-1}) = 0.0$. The algorithm implementation and parameterization are based on the description by Yang [7], with refinement from Geem [4].

```ruby
def objective_function(vector)
  return vector.inject(0.0) {|sum, x| sum + (x ** 2.0)}
end

def rand_in_bounds(min, max)
  return min + ((max-min) * rand())
end

def random_vector(search_space)
  return Array.new(search_space.size) do |i|
    rand_in_bounds(search_space[i][0], search_space[i][1])
  end
end

def create_random_harmony(search_space)
  harmony = {}
  harmony[:vector] = random_vector(search_space)
  harmony[:fitness] = objective_function(harmony[:vector])
```

```ruby
19    return harmony
20  end
21
22  def initialize_harmony_memory(search_space, mem_size, factor=3)
23    memory = Array.new(mem_size*factor){create_random_harmony(search_space)}
24    memory.sort!{|x,y| x[:fitness]<=>y[:fitness]}
25    return memory.first(mem_size)
26  end
27
28  def create_harmony(search_space, memory, consid_rate, adjust_rate, range)
29    vector = Array.new(search_space.size)
30    search_space.size.times do |i|
31      if rand() < consid_rate
32        value = memory[rand(memory.size)][:vector][i]
33        value = value + range*rand_in_bounds(-1.0, 1.0) if rand()<adjust_rate
34        value = search_space[i][0] if value < search_space[i][0]
35        value = search_space[i][1] if value > search_space[i][1]
36        vector[i] = value
37      else
38        vector[i] = rand_in_bounds(search_space[i][0], search_space[i][1])
39      end
40    end
41    return {:vector=>vector}
42  end
43
44  def search(bounds, max_iter, mem_size, consid_rate, adjust_rate, range)
45    memory = initialize_harmony_memory(bounds, mem_size)
46    best = memory.first
47    max_iter.times do |iter|
48      harm = create_harmony(bounds, memory, consid_rate, adjust_rate, range)
49      harm[:fitness] = objective_function(harm[:vector])
50      best = harm if harm[:fitness] < best[:fitness]
51      memory << harm
52      memory.sort!{|x,y| x[:fitness]<=>y[:fitness]}
53      memory.delete_at(memory.size-1)
54      puts " > iteration=#{iter}, fitness=#{best[:fitness]}"
55    end
56    return best
57  end
58
59  if __FILE__ == $0
60    # problem configuration
61    problem_size = 3
62    bounds = Array.new(problem_size) {|i| [-5, 5]}
63    # algorithm configuration
64    mem_size = 20
65    consid_rate = 0.95
66    adjust_rate = 0.7
67    range = 0.05
68    max_iter = 500
69    # execute the algorithm
70    best = search(bounds, max_iter, mem_size, consid_rate, adjust_rate, range)
71    puts "done! Solution: f=#{best[:fitness]}, s=#{best[:vector].inspect}"
72  end
```

Listing 4.3: Harmony Search in Ruby

4.4.8 References

Primary Sources

Geem ct al. proposed the Harmony Search algorithm in 2001, which was applied to a range of optimization problems including a constraint optimization, the Traveling Salesman problem, and the design of a water supply network [6].

Learn More

A book on Harmony Search, edited by Geem provides a collection of papers on the technique and its applications [2], chapter 1 provides a useful summary of the method heuristics for its configuration [7]. Similarly a second edited volume by Geem focuses on studies that provide more advanced applications of the approach [5], and chapter 1 provides a detailed walkthrough of the technique itself [4]. Geem also provides a treatment of Harmony Search applied to the optimal design of water distribution networks [3] and edits yet a third volume on papers related to the application of the technique to structural design optimization problems [1].

4.4.9 Bibliography

[1] Z. W. Geem, editor. *Harmony Search Algorithms for Structural Design Optimization*. Springer, 2009.

[2] Z. W. Geem, editor. *Music-Inspired Harmony Search Algorithm: Theory and Applications*. Springer, 2009.

[3] Z. W. Geem. *Optimal Design of Water Distribution Networks Using Harmony Search*. Lap Lambert Academic Publishing, 2009.

[4] Z. W. Geem. *Recent Advances In Harmony Search Algorithms*, chapter State-of-the-Art in the Structure of Harmony Search Algorithm, pages 1–10. Springer, 2010.

[5] Z. W. Geem, editor. *Recent Advances in Harmony Search Algorithms*. Springer, 2010.

[6] Z. W. Geem, J. H. Kim, and G. V. Loganathan. A new heuristic optimization algorithm: Harmony search. *Simulation*, 76:60–68, 2001.

[7] X-S. Yang. *Music-Inspired Harmony Search Algorithm: Theory and Applications*, chapter Harmony Search as a Metaheuristic, pages 1–14. Springer, 2009.

4.5   Cultural Algorithm

Cultural Algorithm, CA.

4.5.1   Taxonomy

The Cultural Algorithm is an extension to the field of Evolutionary Computation and may be considered a Meta-Evolutionary Algorithm. It more broadly belongs to the field of Computational Intelligence and Metaheuristics. It is related to other high-order extensions of Evolutionary Computation such as the Memetic Algorithm (Section 4.6).

4.5.2   Inspiration

The Cultural Algorithm is inspired by the principle of cultural evolution. Culture includes the habits, knowledge, beliefs, customs, and morals of a member of society. Culture does not exist independent of the environment, and can interact with the environment via positive or negative feedback cycles. The study of the interaction of culture in the environment is referred to as Cultural Ecology.

4.5.3   Metaphor

The Cultural Algorithm may be explained in the context of the inspiring system. As the evolutionary process unfolds, individuals accumulate information about the world which is communicated to other individuals in the population. Collectively this corpus of information is a knowledge base that members of the population may tap-into and exploit. Positive feedback mechanisms can occur where cultural knowledge indicates useful areas of the environment, information which is passed down between generations, exploited, refined, and adapted as situations change. Additionally, areas of potential hazard may also be communicated through the cultural knowledge base.

4.5.4   Strategy

The information processing objective of the algorithm is to improve the learning or convergence of an embedded search technique (typically an evolutionary algorithm) using a higher-order cultural evolution. The algorithm operates at two levels: a population level and a cultural level. The population level is like an evolutionary search, where individuals represent candidate solutions, are mostly distinct and their characteristics are translated into an objective or cost function in the problem domain. The second level is the knowledge or believe space where information acquired by generations is stored, and which is accessible to the current generation.

A communication protocol is used to allow the two spaces to interact and the types of information that can be exchanged.

4.5.5   Procedure

The focus of the algorithm is the `KnowledgeBase` data structure that records different knowledge types based on the nature of the problem. For example, the structure may be used to record the best candidate solution found as well as generalized information about areas of the search space that are expected to payoff (result in good candidate solutions). This cultural knowledge is discovered by the population-based evolutionary search, and is in turn used to influence subsequent generations. The acceptance function constrain the communication of knowledge from the population to the knowledge base.

Algorithm 4.5.1 provides a pseudocode listing of the Cultural Algorithm. The algorithm is abstract, providing flexibility in the interpretation of the processes such as the acceptance of information, the structure of the knowledge base, and the specific embedded evolutionary algorithm.

Algorithm 4.5.1: Pseudocode for the Cultural Algorithm.

Input: $Problem_{size}$, $Population_{num}$
Output: KnowledgeBase

1 Population $\leftarrow$ `InitializePopulation`($Problem_{size}$, $Population_{num}$);
2 KnowledgeBase $\leftarrow$ `InitializeKnowledgebase`($Problem_{size}$, $Population_{num}$);
3 **while** $\neg$`StopCondition()` **do**
4 $\quad$ `Evaluate`(Population);
5 $\quad$ $SituationalKnowledge_{candidate} \leftarrow$ `AcceptSituationalKnowledge`(Population);
6 $\quad$ `UpdateSituationalKnowledge`(KnowledgeBase, $SituationalKnowledge_{candidate}$);
7 $\quad$ Children $\leftarrow$ `ReproduceWithInfluence`(Population, KnowledgeBase);
8 $\quad$ Population $\leftarrow$ `Select`(Children, Population);
9 $\quad$ $NormativeKnowledge_{candidate} \leftarrow$ `AcceptNormativeKnowledge`(Population);
10 $\quad$ `UpdateNormativeKnowledge`(KnowledgeBase, $NormativeKnowledge_{candidate}$);
11 **end**
12 **return** KnowledgeBase;

4.5.6 Heuristics

- The Cultural Algorithm was initially used as a simulation tool to investigate Cultural Ecology. It has been adapted for use as an optimization algorithm for a wide variety of domains not-limited to constraint optimization, combinatorial optimization, and continuous function optimization.

- The knowledge base structure provides a mechanism for incorporating problem-specific information into the execution of an evolutionary search.

- The acceptance functions that control the flow of information into the knowledge base are typically greedy, only including the best information from the current generation, and not replacing existing knowledge unless it is an improvement.

- Acceptance functions are traditionally deterministic, although probabilistic and fuzzy acceptance functions have been investigated.

4.5.7 Code Listing

Listing 4.4 provides an example of the Cultural Algorithm implemented in the Ruby Programming Language. The demonstration problem is an instance of a continuous function optimization that seeks $\min f(x)$ where $f = \sum_{i=1}^{n} x_i^2$, $-5.0 \le x_i \le 5.0$ and $n = 2$. The optimal solution for this basin function is $(v_0, \ldots, v_{n-1}) = 0.0$.

The Cultural Algorithm was implemented based on the description of the Cultural Algorithm Evolutionary Program (CAEP) presented by Reynolds [4]. A real-valued Genetic Algorithm was used as the embedded evolutionary algorithm. The overall best solution is taken as the 'situational' cultural knowledge, whereas the bounds of the top 20% of the best solutions each generation are taken as the 'normative' cultural knowledge. The situational knowledge is returned as the result of the search, whereas the normative knowledge is used to influence the evolutionary process. Specifically, vector bounds in the normative knowledge are used to define a subspace from which new candidate solutions are uniformly sampled during the reproduction step of the evolutionary algorithm's variation mechanism. A real-valued representation and a binary tournament selection strategy are used by the evolutionary algorithm.

```ruby
def objective_function(vector)
  return vector.inject(0.0) {|sum, x| sum + (x ** 2.0)}
end

def rand_in_bounds(min, max)
  return min + ((max-min) * rand())
end
```

```ruby
 8
 9  def random_vector(minmax)
10    return Array.new(minmax.size) do |i|
11      rand_in_bounds(minmax[i][0], minmax[i][1])
12    end
13  end
14
15  def mutate_with_inf(candidate, beliefs, minmax)
16    v = Array.new(candidate[:vector].size)
17    candidate[:vector].each_with_index do |c,i|
18      v[i]=rand_in_bounds(beliefs[:normative][i][0],beliefs[:normative][i][1])
19      v[i] = minmax[i][0] if v[i] < minmax[i][0]
20      v[i] = minmax[i][1] if v[i] > minmax[i][1]
21    end
22    return {:vector=>v}
23  end
24
25  def binary_tournament(pop)
26    i, j = rand(pop.size), rand(pop.size)
27    j = rand(pop.size) while j==i
28    return (pop[i][:fitness] < pop[j][:fitness]) ? pop[i] : pop[j]
29  end
30
31  def initialize_beliefspace(search_space)
32    belief_space = {}
33    belief_space[:situational] = nil
34    belief_space[:normative] = Array.new(search_space.size) do |i|
35      Array.new(search_space[i])
36    end
37    return belief_space
38  end
39
40  def update_beliefspace_situational!(belief_space, best)
41    curr_best = belief_space[:situational]
42    if curr_best.nil? or best[:fitness] < curr_best[:fitness]
43      belief_space[:situational] = best
44    end
45  end
46
47  def update_beliefspace_normative!(belief_space, acc)
48    belief_space[:normative].each_with_index do |bounds,i|
49      bounds[0] = acc.min{|x,y| x[:vector][i]<=>y[:vector][i]}[:vector][i]
50      bounds[1] = acc.max{|x,y| x[:vector][i]<=>y[:vector][i]}[:vector][i]
51    end
52  end
53
54  def search(max_gens, search_space, pop_size, num_accepted)
55    # initialize
56    pop = Array.new(pop_size) { {:vector=>random_vector(search_space)} }
57    belief_space = initialize_beliefspace(search_space)
58    # evaluate
59    pop.each{|c| c[:fitness] = objective_function(c[:vector])}
60    best = pop.sort{|x,y| x[:fitness] <=> y[:fitness]}.first
61    # update situational knowledge
62    update_beliefspace_situational!(belief_space, best)
63    max_gens.times do |gen|
```

```
64    # create next generation
65    children = Array.new(pop_size) do |i|
66      mutate_with_inf(pop[i], belief_space, search_space)
67    end
68    # evaluate
69    children.each{|c| c[:fitness] = objective_function(c[:vector])}
70    best = children.sort{|x,y| x[:fitness] <=> y[:fitness]}.first
71    # update situational knowledge
72    update_beliefspace_situational!(belief_space, best)
73    # select next generation
74    pop = Array.new(pop_size) { binary_tournament(children + pop) }
75    # update normative knowledge
76    pop.sort!{|x,y| x[:fitness] <=> y[:fitness]}
77    acccepted = pop[0...num_accepted]
78    update_beliefspace_normative!(belief_space, acccepted)
79    # user feedback
80    puts " > generation=#{gen}, f=#{belief_space[:situational][:fitness]}"
81    end
82    return belief_space[:situational]
83  end
84
85  if __FILE__ == $0
86    # problem configuration
87    problem_size = 2
88    search_space = Array.new(problem_size) {|i| [-5, +5]}
89    # algorithm configuration
90    max_gens = 200
91    pop_size = 100
92    num_accepted = (pop_size*0.20).round
93    # execute the algorithm
94    best = search(max_gens, search_space, pop_size, num_accepted)
95    puts "done! Solution: f=#{best[:fitness]}, s=#{best[:vector].inspect}"
96  end
```

Listing 4.4: Cultural Algorithm in Ruby

4.5.8   References

Primary Sources

The Cultural Algorithm was proposed by Reynolds in 1994 that combined the method with the Version Space Algorithm (a binary string based Genetic Algorithm), where generalizations of individual solutions were communicated as cultural knowledge in the form of schema patterns (strings of 1's, 0's and #'s, where '#' represents a wildcard) [3].

Learn More

Chung and Reynolds provide a study of the Cultural Algorithm on a testbed of constraint satisfaction problems [1]. Reynolds provides a detailed overview of the history of the technique as a book chapter that presents the state of the art and summaries of application areas including concept learning and continuous function optimization [4]. Coello Coello and Becerra proposed a variation of the Cultural Algorithm that uses Evolutionary Programming as the embedded weak search method, for use with Multi-Objective Optimization problems [2].

4.5.9 Bibliography

[1] C.-J. Chung and R. G. Reynolds. A testbed for solving optimization problems using cultural algorithms. In L. J. Fogel, P. J. Angeline, and T. Bäck, editors, *Evolutionary Programming V: Proceedings of the Fifth Annual Conference on Evolutionary Programming*, pages 225–236, 1996.

[2] C. A. Coello Coello and R. L. Becerra. Evolutionary multiobjective optimization using a cultural algorithm. In *Proceedings of the 2003 IEEE Swarm Intelligence Symposium*, pages 6–13. IEEE Press, 2003.

[3] R. G. Reynolds. An introduction to cultural algorithms. In *Proceedings of the 3rd Annual Conference on Evolutionary Programming*, pages 131–139. World Scienfific Publishing, 1994.

[4] R. G. Reynolds. *New Ideas in Optimization*, chapter Cultural Algorithms: Theory and Applications, pages 367–378. McGraw-Hill Ltd., 1999.

4.6 Memetic Algorithm

Memetic Algorithm, MA.

4.6.1 Taxonomy

Memetic Algorithms have elements of Metaheuristics and Computational Intelligence. Although they have principles of Evolutionary Algorithms, they may not strictly be considered an Evolutionary Technique. Memetic Algorithms have functional similarities to Baldwinian Evolutionary Algorithms, Lamarckian Evolutionary Algorithms, Hybrid Evolutionary Algorithms, and Cultural Algorithms (Section 4.5). Using ideas of memes and Memetic Algorithms in optimization may be referred to as Memetic Computing.

4.6.2 Inspiration

Memetic Algorithms are inspired by the interplay of genetic evolution and memetic evolution. Universal Darwinism is the generalization of genes beyond biological-based systems to any system where discrete units of information can be inherited and be subjected to evolutionary forces of selection and variation. The term 'meme' is used to refer to a piece of discrete cultural information, suggesting at the interplay of genetic and cultural evolution.

4.6.3 Metaphor

The genotype is evolved based on the interaction the phenotype has with the environment. This interaction is metered by cultural phenomena that influence the selection mechanisms, and even the pairing and recombination mechanisms. Cultural information is shared between individuals, spreading through the population as memes relative to their fitness or fitness the memes impart to the individuals. Collectively, the interplay of the geneotype and the memeotype strengthen the fitness of population in the environment.

4.6.4 Strategy

The objective of the information processing strategy is to exploit a population based global search technique to broadly locate good areas of the search space, combined with the repeated usage of a local search heuristic by individual solutions to locate local optimum. Ideally, memetic algorithms embrace the duality of genetic and cultural evolution, allowing the transmission, selection, inheritance, and variation of memes as well as genes.

4.6.5   Procedure

Algorithm 4.6.1 provides a pseudocode listing of the Memetic Algorithm for minimizing a cost function. The procedure describes a simple or first order Memetic Algorithm that shows the improvement of individual solutions separate from a global search, although does not show the independent evolution of memes.

Algorithm 4.6.1: Pseudocode for the Memetic Algorithm.

Input: ProblemSize, Pop_{size}, $MemePop_{size}$
Output: S_{best}

1 Population $\leftarrow$ InitializePopulation(ProblemSize, Pop_{size});
2 **while** ¬StopCondition() **do**
3   **foreach** $S_i \in$ Population **do**
4          $Si_{cost} \leftarrow$ Cost(S_i);
5   **end**
6      $S_{best} \leftarrow$ GetBestSolution(Population);
7   Population $\leftarrow$ StochasticGlobalSearch(Population);
8   MemeticPopulation $\leftarrow$ SelectMemeticPopulation(Population, $MemePop_{size}$);
9   **foreach** $S_i \in$ MemeticPopulation **do**
10         $S_i \leftarrow$ LocalSearch(S_i);
11   **end**
12 **end**
13 **return** S_{best};

4.6.6   Heuristics

- The global search provides the broad exploration mechanism, whereas the individual solution improvement via local search provides an exploitation mechanism.

- Balance is needed between the local and global mechanisms to ensure the system does not prematurely converge to a local optimum and does not consume unnecessary computational resources.

- The local search should be problem and representation specific, where as the global search may be generic and non-specific (black-box).

- Memetic Algorithms have been applied to a range of constraint, combinatorial, and continuous function optimization problem domains.

4.6.7   Code Listing

Listing 4.5 provides an example of the Memetic Algorithm implemented in the Ruby Programming Language. The demonstration problem is an instance of a continuous function optimization that seeks min $f(x)$ where $f = \sum_{i=1}^{n} x_i^2$, $-5.0 \leq x_i \leq 5.0$ and $n = 3$. The optimal solution for this basin function is $(v_0, \ldots, v_{n-1}) = 0.0$. The Memetic Algorithm uses a canonical Genetic Algorithm as the global search technique that operates on binary strings, uses tournament selection, point mutations, uniform crossover and a binary coded decimal decoding of bits to real values. A bit climber local search is used that performs probabilistic bit flips (point mutations) and only accepts solutions with the same or improving fitness.

```ruby
def objective_function(vector)
  return vector.inject(0.0) {|sum, x| sum + (x ** 2.0)}
end

def random_bitstring(num_bits)
  return (0...num_bits).inject(""){|s,i| s<<((rand<0.5) ? "1" : "0")}
end

def decode(bitstring, search_space, bits_per_param)
  vector = []
  search_space.each_with_index do |bounds, i|
    off, sum = i*bits_per_param, 0.0
    param = bitstring[off...(off+bits_per_param)].reverse
    param.size.times do |j|
      sum += ((param[j].chr=='1') ? 1.0 : 0.0) * (2.0 ** j.to_f)
    end
    min, max = bounds
    vector << min + ((max-min)/((2.0**bits_per_param.to_f)-1.0)) * sum
  end
  return vector
end

def fitness(candidate, search_space, param_bits)
  candidate[:vector]=decode(candidate[:bitstring], search_space, param_bits)
  candidate[:fitness] = objective_function(candidate[:vector])
end

def binary_tournament(pop)
  i, j = rand(pop.size), rand(pop.size)
  j = rand(pop.size) while j==i
  return (pop[i][:fitness] < pop[j][:fitness]) ? pop[i] : pop[j]
end

def point_mutation(bitstring, rate=1.0/bitstring.size)
  child = ""
  bitstring.size.times do |i|
    bit = bitstring[i].chr
    child << ((rand()<rate) ? ((bit=='1') ? "0" : "1") : bit)
  end
  return child
end
```

```ruby
42
43  def crossover(parent1, parent2, rate)
44    return ""+parent1 if rand()>=rate
45    child = ""
46    parent1.size.times do |i|
47      child << ((rand()<0.5) ? parent1[i].chr : parent2[i].chr)
48    end
49    return child
50  end
51
52  def reproduce(selected, pop_size, p_cross, p_mut)
53    children = []
54    selected.each_with_index do |p1, i|
55      p2 = (i.modulo(2)==0) ? selected[i+1] : selected[i-1]
56      p2 = selected[0] if i == selected.size-1
57      child = {}
58      child[:bitstring] = crossover(p1[:bitstring], p2[:bitstring], p_cross)
59      child[:bitstring] = point_mutation(child[:bitstring], p_mut)
60      children << child
61      break if children.size >= pop_size
62    end
63    return children
64  end
65
66  def bitclimber(child, search_space, p_mut, max_local_gens, bits_per_param)
67    current = child
68    max_local_gens.times do
69      candidate = {}
70      candidate[:bitstring] = point_mutation(current[:bitstring], p_mut)
71      fitness(candidate, search_space, bits_per_param)
72      current = candidate if candidate[:fitness] <= current[:fitness]
73    end
74    return current
75  end
76
77  def search(max_gens, search_space, pop_size, p_cross, p_mut,
              max_local_gens, p_local, bits_per_param=16)
78    pop = Array.new(pop_size) do |i|
79      {:bitstring=>random_bitstring(search_space.size*bits_per_param)}
80    end
81    pop.each{|candidate| fitness(candidate, search_space, bits_per_param) }
82    gen, best = 0, pop.sort{|x,y| x[:fitness] <=> y[:fitness]}.first
83    max_gens.times do
84      selected = Array.new(pop_size){|i| binary_tournament(pop)}
85      children = reproduce(selected, pop_size, p_cross, p_mut)
86      children.each{|cand| fitness(cand, search_space, bits_per_param)}
87      pop = []
88      children.each do |child|
89        if rand() < p_local
90          child = bitclimber(child, search_space, p_mut, max_local_gens,
                  bits_per_param)
91        end
92        pop << child
93      end
94      pop.sort!{|x,y| x[:fitness] <=> y[:fitness]}
95      best = pop.first if pop.first[:fitness] <= best[:fitness]
```

```
96      puts ">gen=#{gen}, f=#{best[:fitness]}, b=#{best[:bitstring]}"
97    end
98    return best
99  end
100
101 if __FILE__ == $0
102   # problem configuration
103   problem_size = 3
104   search_space = Array.new(problem_size) {|i| [-5, +5]}
105   # algorithm configuration
106   max_gens = 100
107   pop_size = 100
108   p_cross = 0.98
109   p_mut = 1.0/(problem_size*16).to_f
110   max_local_gens = 20
111   p_local = 0.5
112   # execute the algorithm
113   best = search(max_gens, search_space, pop_size, p_cross, p_mut,
            max_local_gens, p_local)
114   puts "done! Solution: f=#{best[:fitness]}, b=#{best[:bitstring]},
            v=#{best[:vector].inspect}"
115 end
```

Listing 4.5: Memetic Algorithm in Ruby

4.6.8   References

Primary Sources

The concept of a Memetic Algorithm is credited to Moscato [5], who was inspired by the description of meme's in Dawkins' "The Selfish Gene" [1]. Moscato proposed Memetic Algorithms as the marriage between population based global search and heuristic local search made by each individual without the constraints of a genetic representation and investigated variations on the Traveling Salesman Problem.

Learn More

Moscato and Cotta provide a gentle introduction to the field of Memetic Algorithms as a book chapter that covers formal descriptions of the approach, a summary of the fields of application, and the state of the art [6]. An overview and classification of the types of Memetic Algorithms is presented by Ong et al. who describe a class of adaptive Memetic Algorithms [7]. Krasnogor and Smith also provide a taxonomy of Memetic Algorithms, focusing on the properties needed to design 'competent' implementations of the approach with examples on a number of combinatorial optimization problems [4]. Work by Krasnogor and Gustafson investigate what they refer to as 'self-generating' Memetic Algorithms that use the memetic principle to co-evolve the local search applied by individual solutions [3]. For a broader overview of the field, see the 2005 book "Recent Advances in Memetic Algorithms" that provides an overview and a number of studies [2].

4.6.9   Bibliography

[1] R. Dawkins. *The selfish gene.* Oxford University Press, 1976.

[2] W. E. Hart, N. Krasnogor, and J. E. Smith. *Recent Advances in Memetic Algorithms.* Springer, 2005.

[3] N. Krasnogor and S. Gustafson. A study on the use of "self-generation" in memetic algorithms. *Natural Computing,* 3(1):53–76, 2004.

[4] N. Krasnogor and J. Smith. A tutorial for competent memetic algorithms: Model, taxonomy and design issues. *IEEE Transactions on Evolutionary Computation,* 9(5):474–488, 2005.

[5] P. Moscato. On evolution, search, optimization, genetic algorithms and martial arts: Towards memetic algorithms. Technical report, California Institute of Technology, 1989.

[6] P. Moscato and C. Cotta. *Handbook of Metaheuristics,* chapter A gentle introduction to memetic algorithms, pages 105–144. Kluwer Academic Publishers, 2003.

[7] Y-S. Ong, M-H. Lim, N. Zhu, and K-W. Wong. Classification of adaptive memetic algorithms: A comparative study. *IEEE Transactions on Systems, Man, and Cybernetics-Part B: Cybernetics,* 36(1):141–152, 2006.

Chapter 5

Probabilistic Algorithms

5.1 Overview

This chapter describes Probabilistic Algorithms

5.1.1 Probabilistic Models

Probabilistic Algorithms are those algorithms that model a problem or search a problem space using an probabilistic model of candidate solutions. Many Metaheuristics and Computational Intelligence algorithms may be considered probabilistic, although the difference with algorithms is the explicit (rather than implicit) use of the tools of probability in problem solving. The majority of the algorithms described in this Chapter are referred to as Estimation of Distribution Algorithms.

5.1.2 Estimation of Distribution Algorithms

Estimation of Distribution Algorithms (EDA) also called Probabilistic Model-Building Genetic Algorithms (PMBGA) are an extension of the field of Evolutionary Computation that model a population of candidate solutions as a probabilistic model. They generally involve iterations that alternate between creating candidate solutions in the problem space from a probabilistic model, and reducing a collection of generated candidate solutions into a probabilistic model.

The model at the heart of an EDA typically provides the probabilistic expectation of a component or component configuration comprising part of an optimal solution. This estimation is typically based on the observed frequency of use of the component in better than average candidate solutions. The probabilistic model is used to generate candidate solutions in the problem space, typically in a component-wise or step-wise manner using a domain specific construction method to ensure validity.

Pelikan et al. provide a comprehensive summary of the field of probabilistic optimization algorithms, summarizing the core approaches and their differences [10]. The edited volume by Pelikan, Sastry, and Cantu-Paz provides a collection of studies on the popular Estimation of Distribution algorithms as well as methodology for designing algorithms and application demonstration studies [13]. An edited volume on studies of EDAs by Larranaga and Lozano [4] and the follow-up volume by Lozano et al. [5] provide an applied foundation for the field.

5.1.3   Extensions

There are many other algorithms and classes of algorithm that were not described from the field of Estimation of Distribution Algorithm, not limited to:

- **Extensions to UMDA**: Extensions to the Univariate Marginal Distribution Algorithm such as the Bivariate Marginal Distribution Algorithm (BMDA) [11, 12] and the Factorized Distribution Algorithm (FDA) [7].

- **Extensions to cGA**: Extensions to the Compact Genetic Algorithm such as the Extended Compact Genetic Algorithm (ECGA) [2, 3].

- **Extensions to BOA**: Extensions to the Bayesian Optimization Algorithm such as the Hierarchal Bayesian Optimization Algorithm (hBOA) [8, 9] and the Incremental Bayesian Optimization Algorithm (iBOA) [14].

- **Bayesian Network Algorithms**: Other Bayesian network algorithms such as The Estimation of Bayesian Network Algorithm [1], and the Learning Factorized Distribution Algorithm (LFDA) [6].

- **PIPE**: The Probabilistic Incremental Program Evolution that uses EDA methods for constructing programs [16].

- **SHCLVND**: The Stochastic Hill-Climbing with Learning by Vectors of Normal Distributions algorithm [15].

5.1.4   Bibliography

[1] R. Etxeberria and P. Larranaga. Global optimization using bayesian networks. In *Proceedings of the Second Symposium on Artificial Intelligence (CIMAF-99)*, pages 151–173, 1999.

[2] G. R. Harik. Linkage learning via probabilistic modeling in the extended compact genetic algorithm (ECGA). Technical Report 99010, Illinois Genetic Algorithms Laboratory, Department of General Engineering, University of Illinois, 1999.

[3] G. R. Harik, F. G. Lobo, and K. Sastry. *Scalable Optimization via Probabilistic Modeling*, chapter Linkage Learning via Probabilistic Modeling in the Extended Compact Genetic Algorithm (ECGA), pages 39–61. Springer, 2006.

[4] P. Larranaga and J. A. Lozano. *Estimation of distribution algorithms: A new tool for evolutionary computation.* Springer, 2002.

[5] J. A. Lozano, P. Larranaga, I. Inza, and E. Bengoetxea. *Towards a new evolutionary computation. Advances in estimation of distribution algorithms.* Springer, 2006.

[6] H. Mühlenbein and T. Mahnig. FDA–a scalable evolutionary algorithm for the optimization of additively decomposed discrete functions. *Evolutionary Compilation*, 7(4):353–376, 1999.

[7] H. Mühlenbein, T. Mahnig, and A. O. Rodriguez. Schemata, distributions and graphical models in evolutionary optimization. *Journal of Heuristics*, 5(2):215–247, 1999.

[8] M. Pelikan and D. E. Goldberg. Hierarchical problem solving and the bayesian optimization algorithms. In *Genetic and Evolutionary Computation Conference 2000 (GECCO-2000)*, pages 267–274, 2000.

[9] M. Pelikan and D. E. Goldberg. Escaping hierarchical traps with competent genetic algorithms. In *Proceedings of the Genetic and Evolutionary Computation Conference (GECCO-2001)*, number 511–518, 2001.

[10] M. Pelikan, D. E. Goldberg, and F. G. Lobo. A survey of optimization by building and using probabilistic models. *Computational Optimization and Applications*, 21:5–20, 2002.

[11] M. Pelikan and H. Mühlenbein. Marginal distributions in evolutionary algorithms. In *Proceedings of the International Conference on Genetic Algorithms Mendel*, 1998.

[12] M. Pelikan and H. Mühlenbein. *Advances in Soft Computing: Engineering Design and Manufacturing*, chapter The Bivariate Marginal Distribution Algorithm, pages 521–535. Springer, 1999.

[13] M. Pelikan, K. Sastry, and E. Cantú-Paz, editors. *Scalable Optimization via Probabilistic Modeling: From Algorithms to Applications.* Springer, 2006.

[14] M. Pelikan, K. Sastry, and D. E. Goldberg. iBOA: The incremental bayesian optimization algorithms. In *Proceedings of the Genetic and Evolutionary Computation Conference (GECCO-2008)*, pages 455–462, 2008.

[15] S. Rudlof and M. Koppen. Stochastic hill climbing with learning by vectors of normal distributions. In *First On-line Workshop on Soft Computing*, Nagoya, Japan, 1996.

[16] R. Salustowicz and J. Schmidhuber. Probabilistic incremental program evolution: Stochastic search through program space. In *Proceedings of the 9th European Conference on Machine Learning Prague*, pages 213–220, 1997.

5.2 Population-Based Incremental Learning

Population-Based Incremental Learning, PBIL.

5.2.1 Taxonomy

Population-Based Incremental Learning is an Estimation of Distribution Algorithm (EDA), also referred to as Population Model-Building Genetic Algorithms (PMBGA) an extension to the field of Evolutionary Computation. PBIL is related to other EDAs such as the Compact Genetic Algorithm (Section 5.4), the Probabilistic Incremental Programing Evolution Algorithm, and the Bayesian Optimization Algorithm (Section 5.5). The fact the the algorithm maintains a single prototype vector that is updated competitively shows some relationship to the Learning Vector Quantization algorithm (Section 8.5).

5.2.2 Inspiration

Population-Based Incremental Learning is a population-based technique without an inspiration. It is related to the Genetic Algorithm and other Evolutionary Algorithms that are inspired by the biological theory of evolution by means of natural selection.

5.2.3 Strategy

The information processing objective of the PBIL algorithm is to reduce the memory required by the genetic algorithm. This is done by reducing the population of a candidate solutions to a single prototype vector of attributes from which candidate solutions can be generated and assessed. Updates and mutation operators are also performed to the prototype vector, rather than the generated candidate solutions.

5.2.4 Procedure

The Population-Based Incremental Learning algorithm maintains a real-valued prototype vector that represents the probability of each component being expressed in a candidate solution. Algorithm 5.2.1 provides a pseudocode listing of the Population-Based Incremental Learning algorithm for maximizing a cost function.

5.2.5 Heuristics

- PBIL was designed to optimize the probability of components from low cardinality sets, such as bit's in a binary string.

Algorithm 5.2.1: Pseudocode for PBIL.

Input: $Bits_{num}$, $Samples_{num}$, $Learn_{rate}$, $P_{mutation}$, $Mutation_{factor}$
Output: S_{best}

1   $V \leftarrow$ InitializeVector($Bits_{num}$);
2   $S_{best} \leftarrow \emptyset$;
3   **while** ¬StopCondition() **do**
4      $S_{current} \leftarrow \emptyset$;
5   **for** i to $Samples_{num}$ **do**
6         $S_i \leftarrow$ GenerateSamples(V);
7   **if** Cost(S_i) $\leq$ Cost($S_{current}$) **then**
8            $S_{current} \leftarrow S_i$;
9   **if** Cost(S_i) $\leq$ Cost(S_{best}) **then**
10               $S_{best} \leftarrow S_i$;
11   **end**
12   **end**
13   **end**
14   **foreach** $S_{bit}^i \in S_{current}$ **do**
15         $V_{bit}^i \leftarrow V_{bit}^i \times (1.0 - Learn_{rate}) + S_{bit}^i \times Learn_{rate}$;
16   **if** Rand() $< P_{mutation}$ **then**
17            $V_{bit}^i \leftarrow V_{bit}^i \times (1.0 - Mutation_{factor}) +$ Rand() $\times$ $Mutation_{factor}$;
18   **end**
19   **end**
20 **end**
21 **return** S_{best};

- The algorithm has a very small memory footprint (compared to some population-based evolutionary algorithms) given the compression of information into a single prototype vector.

- Extensions to PBIL have been proposed that extend the representation beyond sets to real-valued vectors.

- Variants of PBIL that were proposed in the original paper include updating the prototype vector with more than one competitive candidate solution (such as an average of top candidate solutions), and moving the prototype vector away from the least competitive candidate solution each iteration.

- Low learning rates are preferred, such as 0.1.

5.2.6 Code Listing

Listing 5.1 provides an example of the Population-Based Incremental Learning algorithm implemented in the Ruby Programming Language. The demonstration problem is a maximizing binary optimization problem called OneMax that seeks a binary string of unity (all '1' bits). The objective function only provides an indication of the number of correct bits in a candidate string, not the positions of the correct bits. The algorithm is an implementation of the simple PBIL algorithm that updates the prototype vector based on the best candidate solution generated each iteration.

```ruby
def onemax(vector)
  return vector.inject(0){|sum, value| sum + value}
end

def generate_candidate(vector)
  candidate = {}
  candidate[:bitstring] = Array.new(vector.size)
  vector.each_with_index do |p, i|
    candidate[:bitstring][i] = (rand()<p) ? 1 : 0
  end
  return candidate
end

def update_vector(vector, current, lrate)
  vector.each_with_index do |p, i|
    vector[i] = p*(1.0-lrate) + current[:bitstring][i]*lrate
  end
end

def mutate_vector(vector, current, coefficient, rate)
  vector.each_with_index do |p, i|
    if rand() < rate
      vector[i] = p*(1.0-coefficient) + rand()*coefficient
    end
  end
end

def search(num_bits, max_iter, num_samples, p_mutate, mut_factor, l_rate)
  vector = Array.new(num_bits){0.5}
  best = nil
  max_iter.times do |iter|
    current = nil
    num_samples.times do
      candidate = generate_candidate(vector)
      candidate[:cost] = onemax(candidate[:bitstring])
      current = candidate if current.nil? or candidate[:cost]>current[:cost]
      best = candidate if best.nil? or candidate[:cost]>best[:cost]
    end
    update_vector(vector, current, l_rate)
    mutate_vector(vector, current, mut_factor, p_mutate)
    puts " >iteration=#{iter}, f=#{best[:cost]}, s=#{best[:bitstring]}"
    break if best[:cost] == num_bits
  end
  return best
```

```
45  end
46
47  if __FILE__ == $0
48    # problem configuration
49    num_bits = 64
50    # algorithm configuration
51    max_iter = 100
52    num_samples = 100
53    p_mutate = 1.0/num_bits
54    mut_factor = 0.05
55    l_rate = 0.1
56    # execute the algorithm
57    best=search(num_bits, max_iter, num_samples, p_mutate, mut_factor, l_rate)
58    puts "done! Solution: f=#{best[:cost]}/#{num_bits}, s=#{best[:bitstring]}"
59  end
```

Listing 5.1: Population-Based Incremental Learning in Ruby

5.2.7   References

Primary Sources

The Population-Based Incremental Learning algorithm was proposed by
Baluja in a technical report that proposed the base algorithm as well as a
number of variants inspired by the Learning Vector Quantization algorithm
[1].

Learn More

Baluja and Caruana provide an excellent overview of PBIL and compare
it to the standard Genetic Algorithm, released as a technical report [3]
and later published [4]. Baluja provides a detailed comparison between
the Genetic algorithm and PBIL on a range of problems and scales in
another technical report [2]. Greene provided an excellent account on the
applicability of PBIL as a practical optimization algorithm [5]. Höhfeld and
Rudolph provide the first theoretical analysis of the technique and provide
a convergence proof [6].

5.2.8   Bibliography

[1] S. Baluja. Population-based incremental learning: A method for in-
    tegrating genetic search based function optimization and competitive
    learning. Technical Report CMU-CS-94-163, School of Computer Sci-
    ence, Carnegie Mellon University, Pittsburgh, Pennsylvania 15213, June
    1994.

[2] S. Baluja. An empirical comparison of seven iterative and evolutionary
    function optimization heuristics. Technical Report CMU-CS-95-193,

School of Computer Science Carnegie Mellon University, Pittsburgh, Pennsylvania 15213, September 1995.

[3] S. Baluja and R. Caruana. Removing the genetics from the standard genetic algorithm. Technical Report CMU-CS-95-141, School of Computer Science Carnegie Mellon University, Pittsburgh, Pennsylvania 15213, May 1995.

[4] S. Baluja and R. Caruana. Removing the genetics from the standard genetic algorithm. In *Proceedings of the International Conference on Machine Learning*, pages 36–46. Morgan Kaufmann, 1995.

[5] J. R. Greene. Population-based incremental learning as a simple versatile tool for engineering optimization. In *Proceedings of the First International Conference on Evolutionary Computation and Its Applications*, pages 258–269, 1996.

[6] M. Höhfeld and G. Rudolph. Towards a theory of population based incremental learning. In *Proceedings of the IEEE Conference on Evolutionary Computation*, pages 1–5. IEEE Press, 1997.

5.3   Univariate Marginal Distribution Algorithm

Univariate Marginal Distribution Algorithm, UMDA, Univariate Marginal Distribution, UMD.

5.3.1   Taxonomy

The Univariate Marginal Distribution Algorithm belongs to the field of Estimation of Distribution Algorithms (EDA), also referred to as Population Model-Building Genetic Algorithms (PMBGA), an extension to the field of Evolutionary Computation. UMDA is closely related to the Factorized Distribution Algorithm (FDA) and an extension called the Bivariate Marginal Distribution Algorithm (BMDA). UMDA is related to other EDAs such as the Compact Genetic Algorithm (Section 5.4), the Population-Based Incremental Learning algorithm (Section 5.2), and the Bayesian Optimization Algorithm (Section 5.5).

5.3.2   Inspiration

Univariate Marginal Distribution Algorithm is a population technique-based without an inspiration. It is related to the Genetic Algorithm and other Evolutionary Algorithms that are inspired by the biological theory of evolution by means of natural selection.

5.3.3   Strategy

The information processing strategy of the algorithm is to use the frequency of the components in a population of candidate solutions in the construction of new candidate solutions. This is achieved by first measuring the frequency of each component in the population (the univariate marginal probability) and using the probabilities to influence the probabilistic selection of components in the component-wise construction of new candidate solutions.

5.3.4   Procedure

Algorithm 5.3.1 provides a pseudocode listing of the Univariate Marginal Distribution Algorithm for minimizing a cost function.

5.3.5   Heuristics

- UMDA was designed for problems where the components of a solution are independent (linearly separable).

- A selection method is needed to identify the subset of good solutions from which to calculate the univariate marginal probabilities. Many

Algorithm 5.3.1: Pseudocode for the UMDA.

Input: $Bits_{num}$, $Population_{size}$, $Selection_{size}$
Output: S_{best}

1 Population $\leftarrow$ InitializePopulation($Bits_{num}$, $Population_{size}$);
2 EvaluatePopulation(Population);
3 S_{best} $\leftarrow$ GetBestSolution(Population);
4 **while** ¬StopCondition() **do**
5 | Selected $\leftarrow$ SelectFitSolutions(Population, $Selection_{size}$);
6 | V $\leftarrow$ CalculateFrequencyOfComponents(Selected);
7 | Offspring $\leftarrow$ $\emptyset$;
8 | **for** i to $Population_{size}$ **do**
9 | | Offspring $\leftarrow$ ProbabilisticallyConstructSolution(V);
10 | **end**
11 | EvaluatePopulation(Offspring);
12 | S_{best} $\leftarrow$ GetBestSolution(Offspring);
13 | Population $\leftarrow$ Offspring;
14 **end**
15 **return** S_{best};

---

selection methods from the field of Evolutionary Computation may
be used.

5.3.6   Code Listing

Listing 5.2 provides an example of the Univariate Marginal Distribution Algorithm implemented in the Ruby Programming Language. The demonstration problem is a maximizing binary optimization problem called OneMax that seeks a binary string of unity (all '1' bits). The objective function provides only an indication of the number of correct bits in a candidate string, not the positions of the correct bits.

The algorithm is an implementation of UMDA that uses the integers 1 and 0 to represent bits in a binary string representation. A binary tournament selection strategy is used and the whole population is replaced each iteration. The mechanisms from Evolutionary Computation such as elitism and more elaborate selection methods may be implemented as an extension.

```ruby
def onemax(vector)
  return vector.inject(0){|sum, value| sum + value}
end

def random_bitstring(size)
  return Array.new(size){ ((rand()<0.5) ? 1 : 0) }
end

```

```ruby
9  def binary_tournament(pop)
10   i, j = rand(pop.size), rand(pop.size)
11   j = rand(pop.size) while j==i
12   return (pop[i][:fitness] > pop[j][:fitness]) ? pop[i] : pop[j]
13  end
14
15  def calculate_bit_probabilities(pop)
16   vector = Array.new(pop.first[:bitstring].length, 0.0)
17   pop.each do |member|
18     member[:bitstring].each_with_index {|v, i| vector[i] += v}
19   end
20   vector.each_with_index {|f, i| vector[i] = (f.to_f/pop.size.to_f)}
21   return vector
22  end
23
24  def generate_candidate(vector)
25   candidate = {}
26   candidate[:bitstring] = Array.new(vector.size)
27   vector.each_with_index do |p, i|
28     candidate[:bitstring][i] = (rand()<p) ? 1 : 0
29   end
30   return candidate
31  end
32
33  def search(num_bits, max_iter, pop_size, select_size)
34   pop = Array.new(pop_size) do
35     {:bitstring=>random_bitstring(num_bits)}
36   end
37   pop.each{|c| c[:fitness] = onemax(c[:bitstring])}
38   best = pop.sort{|x,y| y[:fitness] <=> x[:fitness]}.first
39   max_iter.times do |iter|
40     selected = Array.new(select_size) { binary_tournament(pop) }
41     vector = calculate_bit_probabilities(selected)
42     samples = Array.new(pop_size) { generate_candidate(vector) }
43     samples.each{|c| c[:fitness] = onemax(c[:bitstring])}
44     samples.sort!{|x,y| y[:fitness] <=> x[:fitness]}
45     best = samples.first if samples.first[:fitness] > best[:fitness]
46     pop = samples
47     puts " >iteration=#{iter}, f=#{best[:fitness]}, s=#{best[:bitstring]}"
48   end
49   return best
50  end
51
52  if __FILE__ == $0
53   # problem configuration
54   num_bits = 64
55   # algorithm configuration
56   max_iter = 100
57   pop_size = 50
58   select_size = 30
59   # execute the algorithm
60   best = search(num_bits, max_iter, pop_size, select_size)
61   puts "done! Solution: f=#{best[:fitness]}, s=#{best[:bitstring]}"
62  end
```

Listing 5.2: Univariate Marginal Distribution Algorithm in Ruby

5.3.7 References

Primary Sources

The Univariate Marginal Distribution Algorithm was described by Mühlenbein in 1997 in which a theoretical foundation is provided (for the field of investigation in general and the algorithm specifically) [2]. Mühlenbein also describes an incremental version of UMDA (IUMDA) that is described as being equivalent to Baluja's Population-Based Incremental Learning (PBIL) algorithm [1].

Learn More

Pelikan and Mühlenbein extended the approach to cover problems that have dependencies between the components (specifically pair-dependencies), referring to the technique as the Bivariate Marginal Distribution Algorithm (BMDA) [3, 4].

5.3.8 Bibliography

[1] S. Baluja. Population-based incremental learning: A method for integrating genetic search based function optimization and competitive learning. Technical Report CMU-CS-94-163, School of Computer Science, Carnegie Mellon University, Pittsburgh, Pennsylvania 15213, June 1994.

[2] H. Mühlenbein. The equation for response to selection and its use for prediction. *Evolutionary Computation*, 5(3):303–346, 1997.

[3] M. Pelikan and H. Mühlenbein. Marginal distributions in evolutionary algorithms. In *Proceedings of the International Conference on Genetic Algorithms Mendel*, 1998.

[4] M. Pelikan and H. Mühlenbein. *Advances in Soft Computing: Engineering Design and Manufacturing*, chapter The Bivariate Marginal Distribution Algorithm, pages 521–535. Springer, 1999.

5.4   Compact Genetic Algorithm

Compact Genetic Algorithm, CGA, cGA.

5.4.1   Taxonomy

The Compact Genetic Algorithm is an Estimation of Distribution Algorithm (EDA), also referred to as Population Model-Building Genetic Algorithms (PMBGA), an extension to the field of Evolutionary Computation. The Compact Genetic Algorithm is the basis for extensions such as the Extended Compact Genetic Algorithm (ECGA). It is related to other EDAs such as the Univariate Marginal Probability Algorithm (Section 5.3), the Population-Based Incremental Learning algorithm (Section 5.2), and the Bayesian Optimization Algorithm (Section 5.5).

5.4.2   Inspiration

The Compact Genetic Algorithm is a probabilistic technique without an inspiration. It is related to the Genetic Algorithm and other Evolutionary Algorithms that are inspired by the biological theory of evolution by means of natural selection.

5.4.3   Strategy

The information processing objective of the algorithm is to simulate the behavior of a Genetic Algorithm with a much smaller memory footprint (without requiring a population to be maintained). This is achieved by maintaining a vector that specifies the probability of including each component in a solution in new candidate solutions. Candidate solutions are probabilistically generated from the vector and the components in the better solution are used to make small changes to the probabilities in the vector.

5.4.4   Procedure

The Compact Genetic Algorithm maintains a real-valued prototype vector that represents the probability of each component being expressed in a candidate solution. Algorithm 5.4.1 provides a pseudocode listing of the Compact Genetic Algorithm for maximizing a cost function. The parameter n indicates the amount to update probabilities for conflicting bits in each algorithm iteration.

5.4.5   Heuristics

- The vector update parameter (n) influences the amount that the probabilities are updated each algorithm iteration.

Algorithm 5.4.1: Pseudocode for the cGA.

Input: $Bits_{num}$, n
Output: S_{best}

1   $V \leftarrow$ InitializeVector($Bits_{num}$, 0.5);
2   $S_{best} \leftarrow \emptyset$;
3   **while** ¬StopCondition() **do**
4     $S_1 \leftarrow$ GenerateSamples(V);
5     $S_2 \leftarrow$ GenerateSamples(V);
6   S_{winner}, $S_{loser} \leftarrow$ SelectWinnerAndLoser(S_1, S_2);
7   **if** Cost(S_{winner}) $\leq$ Cost(S_{best}) **then**
8       $S_{best} \leftarrow S_{winner}$;
9   **end**
10   **for** i to $Bits_{num}$ **do**
11   **if** $S_{winner}^i \neq S_{loser}^i$ **then**
12   **if** $S_{winner}^i \equiv 1$ **then**
13        $V_i^i \leftarrow V_i^i + \frac{1}{n}$;
14   **else**
15        $V_i^i \leftarrow V_i^i - \frac{1}{n}$;
16   **end**
17   **end**
18   **end**
19 **end**
20 **return** S_{best};

- The vector update parameter (n) may be considered to be comparable to the population size parameter in the Genetic Algorithm.

- Early results demonstrate that the cGA may be comparable to a standard Genetic Algorithm on classical binary string optimization problems (such as OneMax).

- The algorithm may be considered to have converged if the vector probabilities are all either 0 or 1.

5.4.6   Code Listing

Listing 5.3 provides an example of the Compact Genetic Algorithm implemented in the Ruby Programming Language. The demonstration problem is a maximizing binary optimization problem called OneMax that seeks a binary string of unity (all '1' bits). The objective function only provides an indication of the number of correct bits in a candidate string, not the positions of the correct bits. The algorithm is an implementation of Compact Genetic Algorithm that uses integer values to represent 1 and 0 bits in a binary string representation.

```ruby
def onemax(vector)
  return vector.inject(0){|sum, value| sum + value}
end

def generate_candidate(vector)
  candidate = {}
  candidate[:bitstring] = Array.new(vector.size)
  vector.each_with_index do |p, i|
    candidate[:bitstring][i] = (rand()<p) ? 1 : 0
  end
  candidate[:cost] = onemax(candidate[:bitstring])
  return candidate
end

def update_vector(vector, winner, loser, pop_size)
  vector.size.times do |i|
    if winner[:bitstring][i] != loser[:bitstring][i]
      if winner[:bitstring][i] == 1
        vector[i] += 1.0/pop_size.to_f
      else
        vector[i] -= 1.0/pop_size.to_f
      end
    end
  end
end

def search(num_bits, max_iterations, pop_size)
  vector = Array.new(num_bits){0.5}
  best = nil
  max_iterations.times do |iter|
    c1 = generate_candidate(vector)
    c2 = generate_candidate(vector)
    winner, loser = (c1[:cost] > c2[:cost] ? [c1,c2] : [c2,c1])
    best = winner if best.nil? or winner[:cost]>best[:cost]
    update_vector(vector, winner, loser, pop_size)
    puts " >iteration=#{iter}, f=#{best[:cost]}, s=#{best[:bitstring]}"
    break if best[:cost] == num_bits
  end
  return best
end

if __FILE__ == $0
  # problem configuration
  num_bits = 32
  # algorithm configuration
  max_iterations = 200
  pop_size = 20
  # execute the algorithm
  best = search(num_bits, max_iterations, pop_size)
  puts "done! Solution: f=#{best[:cost]}/#{num_bits}, s=#{best[:bitstring]}"
end
```

Listing 5.3: Compact Genetic Algorithm in Ruby

5.4.7 References

Primary Sources

The Compact Genetic Algorithm was proposed by Harik, Lobo, and Goldberg in 1999 [3], based on a random walk model previously introduced by Harik et al. [2]. In the introductory paper, the cGA is demonstrated to be comparable to the Genetic Algorithm on standard binary string optimization problems.

Learn More

Harik et al. extended the Compact Genetic Algorithm (called the Extended Compact Genetic Algorithm) to generate populations of candidate solutions and perform selection (much like the Univariate Marginal Probabilist Algorithm), although it used Marginal Product Models [1, 4]. Sastry and Goldberg performed further analysis into the Extended Compact Genetic Algorithm applying the method to a complex optimization problem [5].

5.4.8 Bibliography

[1] G. R. Harik. Linkage learning via probabilistic modeling in the extended compact genetic algorithm (ECGA). Technical Report 99010, Illinois Genetic Algorithms Laboratory, Department of General Engineering, University of Illinois, 1999.

[2] G. R. Harik, E. Cantú-Paz, D. E. Goldberg, and B. L. Miller. The gambler's ruin problem, genetic algorithms, and the sizing of populations. In *IEEE International Conference on Evolutionary Computation*, pages 7–12, 1997.

[3] G. R. Harik, F. G. Lobo, and D. E. Goldberg. The compact genetic algorithm. *IEEE Transactions on Evolutionary Computation*, 3(4):287–297, 1999.

[4] G. R. Harik, F. G. Lobo, and K. Sastry. *Scalable Optimization via Probabilistic Modeling*, chapter Linkage Learning via Probabilistic Modeling in the Extended Compact Genetic Algorithm (ECGA), pages 39–61. Springer, 2006.

[5] K. Sastry and D. E. Goldberg. On extended compact genetic algorithm. In *Late Breaking Paper in Genetic and Evolutionary Computation Conference*, pages 352–359, 2000.

5.5   Bayesian Optimization Algorithm

Bayesian Optimization Algorithm, BOA.

5.5.1   Taxonomy

The Bayesian Optimization Algorithm belongs to the field of Estimation of Distribution Algorithms, also referred to as Population Model-Building Genetic Algorithms (PMBGA) an extension to the field of Evolutionary Computation. More broadly, BOA belongs to the field of Computational Intelligence. The Bayesian Optimization Algorithm is related to other Estimation of Distribution Algorithms such as the Population Incremental Learning Algorithm (Section 5.2), and the Univariate Marginal Distribution Algorithm (Section 5.3). It is also the basis for extensions such as the Hierarchal Bayesian Optimization Algorithm (hBOA) and the Incremental Bayesian Optimization Algorithm (iBOA).

5.5.2   Inspiration

Bayesian Optimization Algorithm is a technique without an inspiration. It is related to the Genetic Algorithm and other Evolutionary Algorithms that are inspired by the biological theory of evolution by means of natural selection.

5.5.3   Strategy

The information processing objective of the technique is to construct a probabilistic model that describes the relationships between the components of fit solutions in the problem space. This is achieved by repeating the process of creating and sampling from a Bayesian network that contains the conditional dependancies, independencies, and conditional probabilities between the components of a solution. The network is constructed from the relative frequencies of the components within a population of high fitness candidate solutions. Once the network is constructed, the candidate solutions are discarded and a new population of candidate solutions are generated from the model. The process is repeated until the model converges on a fit prototype solution.

5.5.4   Procedure

Algorithm 5.5.1 provides a pseudocode listing of the Bayesian Optimization Algorithm for minimizing a cost function. The Bayesian network is constructed each iteration using a greedy algorithm. The network is assessed based on its fit of the information in the population of candidate solutions using either a Bayesian Dirichlet Metric (BD) [9], or a Bayesian Information

Criterion (BIC). Refer to Chapter 3 of Pelikan's book for a more detailed presentation of the pseudocode for BOA [5].

Algorithm 5.5.1: Pseudocode for BOA.

Input: $Bits_{num}$, $Population_{size}$, $Selection_{size}$
Output: S_{best}
1 Population $\leftarrow$ InitializePopulation($Bits_{num}$, $Population_{size}$);
2 EvaluatePopulation(Population);
3 S_{best} $\leftarrow$ GetBestSolution(Population);
4 **while** ¬StopCondition() **do**
5 $\quad$ Selected $\leftarrow$ SelectFitSolutions(Population, $Selection_{size}$);
6 $\quad$ Model $\leftarrow$ ConstructBayesianNetwork(Selected);
7 $\quad$ Offspring $\leftarrow$ $\emptyset$;
8 $\quad$ **for** i to $Population_{size}$ **do**
9 $\quad\quad |$ Offspring $\leftarrow$ ProbabilisticallyConstructSolution(Model);
10 $\quad$ **end**
11 $\quad$ EvaluatePopulation(Offspring);
12 $\quad$ S_{best} $\leftarrow$ GetBestSolution(Offspring);
13 $\quad$ Population $\leftarrow$ Combine(Population, Offspring);
14 **end**
15 **return** S_{best};

5.5.5 Heuristics

- The Bayesian Optimization Algorithm was designed and investigated on binary string-base problems, most commonly representing binary function optimization problems.

- Bayesian networks are typically constructed (grown) from scratch each iteration using an iterative process of adding, removing, and reversing links. Additionally, past networks may be used as the basis for the subsequent generation.

- A greedy hill-climbing algorithm is used each algorithm iteration to optimize a Bayesian network to represent a population of candidate solutions.

- The fitness of constructed Bayesian networks may be assessed using the Bayesian Dirichlet Metric (BD) or a Minimum Description length method called the Bayesian Information Criterion (BIC).

5.5.6 Code Listing

Listing 5.4 provides an example of the Bayesian Optimization Algorithm implemented in the Ruby Programming Language. The demonstration problem is a maximizing binary optimization problem called OneMax that seeks a binary string of unity (all '1' bits). The objective function provides only an indication of the number of correct bits in a candidate string, not the positions of the correct bits.

The Bayesian Optimization Algorithm can be tricky to implement given the use of of a Bayesian Network at the core of the technique. The implementation of BOA provided is based on the the C++ implementation provided by Pelikan, version 1.0 [3]. Specifically, the implementation uses the K2 metric to construct a Bayesian network from a population of candidate solutions [1]. Essentially, this metric is a greedy algorithm that starts with an empty graph and adds the arc with the most gain each iteration until a maximum number of edges have been added or no further edges can be added. The result is a directed acyclic graph. The process that constructs the graph imposes limits, such as the maximum number of edges and the maximum number of in-bound connections per node.

New solutions are sampled from the graph by first topologically ordering the graph (so that bits can be generated based on their dependencies), then probabilistically sampling the bits based on the conditional probabilities encoded in the graph. The algorithm used for sampling the conditional probabilities from the network is Probabilistic Logic Sampling [2]. The stopping condition is either the best solution for the problem is found or the system converges to a single bit pattern.

Given that the implementation was written for clarity, it is slow to execute and provides an great opportunity for improvements and efficiencies.

```ruby
def onemax(vector)
  return vector.inject(0){|sum, value| sum + value}
end

def random_bitstring(size)
  return Array.new(size){ ((rand()<0.5) ? 1 : 0) }
end

def path_exists?(i, j, graph)
  visited, stack = [], [i]
  while !stack.empty?
    return true if stack.include?(j)
    k = stack.shift
    next if visited.include?(k)
    visited << k
    graph[k][:out].each {|m| stack.unshift(m) if !visited.include?(m)}
  end
  return false
end

def can_add_edge?(i, j, graph)
  return !graph[i][:out].include?(j) && !path_exists?(j, i, graph)
end

def get_viable_parents(node, graph)
```

```
26    viable = []
27    graph.size.times do |i|
28      if node!=i and can_add_edge?(node, i, graph)
29        viable << i
30      end
31    end
32    return viable
33  end
34
35  def compute_count_for_edges(pop, indexes)
36    counts = Array.new(2**(indexes.size)){0}
37    pop.each do |p|
38      index = 0
39      indexes.reverse.each_with_index do |v,i|
40        index += ((p[:bitstring][v] == 1) ? 1 : 0) * (2**i)
41      end
42      counts[index] += 1
43    end
44    return counts
45  end
46
47  def fact(v)
48    return v <= 1 ? 1 : v*fact(v-1)
49  end
50
51  def k2equation(node, candidates, pop)
52    counts = compute_count_for_edges(pop, [node]+candidates)
53    total = nil
54    (counts.size/2).times do |i|
55      a1, a2 = counts[i*2], counts[(i*2)+1]
56      rs = (1.0/fact((a1+a2)+1).to_f) * fact(a1).to_f * fact(a2).to_f
57      total = (total.nil? ? rs : total*rs)
58    end
59    return total
60  end
61
62  def compute_gains(node, graph, pop, max=2)
63    viable = get_viable_parents(node[:num], graph)
64    gains = Array.new(graph.size) {-1.0}
65    gains.each_index do |i|
66      if graph[i][:in].size < max and viable.include?(i)
67        gains[i] = k2equation(node[:num], node[:in]+[i], pop)
68      end
69    end
70    return gains
71  end
72
73  def construct_network(pop, prob_size, max_edges=3*pop.size)
74    graph = Array.new(prob_size) {|i| {:out=>[], :in=>[], :num=>i} }
75    gains = Array.new(prob_size)
76    max_edges.times do
77      max, from, to = -1, nil, nil
78      graph.each_with_index do |node, i|
79        gains[i] = compute_gains(node, graph, pop)
80        gains[i].each_with_index {|v,j| from,to,max = i,j,v if v>max}
81      end
```

```
82      break if max <= 0.0
83      graph[from][:out] << to
84      graph[to][:in] << from
85    end
86    return graph
87  end
88
89  def topological_ordering(graph)
90    graph.each {|n| n[:count] = n[:in].size}
91    ordered,stack = [], graph.select {|n| n[:count]==0}
92    while ordered.size < graph.size
93      current = stack.shift
94      current[:out].each do |edge|
95        node = graph.find {|n| n[:num]==edge}
96        node[:count] -= 1
97        stack << node if node[:count] <= 0
98      end
99      ordered << current
100    end
101    return ordered
102  end
103
104  def marginal_probability(i, pop)
105    return pop.inject(0.0){|s,x| s + x[:bitstring][i]} / pop.size.to_f
106  end
107
108  def calculate_probability(node, bitstring, graph, pop)
109    return marginal_probability(node[:num], pop) if node[:in].empty?
110    counts = compute_count_for_edges(pop, [node[:num]]+node[:in])
111    index = 0
112    node[:in].reverse.each_with_index do |v,i|
113      index += ((bitstring[v] == 1) ? 1 : 0) * (2**i)
114    end
115    i1 = index + (1*2**(node[:in].size))
116    i2 = index + (0*2**(node[:in].size))
117    a1, a2 = counts[i1].to_f, counts[i2].to_f
118    return a1/(a1+a2)
119  end
120
121  def probabilistic_logic_sample(graph, pop)
122    bitstring = Array.new(graph.size)
123    graph.each do |node|
124      prob = calculate_probability(node, bitstring, graph, pop)
125      bitstring[node[:num]] = ((rand() < prob) ? 1 : 0)
126    end
127    return {:bitstring=>bitstring}
128  end
129
130  def sample_from_network(pop, graph, num_samples)
131    ordered = topological_ordering(graph)
132    samples = Array.new(num_samples) do
133      probabilistic_logic_sample(ordered, pop)
134    end
135    return samples
136  end
137
```

```
138  def search(num_bits, max_iter, pop_size, select_size, num_children)
139    pop = Array.new(pop_size) { {:bitstring=>random_bitstring(num_bits)} }
140    pop.each{|c| c[:cost] = onemax(c[:bitstring])}
141    best = pop.sort!{|x,y| y[:cost] <=> x[:cost]}.first
142    max_iter.times do |it|
143      selected = pop.first(select_size)
144      network = construct_network(selected, num_bits)
145      arcs = network.inject(0){|s,x| s+x[:out].size}
146      children = sample_from_network(selected, network, num_children)
147      children.each{|c| c[:cost] = onemax(c[:bitstring])}
148      children.each {|c| puts " >>sample, f=#{c[:cost]} #{c[:bitstring]}"}
149      pop = pop[0...(pop_size-select_size)] + children
150      pop.sort! {|x,y| y[:cost] <=> x[:cost]}
151      best = pop.first if pop.first[:cost] >= best[:cost]
152      puts " >it=#{it}, arcs=#{arcs}, f=#{best[:cost]}, [#{best[:bitstring]}]"
153      converged = pop.select {|x| x[:bitstring]!=pop.first[:bitstring]}.empty?
154      break if converged or best[:cost]==num_bits
155    end
156    return best
157  end
158
159  if __FILE__ == $0
160    # problem configuration
161    num_bits = 20
162    # algorithm configuration
163    max_iter = 100
164    pop_size = 50
165    select_size = 15
166    num_children = 25
167    # execute the algorithm
168    best = search(num_bits, max_iter, pop_size, select_size, num_children)
169    puts "done! Solution: f=#{best[:cost]}/#{num_bits}, s=#{best[:bitstring]}"
170  end
```

Listing 5.4: Bayesian Optimization Algorithm in Ruby

5.5.7 References

Primary Sources

The Bayesian Optimization Algorithm was proposed by Pelikan, Goldberg, and Cantú-Paz in the technical report [8], that was later published [10]. The technique was proposed as an extension to the state of Estimation of Distribution algorithms (such as the Univariate Marginal Distribution Algorithm and the Bivariate Marginal Distribution Algorithm) that used a Bayesian Network to model the relationships and conditional probabilities for the components expressed in a population of fit candidate solutions. Pelikan, Goldberg, and Cantú-Paz also described the approach applied to deceptive binary optimization problems (trap functions) in a paper that was published before the seminal journal article [9].

Learn More

Pelikan and Goldberg described an extension to the approach called the Hierarchical Bayesian Optimization Algorithm (hBOA) [6, 7]. The differences in the hBOA algorithm are that it replaces the decision tables (used to store the probabilities) with decision graphs and used a niching method called Restricted Tournament Replacement to maintain diversity in the selected set of candidate solutions used to construct the network models. Pelikan's work on BOA culminated in his PhD thesis that provides a detailed treatment of the approach, its configuration and application [4]. Pelikan, Sastry, and Goldberg proposed the Incremental Bayesian Optimization Algorithm (iBOA) extension of the approach that removes the population and adds incremental updates to the Bayesian network [11].

Pelikan published a book that focused on the technique, walking through the development of probabilistic algorithms inspired by evolutionary computation, a detailed look at the Bayesian Optimization Algorithm (Chapter 3), the hierarchic extension to Hierarchical Bayesian Optimization Algorithm and demonstration studies of the approach on test problems [5].

5.5.8   Bibliography

[1] G. F. Cooper and E. Herskovits. A bayesian method for the induction of probabilistic networks from data. *Machine Learning*, 9(4):309–347, 1992.

[2] M. Henrion. *Uncertainty in Artificial Intelligence 2*, chapter Propagation of Uncertainty by Probabilistic Logic Sampling in Bayes Networks, pages 149–163. Elsevier Science Publishing Company, Inc., 1988.

[3] M. Pelikan. A simple implementation of the bayesian optimization algorithm (boa) in c++ (version 1.0). Technical Report IlliGAL Report No. 99011, University of Illinois at Urbana-Champaign, Illinois Genetic Algorithms Laboratory, Urbana, IL, March 1999.

[4] M. Pelikan. *Bayesian optimization algorithm: From single level to hierarchy*. PhD thesis, University of Illinois at Urbana-Champaign, Urbana, IL, 2002.

[5] M. Pelikan. *Hierarchical Bayesian Optimization Algorithm: Toward a New Generation of Evolutionary Algorithms*. Springer, 2005.

[6] M. Pelikan and D. E. Goldberg. Hierarchical problem solving and the bayesian optimization algorithms. In *Genetic and Evolutionary Computation Conference 2000 (GECCO-2000)*, pages 267–274, 2000.

[7] M. Pelikan and D. E. Goldberg. Escaping hierarchical traps with competent genetic algorithms. In *Proceedings of the Genetic and*

Evolutionary Computation Conference (GECCO-2001), number 511–518, 2001.

[8] M. Pelikan, D. E. Goldberg, and E. Cantú-Paz. Linkage problem, distribution estimation, and bayesian networks. Technical Report IlliGAL Report No. 98013, llinois Genetic Algorithms Laboratory, University of Illinois at Urbana-Champaign, Urbana, IL, 1998.

[9] M. Pelikan, D. E. Goldberg, and E. Cantú-Paz. BOA: The bayesian optimization algorithm. In *Proceedings of the Genetic and Evolutionary Computation Conference (GECCO-99)*, 1999.

[10] M. Pelikan, D. E. Goldberg, and E. Cantú-Paz. Linkage problem, distribution estimation, and bayesian networks. *Evolutionary Computation*, 8(3):311–341, 2002.

[11] M. Pelikan, K. Sastry, and D. E. Goldberg. iBOA: The incremental bayesian optimization algorithms. In *Proceedings of the Genetic and Evolutionary Computation Conference (GECCO-2008)*, pages 455–462, 2008.

5.6   Cross-Entropy Method

Cross-Entropy Method, Cross Entropy Method, CEM.

5.6.1   Taxonomy

The Cross-Entropy Method is a probabilistic optimization belonging to the field of Stochastic Optimization. It is similar to other Stochastic Optimization and algorithms such as Simulated Annealing (Section 4.2), and to Estimation of Distribution Algorithms such as the Probabilistic Incremental Learning Algorithm (Section 5.2).

5.6.2   Inspiration

The Cross-Entropy Method does not have an inspiration. It was developed as an efficient estimation technique for rare-event probabilities in discrete event simulation systems and was adapted for use in optimization. The name of the technique comes from the Kullback-Leibler cross-entropy method for measuring the amount of information (bits) needed to identify an event from a set of probabilities.

5.6.3   Strategy

The information processing strategy of the algorithm is to sample the problem space and approximate the distribution of good solutions. This is achieved by assuming a distribution of the problem space (such as Gaussian), sampling the problem domain by generating candidate solutions using the distribution, and updating the distribution based on the better candidate solutions discovered. Samples are constructed step-wise (one component at a time) based on the summarized distribution of good solutions. As the algorithm progresses, the distribution becomes more refined until it focuses on the area or scope of optimal solutions in the domain.

5.6.4   Procedure

Algorithm 5.6.1 provides a pseudocode listing of the Cross-Entropy Method algorithm for minimizing a cost function.

5.6.5   Heuristics

- The Cross-Entropy Method was adapted for combinatorial optimization problems, although has been applied to continuous function optimization as well as noisy simulation problems.

- A alpha (α) parameter or learning rate $\in [0.1]$ is typically set high, such as 0.7.

Algorithm 5.6.1: Pseudocode for the Cross-Entropy Method.

Input: $Problem_{size}$, $Samples_{num}$, $UpdateSamples_{num}$, $Learn_{rate}$, $Variance_{min}$

Output: S_{best}

1   Means ← InitializeMeans();
2   Variances ← InitializeVariances();
3   S_{best} ← ∅;
4   **while** Max(Variances) $\leq Variance_{min}$ **do**
5   Samples ← 0;
6   **for** $i = 0$ to $Samples_{num}$ **do**
7 | Samples ← GenerateSample(Means, Variances);
8   **end**
9   EvaluateSamples(Samples);
10   SortSamplesByQuality(Samples);
11   **if** Cost($Samples_0$) $\leq$ Cost(S_{best}) **then**
12 | S_{best} ← $Samples_0$;
13   **end**
14     $Samples_{selected}$ ←SelectBestSamples(Samples, $UpdateSamples_{num}$);
15   **for** $i = 0$ to $Problem_{size}$ **do**
16 | $Means_i$ ← $Means_i$ + $Learn_{rate}$ × Mean($Samples_{selected}$, i);
17 | $Variances_i$ ← $Variances_i$ + $Learn_{rate}$ × Variance($Samples_{selected}$, i);
18   **end**
19 **end**
20 **return** S_{best};

- A smoothing function can be used to further control the updates the summaries of the distribution(s) of samples from the problem space. For example, in continuous function optimization a β parameter may replace α for updating the standard deviation, calculated at time t as $\beta_t = \beta - \beta \times (1 - \frac{1}{t})^q$, where β is initially set high $\in [0.8, 0.99]$ and q is a small integer $\in [5, 10]$.

5.6.6   Code Listing

Listing 5.5 provides an example of the Cross-Entropy Method algorithm implemented in the Ruby Programming Language. The demonstration problem is an instance of a continuous function optimization problem that seeks $\min f(x)$ where $f = \sum_{i=1}^{n} x_i^2$, $-5.0 \leq x_i \leq 5.0$ and $n = 3$. The optimal solution for this basin function is $(v_0, \ldots, v_{n-1}) = 0.0$.

The algorithm was implemented based on a description of the Cross-Entropy Method algorithm for continuous function optimization by Rubinstein and Kroese in Chapter 5 and Appendix A of their book on the method [5]. The algorithm maintains means and standard deviations of the distribution of samples for convenience. The means and standard deviations are initialized based on random positions in the problem space and the bounds of the whole problem space respectively. A smoothing parameter is not used on the standard deviations.

```ruby
def objective_function(vector)
  return vector.inject(0.0) {|sum, x| sum + (x ** 2.0)}
end

def random_variable(minmax)
  min, max = minmax
  return min + ((max - min) * rand())
end

def random_gaussian(mean=0.0, stdev=1.0)
  u1 = u2 = w = 0
  begin
    u1 = 2 * rand() - 1
    u2 = 2 * rand() - 1
    w = u1 * u1 + u2 * u2
  end while w >= 1
  w = Math.sqrt((-2.0 * Math.log(w)) / w)
  return mean + (u2 * w) * stdev
end

def generate_sample(search_space, means, stdevs)
  vector = Array.new(search_space.size)
  search_space.size.times do |i|
    vector[i] = random_gaussian(means[i], stdevs[i])
    vector[i] = search_space[i][0] if vector[i] < search_space[i][0]
    vector[i] = search_space[i][1] if vector[i] > search_space[i][1]
  end
  return {:vector=>vector}
end

def mean_attr(samples, i)
  sum = samples.inject(0.0) do |s,sample|
    s + sample[:vector][i]
  end
  return (sum / samples.size.to_f)
end

def stdev_attr(samples, mean, i)
  sum = samples.inject(0.0) do |s,sample|
    s + (sample[:vector][i] - mean)**2.0
  end
  return Math.sqrt(sum / samples.size.to_f)
end

def update_distribution!(samples, alpha, means, stdevs)
  means.size.times do |i|
    means[i] = alpha*means[i] + ((1.0-alpha)*mean_attr(samples, i))
    stdevs[i] = alpha*stdevs[i]+((1.0-alpha)*stdev_attr(samples,means[i],i))
```

```
49      end
50    end
51
52    def search(bounds, max_iter, num_samples, num_update, learning_rate)
53      means = Array.new(bounds.size){|i| random_variable(bounds[i])}
54      stdevs = Array.new(bounds.size){|i| bounds[i][1]-bounds[i][0]}
55      best = nil
56      max_iter.times do |iter|
57        samples = Array.new(num_samples){generate_sample(bounds, means, stdevs)}
58        samples.each {|samp| samp[:cost] = objective_function(samp[:vector])}
59        samples.sort!{|x,y| x[:cost]<=>y[:cost]}
60        best = samples.first if best.nil? or samples.first[:cost] < best[:cost]
61        selected = samples.first(num_update)
62        update_distribution!(selected, learning_rate, means, stdevs)
63        puts " > iteration=#{iter}, fitness=#{best[:cost]}"
64      end
65      return best
66    end
67
68    if __FILE__ == $0
69      # problem configuration
70      problem_size = 3
71      search_space = Array.new(problem_size) {|i| [-5, 5]}
72      # algorithm configuration
73      max_iter = 100
74      num_samples = 50
75      num_update = 5
76      l_rate = 0.7
77      # execute the algorithm
78      best = search(search_space, max_iter, num_samples, num_update, l_rate)
79      puts "done! Solution: f=#{best[:cost]}, s=#{best[:vector].inspect}"
80    end
```

Listing 5.5: Cross-Entropy Method in Ruby

5.6.7 References

Primary Sources

The Cross-Entropy method was proposed by Rubinstein in 1997 [2] for use in optimizing discrete event simulation systems. It was later generalized by Rubinstein and proposed as an optimization method for combinatorial function optimization in 1999 [3]. This work was further elaborated by Rubinstein providing a detailed treatment on the use of the Cross-Entropy method for combinatorial optimization [4].

Learn More

De Boer et al. provide a detailed presentation of Cross-Entropy method including its application in rare event simulation, its adaptation to combinatorial optimization, and example applications to the max-cut, traveling salesman problem, and a clustering numeric optimization example [1]. Rubinstein and Kroese provide a thorough presentation of the approach in their book, summarizing the relevant theory and the state of the art [5].

5.6.8 Bibliography

[1] P. T. De Boer, D. P. Kroese, S. Mannor, and R. Y. Rubinstein. A tutorial on the cross-entropy method. *Annals of Operations Research*, 134(1):19–67, 2005.

[2] R. Y. Rubinstein. Optimization of computer simulation models with rare events. *European Journal of Operations Research*, 99:89–112, 1997.

[3] R. Y. Rubinstein. The simulated entropy method for combinatorial and continuous optimization. *Methodology and Computing in Applied Probability*, 1(2):127–190, 1999.

[4] R. Y. Rubinstein. *Stochastic optimization: algorithms and applications*, chapter Combinatorial optimization, cross-entropy, ants and rare events, pages 303–364. Springer, 2001.

[5] R. Y. Rubinstein and D. P. Kroese. *The Cross-Entropy Method: A Unified Approach to Combinatorial Optimization*. Springer, 2004.

Chapter 6

Swarm Algorithms

6.1 Overview

This chapter describes Swarm Algorithms.

6.1.1 Swarm Intelligence

Swarm intelligence is the study of computational systems inspired by the 'collective intelligence'. Collective Intelligence emerges through the cooperation of large numbers of homogeneous agents in the environment. Examples include schools of fish, flocks of birds, and colonies of ants. Such intelligence is decentralized, self-organizing and distributed through out an environment. In nature such systems are commonly used to solve problems such as effective foraging for food, prey evading, or colony re-location. The information is typically stored throughout the participating homogeneous agents, or is stored or communicated in the environment itself such as through the use of pheromones in ants, dancing in bees, and proximity in fish and birds.

The paradigm consists of two dominant sub-fields 1) *Ant Colony Optimization* that investigates probabilistic algorithms inspired by the stigmergy and foraging behavior of ants, and 2) *Particle Swarm Optimization* that investigates probabilistic algorithms inspired by the flocking, schooling and herding. Like evolutionary computation, swarm intelligence 'algorithms' or 'strategies' are considered adaptive strategies and are typically applied to search and optimization domains.

6.1.2 References

Seminal books on the field of Swarm Intelligence include *"Swarm Intelligence"* by Kennedy, Eberhart and Shi [10], and *"Swarm Intelligence: From Natural to Artificial Systems"* by Bonabeau, Dorigo, and Theraulaz [3]. Another excellent text book on the area is *"Fundamentals of Computational Swarm*

Intelligence" by Engelbrecht [7]. The seminal book reference for the field of Ant Colony Optimization is *"Ant Colony Optimization"* by Dorigo and Stützle [6].

6.1.3 Extensions

There are many other algorithms and classes of algorithm that were not described from the field of Swarm Intelligence, not limited to:

- **Ant Algorithms**: such as Max-Min Ant Systems [15] Rank-Based Ant Systems [4], Elitist Ant Systems [5], Hyper Cube Ant Colony Optimization [2] Approximate Nondeterministic Tree-Search (ANTS) [12] and Multiple Ant Colony System [8].

- **Bee Algorithms**: such as Bee System and Bee Colony Optimization [11], the Honey Bee Algorithm [16], and Artificial Bee Colony Optimization [1, 9].

- **Other Social Insects**: algorithms inspired by other social insects besides ants and bees, such as the Firey Algorithm [18] and the Wasp Swarm Algorithm [14].

- **Extensions to Particle Swarm**: such as Repulsive Particle Swarm Optimization [17].

- **Bacteria Algorithms**: such as the Bacteria Chemotaxis Algorithm [13].

6.1.4 Bibliography

[1] B. Basturk and D. Karaboga. An artificial bee colony (ABC) algorithm for numeric function optimization. In *IEEE Swarm Intelligence Symposium*, 2006.

[2] C. Blum, A. Roli, and M. Dorigo. HC–ACO: The hyper-cube framework for ant colony optimization. In *Proceedings of the Fourth Metaheuristics International Conference*, volume 1, pages 399–403, 2001.

[3] E. Bonabeau, M. Dorigo, and G. Theraulaz. *Swarm Intelligence: From Natural to Artificial Systems*. Oxford University Press US, 1999.

[4] B. Bullnheimer, R. F. Hartl, and C. Strauss. A new rank based version of the ant system: A computational study. *Central European Journal for Operations Research and Economics*, 7(1):25–38, 1999.

[5] M. Dorigo. The ant system: Optimization by a colony of cooperating agents. *IEEE Transactions on Systems, Man, and CyberneticsPart B*, 1:1–13, 1996.

[6] M. Dorigo and T. Stützle. *Ant Colony Optimization.* MIT Press, 2004.

[7] A. P. Engelbrecht. *Fundamentals of Computational Swarm Intelligence.* Wiley & Sons, 2006.

[8] L. M. Gambardella, E. Taillard, and G. Agazzi. *New Ideas in Optimization*, chapter MACS–VRPTW: A Multiple Ant Colony System for Vehicle Routing Problems with Time Windows, pages 63–76. McGraw-Hill, 1999.

[9] D. Karaboga. An idea based on honey bee swarm for numerical optimization. Technical Report TR06, Erciyes University, Engineering Faculty, Computer Engineering Department, 2005.

[10] J. Kennedy, R. C. Eberhart, and Y. Shi. *Swarm Intelligence.* Morgan Kaufmann, 2001.

[11] P. Lučić and D. Teodorović. Bee system: modeling combinatorial optimization transportation engineering problems by swarm intelligence. In *Preprints of the TRISTAN IV Triennial Symposium on Transportation Analysis*, pages 441–445, 2001.

[12] V. Maniezzo. Approximate nondeterministic tree-search procedures for the quadratic assignment problem. *INFORMS Journal on Computing*, 11(4):358–369, 1999.

[13] S. D. Müller, J. Marchetto, S. Airaghi, and P. Koumoutsakos. Optimization based on bacterial chemotaxis. *IEEE Transactions on Evolutionary Computation*, 6(1):16–29, 2002.

[14] P. C. Pinto, T. A. Runkler, and J. M. Sousa. Wasp swarm algorithm for dynamic max-sat problems. In *Proceedings of the 8th international conference on Adaptive and Natural Computing Algorithms, Part I*, pages 350–357. Springer, 2007.

[15] T. Stützle and H. H. Hoos. MAX–MIN ant system, future generation computer systems. *Future Generation Computer Systems*, 16:889–914, 2000.

[16] C. Tovey. The honey bee algorithm: A biological inspired approach to internet server optimization. *Engineering Enterprise, the Alumni Magazine for ISyE at Georgia Institute of Technology*, pages 3–15, 2004.

[17] O Urfalioglu. Robust estimation of camera rotation, translation and focal length at high outlier rates. In *Proceedings of the 1st Canadian Conference on Computer and Robot Vision*, 2004.

[18] X. S. Yang. *Nature-Inspired Metaheuristic Algorithms.* Luniver Press, 2008.

6.2 Particle Swarm Optimization

Particle Swarm Optimization, PSO.

6.2.1 Taxonomy

Particle Swarm Optimization belongs to the field of Swarm Intelligence and Collective Intelligence and is a sub-field of Computational Intelligence. Particle Swarm Optimization is related to other Swarm Intelligence algorithms such as Ant Colony Optimization and it is a baseline algorithm for many variations, too numerous to list.

6.2.2 Inspiration

Particle Swarm Optimization is inspired by the social foraging behavior of some animals such as flocking behavior of birds and the schooling behavior of fish.

6.2.3 Metaphor

Particles in the swarm fly through an environment following the fitter members of the swarm and generally biasing their movement toward historically good areas of their environment.

6.2.4 Strategy

The goal of the algorithm is to have all the particles locate the optima in a multi-dimensional hyper-volume. This is achieved by assigning initially random positions to all particles in the space and small initial random velocities. The algorithm is executed like a simulation, advancing the position of each particle in turn based on its velocity, the best known global position in the problem space and the best position known to a particle. The objective function is sampled after each position update. Over time, through a combination of exploration and exploitation of known good positions in the search space, the particles cluster or converge together around an optima, or several optima.

6.2.5 Procedure

The Particle Swarm Optimization algorithm is comprised of a collection of particles that move around the search space influenced by their own best past location and the best past location of the whole swarm or a close neighbor. Each iteration a particle's velocity is updated using:

$$v_i(t+1) = v_i(t) + \big(c_1 \times rand() \times (p_i^{best} - p_i(t))\big) +$$
$$\big(c_2 \times rand() \times (p_{gbest} - p_i(t))\big)$$

where $v_i(t+1)$ is the new velocity for the ith particle, c_1 and c_2 are the weighting coefficients for the personal best and global best positions respectively, $p_i(t)$ is the ith particle's position at time t, p_i^{best} is the ith particle's best known position, and p_{gbest} is the best position known to the swarm. The $rand()$ function generate a uniformly random variable $\in [0, 1]$. Variants on this update equation consider best positions within a particles local neighborhood at time t.

A particle's position is updated using:

$$p_i(t+1) = p_i(t) + v_i(t) \tag{6.1}$$

Algorithm 6.2.1 provides a pseudocode listing of the Particle Swarm Optimization algorithm for minimizing a cost function.

6.2.6 Heuristics

- The number of particles should be low, around 20-40

- The speed a particle can move (maximum change in its position per iteration) should be bounded, such as to a percentage of the size of the domain.

- The learning factors (biases towards global and personal best positions) should be between 0 and 4, typically 2.

- A local bias (local neighborhood) factor can be introduced where neighbors are determined based on Euclidean distance between particle positions.

- Particles may leave the boundary of the problem space and may be penalized, be reflected back into the domain or biased to return back toward a position in the problem domain. Alternatively, a wrapping strategy may be used at the edge of the domain creating a loop, torrid or related geometrical structures at the chosen dimensionality.

- An inertia or momentum coefficient can be introduced to limit the change in velocity.

6.2.7 Code Listing

Listing 6.1 provides an example of the Particle Swarm Optimization algorithm implemented in the Ruby Programming Language. The demonstration

---

Algorithm 6.2.1: Pseudocode for PSO.

Input: ProblemSize, $Population_{size}$
Output: P_{g_best}

1 Population $\leftarrow \emptyset$;
2 $P_{g\_best} \leftarrow \emptyset$;
3 **for** $i = 1$ **to** $Population_{size}$ **do**
4      $P_{velocity} \leftarrow$ RandomVelocity();
5      $P_{position} \leftarrow$ RandomPosition($Population_{size}$);
6      $P_{cost} \leftarrow$ Cost($P_{position}$);
7      $P_{p\_best} \leftarrow P_{position}$;
8   **if** $P_{cost} \leq P_{g\_best}$ **then**
9          $P_{g\_best} \leftarrow P_{p\_best}$;
10   **end**
11 **end**
12 **while** ¬StopCondition() **do**
13   **foreach** $P \in$ Population **do**
14          $P_{velocity} \leftarrow$ UpdateVelocity($P_{velocity}, P_{g\_best}, P_{p\_best}$);
15          $P_{position} \leftarrow$ UpdatePosition($P_{position}, P_{velocity}$);
16          $P_{cost} \leftarrow$ Cost($P_{position}$);
17   **if** $P_{cost} \leq P_{p\_best}$ **then**
18              $P_{p\_best} \leftarrow P_{position}$;
19   **if** $P_{cost} \leq P_{g\_best}$ **then**
20                  $P_{g\_best} \leftarrow P_{p\_best}$;
21   **end**
22   **end**
23   **end**
24 **end**
25 **return** P_{g_best};

---

problem is an instance of a continuous function optimization that seeks $\min f(x)$ where $f = \sum_{i=1}^{n} x_i^2$, $-5.0 \leq x_i \leq 5.0$ and $n = 3$. The optimal solution for this basin function is $(v_0, \ldots, v_{n-1}) = 0.0$. The algorithm is a conservative version of Particle Swarm Optimization based on the seminal papers. The implementation limits the velocity at a pre-defined maximum, and bounds particles to the search space, reflecting their movement and velocity if the bounds of the space are exceeded. Particles are influenced by the best position found as well as their own personal best position. Natural extensions may consider limiting velocity with an inertia coefficient and including a neighborhood function for the particles.

```
1  def objective_function(vector)
2    return vector.inject(0.0) {|sum, x| sum + (x ** 2.0)}
3  end
4
```

```ruby
def random_vector(minmax)
  return Array.new(minmax.size) do |i|
    minmax[i][0] + ((minmax[i][1] - minmax[i][0]) * rand())
  end
end

def create_particle(search_space, vel_space)
  particle = {}
  particle[:position] = random_vector(search_space)
  particle[:cost] = objective_function(particle[:position])
  particle[:b_position] = Array.new(particle[:position])
  particle[:b_cost] = particle[:cost]
  particle[:velocity] = random_vector(vel_space)
  return particle
end

def get_global_best(population, current_best=nil)
  population.sort{|x,y| x[:cost] <=> y[:cost]}
  best = population.first
  if current_best.nil? or best[:cost] <= current_best[:cost]
    current_best = {}
    current_best[:position] = Array.new(best[:position])
    current_best[:cost] = best[:cost]
  end
  return current_best
end

def update_velocity(particle, gbest, max_v, c1, c2)
  particle[:velocity].each_with_index do |v,i|
    v1 = c1 * rand() * (particle[:b_position][i] - particle[:position][i])
    v2 = c2 * rand() * (gbest[:position][i] - particle[:position][i])
    particle[:velocity][i] = v + v1 + v2
    particle[:velocity][i] = max_v if particle[:velocity][i] > max_v
    particle[:velocity][i] = -max_v if particle[:velocity][i] < -max_v
  end
end

def update_position(part, bounds)
  part[:position].each_with_index do |v,i|
    part[:position][i] = v + part[:velocity][i]
    if part[:position][i] > bounds[i][1]
      part[:position][i]=bounds[i][1]-(part[:position][i]-bounds[i][1]).abs
      part[:velocity][i] *= -1.0
    elsif part[:position][i] < bounds[i][0]
      part[:position][i]=bounds[i][0]+(part[:position][i]-bounds[i][0]).abs
      part[:velocity][i] *= -1.0
    end
  end
end

def update_best_position(particle)
  return if particle[:cost] > particle[:b_cost]
  particle[:b_cost] = particle[:cost]
  particle[:b_position] = Array.new(particle[:position])
end
```

```ruby
61  def search(max_gens, search_space, vel_space, pop_size, max_vel, c1, c2)
62    pop = Array.new(pop_size) {create_particle(search_space, vel_space)}
63    gbest = get_global_best(pop)
64    max_gens.times do |gen|
65      pop.each do |particle|
66        update_velocity(particle, gbest, max_vel, c1, c2)
67        update_position(particle, search_space)
68        particle[:cost] = objective_function(particle[:position])
69        update_best_position(particle)
70      end
71      gbest = get_global_best(pop, gbest)
72      puts " > gen #{gen+1}, fitness=#{gbest[:cost]}"
73    end
74    return gbest
75  end
76
77  if __FILE__ == $0
78    # problem configuration
79    problem_size = 2
80    search_space = Array.new(problem_size) {|i| [-5, 5]}
81    # algorithm configuration
82    vel_space = Array.new(problem_size) {|i| [-1, 1]}
83    max_gens = 100
84    pop_size = 50
85    max_vel = 100.0
86    c1, c2 = 2.0, 2.0
87    # execute the algorithm
88    best = search(max_gens, search_space, vel_space, pop_size, max_vel, c1,c2)
89    puts "done! Solution: f=#{best[:cost]}, s=#{best[:position].inspect}"
90  end
```

Listing 6.1: Particle Swarm Optimization in Ruby

6.2.8   References

Primary Sources

Particle Swarm Optimization was described as a stochastic global optimization method for continuous functions in 1995 by Eberhart and Kennedy [1, 3]. This work was motivated as an optimization method loosely based on the flocking behavioral models of Reynolds [7]. Early works included the introduction of inertia [8] and early study of social topologies in the swarm by Kennedy [2].

Learn More

Poli, Kennedy, and Blackwell provide a modern overview of the field of PSO with detailed coverage of extensions to the baseline technique [6]. Poli provides a meta-analysis of PSO publications that focus on the application the technique, providing a systematic breakdown on application areas [5]. An excellent book on Swarm Intelligence in general with detailed coverage of

Particle Swarm Optimization is "Swarm Intelligence" by Kennedy, Eberhart, and Shi [4].

6.2.9 Bibliography

[1] R. C. Eberhart and J. Kennedy. A new optimizer using particle swarm theory. In *Proceedings of the sixth international symposium on micro machine and human science*, pages 39–43, 1995.

[2] J. Kennedy. Small worlds and mega-minds: Effects of neighborhood topology on particle swarm performance. In *Proceedings of the 1999 Congress on Evolutionary Computation*, 1999.

[3] J. Kennedy and R. C. Eberhart. Particle swarm optimization. In *Proceedings IEEE int'l conf. on neural networks Vol. IV*, pages 1942–1948, 1995.

[4] J. Kennedy, R. C. Eberhart, and Y. Shi. *Swarm Intelligence*. Morgan Kaufmann, 2001.

[5] R. Poli. Analysis of the publications on the applications of particle swarm optimisation. *Journal of Artificial Evolution and Applications*, 1:1–10, 2008.

[6] R. Poli, J. Kennedy, and T. Blackwell. Particle swarm optimization an overview. *Swarm Intelligence*, 1:33–57, 2007.

[7] C. W. Reynolds. Flocks, herds and schools: A distributed behavioral model. In *Proceedings of the 14th annual conference on Computer graphics and interactive techniques*, pages 25–34, 1987.

[8] Y. Shi and R. C. Eberhart. A modified particle swarm optimizers. In *Proceedings of the IEEE International Conference on Evolutionary Computation*, pages 69–73, 1998.

6.3 Ant System

Ant System, AS, Ant Cycle.

6.3.1 Taxonomy

The Ant System algorithm is an example of an Ant Colony Optimization method from the field of Swarm Intelligence, Metaheuristics and Computational Intelligence. Ant System was originally the term used to refer to a range of Ant based algorithms, where the specific algorithm implementation was referred to as Ant Cycle. The so-called Ant Cycle algorithm is now canonically referred to as Ant System. The Ant System algorithm is the baseline Ant Colony Optimization method for popular extensions such as Elite Ant System, Rank-based Ant System, Max-Min Ant System, and Ant Colony System.

6.3.2 Inspiration

The Ant system algorithm is inspired by the foraging behavior of ants, specifically the pheromone communication between ants regarding a good path between the colony and a food source in an environment. This mechanism is called stigmergy.

6.3.3 Metaphor

Ants initially wander randomly around their environment. Once food is located an ant will begin laying down pheromone in the environment. Numerous trips between the food and the colony are performed and if the same route is followed that leads to food then additional pheromone is laid down. Pheromone decays in the environment, so that older paths are less likely to be followed. Other ants may discover the same path to the food and in turn may follow it and also lay down pheromone. A positive feedback process routes more and more ants to productive paths that are in turn further refined through use.

6.3.4 Strategy

The objective of the strategy is to exploit historic and heuristic information to construct candidate solutions and fold the information learned from constructing solutions into the history. Solutions are constructed one discrete piece at a time in a probabilistic step-wise manner. The probability of selecting a component is determined by the heuristic contribution of the component to the overall cost of the solution and the quality of solutions from which the component has historically known to have been included. History is updated proportional to the quality of candidate solutions and is uniformly decreased ensuring the most recent and useful information is retained.

6.3.5   Procedure

Algorithm 6.3.1 provides a pseudocode listing of the main Ant System algorithm for minimizing a cost function. The pheromone update process is described by a single equation that combines the contributions of all candidate solutions with a decay coefficient to determine the new pheromone value, as follows:

$$\tau_{i,j} \leftarrow (1 - \rho) \times \tau_{i,j} + \sum_{k=1}^{m} \Delta_{i,j}^{k} \qquad (6.2)$$

where $\tau_{i,j}$ represents the pheromone for the component (graph edge) (i, j), ρ is the decay factor, m is the number of ants, and $\sum_{k=1}^{m} \Delta_{i,j}^{k}$ is the sum of $\frac{1}{S_{cost}}$ (maximizing solution cost) for those solutions that include component i, j. The Pseudocode listing shows this equation as an equivalent as a two step process of decay followed by update for simplicity.

The probabilistic step-wise construction of solution makes use of both history (pheromone) and problem-specific heuristic information to incrementally construction a solution piece-by-piece. Each component can only be selected if it has not already been chosen (for most combinatorial problems), and for those components that can be selected from (given the current component i), their probability for selection is defined as:

$$P_{i,j} \leftarrow \frac{\tau_{i,j}^{\alpha} \times \eta_{i,j}^{\beta}}{\sum_{k=1}^{c} \tau_{i,k}^{\alpha} \times \eta_{i,k}^{\beta}} \qquad (6.3)$$

where $\eta_{i,j}$ is the maximizing contribution to the overall score of selecting the component (such as $\frac{1.0}{distance_{i,j}}$ for the Traveling Salesman Problem), α is the heuristic coefficient, $\tau_{i,j}$ is the pheromone value for the component, β is the history coefficient, and c is the set of usable components.

6.3.6   Heuristics

- The Ant Systems algorithm was designed for use with combinatorial problems such as the TSP, knapsack problem, quadratic assignment problems, graph coloring problems and many others.

- The history coefficient (α) controls the amount of contribution history plays in a components probability of selection and is commonly set to 1.0.

Algorithm 6.3.1: Pseudocode for Ant System.

Input: ProblemSize, $Population_{size}$, m, ρ, α, β
Output: P_{best}

1   $P_{best} \leftarrow$ CreateHeuristicSolution(ProblemSize);
2   $Pbest_{cost} \leftarrow$ Cost(S_h);
3   Pheromone $\leftarrow$ InitializePheromone($Pbest_{cost}$);
4   **while** $\neg$StopCondition() **do**
5   Candidates $\leftarrow \emptyset$;
6   **for** $i = 1$ **to** m **do**
7         $S_i \leftarrow$ ProbabilisticStepwiseConstruction(Pheromone, ProblemSize, α, β);
8         $Si_{cost} \leftarrow$ Cost(S_i);
9   **if** $Si_{cost} \leq Pbest_{cost}$ **then**
10            $Pbest_{cost} \leftarrow Si_{cost}$;
11            $P_{best} \leftarrow S_i$;
12   **end**
13   Candidates $\leftarrow S_i$;
14   **end**
15   DecayPheromone(Pheromone, ρ);
16   **foreach** $S_i \in$ Candidates **do**
17   UpdatePheromone(Pheromone, S_i, Si_{cost});
18   **end**
19 **end**
20 **return** P_{best};

- The heuristic coefficient (β) controls the amount of contribution problem-specific heuristic information plays in a components probability of selection and is commonly between 2 and 5, such as 2.5.

- The decay factor (ρ) controls the rate at which historic information is lost and is commonly set to 0.5.

- The total number of ants (m) is commonly set to the number of components in the problem, such as the number of cities in the TSP.

6.3.7   Code Listing

Listing 6.2 provides an example of the Ant System algorithm implemented in the Ruby Programming Language. The algorithm is applied to the Berlin52 instance of the Traveling Salesman Problem (TSP), taken from the TSPLIB. The problem seeks a permutation of the order to visit cities (called a tour) that minimized the total distance traveled. The optimal tour distance for Berlin52 instance is 7542 units. Some extensions to the algorithm implementation for speed improvements may consider pre-calculating a distance matrix for all the cities in the problem, and pre-computing a probability matrix for choices during the probabilistic step-wise construction of tours.

```ruby
def euc_2d(c1, c2)
  Math.sqrt((c1[0] - c2[0])**2.0 + (c1[1] - c2[1])**2.0).round
end

def cost(permutation, cities)
  distance =0
  permutation.each_with_index do |c1, i|
    c2 = (i==permutation.size-1) ? permutation[0] : permutation[i+1]
    distance += euc_2d(cities[c1], cities[c2])
  end
  return distance
end

def random_permutation(cities)
  perm = Array.new(cities.size){|i| i}
  perm.each_index do |i|
    r = rand(perm.size-i) + i
    perm[r], perm[i] = perm[i], perm[r]
  end
  return perm
end

def initialise_pheromone_matrix(num_cities, naive_score)
  v = num_cities.to_f / naive_score
  return Array.new(num_cities){|i| Array.new(num_cities, v)}
end

def calculate_choices(cities, last_city, exclude, pheromone, c_heur, c_hist)
  choices = []
  cities.each_with_index do |coord, i|
    next if exclude.include?(i)
    prob = {:city=>i}
    prob[:history] = pheromone[last_city][i] ** c_hist
    prob[:distance] = euc_2d(cities[last_city], coord)
    prob[:heuristic] = (1.0/prob[:distance]) ** c_heur
    prob[:prob] = prob[:history] * prob[:heuristic]
    choices << prob
  end
  choices
end

def select_next_city(choices)
  sum = choices.inject(0.0){|sum,element| sum + element[:prob]}
  return choices[rand(choices.size)][:city] if sum == 0.0
  v = rand()
  choices.each_with_index do |choice, i|
    v -= (choice[:prob]/sum)
    return choice[:city] if v <= 0.0
  end
  return choices.last[:city]
end
```

```ruby
def stepwise_const(cities, phero, c_heur, c_hist)
  perm = []
  perm << rand(cities.size)
  begin
    choices = calculate_choices(cities,perm.last,perm,phero,c_heur,c_hist)
    next_city = select_next_city(choices)
    perm << next_city
  end until perm.size == cities.size
  return perm
end

def decay_pheromone(pheromone, decay_factor)
  pheromone.each do |array|
    array.each_with_index do |p, i|
      array[i] = (1.0 - decay_factor) * p
    end
  end
end

def update_pheromone(pheromone, solutions)
  solutions.each do |other|
    other[:vector].each_with_index do |x, i|
      y=(i==other[:vector].size-1) ? other[:vector][0] : other[:vector][i+1]
      pheromone[x][y] += (1.0 / other[:cost])
      pheromone[y][x] += (1.0 / other[:cost])
    end
  end
end

def search(cities, max_it, num_ants, decay_factor, c_heur, c_hist)
  best = {:vector=>random_permutation(cities)}
  best[:cost] = cost(best[:vector], cities)
  pheromone = initialise_pheromone_matrix(cities.size, best[:cost])
  max_it.times do |iter|
    solutions = []
    num_ants.times do
      candidate = {}
      candidate[:vector] = stepwise_const(cities, pheromone, c_heur, c_hist)
      candidate[:cost] = cost(candidate[:vector], cities)
      best = candidate if candidate[:cost] < best[:cost]
    end
    decay_pheromone(pheromone, decay_factor)
    update_pheromone(pheromone, solutions)
    puts " > iteration #{(iter+1)}, best=#{best[:cost]}"
  end
  return best
end

if __FILE__ == $0
  # problem configuration
  berlin52 = [[565,575],[25,185],[345,750],[945,685],[845,655],
    [880,660],[25,230],[525,1000],[580,1175],[650,1130],[1605,620],
    [1220,580],[1465,200],[1530,5],[845,680],[725,370],[145,665],
    [415,635],[510,875],[560,365],[300,465],[520,585],[480,415],
    [835,625],[975,580],[1215,245],[1320,315],[1250,400],[660,180],
    [410,250],[420,555],[575,665],[1150,1160],[700,580],[685,595],
```

```
109    [685,610],[770,610],[795,645],[720,635],[760,650],[475,960],
110    [95,260],[875,920],[700,500],[555,815],[830,485],[1170,65],
111    [830,610],[605,625],[595,360],[1340,725],[1740,245]]
112  # algorithm configuration
113  max_it = 50
114  num_ants = 30
115  decay_factor = 0.6
116  c_heur = 2.5
117  c_hist = 1.0
118  # execute the algorithm
119  best = search(berlin52, max_it, num_ants, decay_factor, c_heur, c_hist)
120  puts "Done. Best Solution: c=#{best[:cost]}, v=#{best[:vector].inspect}"
121  end
```

Listing 6.2: Ant System in Ruby

6.3.8 References

Primary Sources

The Ant System was described by Dorigo, Maniezzo, and Colorni in an early technical report as a class of algorithms and was applied to a number of standard combinatorial optimization algorithms [4]. A series of technical reports at this time investigated the class of algorithms called Ant System and the specific implementation called Ant Cycle. This effort contributed to Dorigo's PhD thesis published in Italian [2]. The seminal publication into the investigation of Ant System (with the implementation still referred to as Ant Cycle) was by Dorigo in 1996 [3].

Learn More

The seminal book on Ant Colony Optimization in general with a detailed treatment of Ant system is "Ant colony optimization" by Dorigo and Stützle [5]. An earlier book "Swarm intelligence: from natural to artificial systems" by Bonabeau, Dorigo, and Theraulaz also provides an introduction to Swarm Intelligence with a detailed treatment of Ant System [1].

6.3.9 Bibliography

[1] E. Bonabeau, M. Dorigo, and G. Theraulaz. *Swarm Intelligence: From Natural to Artificial Systems*. Oxford University Press US, 1999.

[2] M. Dorigo. *Optimization, Learning and Natural Algorithms (in Italian)*. PhD thesis, Dipartimento di Elettronica, Politecnico di Milano, Milan, Italy, 1992.

[3] M. Dorigo. The ant system: Optimization by a colony of cooperating agents. *IEEE Transactions on Systems, Man, and CyberneticsPart B*, 1:1–13, 1996.

[4] M. Dorigo, V. Maniezzo, and A. Colorni. Positive feedback as a search strategy. Technical report, ipartimento di Elettronica, Politecnico di Milano, Milano, Italy, 1991.

[5] M. Dorigo and T. Stützle. *Ant Colony Optimization*. MIT Press, 2004.

6.4 Ant Colony System

Ant Colony System, ACS, Ant-Q.

6.4.1 Taxonomy

The Ant Colony System algorithm is an example of an Ant Colony Optimization method from the field of Swarm Intelligence, Metaheuristics and Computational Intelligence. Ant Colony System is an extension to the Ant System algorithm and is related to other Ant Colony Optimization methods such as Elite Ant System, and Rank-based Ant System.

6.4.2 Inspiration

The Ant Colony System algorithm is inspired by the foraging behavior of ants, specifically the pheromone communication between ants regarding a good path between the colony and a food source in an environment. This mechanism is called stigmergy.

6.4.3 Metaphor

Ants initially wander randomly around their environment. Once food is located an ant will begin laying down pheromone in the environment. Numerous trips between the food and the colony are performed and if the same route is followed that leads to food then additional pheromone is laid down. Pheromone decays in the environment, so that older paths are less likely to be followed. Other ants may discover the same path to the food and in turn may follow it and also lay down pheromone. A positive feedback process routes more and more ants to productive paths that are in turn further refined through use.

6.4.4 Strategy

The objective of the strategy is to exploit historic and heuristic information to construct candidate solutions and fold the information learned from constructing solutions into the history. Solutions are constructed one discrete piece at a time in a probabilistic step-wise manner. The probability of selecting a component is determined by the heuristic contribution of the component to the overall cost of the solution and the quality of solutions from which the component has historically known to have been included. History is updated proportional to the quality of the best known solution and is decreased proportional to the usage if discrete solution components.

6.4.5 Procedure

Algorithm 6.4.1 provides a pseudocode listing of the main Ant Colony System algorithm for minimizing a cost function. The probabilistic stepwise construction of solution makes use of both history (pheromone) and problem-specific heuristic information to incrementally construct a solution piece-by-piece. Each component can only be selected if it has not already been chosen (for most combinatorial problems), and for those components that can be selected from given the current component i, their probability for selection is defined as:

$$P_{i,j} \leftarrow \frac{\tau_{i,j}^{\alpha} \times \eta_{i,j}^{\beta}}{\sum_{k=1}^{c} \tau_{i,k}^{\alpha} \times \eta_{i,k}^{\beta}} \qquad (6.4)$$

where $\eta_{i,j}$ is the maximizing contribution to the overall score of selecting the component (such as $\frac{1.0}{distance_{i,j}}$ for the Traveling Salesman Problem), β is the heuristic coefficient (commonly fixed at 1.0), $\tau_{i,j}$ is the pheromone value for the component, α is the history coefficient, and c is the set of usable components. A greediness factor ($q0$) is used to influence when to use the above probabilistic component selection and when to greedily select the best possible component.

A local pheromone update is performed for each solution that is constructed to dissuade following solutions to use the same components in the same order, as follows:

$$\tau_{i,j} \leftarrow (1 - \sigma) \times \tau_{i,j} + \sigma \times \tau_{i,j}^{0} \qquad (6.5)$$

where $\tau_{i,j}$ represents the pheromone for the component (graph edge) (i, j), σ is the local pheromone factor, and $\tau_{i,j}^{0}$ is the initial pheromone value.

At the end of each iteration, the pheromone is updated and decayed using the best candidate solution found thus far (or the best candidate solution found for the iteration), as follows:

$$\tau_{i,j} \leftarrow (1 - \rho) \times \tau_{i,j} + \rho \times \Delta\tau i, j \qquad (6.6)$$

where $\tau_{i,j}$ represents the pheromone for the component (graph edge) (i, j), ρ is the decay factor, and $\Delta\tau i, j$ is the maximizing solution cost for the best solution found so far if the component ij is used in the globally best known solution, otherwise it is 0.

6.4.6 Heuristics

- The Ant Colony System algorithm was designed for use with combinatorial problems such as the TSP, knapsack problem, quadratic assignment problems, graph coloring problems and many others.

Algorithm 6.4.1: Pseudocode for Ant Colony System.

Input: ProblemSize, $Population_{size}$, m, ρ, β, σ, $q0$
Output: P_{best}

1   $P_{best} \leftarrow$ CreateHeuristicSolution(ProblemSize);
2   $Pbest_{cost} \leftarrow$ Cost(S_h);
3   $Pheromone_{init} \leftarrow \frac{1.0}{\text{ProblemSize} \times Pbest_{cost}}$;
4   Pheromone $\leftarrow$ InitializePheromone($Pheromone_{init}$);
5   **while** ¬StopCondition() **do**
6   **for** $i = 1$ **to** m **do**
7       $S_i \leftarrow$ ConstructSolution(Pheromone, ProblemSize, β, $q0$);
8       $Si_{cost} \leftarrow$ Cost(S_i);
9   **if** $Si_{cost} \leq Pbest_{cost}$ **then**
10        $Pbest_{cost} \leftarrow Si_{cost}$;
11        $P_{best} \leftarrow S_i$;
12   **end**
13   LocalUpdateAndDecayPheromone(Pheromone, S_i, Si_{cost}, σ);
14   **end**
15   GlobalUpdateAndDecayPheromone(Pheromone, P_{best}, $Pbest_{cost}$, ρ);
16 **end**
17 **return** P_{best};

- The local pheromone (history) coefficient (σ) controls the amount of contribution history plays in a components probability of selection and is commonly set to 0.1.

- The heuristic coefficient (β) controls the amount of contribution problem-specific heuristic information plays in a components probability of selection and is commonly between 2 and 5, such as 2.5.

- The decay factor (ρ) controls the rate at which historic information is lost and is commonly set to 0.1.

- The greediness factor ($q0$) is commonly set to 0.9.

- The total number of ants (m) is commonly set low, such as 10.

6.4.7   Code Listing

Listing 6.3 provides an example of the Ant Colony System algorithm implemented in the Ruby Programming Language. The algorithm is applied to the Berlin52 instance of the Traveling Salesman Problem (TSP), taken from the TSPLIB. The problem seeks a permutation of the order to visit cities (called a tour) that minimized the total distance traveled. The optimal tour

distance for Berlin52 instance is 7542 units. Some extensions to the algorithm implementation for speed improvements may consider pre-calculating
a distance matrix for all the cities in the problem, and pre-computing a
probability matrix for choices during the probabilistic step-wise construction
of tours.

```ruby
def euc_2d(c1, c2)
  Math.sqrt((c1[0] - c2[0])**2.0 + (c1[1] - c2[1])**2.0).round
end

def cost(permutation, cities)
  distance =0
  permutation.each_with_index do |c1, i|
    c2 = (i==permutation.size-1) ? permutation[0] : permutation[i+1]
    distance += euc_2d(cities[c1], cities[c2])
  end
  return distance
end

def random_permutation(cities)
  perm = Array.new(cities.size){|i| i}
  perm.each_index do |i|
    r = rand(perm.size-i) + i
    perm[r], perm[i] = perm[i], perm[r]
  end
  return perm
end

def initialise_pheromone_matrix(num_cities, init_pher)
  return Array.new(num_cities){|i| Array.new(num_cities, init_pher)}
end

def calculate_choices(cities, last_city, exclude, pheromone, c_heur, c_hist)
  choices = []
  cities.each_with_index do |coord, i|
    next if exclude.include?(i)
    prob = {:city=>i}
    prob[:history] = pheromone[last_city][i] ** c_hist
    prob[:distance] = euc_2d(cities[last_city], coord)
    prob[:heuristic] = (1.0/prob[:distance]) ** c_heur
    prob[:prob] = prob[:history] * prob[:heuristic]
    choices << prob
  end
  return choices
end

def prob_select(choices)
  sum = choices.inject(0.0){|sum,element| sum + element[:prob]}
  return choices[rand(choices.size)][:city] if sum == 0.0
  v = rand()
  choices.each_with_index do |choice, i|
    v -= (choice[:prob]/sum)
    return choice[:city] if v <= 0.0
  end
  return choices.last[:city]
```

```ruby
50  end
51
52  def greedy_select(choices)
53    return choices.max{|a,b| a[:prob]<=>b[:prob]}[:city]
54  end
55
56  def stepwise_const(cities, phero, c_heur, c_greed)
57    perm = []
58    perm << rand(cities.size)
59    begin
60      choices = calculate_choices(cities, perm.last, perm, phero, c_heur, 1.0)
61      greedy = rand() <= c_greed
62      next_city = (greedy) ? greedy_select(choices) : prob_select(choices)
63      perm << next_city
64    end until perm.size == cities.size
65    return perm
66  end
67
68  def global_update_pheromone(phero, cand, decay)
69    cand[:vector].each_with_index do |x, i|
70      y = (i==cand[:vector].size-1) ? cand[:vector][0] : cand[:vector][i+1]
71      value = ((1.0-decay)*phero[x][y]) + (decay*(1.0/cand[:cost]))
72      phero[x][y] = value
73      phero[y][x] = value
74    end
75  end
76
77  def local_update_pheromone(pheromone, cand, c_local_phero, init_phero)
78    cand[:vector].each_with_index do |x, i|
79      y = (i==cand[:vector].size-1) ? cand[:vector][0] : cand[:vector][i+1]
80      value = ((1.0-c_local_phero)*pheromone[x][y])+(c_local_phero*init_phero)
81      pheromone[x][y] = value
82      pheromone[y][x] = value
83    end
84  end
85
86  def search(cities, max_it, num_ants, decay, c_heur, c_local_phero, c_greed)
87    best = {:vector=>random_permutation(cities)}
88    best[:cost] = cost(best[:vector], cities)
89    init_pheromone = 1.0 / (cities.size.to_f * best[:cost])
90    pheromone = initialise_pheromone_matrix(cities.size, init_pheromone)
91    max_it.times do |iter|
92      solutions = []
93      num_ants.times do
94        cand = {}
95        cand[:vector] = stepwise_const(cities, pheromone, c_heur, c_greed)
96        cand[:cost] = cost(cand[:vector], cities)
97        best = cand if cand[:cost] < best[:cost]
98        local_update_pheromone(pheromone, cand, c_local_phero, init_pheromone)
99      end
100     global_update_pheromone(pheromone, best, decay)
101     puts " > iteration #{(iter+1)}, best=#{best[:cost]}"
102   end
103   return best
104 end
105
```

```
106  if __FILE__ == $0
107    # problem configuration
108    berlin52 = [[565,575],[25,185],[345,750],[945,685],[845,655],
109      [880,660],[25,230],[525,1000],[580,1175],[650,1130],[1605,620],
110      [1220,580],[1465,200],[1530,5],[845,680],[725,370],[145,665],
111      [415,635],[510,875],[560,365],[300,465],[520,585],[480,415],
112      [835,625],[975,580],[1215,245],[1320,315],[1250,400],[660,180],
113      [410,250],[420,555],[575,665],[1150,1160],[700,580],[685,595],
114      [685,610],[770,610],[795,645],[720,635],[760,650],[475,960],
115      [95,260],[875,920],[700,500],[555,815],[830,485],[1170,65],
116      [830,610],[605,625],[595,360],[1340,725],[1740,245]]
117    # algorithm configuration
118    max_it = 100
119    num_ants = 10
120    decay = 0.1
121    c_heur = 2.5
122    c_local_phero = 0.1
123    c_greed = 0.9
124    # execute the algorithm
125    best = search(berlin52, max_it, num_ants, decay, c_heur, c_local_phero,
           c_greed)
126    puts "Done. Best Solution: c=#{best[:cost]}, v=#{best[:vector].inspect}"
127  end
```

Listing 6.3: Ant Colony System in Ruby

6.4.8   References

Primary Sources

The algorithm was initially investigated by Dorigo and Gambardella under the name Ant-Q [2, 6]. It was renamed Ant Colony System and further investigated first in a technical report by Dorigo and Gambardella [4], and later published [3].

Learn More

The seminal book on Ant Colony Optimization in general with a detailed treatment of Ant Colony System is "Ant colony optimization" by Dorigo and Stützle [5]. An earlier book "Swarm intelligence: from natural to artificial systems" by Bonabeau, Dorigo, and Theraulaz also provides an introduction to Swarm Intelligence with a detailed treatment of Ant Colony System [1].

6.4.9   Bibliography

[1] E. Bonabeau, M. Dorigo, and G. Theraulaz. *Swarm Intelligence: From Natural to Artificial Systems.* Oxford University Press US, 1999.

[2] M. Dorigo and L. M. Gambardella. A study of some properties of ant-q. In H-M. Voigt, W. Ebeling, I. Rechenberg, and H-P. Schwefel, editors,

Proceedings of PPSN IVFourth International Conference on Parallel Problem Solving From Nature, pages 656–665. Springer-Verlag, 1996.

[3] M. Dorigo and L. M. Gambardella. Ant colony system : A cooperative learning approach to the traveling salesman problem. *IEEE Transactions on Evolutionary Computation*, 1(1):53–66, 1997.

[4] M. Dorigo and L. M. Gambardella. Ant colony system: A cooperative learning approach to the traveling salesman problems. Technical Report TR/IRIDIA/1996-5, IRIDIA, Université Libre de Bruxelles, 1997.

[5] M. Dorigo and T. Stützle. *Ant Colony Optimization*. MIT Press, 2004.

[6] L. Gambardella and M. Dorigo. Ant–Q: A reinforcement learning approach to the traveling salesman problems. In A. Prieditis and S. Russell, editors, *Proceedings of ML-95, Twelfth International Conference on Machine Learning*, pages 252–260. Morgan Kaufmann, 1995.

6.5   Bees Algorithm

Bees Algorithm, BA.

6.5.1   Taxonomy

The Bees Algorithm beings to Bee Inspired Algorithms and the field of Swarm Intelligence, and more broadly the fields of Computational Intelligence and Metaheuristics. The Bees Algorithm is related to other Bee Inspired Algorithms, such as Bee Colony Optimization, and other Swarm Intelligence algorithms such as Ant Colony Optimization and Particle Swarm Optimization.

6.5.2   Inspiration

The Bees Algorithm is inspired by the foraging behavior of honey bees. Honey bees collect nectar from vast areas around their hive (more than 10 kilometers). Bee Colonies have been observed to send bees to collect nectar from flower patches relative to the amount of food available at each patch. Bees communicate with each other at the hive via a waggle dance that informs other bees in the hive as to the direction, distance, and quality rating of food sources.

6.5.3   Metaphor

Honey bees collect nectar from flower patches as a food source for the hive. The hive sends out scout's that locate patches of flowers, who then return to the hive and inform other bees about the fitness and location of a food source via a waggle dance. The scout returns to the flower patch with follower bees. A small number of scouts continue to search for new patches, while bees returning from flower patches continue to communicate the quality of the patch.

6.5.4   Strategy

The information processing objective of the algorithm is to locate and explore good sites within a problem search space. Scouts are sent out to randomly sample the problem space and locate good sites. The good sites are exploited via the application of a local search, where a small number of good sites are explored more than the others. Good sites are continually exploited, although many scouts are sent out each iteration always in search of additional good sites.

6.5.5 Procedure

Algorithm 6.5.1 provides a pseudocode listing of the Bees Algorithm for minimizing a cost function.

Algorithm 6.5.1: Pseudocode for the Bees Algorithm.

Input: $Problem_{size}$, $Bees_{num}$, $Sites_{num}$, $EliteSites_{num}$, $PatchSize_{init}$, $EliteBees_{num}$, $OtherBees_{num}$

Output: Bee_{best}

1   Population ← InitializePopulation($Bees_{num}$, $Problem_{size}$);
2   **while** ¬StopCondition() **do**
3   EvaluatePopulation(Population);
4   Bee_{best} ← GetBestSolution(Population);
5   NextGeneration ← ∅;
6      $Patch_{size}$ ← ($PatchSize_{init}$ × $PatchDecrease_{factor}$);
7      $Sites_{best}$ ← SelectBestSites(Population, $Sites_{num}$);
8   **foreach** $Site_i$ ∈ $Sites_{best}$ **do**
9          $RecruitedBees_{num}$ ← ∅;
10   **if** $i < EliteSites_{num}$ **then**
11             $RecruitedBees_{num}$ ← $EliteBees_{num}$;
12   **else**
13             $RecruitedBees_{num}$ ← $OtherBees_{num}$;
14   **end**
15   Neighborhood ← ∅;
16   **for** j to $RecruitedBees_{num}$ **do**
17   Neighborhood ← CreateNeighborhoodBee($Site_i$, $Patch_{size}$);
18   **end**
19   NextGeneration ← GetBestSolution(Neighborhood);
20   **end**
21      $RemainingBees_{num}$ ← ($Bees_{num}$- $Sites_{num}$);
22   **for** j to $RemainingBees_{num}$ **do**
23   NextGeneration ← CreateRandomBee();
24   **end**
25   Population ← NextGeneration;
26 **end**
27 **return** Bee_{best};

6.5.6 Heuristics

- The Bees Algorithm was developed to be used with continuous and combinatorial function optimization problems.

- The $Patch_{size}$ variable is used as the neighborhood size. For example,

in a continuous function optimization problem, each dimension of a
site would be sampled as $x_i \pm (rand() \times Patch_{size})$.

- The $Patch_{size}$ variable is decreased each iteration, typically by a
  constant amount (such as 0.95).

- The number of elite sites ($EliteSites_{num}$) must be < the number
  of sites ($Sites_{num}$), and the number of elite bees ($EliteBees_{num}$) is
  traditionally < the number of other bees ($OtherBees_{num}$).

6.5.7   Code Listing

Listing 6.4 provides an example of the Bees Algorithm implemented in the
Ruby Programming Language. The demonstration problem is an instance of
a continuous function optimization that seeks min $f(x)$ where $f = \sum_{i=1}^{n} x_i^2$,
$-5.0 \leq x_i \leq 5.0$ and $n = 3$. The optimal solution for this basin function
is $(v_0, \ldots, v_{n-1}) = 0.0$. The algorithm is an implementation of the Bees
Algorithm as described in the seminal paper [2]. A fixed patch size decrease
factor of 0.95 was applied each iteration.

```ruby
def objective_function(vector)
  return vector.inject(0.0) {|sum, x| sum + (x ** 2.0)}
end

def random_vector(minmax)
  return Array.new(minmax.size) do |i|
    minmax[i][0] + ((minmax[i][1] - minmax[i][0]) * rand())
  end
end

def create_random_bee(search_space)
  return {:vector=>random_vector(search_space)}
end

def create_neigh_bee(site, patch_size, search_space)
  vector = []
  site.each_with_index do |v,i|
    v = (rand()<0.5) ? v+rand()*patch_size : v-rand()*patch_size
    v = search_space[i][0] if v < search_space[i][0]
    v = search_space[i][1] if v > search_space[i][1]
    vector << v
  end
  bee = {}
  bee[:vector] = vector
  return bee
end

def search_neigh(parent, neigh_size, patch_size, search_space)
  neigh = []
  neigh_size.times do
    neigh << create_neigh_bee(parent[:vector], patch_size, search_space)
  end
  neigh.each{|bee| bee[:fitness] = objective_function(bee[:vector])}
```

```ruby
34    return neigh.sort{|x,y| x[:fitness]<=>y[:fitness]}.first
35  end
36
37  def create_scout_bees(search_space, num_scouts)
38    return Array.new(num_scouts) do
39      create_random_bee(search_space)
40    end
41  end
42
43  def search(max_gens, search_space, num_bees, num_sites, elite_sites,
          patch_size, e_bees, o_bees)
44    best = nil
45    pop = Array.new(num_bees){ create_random_bee(search_space) }
46    max_gens.times do |gen|
47      pop.each{|bee| bee[:fitness] = objective_function(bee[:vector])}
48      pop.sort!{|x,y| x[:fitness]<=>y[:fitness]}
49      best = pop.first if best.nil? or pop.first[:fitness] < best[:fitness]
50      next_gen = []
51      pop[0...num_sites].each_with_index do |parent, i|
52        neigh_size = (i<elite_sites) ? e_bees : o_bees
53        next_gen << search_neigh(parent, neigh_size, patch_size, search_space)
54      end
55      scouts = create_scout_bees(search_space, (num_bees-num_sites))
56      pop = next_gen + scouts
57      patch_size = patch_size * 0.95
58      puts " > it=#{gen+1}, patch_size=#{patch_size}, f=#{best[:fitness]}"
59    end
60    return best
61  end
62
63  if __FILE__ == $0
64    # problem configuration
65    problem_size = 3
66    search_space = Array.new(problem_size) {|i| [-5, 5]}
67    # algorithm configuration
68    max_gens = 500
69    num_bees = 45
70    num_sites = 3
71    elite_sites = 1
72    patch_size = 3.0
73    e_bees = 7
74    o_bees = 2
75    # execute the algorithm
76    best = search(max_gens, search_space, num_bees, num_sites, elite_sites,
            patch_size, e_bees, o_bees)
77    puts "done! Solution: f=#{best[:fitness]}, s=#{best[:vector].inspect}"
78  end
```

Listing 6.4: Bees Algorithm in Ruby

6.5.8   References

Primary Sources

The Bees Algorithm was proposed by Pham et al. in a technical report in 2005 [3], and later published [2]. In this work, the algorithm was applied to standard instances of continuous function optimization problems.

Learn More

The majority of the work on the algorithm has concerned its application to various problem domains. The following is a selection of popular application papers: the optimization of linear antenna arrays by Guney and Onay [1], the optimization of codebook vectors in the Learning Vector Quantization algorithm for classification by Pham et al. [5], optimization of neural networks for classification by Pham et al. [6], and the optimization of clustering methods by Pham et al. [4].

6.5.9   Bibliography

[1] K. Guney and M. Onay. Amplitude-only pattern nulling of linear antenna arrays with the use of bees algorithm. *Progress In Electromagnetics Research*, 70:21–36, 2007.

[2] D. T. Pham, Ghanbarzadeh A., Koc E., Otri S., Rahim S., and M.Zaidi. The bees algorithm - a novel tool for complex optimisation problems. In *Proceedings of IPROMS 2006 Conference*, pages 454–461, 2006.

[3] D. T. Pham, A. Ghanbarzadeh, E. Koc, S. Otri, S. Rahim, and M. Zaidi. The bees algorithm. Technical report, Manufacturing Engineering Centre, Cardiff University, 2005.

[4] D. T. Pham, S. Otri, A. A. Afify, M. Mahmuddin, and H. Al-Jabbouli. Data clustering using the bees algorithm. In *Proc 40th CIRP International Manufacturing Systems Seminar*, 2007.

[5] D. T. Pham, S. Otri, A. Ghanbarzadeh, and E. Koc. Application of the bees algorithm to the training of learning vector quantisation networks for control chart pattern recognition. In *Proceedings of Information and Communication Technologies (ICTTA'06)*, pages 1624–1629, 2006.

[6] D. T. Pham, A. J. Soroka, A. Ghanbarzadeh, E. Koc, S. Otri, and M. Packianather. Optimising neural networks for identification of wood defects using the bees algorithm. In *Proceedings of the 2006 IEEE International Conference on Industrial Informatics*, 2006.

6.6 Bacterial Foraging Optimization Algorithm

Bacterial Foraging Optimization Algorithm, BFOA, Bacterial Foraging Optimization, BFO.

6.6.1 Taxonomy

The Bacterial Foraging Optimization Algorithm belongs to the field of Bacteria Optimization Algorithms and Swarm Optimization, and more broadly to the fields of Computational Intelligence and Metaheuristics. It is related to other Bacteria Optimization Algorithms such as the Bacteria Chemotaxis Algorithm [3], and other Swarm Intelligence algorithms such as Ant Colony Optimization and Particle Swarm Optimization. There have been many extensions of the approach that attempt to hybridize the algorithm with other Computational Intelligence algorithms and Metaheuristics such as Particle Swarm Optimization, Genetic Algorithm, and Tabu Search.

6.6.2 Inspiration

The Bacterial Foraging Optimization Algorithm is inspired by the group foraging behavior of bacteria such as E.coli and M.xanthus. Specifically, the BFOA is inspired by the chemotaxis behavior of bacteria that will perceive chemical gradients in the environment (such as nutrients) and move toward or away from specific signals.

6.6.3 Metaphor

Bacteria perceive the direction to food based on the gradients of chemicals in their environment. Similarly, bacteria secrete attracting and repelling chemicals into the environment and can perceive each other in a similar way. Using locomotion mechanisms (such as flagella) bacteria can move around in their environment, sometimes moving chaotically (tumbling and spinning), and other times moving in a directed manner that may be referred to as swimming. Bacterial cells are treated like agents in an environment, using their perception of food and other cells as motivation to move, and stochastic tumbling and swimming like movement to re-locate. Depending on the cell-cell interactions, cells may swarm a food source, and/or may aggressively repel or ignore each other.

6.6.4 Strategy

The information processing strategy of the algorithm is to allow cells to stochastically and collectively swarm toward optima. This is achieved through a series of three processes on a population of simulated cells: 1) 'Chemotaxis' where the cost of cells is derated by the proximity to other cells and cells move along the manipulated cost surface one at a time (the majority of the work of the algorithm), 2) 'Reproduction' where only those cells that performed well over their lifetime may contribute to the next generation, and 3) 'Elimination-dispersal' where cells are discarded and new random samples are inserted with a low probability.

6.6.5 Procedure

Algorithm 6.6.1 provides a pseudocode listing of the Bacterial Foraging Optimization Algorithm for minimizing a cost function. Algorithm 6.6.2 provides the pseudocode listing for the chemotaxis and swing behaviour of the BFOA algorithm. A bacteria cost is derated by its interaction with other cells. This interaction function ($g()$) is calculated as follows:

$$g(cell_k) = \sum_{i=1}^{S} \left[- d_{attr} \times exp\left(- w_{attr} \times \sum_{m=1}^{P} (cell_m^k - other_m^i)^2 \right) \right] +$$
$$\sum_{i=1}^{S} \left[h_{repel} \times exp\left(- w_{repel} \times \sum_{m=1}^{P} cell_m^k - other_m^i)^2 \right) \right]$$

where $cell_k$ is a given cell, d_{attr} and w_{attr} are attraction coefficients, h_{repel} and w_{repel} are repulsion coefficients, S is the number of cells in the population, P is the number of dimensions on a given cells position vector.

The remaining parameters of the algorithm are as follows $Cells_{num}$ is the number of cells maintained in the population, N_{ed} is the number of elimination-dispersal steps, N_{re} is the number of reproduction steps, N_c is the number of chemotaxis steps, N_s is the number of swim steps for a given cell, $Step_{size}$ is a random direction vector with the same number of dimensions as the problem space, and each value $\in [-1, 1]$, and P_{ed} is the probability of a cell being subjected to elimination and dispersal.

6.6.6 Heuristics

- The algorithm was designed for application to continuous function optimization problem domains.

- Given the loops in the algorithm, it can be configured numerous ways to elicit different search behavior. It is common to have a large number of chemotaxis iterations, and small numbers of the other iterations.

- The default coefficients for swarming behavior (cell-cell interactions) are as follows $d_{attract} = 0.1$, $w_{attract} = 0.2$, $h_{repellant} = d_{attract}$, and $w_{repellant} = 10$.

- The step size is commonly a small fraction of the search space, such as 0.1.

Algorithm 6.6.1: Pseudocode for the BFOA.

Input: $Problem_{size}$, $Cells_{num}$, N_{ed}, N_{re}, N_c, N_s, $Step_{size}$, $d_{attract}$, $w_{attract}$, $h_{repellant}$, $w_{repellant}$, P_{ed}

Output: $Cell_{best}$

1 Population ← InitializePopulation($Cells_{num}$, $Problem_{size}$);
2 **for** $l = 0$ to N_{ed} **do**
3   **for** $k = 0$ to N_{re} **do**
4   **for** $j = 0$ to N_c **do**
5   ChemotaxisAndSwim(Population, $Problem_{size}$, $Cells_{num}$, N_s, $Step_{size}$, $d_{attract}$, $w_{attract}$, $h_{repellant}$, $w_{repellant}$);
6   **foreach** Cell ∈ Population **do**
7   **if** Cost(Cell) ≤ Cost($Cell_{best}$) **then**
8                 $Cell_{best}$ ← Cell;
9   **end**
10   **end**
11   **end**
12   SortByCellHealth(Population);
13   Selected ← SelectByCellHealth(Population, $\frac{Cells_{num}}{2}$);
14   Population ← Selected;
15   Population ← Selected;
16   **end**
17   **foreach** Cell ∈ Population **do**
18   **if** Rand() ≤ P_{ed} **then**
19   Cell ← CreateCellAtRandomLocation();
20   **end**
21   **end**
22 **end**
23 **return** $Cell_{best}$;

- During reproduction, typically half the population with a low health metric are discarded, and two copies of each member from the first (high-health) half of the population are retained.

- The probability of elimination and dispersal (p_{ed}) is commonly set quite large, such as 0.25.

6.6.7 Code Listing

Listing 6.5 provides an example of the Bacterial Foraging Optimization Algorithm implemented in the Ruby Programming Language. The demonstration problem is an instance of a continuous function optimization that seeks $\min f(x)$ where $f = \sum_{i=1}^{n} x_i^2$, $-5.0 \le x_i \le 5.0$ and $n = 2$. The optimal solution for this basin function is $(v_0, \ldots, v_{n-1}) = 0.0$. The algorithm

---

Algorithm 6.6.2: Pseudocode for the `ChemotaxisAndSwim` function.

Input: Population, $Problem_{size}$, $Cells_{num}$, N_s, $Step_{size}$, $d_{attract}$, $w_{attract}$, $h_{repellant}$, $w_{repellant}$

1 **foreach** Cell $\in$ Population **do**
2      $Cell_{fitness} \leftarrow$ Cost(Cell) + Interaction(Cell, Population, $d_{attract}$, $w_{attract}$, $h_{repellant}$, $w_{repellant}$);
3      $Cell_{health} \leftarrow Cell_{fitness}$;
4      $Cell' \leftarrow \emptyset$;
5   **for** $i = 0$ **to** N_s **do**
6   RandomStepDirection $\leftarrow$ CreateStep($Problem_{size}$);
7         $Cell' \leftarrow$ TakeStep(RandomStepDirection, $Step_{size}$);
8         $Cell'_{fitness} \leftarrow$ Cost($Cell'$) + Interaction($Cell'$, Population, $d_{attract}$, $w_{attract}$, $h_{repellant}$, $w_{repellant}$);
9   **if** $Cell'_{fitness} > Cell_{fitness}$ **then**
10           $i \leftarrow N_s$;
11   **else**
12   Cell $\leftarrow Cell'$;
13           $Cell_{health} \leftarrow Cell_{health} + Cell'_{fitness}$;
14   **end**
15   **end**
16 **end**

---

is an implementation based on the description on the seminal work [4]. The parameters for cell-cell interactions (attraction and repulsion) were taken from the paper, and the various loop parameters were taken from the 'Swarming Effects' example.

```
def objective_function(vector)
  return vector.inject(0.0) {|sum, x| sum + (x ** 2.0)}
end

def random_vector(minmax)
  return Array.new(minmax.size) do |i|
    minmax[i][0] + ((minmax[i][1] - minmax[i][0]) * rand())
  end
end

def generate_random_direction(problem_size)
  bounds = Array.new(problem_size){[-1.0,1.0]}
  return random_vector(bounds)
end

def compute_cell_interaction(cell, cells, d, w)
  sum = 0.0
  cells.each do |other|
    diff = 0.0
    cell[:vector].each_index do |i|
```

```
21        diff += (cell[:vector][i] - other[:vector][i])**2.0
22      end
23      sum += d * Math.exp(w * diff)
24    end
25    return sum
26  end
27
28  def attract_repel(cell, cells, d_attr, w_attr, h_rep, w_rep)
29    attract = compute_cell_interaction(cell, cells, -d_attr, -w_attr)
30    repel = compute_cell_interaction(cell, cells, h_rep, -w_rep)
31    return attract + repel
32  end
33
34  def evaluate(cell, cells, d_attr, w_attr, h_rep, w_rep)
35    cell[:cost] = objective_function(cell[:vector])
36    cell[:inter] = attract_repel(cell, cells, d_attr, w_attr, h_rep, w_rep)
37    cell[:fitness] = cell[:cost] + cell[:inter]
38  end
39
40  def tumble_cell(search_space, cell, step_size)
41    step = generate_random_direction(search_space.size)
42    vector = Array.new(search_space.size)
43    vector.each_index do |i|
44      vector[i] = cell[:vector][i] + step_size * step[i]
45      vector[i] = search_space[i][0] if vector[i] < search_space[i][0]
46      vector[i] = search_space[i][1] if vector[i] > search_space[i][1]
47    end
48    return {:vector=>vector}
49  end
50
51  def chemotaxis(cells, search_space, chem_steps, swim_length, step_size,
52      d_attr, w_attr, h_rep, w_rep)
53    best = nil
54    chem_steps.times do |j|
55      moved_cells = []
56      cells.each_with_index do |cell, i|
57        sum_nutrients = 0.0
58        evaluate(cell, cells, d_attr, w_attr, h_rep, w_rep)
59        best = cell if best.nil? or cell[:cost] < best[:cost]
60        sum_nutrients += cell[:fitness]
61        swim_length.times do |m|
62          new_cell = tumble_cell(search_space, cell, step_size)
63          evaluate(new_cell, cells, d_attr, w_attr, h_rep, w_rep)
64          best = cell if cell[:cost] < best[:cost]
65          break if new_cell[:fitness] > cell[:fitness]
66          cell = new_cell
67          sum_nutrients += cell[:fitness]
68        end
69        cell[:sum_nutrients] = sum_nutrients
70        moved_cells << cell
71      end
72      puts " >> chemo=#{j}, f=#{best[:fitness]}, cost=#{best[:cost]}"
73      cells = moved_cells
74    end
75    return [best, cells]
76  end
```

```ruby
76
77  def search(search_space, pop_size, elim_disp_steps, repro_steps,
          chem_steps, swim_length, step_size, d_attr, w_attr, h_rep, w_rep,
          p_eliminate)
78    cells = Array.new(pop_size) { {:vector=>random_vector(search_space)} }
79    best = nil
80    elim_disp_steps.times do |l|
81      repro_steps.times do |k|
82        c_best, cells = chemotaxis(cells, search_space, chem_steps,
              swim_length, step_size, d_attr, w_attr, h_rep, w_rep)
83        best = c_best if best.nil? or c_best[:cost] < best[:cost]
84        puts " > best fitness=#{best[:fitness]}, cost=#{best[:cost]}"
85        cells.sort{|x,y| x[:sum_nutrients]<=>y[:sum_nutrients]}
86        cells = cells.first(pop_size/2) + cells.first(pop_size/2)
87      end
88      cells.each do |cell|
89        if rand() <= p_eliminate
90          cell[:vector] = random_vector(search_space)
91        end
92      end
93    end
94    return best
95  end
96
97  if __FILE__ == $0
98    # problem configuration
99    problem_size = 2
100   search_space = Array.new(problem_size) {|i| [-5, 5]}
101   # algorithm configuration
102   pop_size = 50
103   step_size = 0.1 # Ci
104   elim_disp_steps = 1 # Ned
105   repro_steps = 4 # Nre
106   chem_steps = 70 # Nc
107   swim_length = 4 # Ns
108   p_eliminate = 0.25 # Ped
109   d_attr = 0.1
110   w_attr = 0.2
111   h_rep = d_attr
112   w_rep = 10
113   # execute the algorithm
114   best = search(search_space, pop_size, elim_disp_steps, repro_steps,
          chem_steps, swim_length, step_size, d_attr, w_attr, h_rep, w_rep,
          p_eliminate)
115   puts "done! Solution: c=#{best[:cost]}, v=#{best[:vector].inspect}"
116 end
```

Listing 6.5: Bacterial Foraging Optimization Algorithm in Ruby

6.6.8   References

Primary Sources

Early work by Liu and Passino considered models of chemotaxis as optimization for both E.coli and M.xanthus which were applied to continuous function optimization [2]. This work was consolidated by Passino who presented the Bacterial Foraging Optimization Algorithm that included a detailed presentation of the algorithm, heuristics for configuration, and demonstration applications and behavior dynamics [4].

Learn More

A detailed summary of social foraging and the BFOA is provided in the book by Passino [5]. Passino provides a follow-up review of the background models of chemotaxis as optimization and describes the equations of the Bacterial Foraging Optimization Algorithm in detail in a Journal article [6]. Das et al. present the algorithm and its inspiration, and go on to provide an in depth analysis the dynamics of chemotaxis using simplified mathematical models [1].

6.6.9   Bibliography

[1] S. Das, A. Biswas, S. Dasgupta, and A. Abraham. *Foundations of Computational Intelligence Volume 3: Global Optimization*, chapter Bacterial Foraging Optimization Algorithm: Theoretical Foundations, Analysis, and Applications, pages 23–55. Springer, 2009.

[2] Y. Liu and K. M. Passino. Biomimicry of social foraging bacteria for distributed optimization: Models, principles, and emergent behaviors. *Journal of Optimization Theory and Applications*, 115(3):603–628, 2002.

[3] S. D. Müller, J. Marchetto, S. Airaghi, and P. Koumoutsakos. Optimization based on bacterial chemotaxis. *IEEE Transactions on Evolutionary Computation*, 6(1):16–29, 2002.

[4] K. M. Passino. Biomimicry of bacterial foraging for distributed optimization and control. *IEEE Control Systems Magazine*, 22(3):52–67, 2002.

[5] K. M. Passino. *Biomimicry for Optimization, Control, and Automation*, chapter Part V: Foraging. Springer, 2005.

[6] K. M. Passino. Bacterial foraging optimization. *International Journal of Swarm Intelligence Research*, 1(1):1–16, 2010.

Chapter 7

Immune Algorithms

7.1 Overview

This chapter describes Immune Algorithms.

7.1.1 Immune System

Immune Algorithms belong to the Artificial Immune Systems field of study concerned with computational methods inspired by the process and mechanisms of the biological immune system.

A simplified description of the immune system is an organ system intended to protect the host organism from the threats posed to it from pathogens and toxic substances. Pathogens encompass a range of microorganisms such as bacteria, viruses, parasites and pollen. The traditional perspective regarding the role of the immune system is divided into two primary tasks: the *detection* and *elimination* of pathogen. This behavior is typically referred to as the differentiation of self (molecules and cells that belong to the host organisms) from potentially harmful non-self. More recent perspectives on the role of the system include a maintenance system [3], and a cognitive system [22].

The architecture of the immune system is such that a series of defensive layers protect the host. Once a pathogen makes it inside the host, it must contend with the *innate* and *acquired* immune system. These interrelated immunological sub-systems are comprised of many types of cells and molecules produced by specialized organs and processes to address the self-nonself problem at the lowest level using chemical bonding, where the surfaces of cells and molecules interact with the surfaces of pathogen.

The adaptive immune system, also referred to as the acquired immune system, is named such because it is responsible for specializing a defense for the host organism based on the *specific* pathogen to which it is exposed. Unlike the innate immune system, the acquired immune system is present

only in vertebrates (animals with a spinal column). The system retains a
memory of exposures which it has encountered. This memory is *recalled*
on reinfection exhibiting a *learned* pathogen identification. This learning
process may be divided into two types of response. The first or *primary
response* occurs when the system encounters a novel pathogen. The system is
slow to respond, potentially taking a number of weeks to clear the infection.
On re-encountering the same pathogen again, the system exhibits a *secondary
response*, applying what was learned in the primary response and clearing
up the infection rapidly. The *memory* the system acquires in the primary
response is typically long lasting, providing pathogenic immunity for the
lifetime of the host, two common examples of which are the chickenpox and
measles. White blood cells called lymphocytes (or leukocytes) are the most
important cell in the acquired immune system. Lymphocytes are involved in
both the identification and elimination of pathogen, and recirculate within
the host organisms body in the blood and lymph (the fluid that permeates
tissue).

7.1.2   Artificial Immune Systems

Artificial Immune Systems (AIS) is a sub-field of Computational Intelligence motivated by immunology (primarily mammalian immunology) that
emerged in the early 1990s (for example [1, 15]), based on the proposal in the
late 1980s to apply theoretical immunological models to machine learning
and automated problem solving (such as [9, 12]). The early works in the
field were inspired by exotic theoretical models (immune network theory)
and were applied to machine learning, control and optimization problems.
The approaches were reminiscent of paradigms such as Artificial Neural
Networks, Genetic Algorithms, Reinforcement Learning, and Learning Classifier Systems. The most formative works in giving the field an identity
were those that proposed the immune system as an analogy for information
protection systems in the field of computer security. The classical examples
include Forrest et al.'s Computer Immunity [10, 11] and Kephart's Immune
Anti-Virus [17, 18]. These works were formative for the field because they
provided an intuitive application domain that captivated a broader audience
and assisted in differentiating the work as an independent sub-field.

Modern Artificial Immune systems are inspired by one of three sub-
fields: clonal selection, negative selection and immune network algorithms.
The techniques are commonly used for clustering, pattern recognition,
classification, optimization, and other similar machine learning problem
domains.

The seminal reference for those interested in the field is the text book by
de Castro and Timmis *"Artificial Immune Systems: A New Computational
Intelligence Approach"* [8]. This reference text provides an introduction
to immunology with a level of detail appropriate for a computer scientist,
followed by a summary of the state of the art, algorithms, application areas,

and case studies.

7.1.3 Extensions

There are many other algorithms and classes of algorithm that were not described from the field of Artificial Immune Systems, not limited to:

- **Clonal Selection Algorithms**: such as the B-Cell Algorithm [16], the Multi-objective Immune System Algorithm (MSIRA) [2, 4] and the the Optimization Immune Algorithm (opt-IA, opt-IMMALG) [5, 6] and the Simple Immunological Algorithm [7].

- **Immune Network Algorithms**: such as the approach by Timmis used for clustering called the Artificial Immune Network (AIN) [20] (later extended and renamed the Resource Limited Artificial Immune System [19, 21].

- **Negative Selection Algorithms**: such as an adaptive framework called the *ARTificial Immune System* (ARTIS), with the application to intrusion detection renamed the *Lightweight Intrusion Detection System* (LISYS) [13, 14].

7.1.4 Bibliography

[1] H. Bersini and F. Varela. Hints for adaptive problem solving gleaned from immune networks. In *Lecture Notes In Computer Science*, pages 343–354. Springer-Verlag, London, UK, 1990.

[2] C. A. Coello Coello and N. C. Cortés. An approach to solve multiobjective optimization problems based on an artificial immune system. In P. J. Bentley, editor, *First International Conference on Artificial Immune Systems*, pages 212–221, 2002.

[3] I. R. Cohen. *Tending Adam's Garden: Evolving the Cognitive Immune Self*. Academic Press, New York, 2001.

[4] N. C. Cortés and C. A. Coello Coello. Multiobjective optimization using ideas from the clonal selection principle. In *Lecture Notes in Computer Science*, pages 158–170, Berlin / Heidelberg, 2003. Springer.

[5] V. Cutello and G. Nicosia. An immunological approach to combinatorial optimization problems. In J.C. Riquelme and M. Toro, editors, *Lecture Notes In Computer Science*, pages 361–370, London, UK, 2002. Springer-Verlag.

[6] V. Cutello and G. Nicosia. Multiple learning using immune algorithms. In *Proceedings of 4th International Conference on Recent Advances in Soft Computing, RASC 2002*, pages 102–107, 2002.

[7] V. Cutello and G. Nicosia. Chapter vi. the clonal selection principle for in silico and in vivo computing. In Fernando J. Von Zuben, editor, *Recent Developments in Biologically Inspired Computing*, pages 104–146, Hershey, London, Melbourne, Singapore, 2005. Idea Group Publishing.

[8] L. N. de Castro and J. Timmis. *Artificial Immune Systems: A New Computational Intelligence Approach*. Springer, 2002.

[9] J. D. Farmer, N. H. Packard, and Alan S. Perelson. The immune system, adaptation, and machine learning. *Physica D*, 22:187–204, 1986.

[10] S. Forrest, S. A. Hofmeyr, and A. Somayaji. Computer immunology. *Communications of the ACM*, 40(10):88–96, October 1997.

[11] S. Forrest, A. S. Perelson, L. Allen, and R. Cherukuri. Self-nonself discrimination in a computer. In *Proceedings of the 1992 IEEE Symposium on Security and Privacy*, pages 202–212. IEEE Computer Society Press, 1994.

[12] G. W. Hoffmann. A neural network model based on the analogy with the immune system. *Journal of Theoretical Immunology*, 122(1):33–67, September 1986.

[13] S. Hofmeyr and S. Forrest. Immunity by design: An artificial immune system. In J. Daida, A. E. Eiben, M. H. Garzon, V. Honavar, M. Jakiela, and R. E. Smith, editors, *Proceedings of the Genetic and Evolutionary Computation Conference (GECCO)*, volume 2, pages 1289–1296. Morgan-Kaufmann, 1999.

[14] S. A. Hofmeyr and S. Forrest. Architecture for an artificial immune system. *Evolutionary Computation*, 8(4):443–473, 2000.

[15] Y. Ishida. Fully distributed diagnosis by PDP learning algorithm: towards immune network PDP models. In *IJCNN International Joint Conference on Neural Networks*, volume 1, pages 777–782. IEEE Computer Society, USA, 1990.

[16] J. Kelsey and J. Timmis. Immune inspired somatic contiguous hypermutation for function optimisation. In *Lecture Notes in Computer Science*, pages 207–218. Springer, Berlin / Heidelberg, 2003.

[17] J. O. Kephart. A biologically inspired immune system for computers. In P. Maes, editor, *Artificial Life IV*, pages 130–139. MIT Press, Cambridge, Massachusetts, USA, 1994.

[18] J. O. Kephart, G. B. Sorkin, W. C. Arnold, D. M. Chess, G. J. Tesauro, and S. R. White. Biologically inspired defences against computer viruses. In *Proceedings of the 14th International Joint Conference on Artificial Intelligence*, pages 985–996. Morgan Kaufmann Publishers, Inc., 1995.

[19] J. Timmis and M. Neal. Investigating the evolution and stability of a resource limited artificial immune system. In *Workshop Program*, pages 40–41. AAAI Press, USA, 2000.

[20] J. Timmis, M. Neal, and J. Hunt. An artificial immune system for data analysis. *Biosystems*, 55(1):143–150, 2000.

[21] J. Timmis and M. J. Neal. A resource limited artificial immune system for data analysis. *Knowledge Based Systems Journal: Special Issue*, 14(3-4):121–130, 2001.

[22] F. J. Varela. A cognitive view of the immune system. *World Futures*, 42(1-2):31–40, 1994.

7.2   Clonal Selection Algorithm

Clonal Selection Algorithm, CSA, CLONALG.

7.2.1   Taxonomy

The Clonal Selection Algorithm (CLONALG) belongs to the field of Artificial Immune Systems. It is related to other Clonal Selection Algorithms such as the Artificial Immune Recognition System (Section 7.4), the B-Cell Algorithm (BCA), and the Multi-objective Immune System Algorithm (MISA). There are numerious extensions to CLONALG including tweaks such as the CLONALG1 and CLONALG2 approaches, a version for classification called CLONCLAS, and an adaptive version called Adaptive Clonal Selection (ACS).

7.2.2   Inspiration

The Clonal Selection algorithm is inspired by the Clonal Selection theory of acquired immunity. The clonal selection theory credited to Burnet was proposed to account for the behavior and capabilities of antibodies in the acquired immune system [2, 3]. Inspired itself by the principles of Darwinian natural selection theory of evolution, the theory proposes that antigens select-for lymphocytes (both B and T-cells). When a lymphocyte is selected and binds to an antigenic determinant, the cell proliferates making many thousands more copies of itself and differentiates into different cell types (plasma and memory cells). Plasma cells have a short lifespan and produce vast quantities of antibody molecules, whereas memory cells live for an extended period in the host anticipating future recognition of the same determinant. The important feature of the theory is that when a cell is selected and proliferates, it is subjected to small copying errors (changes to the genome called somatic hypermutation) that change the shape of the expressed receptors and subsequent determinant recognition capabilities of both the antibodies bound to the lymphocytes cells surface, and the antibodies that plasma cells produce.

7.2.3   Metaphor

The theory suggests that starting with an initial repertoire of general immune cells, the system is able to change itself (the compositions and densities of cells and their receptors) in response to experience with the environment. Through a blind process of selection and accumulated variation on the large scale of many billions of cells, the acquired immune system is capable of acquiring the necessary information to protect the host organism from the specific pathogenic dangers of the environment. It also suggests that the system must anticipate (guess) at the pathogen to which it will be exposed, and requires exposure to pathogen that may harm the host before it can acquire the necessary information to provide a defense.

7.2.4 Strategy

The information processing principles of the clonal selection theory describe a general learning strategy. This strategy involves a population of adaptive information units (each representing a problem-solution or component) subjected to a competitive processes for selection, which together with the resultant duplication and variation ultimately improves the adaptive fit of the information units to their environment.

7.2.5 Procedure

Algorithm 7.2.1 provides a pseudocode listing of the Clonal Selection Algorithm (CLONALG) for minimizing a cost function. The general CLONALG model involves the selection of antibodies (candidate solutions) based on affinity either by matching against an antigen pattern or via evaluation of a pattern by a cost function. Selected antibodies are subjected to cloning proportional to affinity, and the hypermutation of clones inversely-proportional to clone affinity. The resultant clonal-set competes with the existent antibody population for membership in the next generation. In addition, low-affinity population members are replaced by randomly generated antibodies. The pattern recognition variation of the algorithm includes the maintenance of a memory solution set which in its entirety represents a solution to the problem. A binary-encoding scheme is employed for the binary-pattern recognition and continuous function optimization examples, and an integer permutation scheme is employed for the Traveling Salesman Problem (TSP).

7.2.6 Heuristics

- The CLONALG was designed as a general machine learning approach and has been applied to pattern recognition, function optimization, and combinatorial optimization problem domains.

- Binary string representations are used and decoded to a representation suitable for a specific problem domain.

- The number of clones created for each selected member is calculated as a function of the repertoire size $N_c = round(\beta \cdot N)$, where β is the user parameter $Clone_{rate}$.

- A rank-based affinity-proportionate function is used to determine the number of clones created for selected members of the population for pattern recognition problem instances.

Algorithm 7.2.1: Pseudocode for CLONALG.

Input: $Population_{size}$, $Selection_{size}$, $Problem_{size}$,
          $RandomCells_{num}$, $Clone_{rate}$, $Mutation_{rate}$
Output: Population
1 Population ← CreateRandomCells($Population_{size}$, $Problem_{size}$);
2 **while** ¬StopCondition() **do**
3   **foreach** $p_i \in$ Population **do**
4   │ Affinity(p_i);
5   **end**
6     $Population_{select}$ ← Select(Population, $Selection_{size}$);
7     $Population_{clones}$ ← $\emptyset$;
8   **foreach** $p_i \in Population_{select}$ **do**
9   │ $Population_{clones}$ ← Clone(p_i, $Clone_{rate}$);
10   **end**
11   **foreach** $p_i \in Population_{clones}$ **do**
12   │ Hypermutate(p_i, $Mutation_{rate}$);
13   │ Affinity(p_i);
14   **end**
15   Population ← Select(Population, $Population_{clones}$,
          $Population_{size}$);
16     $Population_{rand}$ ← CreateRandomCells($RandomCells_{num}$);
17   Replace(Population, $Population_{rand}$);
18 **end**
19 **return** Population;

- The number of random antibodies inserted each iteration is typically very low (1-2).

- Point mutations (bit-flips) are used in the hypermutation operation.

- The function $exp(-\rho \cdot f)$ is used to determine the probability of individual component mutation for a given candidate solution, where f is the candidates affinity (normalized maximizing cost value), and ρ is the user parameter $Mutation_{rate}$.

7.2.7   Code Listing

Listing 7.1 provides an example of the Clonal Selection Algorithm (CLONALG) implemented in the Ruby Programming Language. The demonstration problem is an instance of a continuous function optimization that seeks $\min f(x)$ where $f = \sum_{i=1}^{n} x_i^2$, $-5.0 \leq x_i \leq 5.0$ and $n = 3$. The optimal solution for this basin function is $(v_0, \ldots, v_{n-1}) = 0.0$. The algorithm is implemented as described by de Castro and Von Zuben for function optimization [8].

```ruby
1   def objective_function(vector)
2     return vector.inject(0.0) {|sum, x| sum + (x**2.0)}
3   end
4
5   def decode(bitstring, search_space, bits_per_param)
6     vector = []
7     search_space.each_with_index do |bounds, i|
8       off, sum = i*bits_per_param, 0.0
9       param = bitstring[off...(off+bits_per_param)].reverse
10      param.size.times do |j|
11        sum += ((param[j].chr=='1') ? 1.0 : 0.0) * (2.0 ** j.to_f)
12      end
13      min, max = bounds
14      vector << min + ((max-min)/((2.0**bits_per_param.to_f)-1.0)) * sum
15    end
16    return vector
17  end
18
19  def evaluate(pop, search_space, bits_per_param)
20    pop.each do |p|
21      p[:vector] = decode(p[:bitstring], search_space, bits_per_param)
22      p[:cost] = objective_function(p[:vector])
23    end
24  end
25
26  def random_bitstring(num_bits)
27    return (0...num_bits).inject(""){|s,i| s<<((rand<0.5) ? "1" : "0")}
28  end
29
30  def point_mutation(bitstring, rate)
31    child = ""
32    bitstring.size.times do |i|
33      bit = bitstring[i].chr
34      child << ((rand()<rate) ? ((bit=='1') ? "0" : "1") : bit)
35    end
36    return child
37  end
38
39  def calculate_mutation_rate(antibody, mutate_factor=-2.5)
40    return Math.exp(mutate_factor * antibody[:affinity])
41  end
42
43  def num_clones(pop_size, clone_factor)
44    return (pop_size * clone_factor).floor
45  end
46
47  def calculate_affinity(pop)
48    pop.sort!{|x,y| x[:cost]<=>y[:cost]}
49    range = pop.last[:cost] - pop.first[:cost]
50    if range == 0.0
51      pop.each {|p| p[:affinity] = 1.0}
52    else
53      pop.each {|p| p[:affinity] = 1.0-(p[:cost]/range)}
54    end
55  end
```

```
56
57  def clone_and_hypermutate(pop, clone_factor)
58    clones = []
59    num_clones = num_clones(pop.size, clone_factor)
60    calculate_affinity(pop)
61    pop.each do |antibody|
62      m_rate = calculate_mutation_rate(antibody)
63      num_clones.times do
64        clone = {}
65        clone[:bitstring] = point_mutation(antibody[:bitstring], m_rate)
66        clones << clone
67      end
68    end
69    return clones
70  end
71
72  def random_insertion(search_space, pop, num_rand, bits_per_param)
73    return pop if num_rand == 0
74    rands = Array.new(num_rand) do |i|
75      {:bitstring=>random_bitstring(search_space.size*bits_per_param)}
76    end
77    evaluate(rands, search_space, bits_per_param)
78    return (pop+rands).sort{|x,y| x[:cost]<=>y[:cost]}.first(pop.size)
79  end
80
81  def search(search_space, max_gens, pop_size, clone_factor, num_rand,
                bits_per_param=16)
82    pop = Array.new(pop_size) do |i|
83      {:bitstring=>random_bitstring(search_space.size*bits_per_param)}
84    end
85    evaluate(pop, search_space, bits_per_param)
86    best = pop.min{|x,y| x[:cost]<=>y[:cost]}
87    max_gens.times do |gen|
88      clones = clone_and_hypermutate(pop, clone_factor)
89      evaluate(clones, search_space, bits_per_param)
90      pop = (pop+clones).sort{|x,y| x[:cost]<=>y[:cost]}.first(pop_size)
91      pop = random_insertion(search_space, pop, num_rand, bits_per_param)
92      best = (pop + [best]).min{|x,y| x[:cost]<=>y[:cost]}
93      puts " > gen #{gen+1}, f=#{best[:cost]}, s=#{best[:vector].inspect}"
94    end
95    return best
96  end
97
98  if __FILE__ == $0
99    # problem configuration
100   problem_size = 2
101   search_space = Array.new(problem_size) {|i| [-5, +5]}
102   # algorithm configuration
103   max_gens = 100
104   pop_size = 100
105   clone_factor = 0.1
106   num_rand = 2
107   # execute the algorithm
108   best = search(search_space, max_gens, pop_size, clone_factor, num_rand)
109   puts "done! Solution: f=#{best[:cost]}, s=#{best[:vector].inspect}"
110 end
```

Listing 7.1: CLONALG in Ruby

7.2.8   References

Primary Sources

Hidden at the back of a technical report on the applications of Artificial Immune Systems de Castro and Von Zuben [6] proposed the Clonal Selection Algorithm (CSA) as a computational realization of the clonal selection principle for pattern matching and optimization. The algorithm was later published [7], and investigated where it was renamed to CLONALG (CLONal selection ALGorithm) [8].

Learn More

Watkins et al. proposed to exploit the *inherent distributedness* of the CLONALG and proposed a parallel version of the pattern recognition version of the algorithm [10]. White and Garret also investigated the pattern recognition version of CLONALG and generalized the approach for the task of binary pattern classification renaming it to Clonal Classification (CLONCLAS) where their approach was compared to a number of simple Hamming distance based heuristics [11]. In an attempt to address concerns of algorithm efficiency, parameterization, and representation selection for continuous function optimization Garrett proposed an updated version of CLONALG called Adaptive Clonal Selection (ACS) [9]. In their book, de Castro and Timmis provide a detailed treatment of CLONALG including a description of the approach (starting page 79) and a step through of the algorithm (starting page 99) [5]. Cutello and Nicosia provide a study of the clonal selection principle and algorithms inspired by the theory [4]. Brownlee provides a review of Clonal Selection algorithms providing a taxonomy, algorithm reviews, and a broader bibliography [1].

7.2.9   Bibliography

[1] J. Brownlee. Clonal selection algorithms. Technical Report 070209A, Complex Intelligent Systems Laboratory (CIS), Centre for Information Technology Research (CITR), Faculty of Information and Communication Technologies (ICT), Swinburne University of Technology, Feb 2007.

[2] F. M. Burnet. A modification of jerne's theory of antibody production using the concept of clonal selection. *Australian Journal of Science*, 20:67–69, 1957.

[3] F. M. Burnet. *The clonal selection theory of acquired immunity.* Vanderbilt University Press, 1959.

[4] V. Cutello and G. Nicosia. *Recent Developments in Biologically Inspired Computing*, chapter Chapter VI. The Clonal Selection Principle for In Silico and In Vivo Computing, pages 104–146. Idea Group Publishing, 2005.

[5] L. N. de Castro and J. Timmis. *Artificial immune systems: a new computational intelligence approach.* Springer, 2002.

[6] L. N. de Castro and F. J. Von Zuben. Artificial immune systems - part i: Basic theory and applications. Technical Report TR DCA 01/99, Department of Computer Engineering and Industrial Automation, School of Electrical and Computer Engineering, State University of Campinas, Brazil, 1999.

[7] L. N. de Castro and F. J. Von Zuben. The clonal selection algorithm with engineering applications. In *Proceedings of the Genetic and Evolutionary Computation Conference (GECCO '00), Workshop on Artificial Immune Systems and Their Applications*, pages 36–37, 2000.

[8] L. N. de Castro and F. J. Von Zuben. Learning and optimization using the clonal selection principle. *IEEE Transactions on Evolutionary Computation*, 6:239–251, 2002.

[9] S. M. Garrett. Parameter-free, adaptive clonal selection. In *Congress on Evolutionary Computing (CEC 2004)*, pages 1052–1058, 2004.

[10] A. Watkins, X. Bi, and A. Phadke. Parallelizing an immune-inspired algorithm for efficient pattern recognition. In *Intelligent Engineering Systems through Artificial Neural Networks: Smart Engineering System Design: Neural Networks*, pages 225–230, 2003.

[11] J. White and S. M. Garrett. Improved pattern recognition with artificial clonal selection? In *Proceedings Artificial Immune Systems: Second International Conference, ICARIS 2003*, pages 181–193, 2003.

7.3 Negative Selection Algorithm

Negative Selection Algorithm, NSA.

7.3.1 Taxonomy

The Negative Selection Algorithm belongs to the field of Artificial Immune Systems. The algorithm is related to other Artificial Immune Systems such as the Clonal Selection Algorithm (Section 7.2), and the Immune Network Algorithm (Section 7.5).

7.3.2 Inspiration

The Negative Selection algorithm is inspired by the self-nonself discrimination behavior observed in the mammalian acquired immune system. The clonal selection theory of acquired immunity accounts for the adaptive behavior of the immune system including the ongoing selection and proliferation of cells that select-for potentially harmful (and typically foreign) material in the body. An interesting aspect of this process is that it is responsible for managing a population of immune cells that do not select-for the tissues of the body, specifically it does not create self-reactive immune cells known as auto-immunity. This problem is known as 'self-nonself discrimination' and it involves the preparation and on going maintenance of a repertoire of immune cells such that none are auto-immune. This is achieved by a negative selection process that selects-for and removes those cells that are self-reactive during cell creation and cell proliferation. This process has been observed in the preparation of T-lymphocytes, naïve versions of which are matured using both a positive and negative selection process in the thymus.

7.3.3 Metaphor

The self-nonself discrimination principle suggests that the anticipatory guesses made in clonal selection are filtered by regions of infeasibility (protein conformations that bind to self-tissues). Further, the self-nonself immunological paradigm proposes the modeling of the unknown domain (encountered pathogen) by modeling the complement of what is known. This is unintuitive as the natural inclination is to categorize unknown information by what is different from that which is known, rather than guessing at the unknown information and filtering those guesses by what is known.

7.3.4 Strategy

The information processing principles of the self-nonself discrimination process via negative selection are that of a anomaly and change detection systems that model the anticipation of variation from what is known. The principle is achieved by building a model of changes, anomalies, or unknown (non-normal or non-self) data by generating patterns that do not match an existing corpus of available (self or normal) patterns. The prepared non-normal model is then used to either monitor the existing normal data or streams of new data by seeking matches to the non-normal patterns.

7.3.5 Procedure

Algorithm 7.3.1 provides a pseudocode listing of the detector generation procedure for the Negative Selection Algorithm. Algorithm 7.3.2 provides a pseudocode listing of the detector application procedure for the Negative Selection Algorithm.

Algorithm 7.3.1: Pseudocode for detector generation.

Input: SelfData
Output: Repertoire
1 Repertoire ← ∅;
2 **while** ¬StopCondition() **do**
3   Detectors ← GenerateRandomDetectors();
4   **foreach** $Detector_i$ ∈ Repertoire **do**
5   **if** ¬Matches($Detector_i$, SelfData) **then**
6   Repertoire ← $Detector_i$;
7   **end**
8   **end**
9 **end**
10 **return** Repertoire;

Algorithm 7.3.2: Pseudocode for detector application.

Input: InputSamples, Repertoire
1 **for** $Input_i$ ∈ InputSamples **do**
2      $Input i_{class}$ ← "non-self";
3   **foreach** $Detector_i$ ∈ Repertoire **do**
4   **if** Matches($Input_i$, $Detector_i$) **then**
5              $Input i_{class}$ ← "self";
6   Break;
7   **end**
8   **end**
9 **end**

7.3.6 Heuristics

- The Negative Selection Algorithm was designed for change detection, novelty detection, intrusion detection and similar pattern recognition and two-class classification problem domains.

- Traditional negative selection algorithms used binary representations and binary matching rules such as Hamming distance, and r-contiguous bits.

- A data representation should be selected that is most suitable for a given problem domain, and a matching rule is in turn selected or tailored to the data representation.

- Detectors can be prepared with no prior knowledge of the problem domain other than the known (normal or self) dataset.

- The algorithm can be configured to balance between detector convergence (quality of the matches) and the space complexity (number of detectors).

- The lack of dependence between detectors means that detector preparation and application is inherently parallel and suited for a distributed and parallel implementation, respectively.

7.3.7 Code Listing

Listing 7.2 provides an example of the Negative Selection Algorithm implemented in the Ruby Programming Language. The demonstration problem is a two-class classification problem where samples are drawn from a two-dimensional domain, where $x_i \in [0, 1]$. Those samples in $1.0 > x_i > 0.5$ are classified as self and the rest of the space belongs to the non-self class. Samples are drawn from the self class and presented to the algorithm for the preparation of pattern detectors for classifying unobserved samples from the non-self class. The algorithm creates a set of detectors that do not match the self data, and are then applied to a set of randomly generated samples from the domain. The algorithm uses a real-valued representation. The Euclidean distance function is used during matching and a minimum distance value is specified as a user parameter for approximate matches between patterns. The algorithm includes the additional computationally expensive check for duplicates in the preparation of the self dataset and the detector set.

```ruby
def random_vector(minmax)
  return Array.new(minmax.length) do |i|
    minmax[i][0] + ((minmax[i][1] - minmax[i][0]) * rand())
  end
end
```

```ruby
 7   def euclidean_distance(c1, c2)
 8     sum = 0.0
 9     c1.each_index {|i| sum += (c1[i]-c2[i])**2.0}
10     return Math.sqrt(sum)
11   end
12
13   def contains?(vector, space)
14     vector.each_with_index do |v,i|
15       return false if v<space[i][0] or v>space[i][1]
16     end
17     return true
18   end
19
20   def matches?(vector, dataset, min_dist)
21     dataset.each do |pattern|
22       dist = euclidean_distance(vector, pattern[:vector])
23       return true if dist <= min_dist
24     end
25     return false
26   end
27
28   def generate_detectors(max_detectors, search_space, self_dataset, min_dist)
29     detectors = []
30     begin
31       detector = {:vector=>random_vector(search_space)}
32       if !matches?(detector[:vector], self_dataset, min_dist)
33         detectors << detector if !matches?(detector[:vector], detectors, 0.0)
34       end
35     end while detectors.size < max_detectors
36     return detectors
37   end
38
39   def generate_self_dataset(num_records, self_space, search_space)
40     self_dataset = []
41     begin
42       pattern = {}
43       pattern[:vector] = random_vector(search_space)
44       next if matches?(pattern[:vector], self_dataset, 0.0)
45       if contains?(pattern[:vector], self_space)
46         self_dataset << pattern
47       end
48     end while self_dataset.length < num_records
49     return self_dataset
50   end
51
52   def apply_detectors(detectors, bounds, self_dataset, min_dist, trials=50)
53     correct = 0
54     trials.times do |i|
55       input = {:vector=>random_vector(bounds)}
56       actual = matches?(input[:vector], detectors, min_dist) ? "N" : "S"
57       expected = matches?(input[:vector], self_dataset, min_dist) ? "S" : "N"
58       correct += 1 if actual==expected
59       puts "#{i+1}/#{trials}: predicted=#{actual}, expected=#{expected}"
60     end
61     puts "Done. Result: #{correct}/#{trials}"
62     return correct
```

```
63  end
64
65  def execute(bounds, self_space, max_detect, max_self, min_dist)
66    self_dataset = generate_self_dataset(max_self, self_space, bounds)
67    puts "Done: prepared #{self_dataset.size} self patterns."
68    detectors = generate_detectors(max_detect, bounds, self_dataset, min_dist)
69    puts "Done: prepared #{detectors.size} detectors."
70    apply_detectors(detectors, bounds, self_dataset, min_dist)
71    return detectors
72  end
73
74  if __FILE__ == $0
75    # problem configuration
76    problem_size = 2
77    search_space = Array.new(problem_size) {[0.0, 1.0]}
78    self_space = Array.new(problem_size) {[0.5, 1.0]}
79    max_self = 150
80    # algorithm configuration
81    max_detectors = 300
82    min_dist = 0.05
83    # execute the algorithm
84    execute(search_space, self_space, max_detectors, max_self, min_dist)
85  end
```

Listing 7.2: Negative Selection Algorithm in Ruby

7.3.8   References

Primary Sources

The seminal negative selection algorithm was proposed by Forrest, et al. [5] in which a population of detectors are prepared in the presence of known information, where those randomly generated detectors that match against known data are discarded. The population of pattern guesses in the unknown space then monitors the corpus of known information for changes. The algorithm was applied to the monitoring of files for changes (corruptions and infections by computer viruses), and later formalized as a change detection algorithm [2, 3].

Learn More

The Negative Selection algorithm has been applied to the monitoring of changes in the execution behavior of Unix processes [4, 8], and to monitor changes in remote connections of a network computer (intrusion detection) [6, 7]. The application of the algorithm has been predominantly to virus host intrusion detection and their abstracted problems of classification (two-class) and anomaly detection. Esponda provides some interesting work showing some compression and privacy benefits provided by maintaining a negative model (non-self) [1] Ji and Dasgupta provide a contemporary and detailed review of Negative Selection Algorithms covering topics such as data representations, matching rules, detector generation procedures, computational complexity, hybridization, and theoretical frameworks [9]. Recently, the validity of the application of negative selection algorithms in high-dimensional spaces has been questioned, specifically given the scalability of the approach in the face of the exponential increase in volume within the problem space [10].

7.3.9 Bibliography

[1] C. F. Esponda Darlington. *Negative Representations of Information.* PhD thesis, The University of New Mexico, 2005.

[2] P. D'haeseleer. An immunological approach to change detection: theoretical results. In *Proceedings of the 9th IEEE Computer Security Foundations Workshop*, pages 18–26. IEEE Computer Society, 1996.

[3] P. D'haeseleer, S. Forrest, and P. Helman. An immunological approach to change detection: algorithms, analysis and implications. In *Proceedings of the IEEE Symposium on Security and Privacy*, pages 110–119, 1996.

[4] S. Forrest, S. A. Hofmeyr, A. Somayaji, and T. A. Longstaff. A sense of self for unix processes. In *Proceedings of the 1996 IEEE Symposium on Security and Privacy*, pages 120–128. IEEE Computer Society, 1996.

[5] S. Forrest, A. S. Perelson, L. Allen, and R. Cherukuri. Self-nonself discrimination in a computer. In *Proceedings of the 1992 IEEE Symposium on Security and Privacy*, pages 202–212. IEEE Computer Society Press, 1994.

[6] S. Hofmeyr and S. Forrest. Immunity by design: An artificial immune system. In J. Daida, A. E. Eiben, M. H. Garzon, V. Honavar, M. Jakiela, and R. E. Smith, editors, *Proceedings of the Genetic and Evolutionary Computation Conference (GECCO)*, volume 2, pages 1289–1296. Morgan-Kaufmann, 1999.

[7] S. A. Hofmeyr. *An Immunological Model of Distributed Detection and its Application to Computer Security*. PhD thesis, Department of Computer Sciences, University of New Mexico, 1999.

[8] S. A. Hofmeyr, S. Forrest, and A. Somayaji. Intrusion detection using sequences of system calls. *Journal of Computer Security*, 6(3):151–180, 1998.

[9] Z. Ji and D. Dasgupta. Revisiting negative selection algorithms. *Evolutionary Computation*, 15(2):223–251, 2007.

[10] T. Stibor. *On the Appropriateness of Negative Selection for Anomaly Detection and Network Intrusion Detection.* PhD thesis, Darmstadt University of Technology, Germany, 2006.

7.4   Artificial Immune Recognition System

Artificial Immune Recognition System, AIRS.

7.4.1   Taxonomy

The Artificial Immune Recognition System belongs to the field of Artificial Immune Systems, and more broadly to the field of Computational Intelligence. It was extended early to the canonical version called the Artificial Immune Recognition System 2 (AIRS2) and provides the basis for extensions such as the Parallel Artificial Immune Recognition System [8]. It is related to other Artificial Immune System algorithms such as the Dendritic Cell Algorithm (Section 7.6), the Clonal Selection Algorithm (Section 7.2), and the Negative Selection Algorithm (Section 7.3).

7.4.2   Inspiration

The Artificial Immune Recognition System is inspired by the Clonal Selection theory of acquired immunity. The clonal selection theory credited to Burnet was proposed to account for the behavior and capabilities of antibodies in the acquired immune system [1, 2]. Inspired itself by the principles of Darwinian natural selection theory of evolution, the theory proposes that antigens select-for lymphocytes (both B and T-cells). When a lymphocyte is selected and binds to an antigenic determinant, the cell proliferates making many thousands more copies of itself and differentiates into different cell types (plasma and memory cells). Plasma cells have a short lifespan and produce vast quantities of antibody molecules, whereas memory cells live for an extended period in the host anticipating future recognition of the same determinant. The important feature of the theory is that when a cell is selected and proliferates, it is subjected to small copying errors (changes to the genome called somatic hypermutation) that change the shape of the expressed receptors. It also affects the subsequent determinant recognition capabilities of both the antibodies bound to the lymphocytes cells surface, and the antibodies that plasma cells produce.

7.4.3   Metaphor

The theory suggests that starting with an initial repertoire of general immune cells, the system is able to change itself (the compositions and densities of cells and their receptors) in response to experience with the environment. Through a blind process of selection and accumulated variation on the large scale of many billions of cells, the acquired immune system is capable of acquiring the necessary information to protect the host organism from the specific pathogenic dangers of the environment. It also suggests that the system must anticipate (guess) at the pathogen to which it will be exposed, and requires exposure to pathogen that may harm the host before it can acquire the necessary information to provide a defense.

7.4.4 Strategy

The information processing objective of the technique is to prepare a set of real-valued vectors to classify patterns. The Artificial Immune Recognition System maintains a pool of memory cells that are prepared by exposing the system to a single iteration of the training data. Candidate memory cells are prepared when the memory cells are insufficiently stimulated for a given input pattern. A process of cloning and mutation of cells occurs for the most stimulated memory cell. The clones compete with each other for entry into the memory pool based on stimulation and on the amount of resources each cell is using. This concept of resources comes from prior work on Artificial Immune Networks, where a single cell (an Artificial Recognition Ball or ARB) represents a set of similar cells. Here, a cell's resources are a function of its stimulation to a given input pattern and the number of clones it may create.

7.4.5 Procedure

Algorithm 8.6.1 provides a high-level pseudocode for preparing memory cell vectors using the Artificial Immune Recognition System, specifically the canonical AIRS2. An affinity (distance) measure between input patterns must be defined. For real-valued vectors, this is commonly the Euclidean distance:

$$dist(x, c) = \sum_{i=1}^{n}(x_i - c_i)^2 \tag{7.1}$$

where n is the number of attributes, x is the input vector and c is a given cell vector. The variation of cells during cloning (somatic hypermutation) occurs inversely proportional to the stimulation of a given cell to an input pattern.

7.4.6 Heuristics

- The AIRS was designed as a supervised algorithm for classification problem domains.

- The AIRS is non-parametric, meaning that it does not rely on assumptions about that structure of the function that is is approximating.

- Real-values in input vectors should be normalized such that $x \in [0, 1)$.

Algorithm 7.4.1: Pseudocode for AIRS2.

Input: InputPatterns, $clone_{rate}$, $mutate_{rate}$, $stim_{thresh}$,
       $resources_{max}$, $affinity_{thresh}$
Output: $Cells_{memory}$

1 $Cells_{memory} \leftarrow$ InitializeMemoryPool(InputPatterns);
2 **foreach** $InputPattern_i \in$ InputPatterns **do**
3   Stimulate($Cells_{memory}$, InputPatterns);
4     $Cell_{best} \leftarrow$ GetMostStimulated($InputPattern_i$, $Cells_{memory}$);
5   **if** $Cell_{best}^{class} \neq InputPattern_i^{class}$ **then**
6        $Cells_{memory} \leftarrow$ CreateNewMemoryCell($InputPattern_i$);
7   **else**
8        $Clones_{num} \leftarrow Cell_{best}^{stim} \times clone_{rate} \times mutate_{rate}$;
9        $Cells_{clones} \leftarrow Cell_{best}$;
10   **for** i to $Clones_{num}$ **do**
11         $Cells_{clones} \leftarrow$ CloneAndMutate($Cell_{best}$);
12   **end**
13   **while** AverageStimulation($Cells_{clones}$) $\leq stim_{thresh}$ **do**
14   **foreach** $Cell_i \in Cells_{clones}$ **do**
15           $Cells_{clones} \leftarrow$ CloneAndMutate($Cell_i$);
16   **end**
17   Stimulate($Cells_{clones}$, InputPatterns);
18   ReducePoolToMaximumResources($Cells_{clones}$,
        $resources_{max}$);
19   **end**
20       $Cell_c \leftarrow$ GetMostStimulated($InputPattern_i$, $Cells_{clones}$);
21   **if** $Cell_c^{stim} > Cell_{best}^{stim}$ **then**
22         $Cells_{memory} \leftarrow Cell_c$;
23   **if** Affinity($Cell_c$, $Cell_{best}$) $\leq affinity_{thresh}$ **then**
24   DeleteCell($Cell_{best}$, $Cells_{memory}$);
25   **end**
26   **end**
27   **end**
28 **end**
29 **return** $Cells_{memory}$;

- Euclidean distance is commonly used to measure the distance between real-valued vectors (affinity calculation), although other distance measures may be used (such as dot product), and data specific distance measures may be required for non-scalar attributes.

- Cells may be initialized with small random values or more commonly with values from instances in the training set.

- A cell's affinity is typically minimizing, where as a cells stimulation is maximizing and typically $\in [0, 1]$.

7.4.7 Code Listing

Listing 7.3 provides an example of the Artificial Immune Recognition System implemented in the Ruby Programming Language. The problem is a contrived classification problem in a 2-dimensional domain $x \in [0, 1], y \in [0, 1]$ with two classes: 'A' ($x \in [0, 0.4999999], y \in [0, 0.4999999]$) and 'B' ($x \in [0.5, 1], y \in [0.5, 1]$).

The algorithm is an implementation of the AIRS2 algorithm [7]. An initial pool of memory cells is created, one cell for each class. Euclidean distance divided by the maximum possible distance in the domain is taken as the affinity and stimulation is taken as $1.0 - affinity$. The meta-dynamics for memory cells (competition for input patterns) is not performed and may be added into the implementation as an extension.

```ruby
def random_vector(minmax)
  return Array.new(minmax.size) do |i|
    minmax[i][0] + ((minmax[i][1] - minmax[i][0]) * rand())
  end
end

def generate_random_pattern(domain)
  class_label = domain.keys[rand(domain.keys.size)]
  pattern = {:label=>class_label}
  pattern[:vector] = random_vector(domain[class_label])
  return pattern
end

def create_cell(vector, class_label)
  return {:label=>class_label, :vector=>vector}
end

def initialize_cells(domain)
  mem_cells = []
  domain.keys.each do |key|
    mem_cells << create_cell(random_vector([[0,1],[0,1]]), key)
  end
  return mem_cells
end

def distance(c1, c2)
  sum = 0.0
  c1.each_index {|i| sum += (c1[i]-c2[i])**2.0}
  return Math.sqrt(sum)
end

def stimulate(cells, pattern)
  max_dist = distance([0.0,0.0], [1.0,1.0])
  cells.each do |cell|
    cell[:affinity] = distance(cell[:vector], pattern[:vector]) / max_dist
    cell[:stimulation] = 1.0 - cell[:affinity]
  end
```

```ruby
38    end
39
40    def get_most_stimulated_cell(mem_cells, pattern)
41      stimulate(mem_cells, pattern)
42      return mem_cells.sort{|x,y| y[:stimulation] <=> x[:stimulation]}.first
43    end
44
45    def mutate_cell(cell, best_match)
46      range = 1.0 - best_match[:stimulation]
47      cell[:vector].each_with_index do |v,i|
48        min = [(v-(range/2.0)), 0.0].max
49        max = [(v+(range/2.0)), 1.0].min
50        cell[:vector][i] = min + (rand() * (max-min))
51      end
52      return cell
53    end
54
55    def create_arb_pool(pattern, best_match, clone_rate, mutate_rate)
56      pool = []
57      pool << create_cell(best_match[:vector], best_match[:label])
58      num_clones = (best_match[:stimulation] * clone_rate * mutate_rate).round
59      num_clones.times do
60        cell = create_cell(best_match[:vector], best_match[:label])
61        pool << mutate_cell(cell, best_match)
62      end
63      return pool
64    end
65
66    def competition_for_resournces(pool, clone_rate, max_res)
67      pool.each {|cell| cell[:resources] = cell[:stimulation] * clone_rate}
68      pool.sort!{|x,y| x[:resources] <=> y[:resources]}
69      total_resources = pool.inject(0.0){|sum,cell| sum + cell[:resources]}
70      while total_resources > max_res
71        cell = pool.delete_at(pool.size-1)
72        total_resources -= cell[:resources]
73      end
74    end
75
76    def refine_arb_pool(pool, pattern, stim_thresh, clone_rate, max_res)
77      mean_stim, candidate = 0.0, nil
78      begin
79        stimulate(pool, pattern)
80        candidate = pool.sort{|x,y| y[:stimulation] <=> x[:stimulation]}.first
81        mean_stim = pool.inject(0.0){|s,c| s + c[:stimulation]} / pool.size
82        if mean_stim < stim_thresh
83          candidate = competition_for_resournces(pool, clone_rate, max_res)
84          pool.size.times do |i|
85            cell = create_cell(pool[i][:vector], pool[i][:label])
86            mutate_cell(cell, pool[i])
87            pool << cell
88          end
89        end
90      end until mean_stim >= stim_thresh
91      return candidate
92    end
93
```

```
94   def add_candidate_to_memory_pool(candidate, best_match, mem_cells)
95     if candidate[:stimulation] > best_match[:stimulation]
96       mem_cells << candidate
97     end
98   end
99
100  def classify_pattern(mem_cells, pattern)
101    stimulate(mem_cells, pattern)
102    return mem_cells.sort{|x,y| y[:stimulation] <=> x[:stimulation]}.first
103  end
104
105  def train_system(mem_cells, domain, num_patterns, clone_rate, mutate_rate,
          stim_thresh, max_res)
106    num_patterns.times do |i|
107      pattern = generate_random_pattern(domain)
108      best_match = get_most_stimulated_cell(mem_cells, pattern)
109      if best_match[:label] != pattern[:label]
110        mem_cells << create_cell(pattern[:vector], pattern[:label])
111      elsif best_match[:stimulation] < 1.0
112        pool = create_arb_pool(pattern, best_match, clone_rate, mutate_rate)
113        cand = refine_arb_pool(pool,pattern, stim_thresh, clone_rate, max_res)
114        add_candidate_to_memory_pool(cand, best_match, mem_cells)
115      end
116      puts " > iter=#{i+1}, mem_cells=#{mem_cells.size}"
117    end
118  end
119
120  def test_system(mem_cells, domain, num_trials=50)
121    correct = 0
122    num_trials.times do
123      pattern = generate_random_pattern(domain)
124      best = classify_pattern(mem_cells, pattern)
125      correct += 1 if best[:label] == pattern[:label]
126    end
127    puts "Finished test with a score of #{correct}/#{num_trials}"
128    return correct
129  end
130
131  def execute(domain, num_patterns, clone_rate, mutate_rate, stim_thresh,
          max_res)
132    mem_cells = initialize_cells(domain)
133    train_system(mem_cells, domain, num_patterns, clone_rate, mutate_rate,
          stim_thresh, max_res)
134    test_system(mem_cells, domain)
135    return mem_cells
136  end
137
138  if __FILE__ == $0
139    # problem configuration
140    domain = {"A"=>[[0,0.4999999],[0,0.4999999]],"B"=>[[0.5,1],[0.5,1]]}
141    num_patterns = 50
142    # algorithm configuration
143    clone_rate = 10
144    mutate_rate = 2.0
145    stim_thresh = 0.9
146    max_res = 150
```

```
147   # execute the algorithm
148   execute(domain, num_patterns, clone_rate, mutate_rate, stim_thresh,
          max_res)
149   end
```

Listing 7.3: AIRS in Ruby

7.4.8   References

Primary Sources

The Artificial Immune Recognition System was proposed in the Masters work by Watkins [10], and later published [11]. Early works included the application of the AIRS by Watkins and Boggess to a suite of benchmark classification problems [6], and a similar study by Goodman and Boggess comparing to a conceptually similar approach called Learning Vector Quantization [3].

Learn More

Marwah and Boggess investigated the algorithm seeking issues that affect the algorithms performance [5]. They compared various variations of the algorithm with modified resource allocation schemes, tie-handling within the ARB pool, and ARB pool organization. Watkins and Timmis proposed a new version of the algorithm called AIRS2 which became the replacement for AIRS1 [7]. The updates reduced the complexity of the approach while maintaining the accuracy of the results. An investigation by Goodman et al. into the so called '*source of power*' in AIRS indicated that perhaps the memory cell maintenance procedures played an important role [4]. Watkins et al. provide a detailed review of the technique and its application [9].

7.4.9   Bibliography

[1] F. M. Burnet. A modification of jerne's theory of antibody production using the concept of clonal selection. *Australian Journal of Science*, 20:67–69, 1957.

[2] F. M. Burnet. *The clonal selection theory of acquired immunity*. Vanderbilt University Press, 1959.

[3] D. E. Goodman Jr., L. Boggess, and A. Watkins. Artificial immune system classification of multiple-class problems. In A. Buczak, J. Ghosh, M. Embrechts, O. Ersoy, and S Kercel, editors, *Fuzzy Logic, Evolutionary Programming, Complex Systems and Artificial Life*, volume 12, pages 179–184, New York, 2002. ASME Press.

[4] D. E. Goodman Jr., L. Boggess, and A. Watkins. An investigation into the source of power for AIRS, an artificial immune classification systems. In *Proceedings of the International Joint Conference on Neural Networks (IJCNN'03)*, pages 1678–1683, Portland, Oregon, USA, 2003.

[5] G. Marwah and L. Boggess. Artificial immune systems for classification: Some issues. In *First International Conference on Artificial Immune Systems*, pages 149–153, 2002.

[6] A. Watkins and L. Boggess. A new classifier based on resource limited artificial immune systems. In *Part of the 2002 IEEE World Congress on Computational Intelligence*, pages 1546–1551. IEEE, May 2002.

[7] A. Watkins and J. Timmis. Artificial immune recognition system (AIRS): Revisions and refinements. In P.J. Bentley, editor, *1st International Conference on Artificial Immune Systems (ICARIS2002)*, pages 173–181. University of Kent at Canterbury Printing Unit, UK, 2002.

[8] A. Watkins and J. Timmis. Exploiting parallelism inherent in AIRS, an artificial immune classifier. In V. Cutello, P. Bentley, and J. Timmis, editors, *Lecture Notes in Computer Science (LNCS)*, volume 3239, pages 427–438. Springer-Verlag GmbH, 2004.

[9] A. Watkins, J. Timmis, and L. Boggess. Artificial immune recognition system (AIRS): An immune-inspired supervised learning algorithms. *Genetic Programming and Evolvable Machines*, 5(3):291–317, September 2004.

[10] A. B. Watkins. AIRS: A resource limited artificial immune classifiers. Master's thesis, Mississippi State University, USA, 2001.

[11] A. B. Watkins and L. C. Boggess. A resource limited artificial immune classifier. In *Part of the 2002 IEEE World Congress on Computational Intelligence held in Honolulu*, pages 926–931, USA, May 2002. IEEE Computer Society.

7.5 Immune Network Algorithm

Artificial Immune Network, aiNet, Optimization Artificial Immune Network, opt-aiNet.

7.5.1 Taxonomy

The Artificial Immune Network algorithm (aiNet) is a Immune Network Algorithm from the field of Artificial Immune Systems. It is related to other Artificial Immune System algorithms such as the Clonal Selection Algorithm (Section 7.2), the Negative Selection Algorithm (Section 7.3), and the Dendritic Cell Algorithm (Section 7.6). The Artificial Immune Network algorithm includes the base version and the extension for optimization problems called the Optimization Artificial Immune Network algorithm (opt-aiNet).

7.5.2 Inspiration

The Artificial Immune Network algorithm is inspired by the Immune Network theory of the acquired immune system. The clonal selection theory of acquired immunity accounts for the adaptive behavior of the immune system including the ongoing selection and proliferation of cells that select-for potentially harmful (and typically foreign) material in the body. A concern of the clonal selection theory is that it presumes that the repertoire of reactive cells remains idle when there are no pathogen to which to respond. Jerne proposed an Immune Network Theory (Idiotypic Networks) where immune cells are not at rest in the absence of pathogen, instead antibody and immune cells recognize and respond to each other [6–8].

The Immune Network theory proposes that antibody (both free floating and surface bound) possess idiotopes (surface features) to which the receptors of other antibody can bind. As a result of receptor interactions, the repertoire becomes dynamic, where receptors continually both inhibit and excite each other in complex regulatory networks (chains of receptors). The theory suggests that the clonal selection process may be triggered by the idiotopes of other immune cells and molecules in addition to the surface characteristics of pathogen, and that the maturation process applies both to the receptors themselves and the idiotopes which they expose.

7.5.3 Metaphor

The immune network theory has interesting resource maintenance and signaling information processing properties. The classical clonal selection and negative selection paradigms integrate the accumulative and filtered learning of the acquired immune system, whereas the immune network theory proposes an additional order of complexity between the cells and molecules under selection. In addition to cells that interact directly with pathogen, there are cells that interact with those reactive cells and with pathogen indirectly, in successive layers such that networks of activity for higher-order structures such as internal images of pathogen (promotion), and regulatory networks (so-called anti-idiotopes and anti-anti-idiotopes).

7.5.4 Strategy

The objective of the immune network process is to prepare a repertoire of discrete pattern detectors for a given problem domain, where better performing cells suppress low-affinity (similar) cells in the network. This principle is achieved through an interactive process of exposing the population to external information to which it responds with both a clonal selection response and internal meta-dynamics of intra-population responses that stabilizes the responses of the population to the external stimuli.

7.5.5 Procedure

Algorithm 7.5.1 provides a pseudocode listing of the Optimization Artificial Immune Network algorithm (opt-aiNet) for minimizing a cost function.

7.5.6 Heuristics

- aiNet is designed for unsupervised clustering, where as the opt-aiNet extension was designed for pattern recognition and optimization, specifically multi-modal function optimization.

- The amount of mutation of clones is proportionate to the affinity of the parent cell with the cost function (better fitness, lower mutation).

- The addition of random cells each iteration adds a random-restart like capability to the algorithms.

- Suppression based on cell similarity provides a mechanism for reducing redundancy.

- The population size is dynamic, and if it continues to grow it may be an indication of a problem with many local optima or that the affinity threshold may needs to be increased.

- Affinity proportionate mutation is performed using $c' = c + \alpha \times N(1,0)$ where $\alpha = \frac{1}{\beta} \times exp(-f)$, N is a Guassian random number, and f is the fitness of the parent cell, β controls the decay of the function and can be set to 100.

- The affinity threshold is problem and representation specific, for example a $AffinityThreshold$ may be set to an arbitrary value such

---

Algorithm 7.5.1: Pseudocode for opt-aiNet.

Input: $Population_{size}$, ProblemSize, N_{clones}, N_{random},
AffinityThreshold

Output: S_{best}

1 Population ← InitializePopulation($Population_{size}$, ProblemSize);
2 **while** ¬StopCondition() **do**
3   EvaluatePopulation(Population);
4   S_{best} ← GetBestSolution(Population);
5   Progeny ← ∅;
6     $Cost_{avg}$ ← CalculateAveragePopulationCost(Population);
7   **while** CalculateAveragePopulationCost(Population) >
    $Cost_{avg}$ **do**
8   **foreach** $Cell_i$ ∈ Population **do**
9   Clones ← CreateClones($Cell_i$, N_{clones});
10   **foreach** $Clone_i$ ∈ Clones **do**
11                 $Clone_i$ ←
                MutateRelativeToFitnessOfParent($Clone_i$, $Cell_i$);
12   **end**
13   EvaluatePopulation(Clones);
14   Progeny ← GetBestSolution(Clones);
15   **end**
16   **end**
17   SupressLowAffinityCells(Progeny, AffinityThreshold);
18   Progeny ← CreateRandomCells(N_{random});
19   Population ← Progeny;
20 **end**
21 **return** S_{best};

---

as 0.1 on a continuous function domain, or calculated as a percentage of the size of the problem space.

- The number of random cells inserted may be 40% of the population size.

- The number of clones created for a cell may be small, such as 10.

7.5.7   Code Listing

Listing 7.4 provides an example of the Optimization Artificial Immune Network (opt-aiNet) implemented in the Ruby Programming Language. The demonstration problem is an instance of a continuous function optimization that seeks $\min f(x)$ where $f = \sum_{i=1}^{n} x_i^2$, $-5.0 \leq x_i \leq 5.0$ and $n = 2$. The optimal solution for this basin function is $(v_0, \ldots, v_{n-1}) = 0.0$. The algorithm is an implementation based on the specification by de Castro and Von Zuben [1].

```ruby
def objective_function(vector)
  return vector.inject(0.0) {|sum, x| sum + (x**2.0)}
end

def random_vector(minmax)
  return Array.new(minmax.size) do |i|
    minmax[i][0] + ((minmax[i][1] - minmax[i][0]) * rand())
  end
end

def random_gaussian(mean=0.0, stdev=1.0)
  u1 = u2 = w = 0
  begin
    u1 = 2 * rand() - 1
    u2 = 2 * rand() - 1
    w = u1 * u1 + u2 * u2
  end while w >= 1
  w = Math.sqrt((-2.0 * Math.log(w)) / w)
  return mean + (u2 * w) * stdev
end

def clone(parent)
  v = Array.new(parent[:vector].size) {|i| parent[:vector][i]}
  return {:vector=>v}
end

def mutation_rate(beta, normalized_cost)
  return (1.0/beta) * Math.exp(-normalized_cost)
end

def mutate(beta, child, normalized_cost)
  child[:vector].each_with_index do |v, i|
    alpha = mutation_rate(beta, normalized_cost)
    child[:vector][i] = v + alpha * random_gaussian()
  end
end

def clone_cell(beta, num_clones, parent)
  clones = Array.new(num_clones) {clone(parent)}
  clones.each {|clone| mutate(beta, clone, parent[:norm_cost])}
  clones.each{|c| c[:cost] = objective_function(c[:vector])}
  clones.sort!{|x,y| x[:cost] <=> y[:cost]}
  return clones.first
end

def calculate_normalized_cost(pop)
  pop.sort!{|x,y| x[:cost]<=>y[:cost]}
  range = pop.last[:cost] - pop.first[:cost]
  if range == 0.0
    pop.each {|p| p[:norm_cost] = 1.0}
  else
    pop.each {|p| p[:norm_cost] = 1.0-(p[:cost]/range)}
  end
```

```
54    end
55
56    def average_cost(pop)
57      sum = pop.inject(0.0){|sum,x| sum + x[:cost]}
58      return sum / pop.size.to_f
59    end
60
61    def distance(c1, c2)
62      sum = 0.0
63      c1.each_index {|i| sum += (c1[i]-c2[i])**2.0}
64      return Math.sqrt(sum)
65    end
66
67    def get_neighborhood(cell, pop, aff_thresh)
68      neighbors = []
69      pop.each do |p|
70        neighbors << p if distance(p[:vector], cell[:vector]) < aff_thresh
71      end
72      return neighbors
73    end
74
75    def affinity_supress(population, aff_thresh)
76      pop = []
77      population.each do |cell|
78        neighbors = get_neighborhood(cell, population, aff_thresh)
79        neighbors.sort!{|x,y| x[:cost] <=> y[:cost]}
80        pop << cell if neighbors.empty? or cell.equal?(neighbors.first)
81      end
82      return pop
83    end
84
85    def search(search_space, max_gens, pop_size, num_clones, beta, num_rand,
            aff_thresh)
86      pop = Array.new(pop_size) {|i| {:vector=>random_vector(search_space)} }
87      pop.each{|c| c[:cost] = objective_function(c[:vector])}
88      best = nil
89      max_gens.times do |gen|
90        pop.each{|c| c[:cost] = objective_function(c[:vector])}
91        calculate_normalized_cost(pop)
92        pop.sort!{|x,y| x[:cost] <=> y[:cost]}
93        best = pop.first if best.nil? or pop.first[:cost] < best[:cost]
94        avgCost, progeny = average_cost(pop), nil
95        begin
96          progeny=Array.new(pop.size){|i| clone_cell(beta, num_clones, pop[i])}
97        end until average_cost(progeny) < avgCost
98        pop = affinity_supress(progeny, aff_thresh)
99        num_rand.times {pop << {:vector=>random_vector(search_space)}}
100       puts " > gen #{gen+1}, popSize=#{pop.size}, fitness=#{best[:cost]}"
101     end
102     return best
103   end
104
105   if __FILE__ == $0
106     # problem configuration
107     problem_size = 2
108     search_space = Array.new(problem_size) {|i| [-5, +5]}
```

```
109   # algorithm configuration
110   max_gens = 150
111   pop_size = 20
112   num_clones = 10
113   beta = 100
114   num_rand = 2
115   aff_thresh = (search_space[0][1]-search_space[0][0])*0.05
116   # execute the algorithm
117   best = search(search_space, max_gens, pop_size, num_clones, beta,
           num_rand, aff_thresh)
118   puts "done! Solution: f=#{best[:cost]}, s=#{best[:vector].inspect}"
119   end
```

Listing 7.4: Optimization Artificial Immune Network in Ruby

7.5.8 References

Primary Sources

Early works, such as Farmer et al. [5] suggested at the exploitation of the information processing properties of network theory for machine learning. A seminal network theory based algorithm was proposed by Timmis et al. for clustering problems called the Artificial Immune Network (AIN) [11] that was later extended and renamed the Resource Limited Artificial Immune System [12] and Artificial Immune Network (AINE) [9]. The Artificial Immune Network (aiNet) algorithm was proposed by de Castro and Von Zuben that extended the principles of the Artificial Immune Network (AIN) and the Clonal Selection Algorithm (CLONALG) and was applied to clustering [2]. The aiNet algorithm was further extended to optimization domains and renamed opt-aiNet [1].

Learn More

The authors de Castro and Von Zuben provide a detailed presentation of the aiNet algorithm as a book chapter that includes immunological theory, a description of the algorithm, and demonstration application to clustering problem instances [3]. Timmis and Edmonds provide a careful examination of the opt-aiNet algorithm and propose some modifications and augmentations to improve its applicability and performance for multimodal function optimization problem domains [10]. The authors de Franca, Von Zuben, and de Castro proposed an extension to opt-aiNet that provided a number of enhancements and adapted its capability for for dynamic function optimization problems called dopt-aiNet [4].

7.5.9 Bibliography

[1] L. N. de Castro and J. Timmis. An artificial immune network for multimodal function optimization. In *Proceedings of the 2002 Congress on*

Evolutionary Computation (CEC'02), pages 699–704. IEEE Computer Society, 2002.

[2] L. N. de Castro and F. J. Von Zuben. An evolutionary immune network for data clustering. In Proceedings Sixth Brazilian Symposium on Neural Networks, pages 84–89. IEEE Computer Society, 2000.

[3] L. N. de Castro and F. J. Von Zuben. Data Mining: A Heuristic Approach, chapter Chapter XII: aiNet: An Artificial Immune Network for Data Analysis, pages 231–259. Idea Group Publishing, 2001.

[4] F. O. de França, L. N. de Castro, and F. J. Von Zuben. An artificial immune network for multimodal function optimization on dynamic environments. In Genetic And Evolutionary Computation Conference, pages 289–296. ACM Press, 2005.

[5] J. D. Farmer, N. H. Packard, and Alan S. Perelson. The immune system, adaptation, and machine learning. Physica D, 22:187–204, 1986.

[6] N. K. Jerne. Clonal selection in a lymphocyte network. In Cellular Selection and Regulation in the Immune Response, Society of General Physiologists Series, pages 39–48. Raven Press, 1974.

[7] N. K. Jerne. Towards a network theory of the immune system. Annales d'immunologie (Annals of Immunology), Institut Pasteur (Paris, France), Societe Francaise d'Immunologie, 125(C):373–389, 1974.

[8] N. K. Jerne. Idiotypic networks and other preconceived ideas. Immunological Reviews, 79:5–24, 1984.

[9] T. Knight and J. Timmis. AINE: An immunological approach to data mining. In T. Lin and Xindon Wu, editors, First IEEE International Conference on Data Mining (ICDM'01), pages 297–304. IEEE Computer Society, 2001.

[10] J. Timmis and C. Edmonds. A comment on opt–AINet: An immune network algorithm for optimisation. In Lecture Notes in Computer Science, volume 1, pages 308–317. Springer, 2004.

[11] J. Timmis, M. Neal, and J. Hunt. An artificial immune system for data analysis. Biosystems, 55(1):143–150, 2000.

[12] J. Timmis and M. J. Neal. A resource limited artificial immune system for data analysis. Knowledge Based Systems Journal: Special Issue, 14(3-4):121–130, 2001.

7.6 Dendritic Cell Algorithm

Dendritic Cell Algorithm, DCA.

7.6.1 Taxonomy

The Dendritic Cell Algorithm belongs to the field of Artificial Immune Systems, and more broadly to the field of Computational Intelligence. The Dendritic Cell Algorithm is the basis for extensions such as the Deterministic Dendritic Cell Algorithm (dDCA) [2]. It is generally related to other Artificial Immune System algorithms such as the Clonal Selection Algorithm (Section 7.2), and the Immune Network Algorithm (Section 7.5).

7.6.2 Inspiration

The Dendritic Cell Algorithm is inspired by the Danger Theory of the mammalian immune system, and specifically the role and function of dendritic cells. The Danger Theory was proposed by Matzinger and suggests that the roles of the acquired immune system is to respond to signals of danger, rather than discriminating self from non-self [7, 8]. The theory suggests that antigen presenting cells (such as helper T-cells) activate an alarm signal providing the necessarily co-stimulation of antigen-specific cells to respond. Dendritic cells are a type of cell from the innate immune system that respond to some specific forms of danger signals. There are three main types of dendritic cells: 'immature' that collect parts of the antigen and the signals, 'semi-mature' that are immature cells that internally decide that the local signals represent safe and present the antigen to T-cells resulting in tolerance, and 'mature' cells that internally decide that the local signals represent danger and present the antigen to T-cells resulting in a reactive response.

7.6.3 Strategy

The information processing objective of the algorithm is to prepare a set of mature dendritic cells (prototypes) that provide context specific information about how to classify normal and anomalous input patterns. This is achieved as a system of three asynchronous processes of 1) migrating sufficiently stimulated immature cells, 2) promoting migrated cells to semi-mature (safe) or mature (danger) status depending on their accumulated response, and 3) labeling observed patterns as safe or dangerous based on the composition of the sub-population of cells that respond to each pattern.

7.6.4   Procedure

Algorithm 7.6.1 provides pseudocode for training a pool of cells in the Dendritic Cell Algorithm, specifically the Deterministic Dendritic Cell Algorithm. Mature migrated cells associate their collected input patterns with anomalies, whereas semi-mature migrated cells associate their collected input patterns as normal. The resulting migrated cells can then be used to classify input patterns as normal or anomalous. This can be done through sampling the cells and using a voting mechanism, or more elaborate methods such as a 'mature context antigen value' (MCAV) that uses $\frac{M}{Ag}$ (where M is the number of mature cells with the antigen and Ag is the sum of the exposures to the antigen by those mature cells), which gives a probability of a pattern being an anomaly.

Algorithm 7.6.1: Pseudocode for the Dendritic Cell Algorithm.

Input: InputPatterns, $iterations_{max}$, $cells_{num}$,
$\quad\quad MigrationThresh_{bounds}$
Output: MigratedCells

1 ImmatureCells $\leftarrow$ InitializeCells($cells_{num}$,
$MigrationThresh_{bounds}$);
2 MigratedCells $\leftarrow \emptyset$;
3 **for** $i = 1$ **to** $iterations_{max}$ **do**
4 $\quad$ $P_i \leftarrow$ SelectInputPattern(InputPatterns);
5 $\quad$ $k_i \leftarrow (Pi_{danger} - 2 \times Pi_{safe})$;
6 $\quad$ $cms_i \leftarrow (Pi_{danger} + Pi_{safe})$;
7 $\quad$ **foreach** $Cell_i \in$ ImmatureCells **do**
8 $\quad\quad$ UpdateCellOutputSignals($Cell_i$, k_i, cms_i);
9 $\quad\quad$ StoreAntigen($Cell_i$, $Pi_{antigen}$);
10 $\quad\quad$ **if** $Cell_{lifespan} \leq 0$ **then**
11 $\quad\quad\quad$ ReInitializeCell($Cell_i$);
12 $\quad\quad$ **else if** $Cell_{csm} \geq Cell_{thresh}$ **then**
13 $\quad\quad\quad$ RemoveCell(ImmatureCells, $Cell_i$);
14 $\quad\quad\quad$ ImmatureCells $\leftarrow$
$\quad\quad\quad$ CreateNewCell($MigrationThresh_{bounds}$);
15 $\quad\quad\quad$ **if** $Cell_k < 0$ **then**
16 $\quad\quad\quad\quad$ $Cell_{type} \leftarrow$ Mature;
17 $\quad\quad\quad$ **else**
18 $\quad\quad\quad\quad$ $Cell_{type} \leftarrow$ Semimature;
19 $\quad\quad\quad$ **end**
20 $\quad\quad\quad$ MigratedCells $\leftarrow Cell_i$;
21 $\quad\quad$ **end**
22 $\quad$ **end**
23 **end**
24 **return** MigratedCells;

7.6.5   Heuristics

- The Dendritic Cell Algorithm is not specifically a classification algorithm, it may be considered a data filtering method for use in anomaly detection problems.

- The canonical algorithm is designed to operate on a single discrete, categorical or ordinal input and two probabilistic specific signals indicating the heuristic danger or safety of the input.

- The **danger** and **safe** signals are problem specific signals of the risk that the input pattern is an anomaly or is normal, both typically $\in [0, 100]$.

- The **danger** and **safe** signals do not have to be reciprocal, meaning they may provide conflicting information.

- The system was designed to be used in real-time anomaly detection problems, not just static problem.

- Each cells migration threshold is set separately, typically $\in [5, 15]$

7.6.6   Code Listing

Listing 7.5 provides an example of the Dendritic Cell Algorithm implemented in the Ruby Programming Language, specifically the Deterministic Dendritic Cell Algorithm (dDCA). The problem is a contrived anomaly-detection problem with ordinal inputs $x \in [0, 50)$, where values that divide by 10 with no remainder are considered anomalies. Probabilistic safe and danger signal functions are provided, suggesting danger signals correctly with $P(danger) = 0.70$, and safe signals correctly with $P(safe) = 0.95$.

The algorithm is an implementation of the Deterministic Dendritic Cell Algorithm (dDCA) as described in [2, 9], with verification from [5]. The algorithm was designed to be executed as three asynchronous processes in a real-time or semi-real time environment. For demonstration purposes, the implementation separated out the three main processes and executed the sequentially as a training and cell promotion phase followed by a test (labeling phase).

```ruby
def rand_in_bounds(min, max)
  return min + ((max-min) * rand())
end

def random_vector(search_space)
  return Array.new(search_space.size) do |i|
    rand_in_bounds(search_space[i][0], search_space[i][1])
  end
end

def construct_pattern(class_label, domain, p_safe, p_danger)
```

```ruby
12    set = domain[class_label]
13    selection = rand(set.size)
14    pattern = {}
15    pattern[:class_label] = class_label
16    pattern[:input] = set[selection]
17    pattern[:safe] = (rand() * p_safe * 100)
18    pattern[:danger] = (rand() * p_danger * 100)
19    return pattern
20  end
21
22  def generate_pattern(domain, p_anomaly, p_normal, prob_create_anom=0.5)
23    pattern = nil
24    if rand() < prob_create_anom
25      pattern = construct_pattern("Anomaly", domain, 1.0-p_normal, p_anomaly)
26      puts ">Generated Anomaly [#{pattern[:input]}]"
27    else
28      pattern = construct_pattern("Normal", domain, p_normal, 1.0-p_anomaly)
29    end
30    return pattern
31  end
32
33  def initialize_cell(thresh, cell={})
34    cell[:lifespan] = 1000.0
35    cell[:k] = 0.0
36    cell[:cms] = 0.0
37    cell[:migration_threshold] = rand_in_bounds(thresh[0], thresh[1])
38    cell[:antigen] = {}
39    return cell
40  end
41
42  def store_antigen(cell, input)
43    if cell[:antigen][input].nil?
44      cell[:antigen][input] = 1
45    else
46      cell[:antigen][input] += 1
47    end
48  end
49
50  def expose_cell(cell, cms, k, pattern, threshold)
51    cell[:cms] += cms
52    cell[:k] += k
53    cell[:lifespan] -= cms
54    store_antigen(cell, pattern[:input])
55    initialize_cell(threshold, cell) if cell[:lifespan] <= 0
56  end
57
58  def can_cell_migrate?(cell)
59    return (cell[:cms]>=cell[:migration_threshold] and !cell[:antigen].empty?)
60  end
61
62  def expose_all_cells(cells, pattern, threshold)
63    migrate = []
64    cms = (pattern[:safe] + pattern[:danger])
65    k = pattern[:danger] - (pattern[:safe] * 2.0)
66    cells.each do |cell|
67      expose_cell(cell, cms, k, pattern, threshold)
```

```
68    if can_cell_migrate?(cell)
69      migrate << cell
70      cell[:class_label] = (cell[:k]>0) ? "Anomaly" : "Normal"
71    end
72  end
73  return migrate
74 end
75
76 def train_system(domain, max_iter, num_cells, p_anomaly, p_normal, thresh)
77   immature_cells = Array.new(num_cells){ initialize_cell(thresh) }
78   migrated = []
79   max_iter.times do |iter|
80     pattern = generate_pattern(domain, p_anomaly, p_normal)
81     migrants = expose_all_cells(immature_cells, pattern, thresh)
82     migrants.each do |cell|
83       immature_cells.delete(cell)
84       immature_cells << initialize_cell(thresh)
85       migrated << cell
86     end
87     puts "> iter=#{iter} new=#{migrants.size}, migrated=#{migrated.size}"
88   end
89   return migrated
90 end
91
92 def classify_pattern(migrated, pattern)
93   input = pattern[:input]
94   num_cells, num_antigen = 0, 0
95   migrated.each do |cell|
96     if cell[:class_label] == "Anomaly" and !cell[:antigen][input].nil?
97       num_cells += 1
98       num_antigen += cell[:antigen][input]
99     end
100   end
101   mcav = num_cells.to_f / num_antigen.to_f
102   return (mcav>0.5) ? "Anomaly" : "Normal"
103 end
104
105 def test_system(migrated, domain, p_anomaly, p_normal, num_trial=100)
106   correct_norm = 0
107   num_trial.times do
108     pattern = construct_pattern("Normal", domain, p_normal, 1.0-p_anomaly)
109     class_label = classify_pattern(migrated, pattern)
110     correct_norm += 1 if class_label == "Normal"
111   end
112   puts "Finished testing Normal inputs #{correct_norm}/#{num_trial}"
113   correct_anom = 0
114   num_trial.times do
115     pattern = construct_pattern("Anomaly", domain, 1.0-p_normal, p_anomaly)
116     class_label = classify_pattern(migrated, pattern)
117     correct_anom += 1 if class_label == "Anomaly"
118   end
119   puts "Finished testing Anomaly inputs #{correct_anom}/#{num_trial}"
120   return [correct_norm, correct_anom]
121 end
122
123 def execute(domain, max_iter, num_cells, p_anom, p_norm, thresh)
```

```
124   migrated=train_system(domain, max_iter, num_cells, p_anom, p_norm, thresh)
125   test_system(migrated, domain, p_anom, p_norm)
126   return migrated
127 end
128
129 if __FILE__ == $0
130   # problem configuration
131   domain = {}
132   domain["Normal"] = Array.new(50){|i| i}
133   domain["Anomaly"] = Array.new(5){|i| (i+1)*10}
134   domain["Normal"] = domain["Normal"] - domain["Anomaly"]
135   p_anomaly = 0.70
136   p_normal = 0.95
137   # algorithm configuration
138   iterations = 100
139   num_cells = 10
140   thresh = [5,15]
141   # execute the algorithm
142   execute(domain, iterations, num_cells, p_anomaly, p_normal, thresh)
143 end
```

Listing 7.5: Deterministic Dendritic Cell Algorithm in Ruby

7.6.7 References

Primary Sources

The Dendritic Cell Algorithm was proposed by Greensmith, Aickelin and Cayzer describing the inspiring biological system and providing experimental results on a classification problem [4]. This work was followed shortly by a second study into the algorithm by Greensmith, Twycross, and Aickelin, focusing on computer security instances of anomaly detection and classification problems [6].

Learn More

The Dendritic Cell Algorithm was the focus of Greensmith's thesis, which provides a detailed discussion of the methods abstraction from the inspiring biological system, and a review of the technique's limitations [1]. A formal presentation of the algorithm is provided by Greensmith et al. [5]. Greensmith and Aickelin proposed the Deterministic Dendritic Cell Algorithm (dDCA) that seeks to remove some of the stochastic decisions from the method, and reduce the complexity and to make it more amenable to analysis [2]. Stibor et al. provide a theoretical analysis of the Deterministic Dendritic Cell Algorithm, considering the discrimination boundaries of single dendrite cells in the system [9]. Greensmith and Aickelin provide a detailed overview of the Dendritic Cell Algorithm focusing on the information processing principles of the inspiring biological systems as a book chapter [3].

7.6.8 Bibliography

[1] J. Greensmith. *The Dendritic Cell Algorithm*. PhD thesis, University of Nottingham, 2007.

[2] J. Greensmith and U. Aickelin. The deterministic dendritic cell algorithm. In *Proceedings of the 7th International Conference on Artificial Immune Systems (ICARIS 2007)*, pages 291–302, 2008.

[3] J. Greensmith and U. Aickelin. *Human-Centric Information Processing Through Granular Modelling*, chapter Artificial Dendritic Cells: Multi-faceted Perspectives, pages 375–395. Springer, 2009.

[4] J. Greensmith, U. Aickelin, and S. Cayzer. Introducing dendritic cells as a novel immune-inspired algorithm for anomaly detection. In *Proceedings of the Fourth International Conference on Artificial Immune Systems (ICARIS 2005)*, pages 153–167, 2005.

[5] J. Greensmith, U. Aickelin, and J. Twycross. Articulation and clarification of the dendritic cell algorithm. In *Proceedings of the 5th International Conference on Artificial Immune Systems (ICARIS 2006)*, pages 404–417, 2006.

[6] J. Greensmith, J. Twycross, and U. Aickelin. Dendritic cells for anomaly detection. In *Proceedings of the IEEE Congress on Evolutionary Computation (CEC2006)*, pages 664–671, 2006.

[7] P. Matzinger. Tolerance, danger, and the extended family. *Annual Review of Immunology*, 12:991–1045, 1994.

[8] P. Matzinger. The danger model: A renewed sense of self. *Science*, 296(5566):301–305, 2002.

[9] T. Stibor, R. Oates, G. Kendall, and J. M. Garibaldi. Geometrical insights into the dendritic cell algorithms. In *Proceedings of the 11th Annual conference on Genetic and evolutionary computation*, 2009.

Chapter 8

Neural Algorithms

8.1 Overview

This chapter describes Neural Algorithms.

8.1.1 Biological Neural Networks

A Biological Neural Network refers to the information processing elements of the nervous system, organized as a collection of neural cells, called neurons, that are interconnected in networks and interact with each other using electrochemical signals. A biological neuron is generally comprised of an axon which provides the input signals and is connected to other neurons via synapses. The neuron reacts to input signals and may produce an output signal on its output connection called the dendrites.

The study of biological neural networks falls within the domain of neuroscience which is a branch of biology concerned with the nervous system. Neuroanatomy is a subject that is concerned with the the structure and function of groups of neural networks both with regard to parts of the brain and the structures that lead from and to the brain from the rest of the body. Neuropsychology is another discipline concerned with the structure and function of the brain as they relate to abstract psychological behaviors. For further information, refer to a good textbook on any of these general topics.

8.1.2 Artificial Neural Networks

The field of Artificial Neural Networks (ANN) is concerned with the investigation of computational models inspired by theories and observation of the structure and function of biological networks of neural cells in the brain. They are generally designed as models for addressing mathematical, computational, and engineering problems. As such, there is a lot of interdisciplinary research in mathematics, neurobiology and computer science.

An Artificial Neural Network is generally comprised of a collection of artificial neurons that are interconnected in order to performs some computation on input patterns and create output patterns. They are adaptive systems capable of modifying their internal structure, typically the weights between nodes in the network, allowing them to be used for a variety of function approximation problems such as classification, regression, feature extraction and content addressable memory.

Given that the focus of the field is on performing computation with networks of discrete computing units, the field is traditionally called a 'connectionist' paradigm of Artificial Intelligence and 'Neural Computation'.

There are many types of neural networks, many of which fall into one of two categories:

- **Feed-forward Networks** where input is provided on one side of the network and the signals are propagated forward (in one direction) through the network structure to the other side where output signals are read. These networks may be comprised of one cell, one layer or multiple layers of neurons. Some examples include the Perceptron, Radial Basis Function Networks, and the multi-layer perceptron networks.

- **Recurrent Networks** where cycles in the network are permitted and the structure may be fully interconnected. Examples include the Hopfield Network and Bidirectional Associative Memory.

Artificial Neural Network structures are made up of nodes and weights which typically require training based on samples of patterns from a problem domain. Some examples of learning strategies include:

- **Supervised Learning** where the network is exposed to the input that has a known expected answer. The internal state of the network is modified to better match the expected result. Examples of this learning method include the Back-propagation algorithm and the Hebb rule.

- **Unsupervised Learning** where the network is exposed to input patterns from which it must discern meaning and extract features. The most common type of unsupervised learning is competitive learning where neurons compete based on the input pattern to produce an output pattern. Examples include Neural Gas, Learning Vector Quantization, and the Self-Organizing Map.

Artificial Neural Networks are typically difficult to configure and slow to train, but once prepared are very fast in application. They are generally used for function approximation-based problem domains and prized for their capabilities of generalization and tolerance to noise. They are known to have the limitation of being opaque, meaning there is little explanation to the subject matter expert as to why decisions were made, only how.

There are many excellent reference texts for the field of Artificial Neural Networks, some selected texts include: *"Neural Networks for Pattern Recognition"* by Bishop [1], *"Neural Smithing: Supervised Learning in Feedforward Artificial Neural Networks"* by Reed and Marks II [8] and *"An Introduction to Neural Networks"* by Gurney [2].

8.1.3 Extensions

There are many other algorithms and classes of algorithm that were not described from the field of Artificial Neural Networks, not limited to:

- **Radial Basis Function Network**: A network where activation functions are controlled by Radial Basis Functions [4].

- **Neural Gas**: Another self-organizing and unsupervised competitive learning algorithm. Unlike SOM (and more like LVQ), the nodes are not organized into a lower-dimensional structure, instead the competitive Hebbian-learning like rule is applied to connect, order, and adapt nodes in feature space [5–7].

- **Hierarchical Temporal Memory**: A neural network system based on models of some of the structural and algorithmic properties of the neocortex [3].

8.1.4 Bibliography

[1] C. M. Bishop. *Neural Networks for Pattern Recognition.* Oxford University Press, 1995.

[2] K. Gurney. *An Introduction to Neural Networks.* CRC Press, 1997.

[3] J. Hawkins and S. Blakeslee. *On Intelligence.* Henry Holt and Company, 2005.

[4] Robert J. Howlett and L. C. Jain. *Radial basis function networks 1: recent developments in theory and applications.* Springer, 2001.

[5] T. Martinetz and K. Schulten. A "neural gas" network learns topologies. In *Artificial Neural Networks*, pages 397–402, 1991.

[6] T. Martinetz and K. Schulten. Topology representing networks. *Neural Networks*, 7:507–522, 1994.

[7] T. M. Martinetz, S. G. Berkovich, and K. J. Schulten. 'neural-gas' network for vector quantization and its application to time-series prediction. *IEEE Transactions on Neural Networks*, 4:558–569, 1993.

[8] R. D. Reed and R. J. Marks II. *Neural Smithing: Supervised Learning in Feedforward Artificial Neural Networks*. Mit Press, 1999.

8.2 Perceptron

Perceptron.

8.2.1 Taxonomy

The Perceptron algorithm belongs to the field of Artificial Neural Networks and more broadly Computational Intelligence. It is a single layer feedforward neural network (single cell network) that inspired many extensions and variants, not limited to ADALINE and the Widrow-Hoff learning rules.

8.2.2 Inspiration

The Perceptron is inspired by the information processing of a single neural cell (called a neuron). A neuron accepts input signals via its axon, which pass the electrical signal down to the cell body. The dendrites carry the signal out to synapses, which are the connections of a cell's dendrites to other cell's axons. In a synapse, the electrical activity is converted into molecular activity (neurotransmitter molecules crossing the synaptic cleft and binding with receptors). The molecular binding develops an electrical signal which is passed onto the connected cells axon.

8.2.3 Strategy

The information processing objective of the technique is to model a given function by modifying internal weightings of input signals to produce an expected output signal. The system is trained using a supervised learning method, where the error between the system's output and a known expected output is presented to the system and used to modify its internal state. State is maintained in a set of weightings on the input signals. The weights are used to represent an abstraction of the mapping of input vectors to the output signal for the examples that the system was exposed to during training.

8.2.4 Procedure

The Perceptron is comprised of a data structure (weights) and separate procedures for training and applying the structure. The structure is really just a vector of weights (one for each expected input) and a bias term.

Algorithm 8.6.1 provides a pseudocode for training the Perceptron. A weight is initialized for each input plus an additional weight for a fixed bias constant input that is almost always set to 1.0. The activation of the network to a given input pattern is calculated as follows:

$$activation \leftarrow \sum_{k=1}^{n} \left(w_k \times x_{ki} \right) + w_{bias} \times 1.0 \tag{8.1}$$

where n is the number of weights and inputs, x_{ki} is the kth attribute on the ith input pattern, and w_{bias} is the bias weight. The weights are updated as follows:

$$w_i(t+1) = w_i(t) + \alpha \times (e(t) - a(t)) \times x_i(t) \tag{8.2}$$

where w_i is the ith weight at time t and $t+1$, α is the learning rate, $e(t)$ and $a(t)$ are the expected and actual output at time t, and x_i is the ith input. This update process is applied to each weight in turn (as well as the bias weight with its contact input).

Algorithm 8.2.1: Pseudocode for the Perceptron.

Input: ProblemSize, InputPatterns, $iterations_{max}$, $learn_{rate}$
Output: Weights
1 Weights $\leftarrow$ InitializeWeights(ProblemSize);
2 **for** $i = 1$ **to** $iterations_{max}$ **do**
3      $Pattern_i \leftarrow$ SelectInputPattern(InputPatterns);
4      $Activation_i \leftarrow$ ActivateNetwork($Pattern_i$, Weights);
5      $Output_i \leftarrow$ TransferActivation($Activation_i$);
6   UpdateWeights($Pattern_i$, $Output_i$, $learn_{rate}$);
7 **end**
8 **return** Weights;

8.2.5   Heuristics

- The Perceptron can be used to approximate arbitrary linear functions and can be used for regression or classification problems.

- The Perceptron cannot learn a non-linear mapping between the input and output attributes. The XOR problem is a classical example of a problem that the Perceptron cannot learn.

- Input and output values should be normalized such that $x \in [0, 1)$.

- The learning rate ($\alpha \in [0, 1]$) controls the amount of change each error has on the system, lower learning rages are common such as 0.1.

- The weights can be updated in an online manner (after the exposure to each input pattern) or in batch (after a fixed number of patterns have been observed).

- Batch updates are expected to be more stable than online updates for some complex problems.

- A bias weight is used with a constant input signal to provide stability to the learning process.

- A step transfer function is commonly used to transfer the activation to a binary output value $1 \leftarrow activation \geq 0$, otherwise 0.

- It is good practice to expose the system to input patterns in a different random order each enumeration through the input set.

- The initial weights are typically small random values, typically $\in [0, 0.5]$.

8.2.6   Code Listing

Listing 8.1 provides an example of the Perceptron algorithm implemented in the Ruby Programming Language. The problem is the classical OR boolean problem, where the inputs of the boolean truth table are provided as the two inputs and the result of the boolean OR operation is expected as output.

The algorithm was implemented using an online learning method, meaning the weights are updated after each input pattern is observed. A step transfer function is used to convert the activation into a binary output $\in \{0, 1\}$. Random samples are taken from the domain to train the weights, and similarly, random samples are drawn from the domain to demonstrate what the network has learned. A bias weight is used for stability with a constant input of 1.0.

```ruby
def random_vector(minmax)
  return Array.new(minmax.size) do |i|
    minmax[i][0] + ((minmax[i][1] - minmax[i][0]) * rand())
  end
end

def initialize_weights(problem_size)
  minmax = Array.new(problem_size + 1) {[-1.0,1.0]}
  return random_vector(minmax)
end

def update_weights(num_inputs, weights, input, out_exp, out_act, l_rate)
  num_inputs.times do |i|
    weights[i] += l_rate * (out_exp - out_act) * input[i]
  end
  weights[num_inputs] += l_rate * (out_exp - out_act) * 1.0
end

def activate(weights, vector)
  sum = weights[weights.size-1] * 1.0
  vector.each_with_index do |input, i|
    sum += weights[i] * input
  end
  return sum
end

def transfer(activation)
  return (activation >= 0) ? 1.0 : 0.0
end
```

```
30
31   def get_output(weights, vector)
32     activation = activate(weights, vector)
33     return transfer(activation)
34   end
35
36   def train_weights(weights, domain, num_inputs, iterations, lrate)
37     iterations.times do |epoch|
38       error = 0.0
39       domain.each do |pattern|
40         input = Array.new(num_inputs) {|k| pattern[k].to_f}
41         output = get_output(weights, input)
42         expected = pattern.last.to_f
43         error += (output - expected).abs
44         update_weights(num_inputs, weights, input, expected, output, lrate)
45       end
46       puts "> epoch=#{epoch}, error=#{error}"
47     end
48   end
49
50   def test_weights(weights, domain, num_inputs)
51     correct = 0
52     domain.each do |pattern|
53       input_vector = Array.new(num_inputs) {|k| pattern[k].to_f}
54       output = get_output(weights, input_vector)
55       correct += 1 if output.round == pattern.last
56     end
57     puts "Finished test with a score of #{correct}/#{domain.size}"
58     return correct
59   end
60
61   def execute(domain, num_inputs, iterations, learning_rate)
62     weights = initialize_weights(num_inputs)
63     train_weights(weights, domain, num_inputs, iterations, learning_rate)
64     test_weights(weights, domain, num_inputs)
65     return weights
66   end
67
68   if __FILE__ == $0
69     # problem configuration
70     or_problem = [[0,0,0], [0,1,1], [1,0,1], [1,1,1]]
71     inputs = 2
72     # algorithm configuration
73     iterations = 20
74     learning_rate = 0.1
75     # execute the algorithm
76     execute(or_problem, inputs, iterations, learning_rate)
77   end
```

Listing 8.1: Perceptron in Ruby

8.2.7   References

Primary Sources

The Perceptron algorithm was proposed by Rosenblatt in 1958 [3]. Rosenblatt proposed a range of neural network structures and methods. The 'Perceptron' as it is known is in fact a simplification of Rosenblatt's models by Minsky and Papert for the purposes of analysis [1]. An early proof of convergence was provided by Novikoff [2].

Learn More

Minsky and Papert wrote the classical text titled "Perceptrons" in 1969 that is known to have discredited the approach, suggesting it was limited to linear discrimination, which reduced research in the area for decades afterward [1].

8.2.8   Bibliography

[1] M. L. Minsky and S. A. Papert. *Perceptrons.* MIT Press, 1969.

[2] A. B. Novikoff. On convergence proofs on perceptrons. *Symposium on the Mathematical Theory of Automata*, 12:615–622, 1962.

[3] F. Rosenblatt. The perceptron: A probabilistic model for information storage and organization in the brain. *Cornell Aeronautical Laboratory, Psychological Review*, 6:386–408, 1958.

8.3   Back-propagation

Back-propagation, Backpropagation, Error Back Propagation, Backprop, Delta-rule.

8.3.1   Taxonomy

The Back-propagation algorithm is a supervised learning method for multi-layer feed-forward networks from the field of Artificial Neural Networks and more broadly Computational Intelligence. The name refers to the backward propagation of error during the training of the network. Back-propagation is the basis for many variations and extensions for training multi-layer feed-forward networks not limited to Vogl's Method (Bold Drive), Delta-Bar-Delta, Quickprop, and Rprop.

8.3.2   Inspiration

Feed-forward neural networks are inspired by the information processing of one or more neural cells (called a neuron). A neuron accepts input signals via its axon, which pass the electrical signal down to the cell body. The dendrites carry the signal out to synapses, which are the connections of a cell's dendrites to other cell's axons. In a synapse, the electrical activity is converted into molecular activity (neurotransmitter molecules crossing the synaptic cleft and binding with receptors). The molecular binding develops an electrical signal which is passed onto the connected cells axon. The Back-propagation algorithm is a training regime for multi-layer feed forward neural networks and is not directly inspired by the learning processes of the biological system.

8.3.3   Strategy

The information processing objective of the technique is to model a given function by modifying internal weightings of input signals to produce an expected output signal. The system is trained using a supervised learning method, where the error between the system's output and a known expected output is presented to the system and used to modify its internal state. State is maintained in a set of weightings on the input signals. The weights are used to represent an abstraction of the mapping of input vectors to the output signal for the examples that the system was exposed to during training. Each layer of the network provides an abstraction of the information processing of the previous layer, allowing the combination of sub-functions and higher order modeling.

8.3.4   Procedure

The Back-propagation algorithm is a method for training the weights in a multi-layer feed-forward neural network. As such, it requires a network structure to be defined of one or more layers where one layer is fully connected to the next layer. A standard network structure is one input layer, one hidden layer, and one output layer. The method is primarily concerned with adapting the weights to the calculated error in the presence of input patterns, and the method is applied backward from the network output layer through to the input layer.

Algorithm 8.6.1 provides a high-level pseudocode for preparing a network using the Back-propagation training method. A weight is initialized for each input plus an additional weight for a fixed bias constant input that is almost always set to 1.0. The activation of a single neuron to a given input pattern is calculated as follows:

$$activation = \left(\sum_{k=1}^{n} w_k \times x_{ki} \right) + w_{bias} \times 1.0 \qquad (8.3)$$

where n is the number of weights and inputs, x_{ki} is the kth attribute on the ith input pattern, and w_{bias} is the bias weight. A logistic transfer function (sigmoid) is used to calculate the output for a neuron $\in [0,1]$ and provide nonlinearities between in the input and output signals: $\frac{1}{1+exp(-a)}$, where a represents the neuron activation.

The weight updates use the delta rule, specifically a modified delta rule where error is backwardly propagated through the network, starting at the output layer and weighted back through the previous layers. The following describes the back-propagation of error and weight updates for a single pattern.

An error signal is calculated for each node and propagated back through the network. For the output nodes this is the sum of the error between the node outputs and the expected outputs:

$$es_i = (c_i - o_i) \times td_i \qquad (8.4)$$

where es_i is the error signal for the ith node, c_i is the expected output and o_i is the actual output for the ith node. The td term is the derivative of the output of the ith node. If the sigmod transfer function is used, td_i would be $o_i \times (1 - o_i)$ For the hidden nodes, the error signal is the sum of the weighted error signals from the next layer.

$$es_i = \left(\sum_{k=1}^{n} (w_{ik} \times es_k) \right) \times td_i \qquad (8.5)$$

where es_i is the error signal for the ith node, w_{ik} is the weight between the ith and the kth nodes, and es_k is the error signal of the $k_t h$ node.

The error derivatives for each weight are calculated by combining the input to each node and the error signal for the node.

$$ed_i = \sum_{k=1}^{n} es_i \times x_k \tag{8.6}$$

where ed_i is the error derivative for the ith node, es_i is the error signal for the ith node and x_k is the input from the kth node in the previous layer. This process include the bias input that has a constant value.

Weights are updated in a direction that reduces the error derivative ed_i (error assigned to the weight), metered by a learning coefficient.

$$w_i(t+1) = w_i(t) + (ed_k \times learn_{rate}) \tag{8.7}$$

where $w_i(t+1)$ is the updated i^{th} weight, ed_k is the error derivative for the kth node and $learn_{rate}$ is an update coefficient parameter.

Algorithm 8.3.1: Pseudocode for Back-propagation.

Input: ProblemSize, InputPatterns, $iterations_{max}$, $learn_{rate}$
Output: Network
1 Network ← ConstructNetworkLayers();
2 $Network_{weights}$ ← InitializeWeights(Network, ProblemSize);
3 **for** $i = 1$ **to** $iterations_{max}$ **do**
4    $Pattern_i$ ← SelectInputPattern(InputPatterns);
5    $Output_i$ ← ForwardPropagate($Pattern_i$, Network);
6   BackwardPropagateError($Pattern_i$, $Output_i$, Network);
7   UpdateWeights($Pattern_i$, $Output_i$, Network, $learn_{rate}$);
8 **end**
9 **return** Network;

8.3.5 Heuristics

- The Back-propagation algorithm can be used to train a multi-layer network to approximate arbitrary non-linear functions and can be used for regression or classification problems.

- Input and output values should be normalized such that $x \in [0, 1)$.

- The weights can be updated in an online manner (after the exposure to each input pattern) or in batch (after a fixed number of patterns have been observed).

- Batch updates are expected to be more stable than online updates for some complex problems.

- A logistic (sigmoid) transfer function is commonly used to transfer the activation to a binary output value, although other transfer functions can be used such as the hyperbolic tangent (tanh), Gaussian, and softmax.

- It is good practice to expose the system to input patterns in a different random order each enumeration through the input set.

- The initial weights are typically small random values $\in [0, 0.5]$.

- Typically a small number of layers are used such as 2-4 given that the increase in layers result in an increase in the complexity of the system and the time required to train the weights.

- The learning rate can be varied during training, and it is common to introduce a momentum term to limit the rate of change.

- The weights of a given network can be initialized with a global optimization method before being refined using the Back-propagation algorithm.

- One output node is common for regression problems, where as one output node per class is common for classification problems.

8.3.6   Code Listing

Listing 8.2 provides an example of the Back-propagation algorithm implemented in the Ruby Programming Language. The problem is the classical XOR boolean problem, where the inputs of the boolean truth table are provided as inputs and the result of the boolean XOR operation is expected as output. This is a classical problem for Back-Propagation because it was the problem instance referenced by Minsky and Papert in their analysis of the Perceptron highlighting the limitations of their simplified models of neural networks [3].

The algorithm was implemented using a batch learning method, meaning the weights are updated after each epoch of patterns are observed. A logistic (sigmoid) transfer function is used to convert the activation into an output signal. Weight updates occur at the end of each epoch using the accumulated delta's. A momentum term is used in conjunction with the past weight update to ensure the last update influences the current update, reducing large changes.

A three layer network is demonstrated with 2 nodes in the input layer (two inputs), 2 nodes in the hidden layer and 1 node in the output layer, which is sufficient for the chosen problem. A bias weight is used on each neuron for stability with a constant input of 1.0. The learning process is separated into four steps: forward propagation, backward propagation of error, calculation of error derivatives (assigning blame to the weights) and

the weight update. This separation facilities easy extensions such as adding
a momentum term and/or weight decay to the update process.

```ruby
def random_vector(minmax)
  return Array.new(minmax.size) do |i|
    minmax[i][0] + ((minmax[i][1] - minmax[i][0]) * rand())
  end
end

def initialize_weights(num_weights)
  minmax = Array.new(num_weights) {[-rand(),rand()]}
  return random_vector(minmax)
end

def activate(weights, vector)
  sum = weights[weights.size-1] * 1.0
  vector.each_with_index do |input, i|
    sum += weights[i] * input
  end
  return sum
end

def transfer(activation)
  return 1.0 / (1.0 + Math.exp(-activation))
end

def transfer_derivative(output)
  return output * (1.0 - output)
end

def forward_propagate(net, vector)
  net.each_with_index do |layer, i|
    input=(i==0)? vector : Array.new(net[i-1].size){|k|net[i-1][k][:output]}
    layer.each do |neuron|
      neuron[:activation] = activate(neuron[:weights], input)
      neuron[:output] = transfer(neuron[:activation])
    end
  end
  return net.last[0][:output]
end

def backward_propagate_error(network, expected_output)
  network.size.times do |n|
    index = network.size - 1 - n
    if index == network.size-1
      neuron = network[index][0] # assume one node in output layer
      error = (expected_output - neuron[:output])
      neuron[:delta] = error * transfer_derivative(neuron[:output])
    else
      network[index].each_with_index do |neuron, k|
        sum = 0.0
        # only sum errors weighted by connection to the current k'th neuron
        network[index+1].each do |next_neuron|
          sum += (next_neuron[:weights][k] * next_neuron[:delta])
        end
        neuron[:delta] = sum * transfer_derivative(neuron[:output])
```

```
54          end
55        end
56      end
57    end
58
59    def calculate_error_derivatives_for_weights(net, vector)
60      net.each_with_index do |layer, i|
61        input=(i==0)? vector : Array.new(net[i-1].size){|k|net[i-1][k][:output]}
62        layer.each do |neuron|
63          input.each_with_index do |signal, j|
64            neuron[:deriv][j] += neuron[:delta] * signal
65          end
66          neuron[:deriv][-1] += neuron[:delta] * 1.0
67        end
68      end
69    end
70
71    def update_weights(network, lrate, mom=0.8)
72      network.each do |layer|
73        layer.each do |neuron|
74          neuron[:weights].each_with_index do |w, j|
75            delta = (lrate * neuron[:deriv][j]) + (neuron[:last_delta][j] * mom)
76            neuron[:weights][j] += delta
77            neuron[:last_delta][j] = delta
78            neuron[:deriv][j] = 0.0
79          end
80        end
81      end
82    end
83
84    def train_network(network, domain, num_inputs, iterations, lrate)
85      correct = 0
86      iterations.times do |epoch|
87        domain.each do |pattern|
88          vector,expected=Array.new(num_inputs){|k|pattern[k].to_f},pattern.last
89          output = forward_propagate(network, vector)
90          correct += 1 if output.round == expected
91          backward_propagate_error(network, expected)
92          calculate_error_derivatives_for_weights(network, vector)
93        end
94        update_weights(network, lrate)
95        if (epoch+1).modulo(100) == 0
96          puts "> epoch=#{epoch+1}, Correct=#{correct}/#{100*domain.size}"
97          correct = 0
98        end
99      end
100   end
101
102   def test_network(network, domain, num_inputs)
103     correct = 0
104     domain.each do |pattern|
105       input_vector = Array.new(num_inputs) {|k| pattern[k].to_f}
106       output = forward_propagate(network, input_vector)
107       correct += 1 if output.round == pattern.last
108     end
109     puts "Finished test with a score of #{correct}/#{domain.length}"
```

```ruby
110    return correct
111  end
112
113  def create_neuron(num_inputs)
114    return {:weights=>initialize_weights(num_inputs+1),
115            :last_delta=>Array.new(num_inputs+1){0.0},
116            :deriv=>Array.new(num_inputs+1){0.0}}
117  end
118
119  def execute(domain, num_inputs, iterations, num_nodes, lrate)
120    network = []
121    network << Array.new(num_nodes){create_neuron(num_inputs)}
122    network << Array.new(1){create_neuron(network.last.size)}
123    puts "Topology: #{num_inputs} #{network.inject(""){|m,i|m+"#{i.size} "}}"
124    train_network(network, domain, num_inputs, iterations, lrate)
125    test_network(network, domain, num_inputs)
126    return network
127  end
128
129  if __FILE__ == $0
130    # problem configuration
131    xor = [[0,0,0], [0,1,1], [1,0,1], [1,1,0]]
132    inputs = 2
133    # algorithm configuration
134    learning_rate = 0.3
135    num_hidden_nodes = 4
136    iterations = 2000
137    # execute the algorithm
138    execute(xor, inputs, iterations, num_hidden_nodes, learning_rate)
139  end
```

Listing 8.2: Back-propagation in Ruby

8.3.7   References

Primary Sources

The backward propagation of error method is credited to Bryson and Ho in [1]. It was applied to the training of multi-layer networks and called back-propagation by Rumelhart, Hinton and Williams in 1986 [5, 6]. This effort and the collection of studies edited by Rumelhart and McClelland helped to define the field of Artificial Neural Networks in the late 1980s [7, 8].

Learn More

A seminal book on the approach was "Backpropagation: theory, architectures, and applications" by Chauvin and Rumelhart that provided an excellent introduction (chapter 1) but also a collection of studies applying and extending the approach [2]. Reed and Marks provide an excellent treatment of feed-forward neural networks called "Neural Smithing" that includes chapters dedicated to Back-propagation, the configuration of its parameters, error surface and speed improvements [4].

8.3.8 Bibliography

[1] A. E. Bryson and Y-C. Ho. *Applied optimal control: optimization, estimation, and control.* Taylor & Francis, 1969.

[2] Y. Chauvin and D. E. Rumelhart. *Backpropagation: Theory, architectures, and applications.* Routledge, 1995.

[3] M. L. Minsky and S. A. Papert. *Perceptrons.* MIT Press, 1969.

[4] R. D. Reed and R. J. Marks II. *Neural Smithing: Supervised Learning in Feedforward Artificial Neural Networks.* Mit Press, 1999.

[5] D. E. Rumelhart, G. E. Hinton, and R. J. Williams. Learning representations by back-propagating errors. *Nature*, 323:533–536, 1986.

[6] D. E. Rumelhart, G. E. Hinton, and R. J. Williams. *Parallel distributed processing: explorations in the microstructure of cognition, vol. 1*, chapter Learning internal representations by error propagation, pages 318–362. MIT Press, 1986.

[7] D. E. Rumelhart and J. L. McClelland. *Parallel distributed processing: explorations in the microstructure of cognition. Foundations, Volume 1.* MIT Press, 1986.

[8] D. E. Rumelhart and J. L. McClelland. *Parallel distributed processing: Explorations in the microstructure of cognition. Psychological and biological models, Volume 2.* MIT Press, 1986.

8.4   Hopfield Network

Hopfield Network, HN, Hopfield Model.

8.4.1   Taxonomy

The Hopfield Network is a Neural Network and belongs to the field of Artificial Neural Networks and Neural Computation. It is a Recurrent Neural Network and is related to other recurrent networks such as the Bidirectional Associative Memory (BAM). It is generally related to feedforward Artificial Neural Networks such as the Perceptron (Section 8.2) and the Back-propagation algorithm (Section 8.3).

8.4.2   Inspiration

The Hopfield Network algorithm is inspired by the associated memory properties of the human brain.

8.4.3   Metaphor

Through the training process, the weights in the network may be thought to minimize an energy function and slide down an energy surface. In a trained network, each pattern presented to the network provides an attractor, where progress is made towards the point of attraction by propagating information around the network.

8.4.4   Strategy

The information processing objective of the system is to associate the components of an input pattern with a holistic representation of the pattern called Content Addressable Memory (CAM). This means that once trained, the system will recall whole patterns, given a portion or a noisy version of the input pattern.

8.4.5   Procedure

The Hopfield Network is comprised of a graph data structure with weighted edges and separate procedures for training and applying the structure. The network structure is fully connected (a node connects to all other nodes except itself) and the edges (weights) between the nodes are bidirectional.

The weights of the network can be learned via a one-shot method (one-iteration through the patterns) if all patterns to be memorized by the network are known. Alternatively, the weights can be updated incrementally using the Hebb rule where weights are increased or decreased based on the difference between the actual and the expected output. The one-shot calculation of the network weights for a single node occurs as follows:

$$w_{i,j} = \sum_{k=1}^{N} v_k^i \times v_k^j \tag{8.8}$$

where $w_{i,j}$ is the weight between neuron i and j, N is the number of input patterns, v is the input pattern and v_k^i is the ith attribute on the kth input pattern.

The propagation of the information through the network can be asynchronous where a random node is selected each iteration, or synchronously, where the output is calculated for each node before being applied to the whole network. Propagation of the information continues until no more changes are made or until a maximum number of iterations has completed, after which the output pattern from the network can be read. The activation for a single node is calculated as follows:

$$n_i = \sum_{j=1}^{n} w_{i,j} \times n_j \tag{8.9}$$

where n_i is the activation of the ith neuron, $w_{i,j}$ with the weight between the nodes i and j, and n_j is the output of the jth neuron. The activation is transferred into an output using a transfer function, typically a step function as follows:

$$transfer(n_i) = \begin{cases} 1 & if \geq \theta \\ -1 & if < \theta \end{cases}$$

where the threshold θ is typically fixed at 0.

8.4.6 Heuristics

- The Hopfield network may be used to solve the recall problem of matching cues for an input pattern to an associated pre-learned pattern.

- The transfer function for turning the activation of a neuron into an output is typically a step function $f(a) \in \{-1, 1\}$ (preferred), or more traditionally $f(a) \in \{0, 1\}$.

- The input vectors are typically normalized to boolean values $x \in [-1, 1]$.

- The network can be propagated asynchronously (where a random node is selected and output generated), or synchronously (where the output for all nodes are calculated before being applied).

- Weights can be learned in a one-shot or incremental method based on how much information is known about the patterns to be learned.

- All neurons in the network are typically both input and output neurons, although other network topologies have been investigated (such as the designation of input and output neurons).

- A Hopfield network has limits on the patterns it can store and retrieve accurately from memory, described by $N < 0.15 \times n$ where N is the number of patterns that can be stored and retrieved and n is the number of nodes in the network.

8.4.7   Code Listing

Listing 8.3 provides an example of the Hopfield Network algorithm implemented in the Ruby Programming Language. The problem is an instance of a recall problem where patters are described in terms of a 3×3 matrix of binary values ($\in \{-1, 1\}$). Once the network has learned the patterns, the system is exposed to perturbed versions of the patterns (with errors introduced) and must respond with the correct pattern. Two patterns are used in this example, specifically 'T', and 'U'.

The algorithm is an implementation of the Hopfield Network with a one-shot training method for the network weights, given that all patterns are already known. The information is propagated through the network using an asynchronous method, which is repeated for a fixed number of iterations. The patterns are displayed to the console during the testing of the network, with the outputs converted from $\{-1, 1\}$ to $\{0, 1\}$ for readability.

```ruby
def random_vector(minmax)
  return Array.new(minmax.size) do |i|
    minmax[i][0] + ((minmax[i][1] - minmax[i][0]) * rand())
  end
end

def initialize_weights(problem_size)
  minmax = Array.new(problem_size) {[-0.5,0.5]}
  return random_vector(minmax)
end

def create_neuron(num_inputs)
  neuron = {}
  neuron[:weights] = initialize_weights(num_inputs)
  return neuron
end

def transfer(activation)
  return (activation >= 0) ? 1 : -1
end

def propagate_was_change?(neurons)
  i = rand(neurons.size)
```

```
24    activation = 0
25    neurons.each_with_index do |other, j|
26      activation += other[:weights][i]*other[:output] if i!=j
27    end
28    output = transfer(activation)
29    change = output != neurons[i][:output]
30    neurons[i][:output] = output
31    return change
32  end
33
34  def get_output(neurons, pattern, evals=100)
35    vector = pattern.flatten
36    neurons.each_with_index {|neuron,i| neuron[:output] = vector[i]}
37    evals.times { propagate_was_change?(neurons) }
38    return Array.new(neurons.size){|i| neurons[i][:output]}
39  end
40
41  def train_network(neurons, patters)
42    neurons.each_with_index do |neuron, i|
43      for j in ((i+1)...neurons.size) do
44        next if i==j
45        wij = 0.0
46        patters.each do |pattern|
47          vector = pattern.flatten
48          wij += vector[i]*vector[j]
49        end
50        neurons[i][:weights][j] = wij
51        neurons[j][:weights][i] = wij
52      end
53    end
54  end
55
56  def to_binary(vector)
57    return Array.new(vector.size){|i| ((vector[i]==-1) ? 0 : 1)}
58  end
59
60  def print_patterns(provided, expected, actual)
61    p, e, a = to_binary(provided), to_binary(expected), to_binary(actual)
62    p1, p2, p3 = p[0..2].join(', '), p[3..5].join(', '), p[6..8].join(', ')
63    e1, e2, e3 = e[0..2].join(', '), e[3..5].join(', '), e[6..8].join(', ')
64    a1, a2, a3 = a[0..2].join(', '), a[3..5].join(', '), a[6..8].join(', ')
65    puts "Provided Expected    Got"
66    puts "#{p1}    #{e1}       #{a1}"
67    puts "#{p2}    #{e2}       #{a2}"
68    puts "#{p3}    #{e3}       #{a3}"
69  end
70
71  def calculate_error(expected, actual)
72    sum = 0
73    expected.each_with_index do |v, i|
74      sum += 1 if expected[i]!=actual[i]
75    end
76    return sum
77  end
78
79  def perturb_pattern(vector, num_errors=1)
```

```
80   perturbed = Array.new(vector)
81   indicies = [rand(perturbed.size)]
82   while indicies.size < num_errors do
83     index = rand(perturbed.size)
84     indicies << index if !indicies.include?(index)
85   end
86   indicies.each {|i| perturbed[i] = ((perturbed[i]==1) ? -1 : 1)}
87   return perturbed
88 end
89
90 def test_network(neurons, patterns)
91   error = 0.0
92   patterns.each do |pattern|
93     vector = pattern.flatten
94     perturbed = perturb_pattern(vector)
95     output = get_output(neurons, perturbed)
96     error += calculate_error(vector, output)
97     print_patterns(perturbed, vector, output)
98   end
99   error = error / patterns.size.to_f
100  puts "Final Result: avg pattern error=#{error}"
101  return error
102 end
103
104 def execute(patters, num_inputs)
105   neurons = Array.new(num_inputs) { create_neuron(num_inputs) }
106   train_network(neurons, patters)
107   test_network(neurons, patters)
108   return neurons
109 end
110
111 if __FILE__ == $0
112   # problem configuration
113   num_inputs = 9
114   p1 = [[1,1,1],[-1,1,-1],[-1,1,-1]] # T
115   p2 = [[1,-1,1],[1,-1,1],[1,1,1]] # U
116   patters = [p1, p2]
117   # execute the algorithm
118   execute(patters, num_inputs)
119 end
```

Listing 8.3: Hopfield Network in Ruby

8.4.8   References

Primary Sources

The Hopfield Network was proposed by Hopfield in 1982 where the basic model was described and related to an abstraction of the inspiring biological system [2]. This early work was extended by Hopfield to 'graded' neurons capable of outputting a continuous value through use of a logistic (sigmoid) transfer function [3]. An innovative work by Hopfield and Tank considered the use of the Hopfield network for solving combinatorial optimization problems, with a specific study into the system applied to instances of the Traveling Salesman Problem [4]. This was achieved with a large number of neurons and a representation that decoded the position of each city in the tour as a sub-problem on which a customized network energy function had to be minimized.

Learn More

Popovici and Boncut provide a summary of the Hopfield Network algorithm with worked examples [5]. Overviews of the Hopfield Network are provided in most good books on Artificial Neural Networks, such as [6]. Hertz, Krogh, and Palmer present an in depth study of the field of Artificial Neural Networks with a detailed treatment of the Hopfield network from a statistical mechanics perspective [1].

8.4.9 Bibliography

[1] J. Hertz, Krogh A., and R. G. Palmer. *Introduction to the theory of neural computation*. Westview Press, 1991.

[2] J. J. Hopfield. Neural networks and physical systems with emergent collective computational abilities. In *Proceedings of the National Academy of Sciences of the USA*, volume 79, pages 2554–2558, April 1982.

[3] J. J. Hopfield. Neurons with graded response have collective computational properties like those of two-state neurons. In *Proceedings of the National Academy of Sciences*, volume 81, pages 3088–3092, 1984.

[4] J. J. Hopfield and D. W. Tank. "neural" computation of decisions in optimization problems. *Biological Cybernetics*, 55:141–146, 1985.

[5] N. Popovici and M. Boncut. On the hopfield algorithm. foundations and examples. *General Mathematics*, 2:35–50, 2005.

[6] R. Rojas. *Neural Networks – A Systematic Introduction*, chapter 13. The Hopfield Model. Springer, 1996.

8.5   Learning Vector Quantization

Learning Vector Quantization, LVQ.

8.5.1   Taxonomy

The Learning Vector Quantization algorithm belongs to the field of Artificial Neural Networks and Neural Computation. More broadly to the field of Computational Intelligence. The Learning Vector Quantization algorithm is an supervised neural network that uses a competitive (winner-take-all) learning strategy. It is related to other supervised neural networks such as the Perceptron (Section 8.2) and the Back-propagation algorithm (Section 8.3). It is related to other competitive learning neural networks such as the the Self-Organizing Map algorithm (Section 8.6) that is a similar algorithm for unsupervised learning with the addition of connections between the neurons. Additionally, LVQ is a baseline technique that was defined with a few variants LVQ1, LVQ2, LVQ2.1, LVQ3, OLVQ1, and OLVQ3 as well as many third-party extensions and refinements too numerous to list.

8.5.2   Inspiration

The Learning Vector Quantization algorithm is related to the Self-Organizing Map which is in turn inspired by the self-organizing capabilities of neurons in the visual cortex.

8.5.3   Strategy

The information processing objective of the algorithm is to prepare a set of codebook (or prototype) vectors in the domain of the observed input data samples and to use these vectors to classify unseen examples. An initially random pool of vectors is prepared which are then exposed to training samples. A winner-take-all strategy is employed where one or more of the most similar vectors to a given input pattern are selected and adjusted to be closer to the input vector, and in some cases, further away from the winner for runners up. The repetition of this process results in the distribution of codebook vectors in the input space which approximate the underlying distribution of samples from the test dataset.

8.5.4   Procedure

Vector Quantization is a technique from signal processing where density functions are approximated with prototype vectors for applications such as compression. Learning Vector Quantization is similar in principle, although the prototype vectors are learned through a supervised winner-take-all method.

Algorithm 8.6.1 provides a high-level pseudocode for preparing codebook vectors using the Learning Vector Quantization method. Codebook vectors are initialized to small floating point values, or sampled from an available dataset. The Best Matching Unit (BMU) is the codebook vector from the pool that has the minimum distance to an input vector. A distance measure between input patterns must be defined. For real-valued vectors, this is commonly the Euclidean distance:

$$dist(x, c) = \sum_{i=1}^{n} (x_i - c_i)^2 \qquad (8.10)$$

where n is the number of attributes, x is the input vector and c is a given codebook vector.

Algorithm 8.5.1: Pseudocode for LVQ1.

Input: ProblemSize, InputPatterns, $iterations_{max}$, $CodebookVectors_{num}$, $learn_{rate}$
Output: CodebookVectors

1 CodebookVectors ←
   InitializeCodebookVectors($CodebookVectors_{num}$, ProblemSize);
2 **for** $i = 1$ **to** $iterations_{max}$ **do**
3    $Pattern_i$ ← SelectInputPattern(InputPatterns);
4   Bmu_i ← SelectBestMatchingUnit($Pattern_i$, CodebookVectors);
5   **foreach** $Bmu_i^{attribute} \in Bmu_i$ **do**
6   **if** $Bmu_i^{class} \equiv Pattern_i^{class}$ **then**
7          $Bmu_i^{attribute}$ ← $Bmu_i^{attribute} + learn_{rate} \times (Pattern_i^{attribute} - Bmu_i^{attribute})$
8   **else**
9          $Bmu_i^{attribute}$ ← $Bmu_i^{attribute} - learn_{rate} \times (Pattern_i^{attribute} - Bmu_i^{attribute})$
10   **end**
11   **end**
12 **end**
13 **return** CodebookVectors;

8.5.5 Heuristics

- Learning Vector Quantization was designed for classification problems that have existing data sets that can be used to supervise the learning by the system. The algorithm does not support regression problems.

- LVQ is non-parametric, meaning that it does not rely on assumptions about that structure of the function that it is approximating.

- Real-values in input vectors should be normalized such that $x \in [0, 1)$.

- Euclidean distance is commonly used to measure the distance between real-valued vectors, although other distance measures may be used (such as dot product), and data specific distance measures may be required for non-scalar attributes.

- There should be sufficient training iterations to expose all the training data to the model multiple times.

- The learning rate is typically linearly decayed over the training period from an initial value to close to zero.

- The more complex the class distribution, the more codebook vectors that will be required, some problems may need thousands.

- Multiple passes of the LVQ training algorithm are suggested for more robust usage, where the first pass has a large learning rate to prepare the codebook vectors and the second pass has a low learning rate and runs for a long time (perhaps 10-times more iterations).

8.5.6 Code Listing

Listing 8.4 provides an example of the Learning Vector Quantization algorithm implemented in the Ruby Programming Language. The problem is a contrived classification problem in a 2-dimensional domain $x \in [0, 1], y \in [0, 1]$ with two classes: 'A' ($x \in [0, 0.4999999], y \in [0, 0.4999999]$) and 'B' ($x \in [0.5, 1], y \in [0.5, 1]$).

The algorithm was implemented using the LVQ1 variant where the best matching codebook vector is located and moved toward the input vector if it is the same class, or away if the classes differ. A linear decay was used for the learning rate that was updated after each pattern was exposed to the model. The implementation can easily be extended to the other variants of the method.

```ruby
def random_vector(minmax)
  return Array.new(minmax.size) do |i|
    minmax[i][0] + ((minmax[i][1] - minmax[i][0]) * rand())
  end
end

def generate_random_pattern(domain)
  classes = domain.keys
  selected_class = rand(classes.size)
  pattern = {:label=>classes[selected_class]}
  pattern[:vector] = random_vector(domain[classes[selected_class]])
  return pattern
end

def initialize_vectors(domain, num_vectors)
```

```ruby
16    classes = domain.keys
17    codebook_vectors = []
18    num_vectors.times do
19      selected_class = rand(classes.size)
20      codebook = {}
21      codebook[:label] = classes[selected_class]
22      codebook[:vector] = random_vector([[0,1],[0,1]])
23      codebook_vectors << codebook
24    end
25    return codebook_vectors
26  end
27
28  def euclidean_distance(c1, c2)
29    sum = 0.0
30    c1.each_index {|i| sum += (c1[i]-c2[i])**2.0}
31    return Math.sqrt(sum)
32  end
33
34  def get_best_matching_unit(codebook_vectors, pattern)
35    best, b_dist = nil, nil
36    codebook_vectors.each do |codebook|
37      dist = euclidean_distance(codebook[:vector], pattern[:vector])
38      best,b_dist = codebook,dist if b_dist.nil? or dist<b_dist
39    end
40    return best
41  end
42
43  def update_codebook_vector(bmu, pattern, lrate)
44    bmu[:vector].each_with_index do |v,i|
45      error = pattern[:vector][i]-bmu[:vector][i]
46      if bmu[:label] == pattern[:label]
47        bmu[:vector][i] += lrate * error
48      else
49        bmu[:vector][i] -= lrate * error
50      end
51    end
52  end
53
54  def train_network(codebook_vectors, domain, iterations, learning_rate)
55    iterations.times do |iter|
56      pat = generate_random_pattern(domain)
57      bmu = get_best_matching_unit(codebook_vectors, pat)
58      lrate = learning_rate * (1.0-(iter.to_f/iterations.to_f))
59      if iter.modulo(10)==0
60        puts "> iter=#{iter}, got=#{bmu[:label]}, exp=#{pat[:label]}"
61      end
62      update_codebook_vector(bmu, pat, lrate)
63    end
64  end
65
66  def test_network(codebook_vectors, domain, num_trials=100)
67    correct = 0
68    num_trials.times do
69      pattern = generate_random_pattern(domain)
70      bmu = get_best_matching_unit(codebook_vectors, pattern)
71      correct += 1 if bmu[:label] == pattern[:label]
```

```
72    end
73    puts "Done. Score: #{correct}/#{num_trials}"
74    return correct
75  end
76
77  def execute(domain, iterations, num_vectors, learning_rate)
78    codebook_vectors = initialize_vectors(domain, num_vectors)
79    train_network(codebook_vectors, domain, iterations, learning_rate)
80    test_network(codebook_vectors, domain)
81    return codebook_vectors
82  end
83
84  if __FILE__ == $0
85    # problem configuration
86    domain = {"A"=>[[0,0.4999999],[0,0.4999999]],"B"=>[[0.5,1],[0.5,1]]}
87    # algorithm configuration
88    learning_rate = 0.3
89    iterations = 1000
90    num_vectors = 20
91    # execute the algorithm
92    execute(domain, iterations, num_vectors, learning_rate)
93  end
```

Listing 8.4: Learning Vector Quantization in Ruby

8.5.7   References

Primary Sources

The Learning Vector Quantization algorithm was described by Kohonen in 1988 [2], and was further described in the same year by Kohonen [1] and benchmarked by Kohonen, Barna, and Chrisley [5].

Learn More

Kohonen provides a detailed overview of the state of LVQ algorithms and variants (LVQ1, LVQ2, and LVQ2.1) [3]. The technical report that comes with the LVQ_PAK software (written by Kohonen and his students) provides both an excellent summary of the technique and its main variants, as well as summarizing the important considerations when applying the approach [6]. The seminal book on Learning Vector Quantization and the Self-Organizing Map is "Self-Organizing Maps" by Kohonen, which includes a chapter (Chapter 6) dedicated to LVQ and its variants [4].

8.5.8   Bibliography

[1] T. Kohonen. An introduction to neural computing. *Neural Networks*, 1(1):3–16, 1988.

[2] T. Kohonen. Learning vector quantization. *Neural Networks*, 1:303, 1988.

[3] T. Kohonen. Improved versions of learning vector quantization. In *IJCNN International Joint Conference on Neural Networks*, volume 1, pages 545–550. IEEE Press, 1990.

[4] T. Kohonen. *Self-Organizing Maps*. Springer, 1995.

[5] T. Kohonen, G. Barna, and R. Chrisley. Statistical pattern recognition with neural networks: benchmarking studies. In *IEEE International Conference on Neural Networks*, volume 1, pages 61–68, 1988.

[6] T. Kohonen, J. Hynninen, J. Kangas, J. Laaksonen, and K. Torkkola. LVQ–PAK: The learning vector quantization program package. Technical Report A30, Helsinki University of Technology, Laboratory of Computer and Information Science, Rakentajanaukio, 1996.

8.6   Self-Organizing Map

Self-Organizing Map, SOM, Self-Organizing Feature Map, SOFM, Kohonen Map, Kohonen Network.

8.6.1   Taxonomy

The Self-Organizing Map algorithm belongs to the field of Artificial Neural Networks and Neural Computation. More broadly it belongs to the field of Computational Intelligence. The Self-Organizing Map is an unsupervised neural network that uses a competitive (winner-take-all) learning strategy. It is related to other unsupervised neural networks such as the Adaptive Resonance Theory (ART) method. It is related to other competitive learning neural networks such as the the Neural Gas Algorithm, and the Learning Vector Quantization algorithm (Section 8.5), which is a similar algorithm for classification without connections between the neurons. Additionally, SOM is a baseline technique that has inspired many variations and extensions, not limited to the Adaptive-Subspace Self-Organizing Map (ASSOM).

8.6.2   Inspiration

The Self-Organizing Map is inspired by postulated feature maps of neurons in the brain comprised of feature-sensitive cells that provide ordered projections between neuronal layers, such as those that may exist in the retina and cochlea. For example, there are acoustic feature maps that respond to sounds to which an animal is most frequently exposed, and tonotopic maps that may be responsible for the order preservation of acoustic resonances.

8.6.3   Strategy

The information processing objective of the algorithm is to optimally place a topology (grid or lattice) of codebook or prototype vectors in the domain of the observed input data samples. An initially random pool of vectors is prepared which are then exposed to training samples. A winner-take-all strategy is employed where the most similar vector to a given input pattern is selected, then the selected vector and neighbors of the selected vector are updated to closer resemble the input pattern. The repetition of this process results in the distribution of codebook vectors in the input space which approximate the underlying distribution of samples from the test dataset. The result is the mapping of the topology of codebook vectors to the underlying structure in the input samples which may be summarized or visualized to reveal topologically preserved features from the input space in a low-dimensional projection.

8.6.4   Procedure

The Self-Organizing map is comprised of a collection of codebook vectors connected together in a topological arrangement, typically a one dimensional line or a two dimensional grid. The codebook vectors themselves represent prototypes (points) within the domain, whereas the topological structure imposes an ordering between the vectors during the training process. The result is a low dimensional projection or approximation of the problem domain which may be visualized, or from which clusters may be extracted.

Algorithm 8.6.1 provides a high-level pseudocode for preparing codebook vectors using the Self-Organizing Map method. Codebook vectors are initialized to small floating point values, or sampled from the domain. The Best Matching Unit (BMU) is the codebook vector from the pool that has the minimum distance to an input vector. A distance measure between input patterns must be defined. For real-valued vectors, this is commonly the Euclidean distance:

$$dist(x, c) = \sum_{i=1}^{n} (x_i - c_i)^2 \tag{8.11}$$

where n is the number of attributes, x is the input vector and c is a given codebook vector.

The neighbors of the BMU in the topological structure of the network are selected using a neighborhood size that is linearly decreased during the training of the network. The BMU and all selected neighbors are then adjusted toward the input vector using a learning rate that too is decreased linearly with the training cycles:

$$c_i(t + 1) = learn_{rate}(t) \times (c_i(t) - x_i) \tag{8.12}$$

where $c_i(t)$ is the ith attribute of a codebook vector at time t, $learn_{rate}$ is the current learning rate, an x_i is the ith attribute of a input vector.

The neighborhood is typically square (called bubble) where all neighborhood nodes are updated using the same learning rate for the iteration, or Gaussian where the learning rate is proportional to the neighborhood distance using a Gaussian distribution (neighbors further away from the BMU are updated less).

8.6.5   Heuristics

- The Self-Organizing Map was designed for unsupervised learning problems such as feature extraction, visualization and clustering. Some extensions of the approach can label the prepared codebook vectors which can be used for classification.

- SOM is non-parametric, meaning that it does not rely on assumptions about that structure of the function that it is approximating.

Algorithm 8.6.1: Pseudocode for the SOM.

Input: InputPatterns, $iterations_{max}$, $learn_{rate}^{init}$, $neighborhood_{size}^{init}$,
$\quad Grid_{width}$, $Grid_{height}$
Output: CodebookVectors

1 CodebookVectors $\leftarrow$ InitializeCodebookVectors($Grid_{width}$,
$Grid_{height}$, InputPatterns);
2 **for** $i = 1$ **to** $iterations_{max}$ **do**
3 $\quad$ $learn_{rate}^i \leftarrow$ CalculateLearningRate(i, $learn_{rate}^{init}$);
4 $\quad$ $neighborhood_{size}^i \leftarrow$ CalculateNeighborhoodSize(i,
$\quad neighborhood_{size}^{init}$);
5 $\quad$ $Pattern_i \leftarrow$ SelectInputPattern(InputPatterns);
6 $\quad$ $Bmu_i \leftarrow$ SelectBestMatchingUnit($Pattern_i$,
$\quad$ CodebookVectors);
7 $\quad$ Neighborhood $\leftarrow$ Bmu_i;
8 $\quad$ Neighborhood $\leftarrow$ SelectNeighbors(Bmu_i, CodebookVectors,
$\quad neighborhood_{size}^i$);
9 $\quad$ **foreach** $Vector_i \in$ Neighborhood **do**
10 $\quad\quad$ **foreach** $Vector_i^{attribute} \in Vector_i$ **do**
11 $\quad\quad\quad$ $Vector_i^{attribute} \leftarrow Vector_i^{attribute} + learn_{rate}^i \times$
$\quad\quad\quad$ $(Pattern_i^{attribute} - Vector_i^{attribute})$
12 $\quad\quad$ **end**
13 $\quad$ **end**
14 **end**
15 **return** CodebookVectors;

- Real-values in input vectors should be normalized such that $x \in [0, 1)$.

- Euclidean distance is commonly used to measure the distance between real-valued vectors, although other distance measures may be used (such as dot product), and data specific distance measures may be required for non-scalar attributes.

- There should be sufficient training iterations to expose all the training data to the model multiple times.

- The more complex the class distribution, the more codebook vectors that will be required, some problems may need thousands.

- Multiple passes of the SOM training algorithm are suggested for more robust usage, where the first pass has a large learning rate to prepare the codebook vectors and the second pass has a low learning rate and runs for a long time (perhaps 10-times more iterations).

- The SOM can be visualized by calculating a Unified Distance Matrix (U-Matrix) shows highlights the relationships between the nodes in the chosen topology. A Principle Component Analysis (PCA) or Sammon's Mapping can be used to visualize just the nodes of the network without their inter-relationships.

- A rectangular 2D grid topology is typically used for a SOM, although toroidal and sphere topologies can be used. Hexagonal grids have demonstrated better results on some problems and grids with higher dimensions have been investigated.

- The neuron positions can be updated incrementally or in a batch model (each epoch of being exposed to all training samples). Batch-mode training is generally expected to result in a more stable network.

- The learning rate and neighborhood size parameters typically decrease linearly with the training iterations, although non-linear functions may be used.

8.6.6 Code Listing

Listing 8.5 provides an example of the Self-Organizing Map algorithm implemented in the Ruby Programming Language. The problem is a feature detection problem, where the network is expected to learn a predefined shape based on being exposed to samples in the domain. The domain is two-dimensional $x, y \in [0, 1]$, where a shape is pre-defined as a square in the middle of the domain $x, y \in [0.3, 0.6]$. The system is initialized to vectors within the domain although is only exposed to samples within the pre-defined shape during training. The expectation is that the system will model the shape based on the observed samples.

The algorithm is an implementation of the basic Self-Organizing Map algorithm based on the description in Chapter 3 of the seminal book on the technique [5]. The implementation is configured with a 4×5 grid of nodes, the Euclidean distance measure is used to determine the BMU and neighbors, a Bubble neighborhood function is used. Error rates are presented to the console, and the codebook vectors themselves are described before and after training. The learning process is incremental rather than batch, for simplicity.

An extension to this implementation would be to visualize the resulting network structure in the domain - shrinking from a mesh that covers the whole domain, down to a mesh that only covers the pre-defined shape within the domain.

```ruby
def random_vector(minmax)
  return Array.new(minmax.size) do |i|
    minmax[i][0] + ((minmax[i][1] - minmax[i][0]) * rand())
  end
end

def initialize_vectors(domain, width, height)
```

```ruby
 8    codebook_vectors = []
 9    width.times do |x|
10      height.times do |y|
11        codebook = {}
12        codebook[:vector] = random_vector(domain)
13        codebook[:coord] = [x,y]
14        codebook_vectors << codebook
15      end
16    end
17    return codebook_vectors
18  end
19
20  def euclidean_distance(c1, c2)
21    sum = 0.0
22    c1.each_index {|i| sum += (c1[i]-c2[i])**2.0}
23    return Math.sqrt(sum)
24  end
25
26  def get_best_matching_unit(codebook_vectors, pattern)
27    best, b_dist = nil, nil
28    codebook_vectors.each do |codebook|
29      dist = euclidean_distance(codebook[:vector], pattern)
30      best,b_dist = codebook,dist if b_dist.nil? or dist<b_dist
31    end
32    return [best, b_dist]
33  end
34
35  def get_vectors_in_neighborhood(bmu, codebook_vectors, neigh_size)
36    neighborhood = []
37    codebook_vectors.each do |other|
38      if euclidean_distance(bmu[:coord], other[:coord]) <= neigh_size
39        neighborhood << other
40      end
41    end
42    return neighborhood
43  end
44
45  def update_codebook_vector(codebook, pattern, lrate)
46    codebook[:vector].each_with_index do |v,i|
47      error = pattern[i]-codebook[:vector][i]
48      codebook[:vector][i] += lrate * error
49    end
50  end
51
52  def train_network(vectors, shape, iterations, l_rate, neighborhood_size)
53    iterations.times do |iter|
54      pattern = random_vector(shape)
55      lrate = l_rate * (1.0-(iter.to_f/iterations.to_f))
56      neigh_size = neighborhood_size * (1.0-(iter.to_f/iterations.to_f))
57      bmu,dist = get_best_matching_unit(vectors, pattern)
58      neighbors = get_vectors_in_neighborhood(bmu, vectors, neigh_size)
59      neighbors.each do |node|
60        update_codebook_vector(node, pattern, lrate)
61      end
62      puts ">training: neighbors=#{neighbors.size}, bmu_dist=#{dist}"
63    end
```

```ruby
64   end
65
66   def summarize_vectors(vectors)
67     minmax = Array.new(vectors.first[:vector].size){[1,0]}
68     vectors.each do |c|
69       c[:vector].each_with_index do |v,i|
70         minmax[i][0] = v if v<minmax[i][0]
71         minmax[i][1] = v if v>minmax[i][1]
72       end
73     end
74     s = ""
75     minmax.each_with_index {|bounds,i| s << "#{i}=#{bounds.inspect} "}
76     puts "Vector details: #{s}"
77     return minmax
78   end
79
80   def test_network(codebook_vectors, shape, num_trials=100)
81     error = 0.0
82     num_trials.times do
83       pattern = random_vector(shape)
84       bmu,dist = get_best_matching_unit(codebook_vectors, pattern)
85       error += dist
86     end
87     error /= num_trials.to_f
88     puts "Finished, average error=#{error}"
89     return error
90   end
91
92   def execute(domain, shape, iterations, l_rate, neigh_size, width, height)
93     vectors = initialize_vectors(domain, width, height)
94     summarize_vectors(vectors)
95     train_network(vectors, shape, iterations, l_rate, neigh_size)
96     test_network(vectors, shape)
97     summarize_vectors(vectors)
98     return vectors
99   end
100
101  if __FILE__ == $0
102    # problem configuration
103    domain = [[0.0,1.0],[0.0,1.0]]
104    shape = [[0.3,0.6],[0.3,0.6]]
105    # algorithm configuration
106    iterations = 100
107    l_rate = 0.3
108    neigh_size = 5
109    width, height = 4, 5
110    # execute the algorithm
111    execute(domain, shape, iterations, l_rate, neigh_size, width, height)
112  end
```

Listing 8.5: Self-Organizing Map in Ruby

8.6.7 References

Primary Sources

The Self-Organizing Map was proposed by Kohonen in 1982 in a study that included the mathematical basis for the approach, summary of related physiology, and simulation on demonstration problem domains using one and two dimensional topological structures [3]. This work was tightly related two other papers published at close to the same time on topological maps and self-organization [1, 2].

Learn More

Kohonen provides a detailed introduction and summary of the Self-Organizing Map in a journal article [4]. Kohonen et al. provide a practical presentation of the algorithm and heuristics for configuration in the technical report written to accompany the released SOM-PAK implementation of the algorithm for academic research [6]. The seminal book on the technique is "Self-Organizing Maps" by Kohonen, which includes chapters dedicated to the description of the basic approach, physiological interpretations of the algorithm, variations, and summaries of application areas [5].

8.6.8 Bibliography

[1] T. Kohonen. Automatic formation of topological maps of patterns in a self-organizing system. In *Proceedings of 2nd Scandinavian Conf. on Image Analysis*, pages 214–220, 1981.

[2] T. Kohonen. Clustering, taxonomy, and topological maps of patterns. In *International Conference on Pattern Recognition*, pages 114–128, 1982.

[3] T. Kohonen. Self-organized formation of topologically correct feature maps. *Biological Cybernetics*, 43:59–69, 1982.

[4] T. Kohonen. The self-organizing map. *Proceedings of the IEEE*, 78(9):1464–1480, 1990.

[5] T. Kohonen. *Self-Organizing Maps*. Springer, 1995.

[6] T. Kohonen, J. Hynninen, J. Kangas, and J. Laaksonen. SOM–PAK: The self-organizing map program package. Technical Report A31, Helsinki University of Technology, Laboratory of Computer and Information Science, 1996.

Part III

Extensions

Chapter 9

Advanced Topics

This chapter discusses a number of advanced topics that may be considered once one or more of the algorithms described in this book have been mastered.

The topics in this section consider some practical concerns such as:

- How to implement an algorithm using a different programming paradigm (Section 9.1).

- How to devise and investigate a new biologically-inspired algorithm (Section 9.2).

- How to test algorithm implementations to ensure they are implemented correctly (Section 9.3).

- How to visualize problems, algorithm behavior and candidate solutions (Section 9.4).

- How to direct these algorithms toward practical problem solving (Section 9.5).

- Issues to consider when benchmarking and comparing the capabilities of algorithms (Section 9.6).

The objective of this chapter is to illustrate the concerns and skills necessary for taking the algorithms described in this book into the real-world.

9.1   Programming Paradigms

This section discusses three standard programming paradigms that may be used to implement the algorithms described throughput the book:

- Procedural Programming (Section 9.1.1)

- Object-Oriented Programming (Section 9.1.2)

- Flow Programming (Section 9.1.3)

Each paradigm is described and an example implementation is provided using the Genetic Algorithm (described in Section 3.2) as a context.

9.1.1   Procedural Programming

This section considers the implementation of algorithms from the Clever Algorithms project in the Procedural Programming Paradigm.

Description

The procedural programming paradigm (also called imperative programming) is concerned with defining a linear procedure or sequence of programming statements. A key feature of the paradigm is the partitioning of functionality into small discrete re-usable modules called procedures (subroutines or functions) that act like small programs themselves with their own scope, inputs and outputs. A procedural code example is executed from a single point of control or entry point which calls out into declared procedures, which in turn may call other procedures.

Procedural programming was an early so-called 'high-level programming paradigm' (compared to lower-level machine code) and is the most common and well understood form of programming. Newer paradigms (such as Object-Oriented programming) and modern businesses programming languages (such as C++, Java and C#) are built on the principles of procedural programming.

All algorithms in this book were implemented using a procedural programming paradigm in the Ruby Programming Language. A procedural representation was chosen to provide the most transferrable instantiation of the algorithm implementations. Many languages support the procedural paradigm and procedural code examples are expected to be easily ported to popular paradigms such as object-oriented and functional.

Example

Listing 3.1 in Section 3.2 provides an example of the Genetic Algorithm implemented in the Ruby Programming Language using the procedural programming paradigm.

9.1.2 Object-Oriented Programming

This section considers the implementation of algorithms from the Clever Algorithms project in the Object-Oriented Programming Paradigm.

Description

The Object-Oriented Programming (OOP) paradigm is concerned with modeling problems in terms of entities called objects that have attributes and behaviors (data and methods) and interact with other entities using message passing (calling methods on other entities). An object developer defines a class or template for the entity, which is instantiated or constructed and then may be used in the program.

Objects can extend other objects, inheriting some or all of the attributes and behaviors from the parent providing specific modular reuse. Objects can be treated as a parent type (an object in its inheritance tree) allowing the use or application of the objects in the program without the caller knowing the specifics of the behavior or data inside the object. This general property is called polymorphism, which exploits the encapsulation of attributes and behavior within objects and their capability of being treated (viewed or interacted with) as a parent type.

Organizing functionality into objects allows for additional constructs such as abstract types where functionality is only partially defined and must be completed by descendant objects, overriding where descending objects re-define behavior defined in a parent object, and static classes and behaviors where behavior is executed on the object template rather than the object instance. For more information on Object-Oriented programming and software design refer to a good textbook on the subject, such as Booch [1] or Meyer [3].

There are common ways of solving discrete problems using object-oriented programs called patterns. They are organizations of behavior and data that have been abstracted and presented as a solution or idiom for a class of problem. The Strategy Pattern is an object-oriented pattern that is suited to implementing an algorithm. This pattern is intended to encapsulate the behavior of an algorithm as a strategy object where different strategies can be used interchangeably on a given context or problem domain. This strategy can be useful in situations where the performance or capability of a range of different techniques needs to be assessed on a given problem (such as algorithm racing or bake-offs). Additionally, the problem or context can also be modeled as an interchangeable object, allowing both algorithms and problems to be used interchangeably. This method is used in object-oriented algorithm frameworks. For more information on the strategy pattern or object-oriented design patterns in general, refer to Gamma et al. [2].

Example

Listing 9.1 provides an example of the Genetic Algorithm implemented in the Ruby Programming Language using the Object-Oriented Programming Paradigm.

The implementation provides general problem and strategy classes that define their behavioral expectations. A `OneMax` problem class and a `Genetic-Algorithm` strategy class are specified. The algorithm makes few assumptions of the problem other than it can assess candidate solutions and determine whether a given solution is optimal. The problem makes very few assumptions about candidate solutions other than they are map data structures that contain a binary string and fitness key-value pairs. The use of the Strategy Pattern allows a new algorithm to easily be defined to work with the existing problem, and that new problems could be defined for the Genetic Algorithm to execute.

Note that Ruby does not support abstract classes, so this construct is simulated by defining methods that raise an exception if they are not overridden by descendant classes.

```ruby
 1  # A problem template
 2  class Problem
 3    def assess(candidate_solution)
 4      raise "A problem has not been defined"
 5    end
 6
 7    def is_optimal?(candidate_solution)
 8      raise "A problem has not been defined"
 9    end
10  end
11
12  # An strategy template
13  class Strategy
14    def execute(problem)
15      raise "A strategy has not been defined!"
16    end
17  end
18
19  # An implementation of the OneMax problem using the problem template
20  class OneMax < Problem
21
22    attr_reader :num_bits
23
24    def initialize(num_bits=64)
25      @num_bits = num_bits
26    end
27
28    def assess(candidate_solution)
29      if candidate_solution[:bitstring].length != @num_bits
30        raise "Expected #{@num_bits} in candidate solution."
31      end
32      sum = 0
33      candidate_solution[:bitstring].size.times do |i|
34        sum += 1 if candidate_solution[:bitstring][i].chr =='1'
```

```
35        end
36        return sum
37      end
38
39      def is_optimal?(candidate_solution)
40        return candidate_solution[:fitness] == @num_bits
41      end
42    end
43
44    # An implementation of the Genetic algorithm using the strategy template
45    class GeneticAlgorithm < Strategy
46
47      attr_reader :max_generations, :population_size, :p_crossover, :p_mutation
48
49      def initialize(max_gens=100, pop_size=100, crossover=0.98,
                mutation=1.0/64.0)
50        @max_generations = max_gens
51        @population_size = pop_size
52        @p_crossover = crossover
53        @p_mutation = mutation
54      end
55
56      def random_bitstring(num_bits)
57        return (0...num_bits).inject(""){|s,i| s<<((rand<0.5) ? "1" : "0")}
58      end
59
60      def binary_tournament(pop)
61        i, j = rand(pop.size), rand(pop.size)
62        j = rand(pop.size) while j==i
63        return (pop[i][:fitness] > pop[j][:fitness]) ? pop[i] : pop[j]
64      end
65
66      def point_mutation(bitstring)
67        child = ""
68         bitstring.size.times do |i|
69          bit = bitstring[i].chr
70          child << ((rand()<@p_mutation) ? ((bit=='1') ? "0" : "1") : bit)
71        end
72        return child
73      end
74
75      def uniform_crossover(parent1, parent2)
76        return ""+parent1 if rand()>=@p_crossover
77        child = ""
78        parent1.length.times do |i|
79          child << ((rand()<0.5) ? parent1[i].chr : parent2[i].chr)
80        end
81        return child
82      end
83
84      def reproduce(selected)
85        children = []
86        selected.each_with_index do |p1, i|
87          p2 = (i.modulo(2)==0) ? selected[i+1] : selected[i-1]
88          p2 = selected[0] if i == selected.size-1
89          child = {}
```

```
90      child[:bitstring] = uniform_crossover(p1[:bitstring], p2[:bitstring])
91      child[:bitstring] = point_mutation(child[:bitstring])
92      children << child
93      break if children.size >= @population_size
94    end
95    return children
96  end
97
98  def execute(problem)
99    population = Array.new(@population_size) do |i|
100     {:bitstring=>random_bitstring(problem.num_bits)}
101   end
102   population.each{|c| c[:fitness] = problem.assess(c)}
103   best = population.sort{|x,y| y[:fitness] <=> x[:fitness]}.first
104   @max_generations.times do |gen|
105     selected = Array.new(population_size){|i|
                binary_tournament(population)}
106     children = reproduce(selected)
107     children.each{|c| c[:fitness] = problem.assess(c)}
108     children.sort!{|x,y| y[:fitness] <=> x[:fitness]}
109     best = children.first if children.first[:fitness] >= best[:fitness]
110     population = children
111     puts " > gen #{gen}, best: #{best[:fitness]}, #{best[:bitstring]}"
112     break if problem.is_optimal?(best)
113   end
114   return best
115  end
116 end
117
118 if __FILE__ == $0
119   # problem configuration
120   problem = OneMax.new
121   # algorithm configuration
122   strategy = GeneticAlgorithm.new
123   # execute the algorithm
124   best = strategy.execute(problem)
125   puts "done! Solution: f=#{best[:fitness]}, s=#{best[:bitstring]}"
126 end
```

Listing 9.1: Genetic Algorithm in Ruby using OOP

9.1.3   Flow Programming

This section considers the implementation of algorithms from the Clever Algorithms project in the Flow Programming paradigm.

Description

Flow, data-flow, or pipeline programming involves chaining a sequence of smaller processes together and allowing a flow of information through the sequence in order to perform the desired computation. Units in the flow are considered black-boxes that communicate with each other using message passing. The information that is passed between the units is considered a stream and a given application may have one or more streams of potentially varying direction. Discrete information in a stream is partitioned into information packets which are passed from unit-to-unit via message buffers, queues or similar data structures.

A flow organization allows computing units to be interchanged readily. It also allows for variations of the pipeline to be considered with minor reconfiguration. A flow or pipelining structure is commonly used by software frameworks for the organization within a given algorithm implementation, allowing the specification of operators that manipulate candidate solutions to be varied and interchanged.

For more information on Flow Programming see a good textbook on the subject, such as Morrison [4].

Example

Listing 9.2 provides an example of the Genetic Algorithm implemented in the Ruby Programming Language using the Flow Programming paradigm. Each unit is implemented as an object that executes its logic within a standalone thread that reads input from the input queue and writes data to its output queue. The implementation shows four flow units organized into a cyclic graph where the output queue of one unit is used as the input of the next unit in the cycle (`EvalFlowUnit` to `StopConditionUnit` to `SelectFlowUnit` to `VariationFlowUnit`).

Candidate solutions are the unit of data that is passed around in the flow between units. When the system is started it does not have any information to process until a set of random solutions are injected into the evaluation unit's input queue. The solution are evaluated and sent to the stop condition unit where the constraints of the algorithm execution are tested (optima found or maximum number of evaluations) and the candidates are passed on to the selection flow unit. The selection unit collects a predefined number of candidate solutions then passes the better solutions onto the variation unit. The variation unit performs crossover and mutation on each pair of candidate solutions and sends the results to the evaluation unit, completing the cycle.

```
1   require 'thread'
2
3   # Generic flow unit
4   class FlowUnit
5     attr_reader :queue_in, :queue_out, :thread
6
7     def initialize(q_in=Queue.new, q_out=Queue.new)
8       @queue_in, @queue_out = q_in, q_out
9       start()
10    end
11
12    def execute
13      raise "FlowUnit not defined!"
```

```
14      end
15
16      def start
17        puts "Starting flow unit: #{self.class.name}!"
18        @thread = Thread.new do
19          execute() while true
20        end
21      end
22    end
23
24    # Evaluation of solutions flow unit
25    class EvalFlowUnit < FlowUnit
26      def onemax(bitstring)
27        sum = 0
28        bitstring.size.times {|i| sum+=1 if bitstring[i].chr=='1'}
29        return sum
30      end
31
32      def execute
33        data = @queue_in.pop
34        data[:fitness] = onemax(data[:bitstring])
35        @queue_out.push(data)
36      end
37    end
38
39    # Stop condition flow unit
40    class StopConditionUnit < FlowUnit
41      attr_reader :best, :num_bits, :max_evaluations, :evals
42
43      def initialize(q_in=Queue.new, q_out=Queue.new, max_evaluations=10000,
            num_bits=64)
44        @best, @evals = nil, 0
45        @num_bits = num_bits
46        @max_evaluations = max_evaluations
47        super(q_in, q_out)
48      end
49
50      def execute
51        data = @queue_in.pop
52        if @best.nil? or data[:fitness] > @best[:fitness]
53          @best = data
54          puts " >new best: #{@best[:fitness]}, #{@best[:bitstring]}"
55        end
56        @evals += 1
57        if @best[:fitness]==@num_bits or @evals>=@max_evaluations
58          puts "done! Solution: f=#{@best[:fitness]}, s=#{@best[:bitstring]}"
59          @thread.exit()
60        end
61        @queue_out.push(data)
62      end
63    end
64
65    # Fitness-based selection flow unit
66    class SelectFlowUnit < FlowUnit
67      def initialize(q_in=Queue.new, q_out=Queue.new, pop_size=100)
68        @pop_size = pop_size
```

```
69        super(q_in, q_out)
70      end
71
72      def binary_tournament(pop)
73        i, j = rand(pop.size), rand(pop.size)
74        j = rand(pop.size) while j==i
75        return (pop[i][:fitness] > pop[j][:fitness]) ? pop[i] : pop[j]
76      end
77
78      def execute
79        population = Array.new
80        population << @queue_in.pop while population.size < @pop_size
81        @pop_size.times do |i|
82          @queue_out.push(binary_tournament(population))
83        end
84      end
85    end
86
87    # Variation flow unit
88    class VariationFlowUnit < FlowUnit
89      def initialize(q_in=Queue.new, q_out=Queue.new, crossover=0.98,
                mutation=1.0/64.0)
90        @p_crossover = crossover
91        @p_mutation = mutation
92        super(q_in, q_out)
93      end
94
95      def uniform_crossover(parent1, parent2)
96        return ""+parent1 if rand()>=@p_crossover
97        child = ""
98        parent1.length.times do |i|
99          child << ((rand()<0.5) ? parent1[i].chr : parent2[i].chr)
100       end
101       return child
102     end
103
104     def point_mutation(bitstring)
105       child = ""
106       bitstring.size.times do |i|
107         bit = bitstring[i].chr
108         child << ((rand()<@p_mutation) ? ((bit=='1') ? "0" : "1") : bit)
109       end
110       return child
111     end
112
113     def reproduce(p1, p2)
114       child = {}
115       child[:bitstring] = uniform_crossover(p1[:bitstring], p2[:bitstring])
116       child[:bitstring] = point_mutation(child[:bitstring])
117       return child
118     end
119
120     def execute
121       parent1 = @queue_in.pop
122       parent2 = @queue_in.pop
123       @queue_out.push(reproduce(parent1, parent2))
```

```
124       @queue_out.push(reproduce(parent2, parent1))
125     end
126   end
127
128   def random_bitstring(num_bits)
129     return (0...num_bits).inject(""){|s,i| s<<((rand<0.5) ? "1" : "0")}
130   end
131
132   def search(population_size=100, num_bits=64)
133     # create the pipeline
134     eval = EvalFlowUnit.new
135     stopcondition = StopConditionUnit.new(eval.queue_out)
136     selection = SelectFlowUnit.new(stopcondition.queue_out)
137     variation = VariationFlowUnit.new(selection.queue_out, eval.queue_in)
138     # push random solutions into the pipeline
139     population_size.times do
140       solution = {:bitstring=>random_bitstring(num_bits)}
141       eval.queue_in.push(solution)
142     end
143     stopcondition.thread.join
144     return stopcondition.best
145   end
146
147   if __FILE__ == $0
148     best = search()
149     puts "done! Solution: f=#{best[:fitness]}, s=#{best[:bitstring]}"
150   end
```

Listing 9.2: Genetic Algorithm in Ruby using the Flow Programming

9.1.4   Other Paradigms

A number of popular and common programming paradigms have been considered in this section, although many more have not been described.

Many programming paradigms are not appropriate for implementing algorithms as-is, but may be useful with the algorithm as a component in a broader system, such as Agent-Oriented Programming where the algorithm may be a procedure available to the agent. Meta-programming a case where the capabilities of the paradigm may be used for parts of an algorithm implementation, such as the manipulation of candidate programs in Genetic Programming (Section 3.3). Aspect-Oriented Programming could be layered over an object oriented algorithm implementation and used to separate the concerns of termination conditions and best solution logging.

Other programming paradigms provide variations on what has already been described, such as Functional Programming which would be similar to the procedural example, and Event-Driven Programming that would not be too dissimilar in principle to the Flow-Based Programming. Another example is the popular idiom of Map-Reduce which is an application of functional programming principles organized into a data flow model.

Finally, there are programming paradigms that are not relevant or feasible to consider implementing algorithms, such as Logic Programming.

9.1.5   Bibliography

[1] G. Booch, R. Maksimchuk, M. Engle, B. Young, J. Conallen, and K. Houston. *Object-Oriented Analysis and Design with Applications*. Addison-Wesley, 1997.

[2] E. Gamma, R. Helm, R. Johnson, and J. Vlissides. *Design Patterns: Elements of Reusable Object Oriented Software*. Addison-Wesley, 1995.

[3] B. Meyer. *Object-Oriented Software Construction*. Prentice Hall, 1997.

[4] J-P. Morrison. *Flow-Based Programming: A New Approach to Application Developments*. CreateSpace, 2nd edition, 2010.

9.2 Devising New Algorithms

This section provides a discussion of some of the approaches that may be used to devise new algorithms and systems inspired by biological systems for addressing mathematical and engineering problems. This discussion covers:

- An introduction to adaptive systems and complex adaptive systems as an approach for studying natural phenomenon and deducing adaptive strategies that may be the basis for algorithms (Section 9.2.1).

- An introduction to some frameworks and methodologies for reducing natural systems into abstract information processing procedures and ultimately algorithms (Section 9.2.2).

- A summary of a methodology that may be used to investigate a devised adaptive system that considers the trade-off in model fidelity and descriptive power proposed by Goldberg, a pioneer in the Evolutionary Computation field (Section 9.2.3).

9.2.1 Adaptive Systems

Many algorithms, such as the Genetic Algorithm have come from the study and models of complex and adaptive systems. Adaptive systems research provides a methodology by which these systems can be systematically investigated resulting in adaptive plans or strategies that can provide the basis for new and interesting algorithms.

Holland proposed a formalism in his seminal work on adaptive systems that provides a general manner in which to define an adaptive system [7]. Phrasing systems in this way provides a framework under which adaptive systems may be evaluated and compared relative to each other, the difficulties and obstacles of investigating specific adaptive systems are exposed, and the abstracted principles of different system types may be distilled. This section provides a summary of the Holland's seminal adaptive systems formalism and considers clonal selection as an example of an adaptive plan.

Adaptive Systems Formalism

This section presents a brief review of Holland's adaptive systems formalism described in [7] (Chapter 2). This presentation focuses particularly on the terms and their description, and has been hybridized with the concise presentation of the formalism by De Jong [9] (page 6). The formalism is divided into sections: 1) *Primary Objects* summarized in Table 9.1, and 2) *Secondary Objects* summarized in Table 9.2. Primary Objects are the conventional objects of an adaptive system: the environment e, the strategy or adaptive plan that creates solutions in the environment s, and the utility assigned to created solutions U.

Term	Object	Description
e	Environment	The environment of the system undergoing adaptation.
s	Strategy	The adaptive plan which determines successive structural modifications in response to the environment.
U	Utility	A measure of performance or payoff of different structures in the environment. Maps a given solution (A) to a real number evaluation.

Table 9.1: Primary Objects in the adaptive systems formalism.

Secondary Objects extend beyond the primary objects providing the detail of the formalism. These objects suggest a broader context than that of the instance specific primary objects, permitting the evaluation and comparison of sets of objects such as plans (S), environments (E), search spaces (A), and operators (O).

A given adaptive plan acts in discrete time t, which is a useful simplification for analysis and computer simulation. A framework for a given adaptive system requires the definition of a set of strategies S, a set of environments E, and criterion for ranking strategies X. A given adaptive plan is specified within this framework given the following set of objects: a search space A, a set of operators O, and feedback from the environment I. Holland proposed a series of fundamental questions when considering the definition for an adaptive system, which he rephrases within the context of the formalism (see Table 9.3).

Some Examples

Holland provides a series of illustrations rephrasing common adaptive systems in the context of the formalism [7] (pages 35-36). Examples include: genetics, economics, game playing, pattern recognition, control, function optimization, and the central nervous system. The formalism is applied to investigate his schemata theorem, reproductive plans, and genetic plans. These foundational models became the field of Evolutionary Computation (Chapter 3).

From working within the formalism, Holland makes six observations regarding obstacles that may be encountered whilst investigating adaptive systems [7] (pages 159-160):

- *High cardinality of A*: makes searches long and storage of relevant data difficult.

- *Appropriateness of credit*: knowledge of the properties about 'successful' structures is incomplete, making it hard to predict good future structures from past structures.

Term	Object	Description
A	Search Space	The set of attainable structures, solutions, and the domain of action for an adaptive plan.
E	Environments	The range of different environments, where e is an instance. It may also represent the unknowns of the strategy about the environment.
O	Operators	Set of operators applied to an instance of A at time t (A_t) to transform it into A_{t+1}.
S	Strategies	Set of plans applicable for a given environment (where s is an instance), that use operators from the set O.
X	Criterion	Used to compare strategies (in the set S), under the set of environments (E). Takes into account the efficiency of a plan in different environments.
I	Feedback	Set of possible environmental inputs and signals providing dynamic information to the system about the performance of a particular solution A in a particular environment E.
M	Memory	The memory or retained parts of the input history (I) for a solution (A).

Table 9.2: Secondary Objects in the adaptive systems formalism.

- *High dimensionality of U on an e*: performance is a function of a large number of variables which is difficult for classical optimization methods.

- *Non-linearity of U on an e*: many false optima or false peaks, resulting in the potential for a lot of wasted computation.

- *Mutual interference of search and exploitation*: the exploration (acquisition of new information), exploitation (application of known information) trade-off.

- *Relevant non-payoff information*: the environment may provide a lot more information in addition to payoff, some of which may be relevant to improved performance.

Cavicchio provides perhaps one of the first applications of the formalism (after Holland) in his dissertation investigating Holland's reproductive plans [10] (and to a lesser extent in [11]). The work summarizes the formalism, presenting essentially the same framework, although he provides a specialization of the search space A. The search space is broken down into a representation (codes), solutions (devices), and a mapping function from

Question	Formal
To what parts of its environment is the organism (system, organization) adapting?	What is E?
How does the environment act upon the adapting organism (system, organization)?	What is I?
What structures are undergoing adaptation?	What is A?
What are the mechanisms of adaptation?	What is O?
What part of the history of its interaction with the environment does the organism (system, organization) retain in addition to that summarized in the structure tested?	What is M?
What limits are there to the adaptive process?	What is S?
How are different (hypotheses about) adaptive processes to be compared?	What is X?

Table 9.3: Questions when investigating adaptive systems, taken from [7] (pg. 29).

representation to solutions. The variation highlights the restriction the representation and mapping have on the designs available to the adaptive plan. Further, such mappings may not be one-to-one, there may be many instances in the representation space that map to the same solution (or the reverse).

Although not explicitly defined, Holland's specification of structures A is clear in pointing out that the structures are not bound to a level of abstraction; the definition covers structures at all levels. Nevertheless, Cavicchio's specialization for a representation-solution mapping was demonstrated to be useful in his exploration of reproductive plans (early Genetic Algorithms). He proposed that an adaptive system is *first order* if the utility function U for structures on an environment encompasses feedback I.

Cavicchio described the potential independence (component-wise) and linearity of the utility function with respect to the representation used. De Jong also employed the formalism to investigate reproductive plans in his dissertation research [9]. He indicated that the formalism covers the essential characteristics of adaptation, where the performance of a solution is a function of its characteristics and its environment. Adaptation is defined as a strategy for generating better-performing solutions to a problem by reducing initial uncertainty about the environment via feedback from the evaluation of individual solutions. De Jong used the formalism to define a series of genetic reproductive plans, which he investigated in the context of function optimization.

Complex Adaptive Systems

Adaptive strategies are typically complex because they result in irreducible
emergent behaviors that occur as a result of the non-linear interactions of
system components. The study of Complex Adaptive Systems (CAS) is
the study of high-level abstractions of natural and artificial systems that
are generally impervious to traditional analysis techniques. Macroscopic
patterns emerge from the dynamic and non-linear interactions of the system's low-level (microscopic) adaptive agents. The emergent patterns are
more than the sum of their parts. As such, traditional reductionist methodologies fail to describe how the macroscopic patterns emerge. Holistic and
totalistic investigatory approaches are applied that relate the simple rules
and interactions of the simple adaptive agents to their emergent effects in a
'bottom-up' manner.

Some relevant examples of CAS include: the development of embryos,
ecologies, genetic evolution, thinking and learning in the brain, weather
systems, social systems, insect swarms, bacteria becoming resistant to an
antibiotic, and the function of the adaptive immune system.

The field of CAS was founded at the Santa Fe Institute (SFI), in the
late 1980s by a group of physicists, economists, and others interested in
the study of complex systems in which the agents of those systems change
[1]. One of the most significant contributors to the inception of the field
from the perspective of adaptation was Holland. He was interested in the
question of how computers could be programmed so that problem-solving
capabilities are built up by specifying: *"what is to be done"* (inductive
information processing) rather than *"how to do it"* (deductive information
processing). In the 1992 reprint of his book he provided a summary of CAS
with a computational example called ECHO [7]. His work on CAS was
expanded in a later book which provided an in depth study of the topic [8].

There is no clear definition of a Complex Adaptive System, rather sets
of parsimonious principles and properties, many different researches in the
field defining their own nomenclature. Popular definitions beyond Holland's
work include that of Gell-Mann [4] and Arthur [2].

9.2.2   Biologically Inspired Algorithms

Explicit methodologies have been devised and used for investigating natural
systems with the intent of devising new computational intelligence techniques. This section introduces two such methodologies taken from the field
of Artificial Immune Systems (Chapter 7).

Conceptual Framework

Although the progression from an inspiring biological system to an inspired
computation system may appear to be an intuitive process, it can involve

problems of standardization of nomenclature, effective abstraction and departure from biology, and rigor. Stepney, et al. caution that by following a process that lacks the detail of *modeling*, one may fall into the trap of *reasoning by metaphor* [12–14].

Besides the lack of rigor, the trap suggests that such reasoning and lack of objective analysis limits and biases the suitability and applicability of resultant algorithms. They propose that many algorithms in the field of Artificial Immune Systems (and beyond) have succumbed to this trap. This observation resulted in the development and application of a conceptual framework to provide a general process that may be applied in the field of Biological Inspired Computation toward realizing Biological Inspired Computational Intelligence systems.

The conceptual framework is comprised of the following actors and steps:

1. *Biological System*: The driving motivation for the work that possesses some innate information processing qualities.

2. *Probes*: Observations and experiments that provide a partial or noisy perspective of the biological system.

3. *Models*: From probes, abstract and simplified models of the information processing qualities of the system are built and validated.

4. *Framework*: Built and validated analytical computational frameworks. Validation may use mathematical analysis, benchmark problems, and engineering demonstration.

5. *Algorithms*: The framework provides the principles for designing and analyzing algorithms that may be general and applicable to domains unrelated to the biological motivation.

Immunology as Information Processing

Forrest and Hofmeyr summarized their AIS research efforts at the University of New Mexico and the Santa Fe Institute as *"immunology as information processing"* [3]. They define information as spatio-temporal patterns that can be abstracted and described independent of the biological system and information processing as computation with these patterns. They proposed that such patterns are encoded in the proteins and other molecules of the immune system, and that they govern the behavior of the biological system. They suggest that their information processing perspective can be contrasted with the conventional structural perspective of cellular interactions as mechanical devices. They consider a simple four-step procedure for the investigation of *immunology as information processing*, transitioning from the biological system to a usable computational tool:

1. Identify a specific mechanism that appears to be interesting computationally.

2. Write a computer program that implements or models the mechanism.

3. Study its properties through simulation and mathematical analysis.

4. Demonstrate capabilities either by applying the model to a biological question of interest or by showing how it can be used profitably in a computer science setting.

The procedure is similar to the outlined in the conceptual framework for Biologically Inspired Algorithms in that in addition to identifying biological mechanisms (input) and demonstrating a resultant algorithms (output), the procedure 1) highlights the need for abstraction involving modeling the identified mechanism, and 2) highlights the need to analyze the models and abstractions. The procedure of Forrest and Hofmeyr can be used to specialize the conceptual framework of Stepney et al. by clearly specifying the immunological information processing focus.

9.2.3   Modeling a New Strategy

Once an abstract information processing system is devised it must be investigated in a systematic manner. There are a range of modeling techniques for such a system from weak and rapid to realize to strong and slow to realize. This section considers the trade-off's in modeling an adaptive technique.

Engineers and Mathematicians

Goldberg describes the airplane and other products of engineering as *material machines*, and distinguishes them from the engineering of genetic algorithms and other adaptive systems as *conceptual machines*. He argues the methodological distinction between the two is counter-productive and harmful from the perspective of conceptual machines, specifically that the methodology of the material is equally applicable to that of the conceptual [5].

The obsession of mathematical rigor in computer science, although extremely valuable, is not effective in the investigation of adaptive systems given their complexity. Goldberg sites the airplane as an example where the engineering invention is used and trusted without a formal proof that the invention works (that an airplane can fly).[1]

This defense leads to what Goldberg refers to the *economy of design*, which is demonstrated with a trade-off that distinguishes 'model description' (mathematician-scientists) that is concerned with model fidelity, and model prescription (engineer-inventor) that is concerned with a working product. In descriptive modeling *the model is the thing* whereas in 'prescriptive modeling', *the object is the thing*. In the latter, the model (and thus its

---

[1]Goldberg is quick to point out that sets of equations do exist for various aspects of flight, although no integrated mathematical proof for airplane flight exists.

utility) serves the object, in the former model accuracy may be of primary concern. This economy of modeling provides a perspective that distinguishes the needs of the prescriptive and descriptive fields of investigation.

The mathematician-scientist is interested in increasing model accuracy at the expense of speed (slow), whereas the engineer may require a marginally predictive (less accurate) model relatively quickly. This trade-off between high-cost high-accuracy models and low-cost low-fidelity models is what may be referred to as the *modeling spectrum* that assists in selecting an appropriate level of modeling. Goldberg proposes that the field of Genetic Algorithms expend too much effort at either ends of this spectrum. There is much work where there is an obsession with blind-prototyping many different tweaks in the hope of striking it lucky with the *right* mechanism, operator, or parameter. Alternatively, there is also an obsession with detailed mathematical models such as differential equations and Markov chains. The middle ground of the spectrum, what Goldberg refers to as *little models* is a valuable economic modeling consideration for the investigation of conceptual machines to "*do good science through good engineering*".

Methodology

The methodology has been referred to as post-modern systems engineering and is referred to by Goldberg as a methodology of innovation [6]. The core principles of the process are as follows:

1. *Decomposition*: Decompose the large problem approximately and intuitively, breaking into quasi-separate sub-problems (as separate as possible).

2. *Modeling*: Investigate each sub-problem separately (or as separate as possible) using empirical testing coupled with adequately predictive, low-cost models.

3. *Integration*: Assemble the sub-solutions and test the overall invention, paying attention to unforeseen interactions between the sub-problems.

Decomposition Problem decomposition and decomposition design is an axiom of reductionism and is at the very heart of problem solving in computer science. In the context of adaptive systems, one may consider the base or medium on which the system is performing its computation mechanisms the so-called building blocks of information processing. A structural decomposition may involve the architecture and data structures of the system. Additionally, one may also consider a functional breakdown of mechanisms such as the operators applied at each discrete step of an algorithmic process. The reductions achieved provide the basis of investigation and modeling.

Small Models   Given the principle of the economy of modeling presented as a spectrum, one may extend the description of each of the five presented model types. *Small Models* refers to the middle of the spectrum, specifically to the application of dimensional and facet-wise models. These are mid-range quantitative models that make accurate prediction over a limited range of states at moderate cost. Once derived, this class of models generally require a small amount of formal manipulation and large amounts of data for calibration and verification. The following summarizes the modeling spectrum:

- *Unarticulated Wisdom*: (low-cost, high-error) Intuition, what is used when there is nothing else.

- *Articulated Qualitative Models*: Descriptions of mechanisms, graphical representations of processes and/or relationships, empirical observation or statistical data collection and analysis.

- *Dimensional Models*: Investigate dimensionless parameters of the system.

- *Facet-wise Models*: Investigation of a decomposition element of a model in relative isolation.

- *Equations of Motion*: (high-cost, low-error) Differential equations and Markov chains.

Facet-wise models are an exercise in simple mathematics that may be used to investigate a decomposition element of a model in relative isolation. They are based on the idea of *bracketing high-order phenomena* by simplifying or making assumptions about the state of the system. An example used by Goldberg from fluid mechanics is a series of equations that simplify the model by assuming that a fluid or gas has no viscosity, which matches no known substance. A common criticism of this modeling approach is *"system X doesn't work like that, the model is unrealistic."* The source of such concerns with adaptive systems is that their interactions are typically high-dimensional and non-linear. Goldberg's response is that for a given poorly understood area of research, any 'useful' model is better than no model. Dimensional analysis or the so-called dimensional reasoning and scaling laws are another common conceptual tool in engineering and the sciences. Such models may be used to investigate dimensionless parameters of the system, which may be considered the formalization of the systemic behaviors.

Integration   Integration is a unification process of combining the findings of various models together to form a *patch-quilt* coherent theory of the system. Integration is not limited to holistic unification, and one may address specific hypothesis regarding the system resulting in conclusions about existing systems and design decisions pertaining to the next generation of systems.

Application In addition to elucidating the methodology, Goldberg specifies a series of five useful heuristics for the application of the methodology (taken from [5], page 8):

1. *Keep the goal of a working conceptual machine in mind.* Experimenters commonly get side tracked by experimental design and statistical verification; theoreticians get side tracked with notions of mathematical rigor and model fidelity.

2. *Decompose the design ruthlessly.* One cannot address the analytical analysis of a system like a Genetic Algorithm in one big 'gulp'.

3. *Use facet-wise models with almost reckless abandon.* One should build easy models that can be solved by bracketing everything that gets in the way.

4. *Integrate facet-wise models using dimensional arguments.* One can combine many small models together in a patch-quilt manner and defend the results of such models using dimensional analysis.

5. *Build high-order models when small models become inadequate.* Add complexity to models as complexity is needed (economy of modeling).

9.2.4 Bibliography

[1] P. W. Anderson, K. J. Arrow, and D. Pines. *Proceedings of The Santa Fe Institute Studies in the Sciences of Complexity - Economy As an Evolving Complex System.* Addison Wesley Publishing Company, USA, 1988.

[2] W. B. Arthur. Introduction: Process and emergence in the economy. In S. Durlauf and D. A. Lane, editors, *The Economy as an Evolving Complex System II*, volume Volume XXVII. Addison-Wesley Pub. Co, Reading, Mass, USA, 1997.

[3] S. Forrest and S. A. Hofmeyr. Immunology as information processing. In *Design Principles for the Immune System and Other Distributed Autonomous Systems*, pages 361–388. Oxford University Press, New York, 2001.

[4] M. Gell-Mann. Complex adaptive systems. In D. Pines and D. Meltzer, editors, *Complexity: metaphors, models, and reality*, pages 17–45. Addison-Wesley, USA, 1994.

[5] D. E. Goldberg. From genetic and evolutionary optimization to the design of conceptual machines. *Evolutionary Optimization*, 1(1):1–12, 1999.

[6] D. E. Goldberg. The design of innovating machines: A fundamental discipline for a postmodern systems engineering. In *Engineering Systems Symposium*. MIT Engineering Systems Division, USA, 2004.

[7] J. H. Holland. *Adaptation in natural and artificial systems: An introductory analysis with applications to biology, control, and artificial intelligence*. University of Michigan Press, 1975.

[8] J. H. Holland. *Hidden Order: How Adaptation Builds Complexity*. Addison Wesley Publishing Company, USA, 1995.

[9] K. A. De Jong. *An analysis of the behavior of a class of genetic adaptive systems*. PhD thesis, University of Michigan Ann Arbor, MI, USA, 1975.

[10] D. J. Cavicchio Jr. *Adaptive Search Using Simulated Evolution*. PhD thesis, The University of Michigan, 1970.

[11] D. J. Cavicchio Jr. Reproductive adaptive plans. In *Proceedings of the ACM annual conference*, volume 1, New York, NY, USA, 1972. ACM.

[12] S. Stepney, R. E. Smith, J. Timmis, and A. M. Tyrrell. Towards a conceptual framework for artificial immune systems. In V. Cutello, P. J. Bentley, and J. Timmis, editors, *Lecture Notes in Computer Science*, pages 53–64. Springer-Verlag, Germany, 2004.

[13] S. Stepney, R. E. Smith, J. Timmis, A. M. Tyrrell, M. J. Neal, and A. N. W. Hone. Conceptual frameworks for artificial immune systems. *International Journal of Unconventional Computing*, 1(3):315–338, July 2005.

[14] J. Twycross and U. Aickelin. Towards a conceptual framework for innate immunity. In *Lecture Notes in Computer Science*, pages 112–125. Springer, Germany, 2005.

9.3 Testing Algorithms

This section provides an introduction to software testing and the testing of Artificial Intelligence algorithms. Section 9.3.1 introduces software testing and focuses on a type of testing relevant to algorithms called unit testing. Section 9.3.2 provides a specific example of an algorithm and a prepared suite of unit tests, and Section 9.3.3 provides some rules-of-thumb for testing algorithms in general.

9.3.1 Software Testing

Software testing in the field of Software Engineering is a process in the life-cycle of a software project that verifies that the product or service meets quality expectations and validates that software meets the requirements specification. Software testing is intended to locate defects in a program, although a given testing method cannot guarantee to locate all defects. As such, it is common for an application to be subjected to a range of testing methodologies throughout the software life-cycle, such as unit testing during development, integration testing once modules and systems are completed, and user acceptance testing to allow the stakeholders to determine if their needs have been met.

Unit testing is a type of software testing that involves the preparation of well-defined procedural tests of discrete functionality of a program that provide confidence that a module or function behaves as intended. Unit tests are referred to as 'white-box' tests (contrasted to 'black-box' tests) because they are written with full knowledge of the internal structure of the functions and modules under tests. Unit tests are typically prepared by the developer that wrote the code under test and are commonly automated, themselves written as small programmers that are executed by a unit testing framework (such as JUnit for Java or the Test framework in Ruby). The objective is not to test each path of execution within a unit (called complete-test or complete-code coverage), but instead to focus tests on areas of risk, uncertainty, or criticality. Each test focuses on one aspect of the code (test one thing) and are commonly organized into test suites of commonality.

Some of the benefits of unit testing include:

- *Documentation*: The preparation of a suite of tests for a given system provide a type of programming documentation highlighting the expected behavior of functions and modules and providing examples of how to interact with key components.

- *Readability*: Unit testing encourages a programming style of small modules, clear input and output and fewer inter-component dependencies. Code written for easy of testing (testability) may be easier to read and follow.

- *Regression*: Together, the suite of tests can be executed as a regression-test of the system. The automation of the tests means that any defects caused by changes to the code can easily be identified. When a defect is found that slipped through, a new test can be written to ensure it will be identified in the future.

Unit tests were traditionally written after the program was completed. A popular alternative is to prepare the tests before the functionality of the application is prepared, called Test-First or Test-Driven Development (TDD). In this method, the tests are written and executed, failing until the application functionality is written to make the test pass. The early preparation of tests allow the programmer to consider the behavior required from the program and the interfaces and functions the program needs to expose before they are written.

The concerns of software testing are very relevant to the development, investigation, and application of Metaheuristic and Computational Intelligence algorithms. In particular, the strong culture of empirical investigation and prototype-based development demands a baseline level of trust in the systems that are presented in articles and papers. Trust can be instilled in an algorithm by assessing the quality of the algorithm implementation itself. Unit testing is lightweight (requiring only the writing of automated test code) and meets the needs of promoting quality and trust in the code while prototyping and developing algorithms. It is strongly suggested as a step in the process of empirical algorithm research in the fields of Metaheuristics, Computational Intelligence, and Biologically Inspired Computation.

9.3.2 Unit Testing Example

This section provides an example of an algorithm and its associated unit tests as an illustration of the presented concepts. The implementation of the Genetic Algorithm is discussed from the perspective of algorithm testing and an example set of unit tests for the Genetic Algorithm implementation are presented as a case study.

Algorithm

Listing 3.1 in Section 3.2 provides the source code for the Genetic Algorithm in the Ruby Programming Language. Important considerations when in using the Ruby test framework, is ensuring that the functions of the algorithm are exposed for testing and that the algorithm demonstration itself does not execute. This is achieved through the use of the (if _FILE_ == $0) condition, which ensures the example only executes when the file is called directly, allowing the functions to be imported and executed independently by a unit test script. The algorithm is very modular with its behavior partitioned into small functions, most of which are independently testable.

The `reproduce` function has some dependencies although its orchestration of sub-functions is still testable. The `search` function is the only monolithic function, which both depends on all other functions in the implementation (directly or indirectly) and hence is difficult to unit test. At best, the `search` function may be a case for system testing addressing functional requirements, such as *"does the algorithm deliver optimized solutions"*.

Unit Tests

Listing 9.3 provides the `TC_GeneticAlgorithm` class that makes use of the built-in Ruby unit testing framework by extending the `TestCase` class. The listing provides an example of ten unit tests for six of the functions in the Genetic Algorithm implementation. Two types of unit tests are provided:

- *Deterministic*: Directly test the function in question, addressing questions such as: does `onemax` add correctly? and does `point_mutation` behave correctly?

- *Probabilistic*: Test the probabilistic properties of the function in question, addressing questions such as: does `random_bitstring` provide an expected 50/50 mixture of 1s and 0s over a large number of cases? and does `point_mutation` make an expected number of changes over a large number of cases?

The tests for probabilistic expectations is a weaker form of unit testing that can be used to either provide additional confidence to deterministically tested functions, or to be used as a last resort when direct methods cannot be used.

Given that a unit test should 'test one thing' it is common for a given function to have more than one unit tests. The `reproduce` function is a good example of this with three tests in the suite. This is because it is a larger function with behavior called in dependent functions which is varied based on parameters.

```ruby
class TC_GeneticAlgorithm < Test::Unit::TestCase

  # test that the objective function behaves as expected
  def test_onemax
    assert_equal(0, onemax("0000"))
    assert_equal(4, onemax("1111"))
    assert_equal(2, onemax("1010"))
  end

  # test the creation of random strings
  def test_random_bitstring
    assert_equal(10, random_bitstring(10).size)
    assert_equal(0, random_bitstring(10).delete('0').delete('1').size)
  end

```

```
16     # test the approximate proportion of 1's and 0's
17     def test_random_bitstring_ratio
18       s = random_bitstring(1000)
19       assert_in_delta(0.5, (s.delete('1').size/1000.0), 0.05)
20       assert_in_delta(0.5, (s.delete('0').size/1000.0), 0.05)
21     end
22
23     # test that members of the population are selected
24     def test_binary_tournament
25       pop = Array.new(10) {|i| {:fitness=>i} }
26       10.times {assert(pop.include?(binary_tournament(pop)))}
27     end
28
29     # test point mutations at the limits
30     def test_point_mutation
31       assert_equal("0000000000", point_mutation("0000000000", 0))
32       assert_equal("1111111111", point_mutation("1111111111", 0))
33       assert_equal("1111111111", point_mutation("0000000000", 1))
34       assert_equal("0000000000", point_mutation("1111111111", 1))
35     end
36
37     # test that the observed changes approximate the intended probability
38     def test_point_mutation_ratio
39       changes = 0
40       100.times do
41         s = point_mutation("0000000000", 0.5)
42         changes += (10 - s.delete('1').size)
43       end
44       assert_in_delta(0.5, changes.to_f/(100*10), 0.05)
45     end
46
47     # test cloning with crossover
48     def test_crossover_clone
49       p1, p2 = "0000000000", "1111111111"
50       100.times do
51         s = crossover(p1, p2, 0)
52         assert_equal(p1, s)
53         assert_not_same(p1, s)
54       end
55     end
56
57     # test recombination with crossover
58     def test_crossover_recombine
59       p1, p2 = "0000000000", "1111111111"
60       100.times do
61         s = crossover(p1, p2, 1)
62         assert_equal(p1.size, s.size)
63         assert_not_equal(p1, s)
64         assert_not_equal(p2, s)
65         s.size.times {|i| assert( (p1[i]==s[i]) || (p2[i]==s[i]) ) }
66       end
67     end
68
69     # test odd sized population
70     def test_reproduce_odd
71       pop = Array.new(9) {|i| {:fitness=>i,:bitstring=>"0000000000"} }
```

```
72    children = reproduce(pop, pop.size, 0, 1)
73    assert_equal(9, children.size)
74  end
75
76  # test reproduce size mismatch
77  def test_reproduce_mismatch
78    pop = Array.new(10) {|i| {:fitness=>i,:bitstring=>"0000000000"} }
79    children = reproduce(pop, 9, 0, 0)
80    assert_equal(9, children.size)
81  end
82 end
```

Listing 9.3: Unit Tests for the Genetic Algorithm in Ruby

9.3.3 Rules-of-Thumb

Unit testing is easy, although writing good unit tests is difficult given the complex relationship the tests have with the code under test. Testing Metaheuristics and Computational Intelligence algorithms is harder again given their probabilistic nature and their ability to 'work in spite of you', that is, provide some kind of result even when implemented with defects.

The following guidelines may help when unit testing an algorithm:

- *Start Small*: Some unit tests are better than no unit test and each additional test can improve the trust and the quality of the code. For an existing algorithm implementation, start by writing a test for a small and simple behavior and slowly build up a test suite.

- *Test one thing*: Each test should focus on verifying the behavior of one aspect of one unit of code. Writing concise and behavior-focused unit tests are the objective of the methodology.

- *Test once*: A behavior or expectation only needs to be tested once, do not repeat a test each time a given unit is tested.

- *Don't forget the I/O*: Remember to test the inputs and outputs of a unit of code, specifically the pre-conditions and post-conditions. It can be easy to focus on the decision points within a unit and forget its primary purpose.

- *Write code for testability*: The tests should help to shape the code they test. Write small functions or modules, think about testing while writing code (or write tests first), and refactor code (update code after the fact) to make it easier to test.

- *Function independence*: Attempt to limit the direct dependence between functions, modules, objects and other constructs. This is related to testability and writing small functions although suggests limits on how much interaction there is between units of code in the algorithm.

Less dependence means less side-effects of a given unit of code and ultimately less complicated tests.

- *Test Independence*: Test should be independent from each other. Frameworks provide hooks to set-up and tear-down state prior to the execution of each test, there should be no needed to have one test prepare data or state for other tests. Tests should be able to execute independently and in any order.

- *Test your own code*: Avoid writing tests that verify the behavior of framework or library code, such as the randomness of a random number generator or whether a math or string function behaves as expected. Focus on writing test for the manipulation of data performed by the code you have written.

- *Probabilistic testing*: Metaheuristics and Computational Intelligence algorithms generally make use of stochastic or probabilistic decisions. This means that some behaviors are not deterministic and are more difficult to test. As with the example, write probabilistic tests to verify that such processes behave as intended. Given that probabilistic tests are weaker than deterministic tests, consider writing deterministic tests first. A probabilistic behavior can be made deterministic by replacing the random number generator with a proxy that returns deterministic values, called a mock. This level of testing may require further impact to the original code to allow for dependent modules and objects to be mocked.

- *Consider test-first*: Writing the tests first can help to crystallize expectations when implementing an algorithm from the literature, and help to solidify thoughts when developing or prototyping a new idea.

9.3.4   References

For more information on software testing, consult a good book on software engineering. Two good books dedicated to testing are *"Beautiful Testing: Leading Professionals Reveal How They Improve Software"* that provides a compendium of best practices from professional programers and testers [2], and *"Software testing"* by Patton that provides a more traditional treatment [4].

Unit testing is covered in good books on software engineering or software testing. Two good books that focus on unit testing include *"Test Driven Development: By Example"* on the TDD methodology by Beck, a pioneer of Extreme Programming and Test Drive Development [1] and *"Pragmatic unit testing in Java with JUnit"* by Hunt and Thomas [3].

9.3.5   Bibliography

[1] K. Beck. *Test Driven Development: By Example.* Addison-Wesley Professional, 2002.

[2] A. Goucher and T. Riley, editors. *Beautiful Testing: Leading Professionals Reveal How They Improve Software.* O'Reilly Media, 2009.

[3] A. Hunt and D. Thomas. *Pragmatic unit testing in Java with JUnit.* Pragmatic Bookshelf, 2003.

[4] R. Patton. *Software testing.* Sams, 2nd edition, 2005.

9.4   Visualizing Algorithms

This section considers the role of visualization in the development and application of algorithms from the fields of Metaheuristics, Computational Intelligence, and Biologically Inspired Computation. Visualization can be a powerful technique for exploring the spatial relationships between data (such as an algorithm's performance over time) and investigatory tool (such as plotting an objective problem domain or search space). Visualization can also provide a weak form of algorithm testing, providing observations of efficiency or efficacy that may be indicative of the expected algorithm behavior.

This section provides a discussion of the techniques and methods that may be used to explore and evaluate the problems and algorithms described throughout this book. The discussion and examples in this section are primarily focused on function optimization problems, although the principles of visualization as exploration (and a weak form of algorithm testing) are generally applicable to function approximation problem instances.

9.4.1   Gnuplot

Gnuplot is a free open source command line tool used to generate plots from data. It supports a large number of different plot types and provides seemingly limitless configurability. Plots are shown to the screen by default, but the tool can easily be configured to generate image files as well as LaTeX, PostScript and PDF documents.

Gnuplot can be downloaded from the website[2] that also provides many demonstrations of different plot types with sample scripts showing how the plots were created. There are many tutorials and examples on the web, and help is provided inside the Gnuplot software by typing **help** followed by the command name (for example: **help plot**). For a more comprehensive reference on Gnuplot, see Janert's introductory book to the software, *"Gnuplot in Action"* [1].

Gnuplot was chosen for the demonstrations in this section as useful plots can be created with a minimum number of commands. Additionally, it is easily integrated into a range of scripting languages is supported on a range of modern operating systems. All examples in this section include both the resulting plot and the script used to generate it. The scripts may be typed directly into the Gnuplot interpreter or into a file which is processed by the Gnuplot command line tool. The examples in this section provide a useful starting point for visualizing the problems and algorithms described throughout this book.

---

[2]Gnuplot URL: http://www.gnuplot.info

9.4.2 Plotting Problems

The visualization of the problem under study is an excellent start in learning about a given domain. A simple spatial representation of the search space or objective function can help to motivate the selection and configuration of an appropriate technique.

The visualization method is specific to the problem type and instance being considered. This section provides examples of visualizing problems from the fields of continuous and combinatorial function optimization, two classes of problems that appear frequently in the described algorithms.

Continuous Function Optimization

A continuous function optimization problem is typically visualized in two dimensions as a line where $x = input, y = f(input)$ or three dimensions as a surface where $x, y = input, z = f(input)$.

Some functions may have many more dimensions, which if the function is linearly separable can be visualized in lower dimensions. Functions that are not linearly-separable may be able to make use of projection techniques such as Principle Component Analysis (PCA). For example, preparing a stratified sample of the search space as vectors with associated cost function value and using PCA to project the vectors onto a two-dimensional plane for visualization.

Similarly, the range of each variable input to the function may be large. This may mean that some of the complexity or detail may be lost when the function is visualized as a line or surface. An indication of this detail may be achieved by creating spot-sample plots of narrow sub-sections of the function.

Figure 9.1 provides an example of the Basin function in one dimension. The Basin function is a continuous function optimization that seeks $\min f(x)$ where $f = \sum_{i=1}^{n} x_i^2$, $-5.0 \leq x_i \leq 5.0$. The optimal solution for this function is $(v_0, \ldots, v_{n-1}) = 0.0$. Listing 9.4 provides the Gnuplot script used to prepare the plot ($n = 1$).

```
set xrange [-5:5]
plot x*x
```

Listing 9.4: Gnuplot script for plotting a function in one-dimension.

Figure 9.2 provides an example of the basin function in two-dimensions as a three-dimensional surface plot. Listing 9.5 provides the Gnuplot script used to prepare the surface plot.

```
set xrange [-5:5]
set yrange [-5:5]
set zrange [0:50]
splot x*x+y*y
```

Listing 9.5: Gnuplot script for plotting a function in two-dimensions

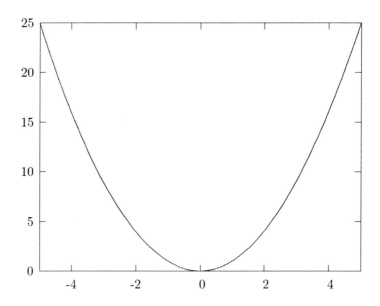

Figure 9.1: Plot of the Basin function in one-dimension.

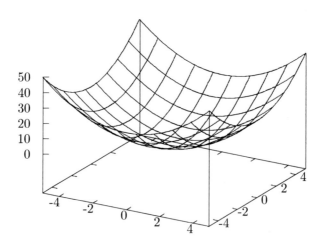

Figure 9.2: Plot of the Basin function in two-dimensions.

Both plots show the optimum in the center of the domain at $x = 0.0$ in one-dimension and $x, y = 0.0$ in two-dimensions.

Traveling Salesman Problem

The Traveling Salesman Problem (TSP) description is comprised of a list of cities, each with a different coordinate (at least in the case of the symmetric TSP). This can easily be visualized as a map if the coordinates at latitudes and longitudes, or as a scatter plot.

A second possible visualization is to prepare a distance matrix (distance between each point and all other points) and visualize the matrix directly, with each cell shaded relative to the distances of all other cells (largest distances darker and the shorter distances lighter). The light areas in the matrix highlight short or possible nearest-neighbor cities.

Figure 9.3 provides a scatter plot of the Berlin52 TSP used through out the algorithm descriptions in this book. The Berlin52 problem seeks a permutation of the order to visit cities (called a tour) that minimize the total distance traveled. The optimal tour distance for Berlin52 is 7542 units.

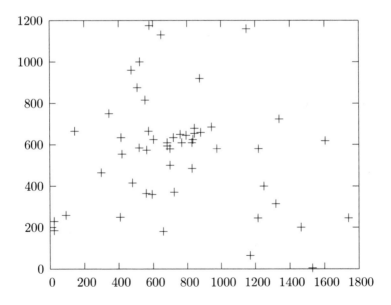

Figure 9.3: Plot of the cities of the Berlin52 TSP.

Listing 9.6 provides the Gnuplot script used to prepare the plot, where `berlin52.tsp` is a file that contains a listing of the coordinates of all cities, one city per line separated by white space. Listing 9.7 provides a snippet of the first five lines of the `berlin52.tsp` file.

```
1  plot "berlin52.tsp"
```

Listing 9.6: Gnuplot script for plotting the Berlin52 TSP.

```
1  565.0 575.0
2  25.0 185.0
3  345.0 750.0
4  945.0 685.0
5  845.0 655.0
6  ...
```

Listing 9.7: Snippet of the `berlin52.tsp` file.

The scatter plot shows some clustering of points toward the middle of the domain as well as many points spaced out near the periphery of the plot. An optimal solution is not obvious from looking at the plot, although one can see the potential for nearest-neighbor heuristics and importance of structure preserving operations on candidate solutions.

9.4.3   Plotting Algorithm Performance

Visualizing the performance of an algorithm can give indications that it is converging (implemented correctly) and provide insight into its dynamic behavior. Many algorithms are very simple to implement but exhibit complex dynamic behavior that is difficult to model and predict beforehand. An understanding of such behavior and the effects of changing an algorithm's parameters can be understood through systematic and methodological investigation. Exploring parameter configurations and plots of an algorithm's performance can give a quick first-pass approximation of the algorithms capability and potentially highlight fruitful areas for focused investigation.

Two quite different perspectives on visualizing algorithm performance are: a single algorithm run and a comparison between multiple algorithm runs. The visualization of algorithm runs is explored in this section in the context of the Genetic Algorithm applied to a binary optimization problem called OneMax (see Section 3.2).

Single Algorithm Run

The performance of an algorithm over the course of a single run can easily be visualized as a line graph, regardless of the specific measures used. The graph can be prepared after algorithm execution has completed, although, many algorithm frameworks provide dynamic line graphs.

Figure 9.4 provides an example line graph, showing the quality of the best candidate solution located by the Genetic Algorithm each generation for a single run applied to a 64-bit OneMax problem. Listing 9.8 provides the Gnuplot script used to prepare the plot, where `ga1.txt` is a text file that provides the fitness of the best solution each algorithm iteration on a new line. Listing 9.9 provides a snippet of the first five lines of the `ga1.txt` file.

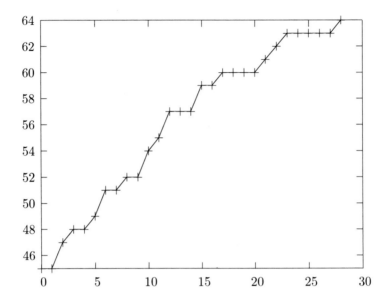

Figure 9.4: Line graph of the best solution found by the Genetic Algorithm.

```
1  set yrange [45:64]
2  plot "ga1.txt" with linespoints
```
Listing 9.8: Gnuplot script for creating a line graph.

```
1  45
2  45
3  47
4  48
5  48
6  ...
```
Listing 9.9: Snippet of the `ga1.txt` file.

Multiple Algorithm Runs

Multiple algorithm runs can provide insight into the tendency of an algorithm or algorithm configuration on a problem, given the stochastic processes that underlie many of these techniques. For example, a collection of the best result observed over a number of runs may be taken as a distribution indicating the capability of an algorithm for solving a given instance of a problem. This distribution may be visualized directly.

Figure 9.5 provides a histogram plot showing the best solutions found and the number of times they were located by Genetic Algorithm over 100 runs on a 300-bit OneMax function.

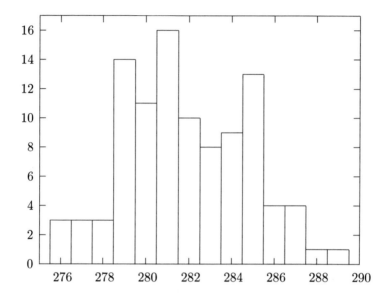

Figure 9.5: Histogram of the best solutions found by a Genetic Algorithm.

Listing 9.10 provide the Gnuplot script used to prepare the plot, where `ga2.histogram.txt` is a text file that contains discrete fitness values and the number of times it was discovered by the algorithm over 100 runs.

```
set yrange [0:17]
set xrange [275:290]
plot "ga2.histogram.txt" with boxes
```

Listing 9.10: Gnuplot script for creating a histogram.

Listing 9.11 provides a snippet of the first five lines of the `ga2.histogram.txt` file.

```
276 3
277 3
278 3
279 14
280 11
...
```

Listing 9.11: Snippet of the `ga2.histogram.txt` file.

Multiple Distributions of Algorithm Runs

Algorithms can be compared against each other based on the distributions of algorithm performance over a number of runs. This comparison usually takes the form of statistical tests that can make meaningful statements about the differences between distributions. A visualization of the relative difference between the distributions can aid in an interpretation of such statistical measures.

A compact way for representing a distribution is to use a box-and-whisker plot that partitions the data into quartiles, showing the central tendency of the distribution, the middle mass of the data (the second and third quartiles), the limits of the distribution and any outliers. Algorithm run distributions may be summarized as a box-and-whisker plots and plotted together to spatially show relative performance relationships.

Figure 9.6 provides box-and-whisker plots of the best score distribution of 100 runs for the Genetic Algorithm applied to a 300-bit OneMax problem with three different mutation configurations. The measure collected from each run was the quality of the best candidate solution found.

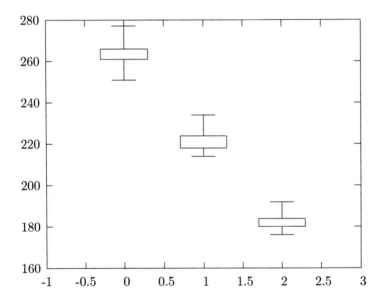

Figure 9.6: Box-and-whisker plots of the Genetic Algorithm's performance.

Listing 9.12 provide the Gnuplot script used to prepare the plot, where the file boxplots1.txt contains summaries of the results one run per line, each each line containing the min, first, second, and third quartiles and the max values separated by a space. Listing 9.13 provides a complete listing of the three lines of the boxplots1.txt file.

```
1  set bars 15.0
2  set xrange [-1:3]
3  plot 'boxplots1.txt' using 0:2:1:5:4 with candlesticks whiskerbars 0.5
```

Listing 9.12: Gnuplot script for creating a Box-and-whisker plot.

```
1  251.0 261.0 263.0 266.0 277.0
2  214.0 218.0 220.0 224.0 234.0
3  176.0 180.0 182.0 184.0 192.0
```

Listing 9.13: Complete listing of the `boxplots1.txt` file.

9.4.4   Plotting Candidate Solutions

Visualizing candidate solutions can provide an insight into the complexity
of the problem and the behavior of an algorithm. This section provides
examples of visualizing candidate solutions in the context of their problem
domains from both continuous and combinatorial function optimization.

Continuous Function Optimization

Visualizing candidate solutions from a continuous function optimization
domain at periodic times over the course of a run can provide an indication of
the algorithms behavior in moving through a search space. In low dimensions
(such as one or two dimensions) this can provide qualitative insights into
the relationship between algorithm configurations and behavior.

Figure 9.7 provides a plot of the best solution found each iteration by
the Particle Swarm Optimization algorithm on the Basin function in two
dimensions (see Section 6.2). The positions of the candidate solutions are
projected on top of a heat map of the Basin function in two-dimensions, with
the gradient representing the cost of solutions at each point. Listing 9.14
provides the Gnuplot script used to prepare the plot, where `pso1.txt` is a
file that contains the coordinates of the best solution found by the algorithm,
with one coordinate per line separated by a space. Listing 9.15 provides a
snippet of the first five lines of the `pso1.txt` file.

```
1  set xrange [-5:5]
2  set yrange [-5:5]
3  set pm3d map
4  set palette gray negative
5  set samples 20
6  set isosamples 20
7  splot x*x+y*y, "pso1.txt" using 1:2:(0) with points
```

Listing 9.14: Gnuplot script use to create a heat map and selected samples.

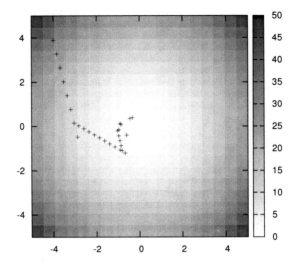

Figure 9.7: Heat map plot showing selected samples in the domain.

```
1   -3.9986483808224222 3.8910758979126956 31.12966051677087
2   -3.838580364459159 3.266132168962991 25.402318559546302
3   -3.678512348095896 2.6411884400132863 20.507329470753803
4   -3.518444331732633 2.0162447110635817 16.44469325039336
5   -3.35837631536937 1.391300982113877 13.214409898464986
6   ...
```

Listing 9.15: Snippet of the pso1.txt file.

Traveling Salesman Problem

Visualizing the results of a combinatorial optimization can provide insight into the areas of the problem that a selected technique is handling well, or poorly. Candidate solutions can be visualized over the course of a run to observe how the complexity of solutions found by a technique change over time. Alternatively, the best candidate solutions can be visualized at the end of a run.

Candidate solutions for the TSP are easily visualized as tours (order of city visits) in the context of the city coordinates of the problem definition.

Figure 9.8 provides a plot of an example Nearest-Neighbor solution for the Berlin52 TSP. A Nearest-Neighbor solution is constructed by randomly selecting the first city in the tour then selecting the next city in the tour with the minimum distance to the current city until a complete tour is created.

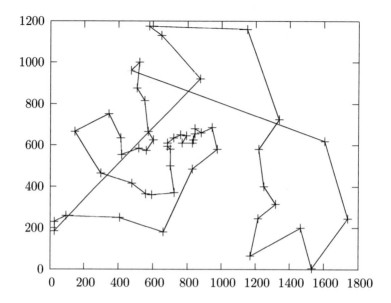

Figure 9.8: Plot of a Nearest-Neighbor tour for the Berlin52 TSP.

Listing 9.16 provides the Gnuplot script used to prepare the plot, where berlin52.nn.tour is a file that contains a listing of the coordinates of all cities separated by white space in order that the cities are visited with one city per line. The first city in the tour is repeated as the last city in the tour to provide a closed polygon in the plot. Listing 9.17 provides a snippet of the first five lines of the berlin52.nn.tour file.

```
plot "berlin52.nn.tour" with linespoints
```

Listing 9.16: Gnuplot script for plotting a tour for a TSP.

```
475 960
525 1000
510 875
555 815
575 665
...
```

Listing 9.17: Snippet of the berlin52.nn.tour file.

Figure 9.9 provides a plot of the known optimal solution for the Berlin52 Traveling Salesman problem.

Listing 9.18 provides the Gnuplot script used to prepare the plot, where berlin52.optimal is a file that contains a listing of the coordinates of all cities in order that the cities are visited with one city per line separated by

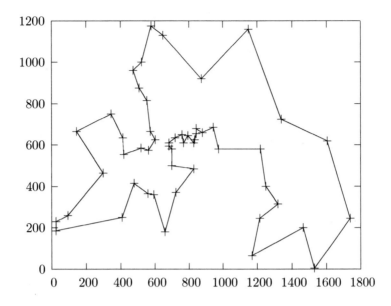

Figure 9.9: Plot of the optimal tour for the Berlin52 TSP.

white space. The first city in the tour is repeated as the last city in the tour
to provide a closed polygon in the plot.

```
plot "berlin52.optimal" with linespoints
```

Listing 9.18: Gnuplot script for plotting a tour for a TSP.

Listing 9.19 provides a snippet of the first five lines of the berlin52.optimal
file.

```
565.0 575.0
605.0 625.0
575.0 665.0
555.0 815.0
510.0 875.0
...
```

Listing 9.19: Snippet of the berlin52.optimal file.

9.4.5   Bibliography

[1] P. Janert. *Gnuplot in Action: Understanding Data with Graphs*. Manning
    Publications, 2009.

9.5   Problem Solving Strategies

The field of Data Mining has clear methodologies that guide a practitioner
to solve problems, such as Knowledge Discovery in Databases (KDD) [16].
Metaheuristics and Computational Intelligence algorithms have no such
methodology.[3]

This section describes some of the considerations when applying algorithms from the fields of Metaheuristics, Computational Intelligence, and
Biologically Inspired Computation to practical problem domains. This
discussion includes:

- The suitability of application of a given technique to a given problem and the transferability of algorithm and problem features (Section 9.5.1)

- The distinction between strong and weak methods which use more
  or less problem specific information respectively, and the continuum
  between these extremes (Section 9.5.2).

- A summary of problem solving strategies that suggest different ways
  of applying a given technique to the function optimization and approximation fields (Section 9.5.3).

9.5.1   Suitability of Application

From a problem-solving perspective, the tools that emerge from the field
of Computational Intelligence are generally assessed with regard to their
utility as *efficiently* or *effectively* solving problems. An important lesson
from the No-Free-Lunch Theorem was to *bound claims of applicability* (see
Section subsec:nfl), that is to consider the suitability of a given strategy
with regard to the feature overlap with the attributes of a given problem
domain. From a Computational Intelligence perspective, one may consider
the architecture, processes, and constraints of a given strategy as the features
of an approach.

The suitability of the application of a particular approach to a problem
takes into considerations concerns such as the *appropriateness* (can the
approach address the problem), the *feasibility* (available resources and
related efficiency concerns), and the *flexibility* (ability to address unexpected
or unintended effects). This section summarizes a general methodology
toward addressing the problem of suitability in the context of Computational
Intelligence tools. This methodology involves 1) the systematic elicitation
of system and problem features, and 2) the consideration of the overlap of
problem-problem, algorithm-algorithm, and problem-algorithm overlap of
feature sets.

---

[3]Some methods can be used for classification and regression and as such may fit into
methodologies such as KDD.

Systematic Feature Elicitation

A *feature* of a system (tool, strategy, model) or a problem is a distinctive element or property that may be used to differentiate it from similar and/or related cases. Examples may include functional concerns such as: processes, data structures, architectures, and constraints, as well as emergent concerns that may have a more subjective quality such as general behaviors, organizations, and higher-order structures. The process of the elicitation of features may be taken from a system or problem perspective:

- *System Perspective*: This requires a strong focus on the lower level functional elements and investigations that work toward correlating specific controlled procedures towards predictable emergent behaviors.

- *Problem Perspective*: May require both a generalization of the specific case to the general problem case, as well as a functional or logical decomposition into constituent parts.

Problem *generalization* and *functional decomposition* are important and commonly used patterns for problem solving in the broader fields of Artificial Intelligence and Machine Learning. The promotion of simplification and modularity can reduce the cost and complexity of achieving solutions [10, 43].

Feature Overlap

Overlap in elicited features may be considered from three important perspectives: *between systems*, *between problems*, and *between a system and a problem*. Further, such overlap may be considered at different levels of detail with regard to generalized problem solving strategies and problem definitions. These overlap cases are considered as follows:

- *System Overlap* defines the suitability of comparing one system to another, referred to as *comparability*. For example, systems may be considered for the same general problems and compared in terms of theoretical or empirical capability, the results of which may only be meaningful if the systems are significantly similar to each other as assessed in terms of feature overlap.

- *Problem Overlap* defines the suitability of comparing one problem to another, referred to as *transferability*. From a systems focus, transferability refers to the capability of a technique on a given problem to be successfully applied to another problem, the result of which is only meaningful if there is a strong overlap between the problems under consideration.

- *System-Problem Overlap* defines the suitability of a system on a given problem, referred to as *applicability*. For example, a system is considered suitable for a given problem if it has a significant overlap in capabilities with the requirements of the problem definition.

Such mappings are imprecise given the subjective assessment and complexity required in both the elicitation and consideration overlap of the of features, the hardest of which is expected to be the mapping between systems and problems. The mapping of salient features of algorithms and problems was proposed as an important reconciliation of the No-Free-Lunch Theorem by Wolpert and Macready [58], although the important difference of this approach is that the system and algorithm are given prior to the assessment. In their first work on the theorem, Wolpert and Macready specifically propose the elicitation of the features from a problem-first perspective, for which specialized algorithms can be defined [57]. Therefore, this methodology of suitability may be considered a generalization of this reconciliation suitable for the altered Computational Intelligence (strategy first) perspective on Artificial Intelligence.

9.5.2   Strong and Weak Methods

Generally, the methods from the fields of Metaheuristics, Computational Intelligence, and Biologically Inspired Computation may be considered weak methods. They are general purpose and are typically considered black-box solvers for a range of problem domains. The stronger the method, the more that must be known about the problem domain. Rather than discriminating techniques into weak and strong it is more useful to consider a continuum of methods from pure block box techniques that have few assumptions about the problem domain, to strong methods that exploit most or all of the problem specific information available.

For example, the Traveling Salesman Problem is an example of a combinatorial optimization problem. A naïve (such a Random Search) black box method may simply explore permutations of the cities. Slightly stronger methods may initialize the search with a heuristic-generated technique (such as nearest neighbor) and explore the search space using a variation method that also exploits heuristic information about the domain (such as a 2-opt variation). Continuing along this theme, a stochastic method may explore the search space using a combination of probabilistic and heuristic information (such as Ant Colony Optimization algorithms). At the other end of the scale the stochastic elements are decreased or removed until one is left with pure heuristic methods such as the Lin-Kernighan heuristic [31] and exact algorithms from linear and dynamic programming that focus on the structure and nature of the problem [55].

Approaching a problem is not as simple as selecting the strongest method available and solving it. The following describes two potential strategies:

- *Start Strong*: Select the strongest technique available and apply it to the problem. Difficult problems can be resistant to traditional methods for many intrinsic and extrinsic reasons. Use products from a strong technique (best solution found, heuristics) to seed the next weaker method in line.

- *Start Weak*: Strong methods do not exist for all problems, and if they do exist, the computation, skill, and/or time resources may not be available to exploit them. Start with a weak technique and use it to learn about the problem domain. Use this information to make better decisions about subsequent techniques to try that can exploit what has been learned.

In a real-world engineering or business scenario, the objective is to solve a problem or achieve the best possible solution to the problem within the operating constraints. Concerns of algorithm and technique purity become less important than they may be in their respective fields of research. Both of the above strategies suggest an iterative methodology, where the product or knowledge gained from one technique may be used to prime a subsequent stronger or weaker technique.

9.5.3 Domain-Specific Strategies

An algorithm may be considered a strategy for problem solving. There are a wide range of ways in which a given algorithm can be used to solve a problem. Function Optimization and Function Approximation were presented as two general classes of problems to which the algorithms from the fields of Metaheuristics, Computational Intelligence, and Biologically Inspired Computation are applied. This section reviews general problem problem solving strategies that may be adopted for a given technique in each of these general problem domains.

Function Optimization

This section reviews a select set of strategies for addressing optimization problems from the field of Metaheuristics and Computational Intelligence to provide general insight into the state of the interaction between stochastic algorithms and the field of optimization. This section draws heavily from the field of Evolutionary Computation, Swarm Intelligence, and related Computational Intelligence sub-fields.

Global and Local Optimization   Global Optimization refers to seeking a globally optimal structure or approximation thereof in a given problem domain. Global is differentiated from Local Optimization in that the latter focuses on locating an optimal structure within a constrained region of the decision variable search space, such as a single peak or valley (basin of attraction). In the literature, global optimization problems refers to the class of optimization problems that generally cannot be addressed through more conventional approaches such as gradient descent methods (that require mathematical derivatives) and pattern search (that can get 'stuck' in local optima and never converge) [41, 53].

A global search strategy provides the benefit of making few if any assumptions about where promising areas of the search space may be, potentially highlighting unintuitive combinations of parameters. A local search strategy provides the benefit of focus and refinement of an existing candidate solution. It is common to apply a local search method to the solutions located by a global search procedure as a refinement strategy (such as using a Hill Climber (Section 2.4) after a Genetic Algorithm (Section 3.2)), and some methods have both techniques built in (such as GRASP in Section 2.8).

Parallel Optimization   A natural step toward addressing difficult (large and rugged cost landscapes) is to exploit parallel and distributed hardware, to get an improved result in the same amount of time, the same result in less time, or both [12]. Towards unifying the myriad of approaches and hardware configurations, a general consensus and taxonomy has been defined by the Parallel Evolutionary Algorithms (PEA) and Parallel Metaheuristics fields that considers the ratio of *communication* to *computation* called *granularity* [4, 11].

This taxonomy is presented concisely by Alba and Tomassini as a plot or trade-off of three concerns: 1) the number of sub-populations (models or parallel strategies working on the problem), 2) the coupling between the sub-populations (frequency and amplitude of communication), and 3) the size of the sub-populations (size or extent of the sub-models) [5].

Two important and relevant findings from the narrower field of Parallel Evolutionary Algorithms include 1) that tight coupling (frequent inter-system migration of candidate solutions) between coarse-grained models typically results in worse performance than a non-distributed approach [6], and 2) that loose coupling (infrequent migration) between coarse-grained models has been consistently shown to provide a super-linear increase in performance [3, 7, 11].

Cooperative Search   This is a more general approach that considers the use of multiple models that work together to address a difficult optimization problems. Durfee et al. consider so-called Cooperative Distributed Problem Solving (CDPS) in which a network of loosely coupled solvers are employed to address complex distributed problems. In such systems, it is desirable to match the processing capabilities of the solver to the attributes of the problem. For example, a given problem may have spatially distributed, functionally distributed, or temporally distributed sub-problems to which a centralized and monolithic system may not be suitable.

Lesser [30] considers CDPS and proposes such models perform *distributed search* on dependent or independent and potentially overlapping sub-problems as a motivating perspective for conducting research into Distributed Artificial Intelligence (DAI)[4]. Lesser points out that in real world applications, it is hard to get a optimal mapping between the allocated resources and the needs or availability of information for a given problem, suggesting that such problems may be caused by a mismatch in processing times and/or number of sub-problems, interdependencies between sub-problems, and local experts whose expertise cannot be effectively communicated. For a more detail on the relationships between parallel and cooperative search, El-Abd and Kamel provide a rigorous taxonomy [15].

Hybrid Search   Hybrid Search is a perspective on optimization that focuses on the use of multiple and likely different approaches either sequentially (as in the canonical global and local search case), or in parallel (such as in Cooperative Search). For example in this latter case, it is common in the field of PEA to encourage different levels of exploration and exploitation across island populations by varying the operators or operator configurations used [2, 51].

Talbi proposed a detailed 4-level taxonomy of Hybrid Metaheuristics that concerns parallel and cooperating approaches [50]. The taxonomy encompasses parallel and cooperative considerations for optimization and focuses on the discriminating features in the lowest level such as heterogeneity, and specialization of approaches.

Functional Decomposition   Three examples of a functional decomposition of optimization include 1) multiple objectives, 2) multiple constraints, and 3) partitions of the decision variable search space.

Multi-Objective Optimization (MOO) is a sub-field that is concerned with the optimization of two or more objective functions. A solution to a MOO conventionally involves locating and returning a set of candidate solutions called the non-dominated set [13]. The Pareto optimal set, is the set of optimal non-dominated solutions. For a given problem no feasible solution exists that dominates a Pareto optimal solution. All solutions that are Pareto optimal belong to the Pareto set, and the points that these solutions map to in the objective space is called the Pareto front. The complexity with MOO problems is in the typically unknown dependencies between decision variables across objectives, that in the case of conflicts, must be traded off (Purshouse and Fleming provide a taxonomy of such complexity [42]).

Constraint Satisfaction Problem's (CSP) involve the optimization of decision variables under a set of constraints. The principle complexity in

---

[4]This perspective provided the basis for what became the field of Multi-Agent Systems (MAS).

such problems is in locating structures that are feasible or violate the least number of constraints, optimizing such feasibility [27, 54].

Search Space Partitioning involves partitioning of the decision variable search space (for example see Multispace Search by Gu et al. [14, 21, 22]). This is a critical consideration given that for equal-sized dimensional bounds on parameters, an increase in decision variables results in an exponential increase in the volume of the space to search.

Availability Decomposition   Optimization problems may be partitioned by the concerns of temporal and spatial distribution of 1) information availability, and 2) computation availability. An interesting area of research regarding variable information availability for optimization problems is called Interactive Evolutionary Computation, in which one or a collection of human operators dynamically interact with an optimization process [49]. Example problem domains include but are not limited to computer graphics, industrial design, image processing, and drug design.

There is an increasing demand to exploit clusters of heterogeneous workstations to complete large-scale distributed computation tasks like optimization, typically in an opportunistic manner such as when individual machines are underutilized. The effect is that optimization strategies such as random partitioning of the search space (independent non-interacting processing) are required to take advantage of such environments for optimization problems [32, 46].

Meta Optimization   One may optimize at a level above that considered in previous sections. Specifically, 1) the iterative generation of an inductive model called multiple restart optimization, and 2) the optimization of the parameters of the process that generates an inductive model of an optimization problem. Multiple or iterative restarts involves multiple independent algorithm executions from different (random) starting conditions. It is generally considered as a method for achieving an improved result in difficult optimization problems where a given strategy is deceived by local or false optima [24, 34], typically requiring a restart schedule [17].

A second and well studied form of meta optimization involves the optimization of the search process itself. Classical examples include the self-adaptation of mutation parameters (step sizes) in the Evolutionary Strategies (ES) and Evolutionary Programming (EP) approaches. Smith and Fogarty provided a review of genetic algorithms with adaptive strategies including a taxonomy in which the meta-adaptations are applied at one of three levels: 1) the population (adapting the overall sampling strategy), 2) the individual (adapting the creation of new samples in the decision variable space), and 3) components (modifying component contributions and/or individual step sizes as in ES and EP) [48].

Function Approximation

This section reviews a select set of strategies for addressing Function Approximation problems from the fields of Artificial Intelligence and Computational Intelligence to to provide general insight into the state of the interaction between stochastic algorithms and the field. The review draws heavily from the fields of Artificial Neural Networks, specifically Competitive Learning, as well as related inductive Machine Learning fields such as Instance Based Learning.

Vector Quantization Vector Quantization (VQ) refers to a method of approximating a target function using a set of exemplar (prototype or codebook) vectors. The exemplars represent a discrete subset of the problem, generally restricted to the features of interest using the natural representation of the observations in the problem space, typically an an unconstrained n-dimensional real valued space. The VQ method provides the advantage of a non-parametric model of a target function (like instance-based and lazy learning such as the k-Nearest-Neighbor method (kNN)) using a symbolic representation that is meaningful in the domain (like tree-based approaches).

The promotion of compression addresses the storage and retrieval concerns of kNN, although the selection of codebook vectors (the so-called quantization problem) is a hard problem that is known to be NP-complete [18]. More recently Kuncheva and Bezdek have worked towards unifying quantization methods in the application to classification problems, referring to the approaches as Nearest Prototype Classifiers (NPC) and proposing a generalized nearest prototype classifier [28, 29].

Parallelization Instance-based approaches are inherently parallel given the generally discrete independent nature in which they are used, specifically in a case or per-query manner. As such, parallel hardware can be exploited in the preparation of the corpus of prototypes (parallel preparation), and more so in the application of the corpus given its read-only usage [1, 35, 39]. With regard to vector quantization specifically, there is an industry centered around the design and development of VQ and WTA algorithms and circuits given their usage to compress digital audio and video data [36, 38].

Cooperative Methods Classical cooperative methods in the broader field of statistical machine learning are referred to as *Ensemble Methods* [37, 40] or more recently *Multiclassifier Systems* [20].

Boosting is based on the principle of combining a set of quasi-independent weak learners that collectively are as effective as a single strong learner [26, 44]. The seminal approach is called Adaptive Boosting (AdaBoost) that involves the preparation of a series of classifiers, where subsequent classifiers are prepared for the observations that are misclassified by the proceeding classifier models (creation of specialists) [45].

Bootstrap Aggregation (bagging) involves partitioning the observations into N randomly chosen subsets (with re-selection), and training a different model on each [9]. Although robust to noisy datasets, the approach requires careful consideration as to the consensus mechanism between the independent models for decision making.

Stacked Generalization (stacking) involves creating a sequence of models of generally different types arranged into a stack, where subsequently added models generalize the behavior (success or failure) of the model before it with the intent of correcting erroneous decision making [52, 56].

Functional Decomposition   As demonstrated, it is common in ensemble methods to partition the dataset either explicitly or implicitly to improve the approximation of the underlying target function. A first important decomposition involves partitioning the problem space into sub-spaces based on the attributes, regular groups of attributes called features, and decision attributes such as class labels. A popular method for attribute-based partitioning is called the Random Subspace Method, involving the random partitioning of attributes to which specialized model is prepared for each (commonly used on tree-based approaches) [23].

A related approach involves a hierarchical partitioning of attributes space into sub-vectors (sub-spaces) used to improve VQ-based compression [19]. Another important functional decomposition methods involve the partitioning of the set of observations. The are many ways in which observations may be divided, although common approaches include pre-processing using clustering techniques to divide the set into natural groups, additional statistical approaches that partition based on central tendency and outliers, and re-sampling methods that are required to reduce the volume of observations.

Availability Decomposition   The availability observations required to address function approximation in real-world problem domains motivate the current state of the art in Distributed Data Mining (DDM, or sometimes Collective Data Mining), Parallel Data Mining (PDM), and Distributed Knowledge Discovery in Database (DKDD) [25]. The general information availability concerns include 1) the *intractable volume of observations*, and 2) the *spatial (geographical) and temporal distribution of information* [59]. In many real-world problems it is infeasible to centralize relevant observations for modeling, requiring scalable, load balancing, and incremental acquisition of information [47].

Meta-Approximation   The so-called ensemble or multiple-classifier methods may be considered meta approximation approaches as they are not specific to a given modeling technique. As with function optimization, meta-approaches may be divided into restart methods and meta-learning algorithms. The use of restart methods is a standard practice for connectionist approaches, and more generally in approaches that use random starting conditions and a gradient or local search method of refinement.

The method provides an opportunity for over-coming local optima in the error-response surface, when there is an unknown time remaining until convergence [33], and can exploit parallel hardware to provide a speed advantage [8]. Ensemble methods and variants are examples of meta approximation approaches, as well as the use of consensus classifiers (gate networks in mixtures of experts) to integrate and weight the decision making properties from ensembles.

9.5.4 Bibliography

[1] A. Aamodt and E. Plaza. Case-based reasoning: Foundational issues, methodological variations, and system approaches. *Artificial Intelligence Communications*, 7(1):39–59, 1994.

[2] P. Adamidis, P. Adamidis, and V. Petridis. Co–operating populations with different evolution behaviours. In V. Petridis, editor, *Proceedings IEEE International Conference on Evolutionary Computation*, pages 188–191, 1996.

[3] E. Alba. Parallel evolutionary algorithms can achieve super-linear performance. *Information Processing Letters*, 82:7–13, 2002.

[4] E. Alba. *Parallel Metaheuristics: A New Class of Algorithms*. John Wiley, 2005.

[5] E. Alba and M. Tomassini. Parallelism and evolutionary algorithms. *IEEE Transactions on Evolutionary Computation*, 6(5):443–462, 2002.

[6] E. Alba and J. M. Troya. Influence of the migration policy in parallel distributed gas with structured and panmictic populations. *Applied Intelligence*, 12:163–181, 2000.

[7] T. C. Belding. The distributed genetic algorithm revisited. In *Proceedings of the 6th International Conference on Genetic Algorithms*, 1995.

[8] A. Di Blas, A. Jagota, and R. Hughey. Optimizing neural networks on SIMD parallel computers. *Parallel Computing*, 31:97–115, 2005.

[9] L. Breiman. Bagging predictors. *Machine Learning*, 24(2):123–140, 1996.

[10] R. Brooks. A robust layered control system for a mobile robot. *IEEE Journal Of Robotics And Automation*, 2(1):14–23, 1986.

[11] E. Cantú-Paz. *Efficient and Accurate Parallel Genetic Algorithms.* Kluwer Academic Publishers (Springer), 2000.

[12] T. G. Crainic and N. Hail. Parallel metaheuristics applications. In *Parallel Metaheuristics.* John Wiley & Sons, Inc., 2005.

[13] K. Deb. *Multi-Objective Optimization Using Evolutionary Algorithms.* John Wiley and Sons, 2001.

[14] B. Du, J. Gu, W. Wang, and D. H. K. Tsang. Multispace search for minimizing the maximum nodal degree. In J. Gu, editor, *Proceedings Sixth International Conference on Computer Communications and Networks*, pages 364–367, 1997.

[15] M. El-Abd and M. Kamel. A taxonomy of cooperative search algorithms. In *Hybrid Metaheuristics*, 2005.

[16] U. Fayyad, G. Piatetsky-Shapiro, and P. Smyth. The KDD process for extracting useful knowledge from volumes of data. *Communications of the ACM*, 39(11):27–34, 1996.

[17] A. S. Fukunaga. Restart scheduling for genetic algorithms. In *Parallel Problem Solving from Nature - PPSN V*, pages 357–366, 1998.

[18] M. Garey, D. Johnson, and H. Witsenhausen. The complexity of the generalized Lloyd–Max problem (corresp.). *IEEE Transactions on Information Theory*, 28(2):255–256, Mar 1982.

[19] A. Gersho, A. Gersho, and Y. Shoham. Hierarchical vector quantization of speech with dynamic codebook allocation. In Y. Shoham, editor, *Proceedings of the IEEE International Conference on ICASSP '84. Acoustics, Speech, and Signal Processing*, volume 9, pages 416–419, 1984.

[20] J. Ghosh. Multiclassifier systems: Back to the future. In *Proceedings of the Third International Workshop on Multiple Classifier Systems*, 2002.

[21] J. Gu. Multispace search: A new optimization approach. In *Algorithms and Computation*, 1994.

[22] J. Gu. Multispace search for satisfiability and NP–Hard problems. In *Satisfiability Problem: Theory and Applications : DIMACS Workshop*, 1997.

[23] T. K. Ho. The random subspace method for constructing decision forests. *IEEE Transactions on Pattern Analysis and Machine Intelligence*, 20:832–844, 1998.

[24] X. Hu, R. Shonkwiler, and M. Spruill. Random restarts in global optimization. Technical Report 110592-015, School of Mathematics, Georgia Institute of Technology, January 1994.

[25] H. Kargupta and P. Chan. *Advances in Distributed and Parallel Knowledge Discovery.* AAAI Press/MIT Press, 2000.

[26] M. Kearns. Thoughts on hypothesis boosting. Unpublished manuscript, 1988.

[27] V. Kumar. Algorithms for constraint–satisfaction problems : a survey. *The AI magazine (AI mag.)*, 13:32–44, 1992.

[28] L. Kuncheva and J. Bezdek. An integrated framework for generalized nearest prototype classifier design. *Int. Journal of Uncertaintly, Fuzziness and Knowledge-Based Systems*, 6:437–457, 1998.

[29] L. I. Kuncheva and J. C. Bezdek. Nearest prototype classification: clustering, genetic algorithms, or random search? *IEEE Transactions on Systems, Man and Cybernetics, Part C*, 28(1):160–164, 1998.

[30] V. R. Lesser. An overview of DAI: Viewing distributed AI as distributed search. *Journal of Japanese Society for Artificial Intelligence-Special Issue on Distributed Artificial Intelligence*, 5(4):392–400, January 1990.

[31] S. Lin and B. W Kernighan. An effective heuristic algorithm for the traveling-salesman problems. *Operations Research*, 21:498–516, 1973.

[32] P. Liu and D. W. Wang. Reduction optimization in heterogeneous cluster environments. In D-W. Wang, editor, *Proceedings 14th International Parallel and Distributed Processing Symposium IPDPS 2000*, pages 477–482, 2000.

[33] M. Magdon-Ismail and A. F. Atiya. The early restart algorithm. *Neural Computation*, 12:1303–1312, 2000.

[34] M. Muselli. A theoretical approach to restart in global optimization. *Journal of Global Optimization*, 10:1–16, 1997.

[35] M. V. Nagendra Prasad, V. R. Lesser, and S. E. Lander. Retrieval and reasoning in distributed case bases. *Journal of Visual Communication and Image Representation, Special Issue on Digital Libraries*, 7(1):74–87, 1996.

[36] A. Nakada, T. Shibata, M. Konda, T. Morimoto, and T. Ohmi. A fully parallel vector-quantization processor for real-time motion-picture compression. *IEEE Journal of Solid-State Circuits*, 34(6):822–830, 1999.

[37] D. Opitz and R. Maclin. Popular ensemble methods: An empirical study. *Journal of Artificial Intelligence Research*, 11:169–198, 1999.

[38] K. K. Parhi, F. H. Wu, and K. Genesan. Sequential and parallel neural network vector quantizers. *IEEE Transactions on Computers*, 43(1):104–109, 1994.

[39] E. Plaza, J. Lluis, and A. F. Martin. Cooperative case-based reasoning. In *Distributed Artificial Intelligence Meets Machine Learning Learning in Multi-Agent Environments*, 1997.

[40] R. Polikar. Ensemble based systems in decision making. *IEEE Circuits and Systems Magazine*, 6(3):21–45, 2006.

[41] W. L. Price. A controlled random search procedure for global optimisation. *The Computer Journal*, 20(4):367–370, 1977.

[42] R. C. Purshouse and P. J. Fleming. Conflict, harmony, and independence: Relationships in evolutionary multi-criterion optimisation. In *Proceedings of the Second International Conference on Evolutionary Multi-Criterion Optimization (EMO)*, pages 16–30, 2003.

[43] S. Russell and P. Norvig. *Artificial Intelligence: A Modern Approach*. Prentice Hall, third edition, 2009.

[44] R. E. Schapire. The strength of weak learnability. *Machine Learning*, 5(2):197–227, 1992.

[45] R. E. Schapire. The boosting approach to machine learning: An overview. In D. D. Denison, M. H. Hansen, C. Holmes, B. Mallick, and B. Yu, editors, *Nonlinear Estimation and Classification*, 2003.

[46] T. Schnekenburger. Parallel randomized algorithms in heterogeneous environments. In *Int. Conference on Systems Engineering*, 1993.

[47] D. Skillicorn. Strategies for parallel data mining. *IEEE Concurrency*, 7(4):26–35, 1999.

[48] J. E. Smith and T. C. Fogarty. Operator and parameter adaptation in genetic algorithms. *Soft Computing - A Fusion of Foundations, Methodologies and Applications*, 1:81–87, 1997.

[49] H. Takagi. Interactive evolutionary computation: Fusion of the capabilities of EC optimization and human evaluations. *Proceedings of the IEEE*, 89(9):1275–1296, September 2001.

[50] E. Talbi. A taxonomy of hybrid metaheuristics. *Journal of Heuristics*, 8:541–564, 2001.

[51] R. Tanese. Distributed genetic algorithms. In *Proceedings of the third international conference on Genetic algorithms*, pages 434–439. Morgan Kaufmann Publishers Inc., 1989.

[52] K. M. Ting and I. H. Witten. Issues in stacked generalization. *Journal of Artificial Intelligence Research*, 10:271–289, 1999.

[53] A. Törn, M. M. Ali, and S. Viitanen. Stochastic global optimization: Problem classes and solution techniques. *Journal of Global Optimization*, 14:437–447, 1999.

[54] E. Tsang. *Foundations of Constraint Satisfaction*. Academic Press, 1993.

[55] G. J. Woeginger. Exact algorithms for NP–hard problems: A surveys. *Combinatorial Optimization – Eureka, You Shrink!*, 2570:185–207, 2003.

[56] D. H. Wolpert. Stacked generalization. *Neural Networks*, 5(LA-UR-90-3460):241–259, 1992.

[57] D. H. Wolpert and W. G. Macready. No free lunch theorems for search. Technical report, Santa Fe Institute, Sante Fe, NM, USA, 1995.

[58] D. H. Wolpert and W. G. Macready. No free lunch theorems for optimization. *IEEE Transactions on Evolutionary Computation*, 1(67):67–82, 1997.

[59] M. J. Zaki. Parallel and distributed data mining: An introduction. In *Revised Papers from Large-Scale Parallel Data Mining, Workshop on Large-Scale Parallel KDD Systems, SIGKDD*, pages 1–23, 1999.

9.6 Benchmarking Algorithms

When it comes to evaluating an optimization algorithm, every researcher has their own thoughts on the way it should be done. Unfortunately, many empirical evaluations of optimization algorithms are performed and reported without addressing basic experimental design considerations. This section provides a summary of the literature on experimental design and empirical algorithm comparison methodology. This summary contains rules of thumb and the seeds of best practice when attempting to configure and compare optimization algorithms, specifically in the face of the no-free-lunch theorem.

9.6.1 Issues of Benchmarking Methodology

Empirically comparing the performance of algorithms on optimization problem instances is a staple for the fields of Heuristics and Biologically Inspired Computation, and the problems of effective comparison methodology have been discussed since the inception of these fields. Johnson suggests that the coding of an algorithm is the easy part of the process; the difficult work is getting meaningful and publishable results [24]. He goes on to provide a very through list of questions to consider before racing algorithms, as well as what he describes as his "pet peeves" within the field of empirical algorithm research.

Hooker [22] (among others) practically condemns what he refers to as competitive testing of heuristic algorithms, calling it *"fundamentally anti-intellectual"*. He goes on to strongly encourag a rigorous methodology of what he refers to as scientific testing where the aim is to investigate algorithmic behaviors.

Barr, Golden et al. [1] list a number of properties worthy of a heuristic method making a contribution, which can be paraphrased as; efficiency, efficacy, robustness, complexity, impact, generalizability, and innovation. This is interesting given that many (perhaps a majority) of conference papers focus on solution quality alone (one aspect of efficacy). In their classical work on reporting empirical results of heuristics Barr, Golden et al. specify a loose experimental setup methodology with the following steps:

1. Define the goals of the experiment.

2. Select measure of performance and factors to explore.

3. Design and execute the experiment.

4. Analyze the data and draw conclusions.

5. Report the experimental results.

They then suggest eight guidelines for reporting results, in summary they are; reproducibility, specify all influential factors (code, computing environment, etc), be precise regarding measures, specify parameters, use statistical experimental design, compare with other methods, reduce variability of results, and ensure results are comprehensive. They then clarify these points with examples.

Peer, Engelbrecht et al. [32] summarize the problems of algorithm benchmarking (with a bias toward particle swarm optimization) to the following points: duplication of effort, insufficient testing, failure to test against state-of-the-art, poor choice of parameters, conflicting results, and invalid statistical inference. Eiben and Jelasity [14] sight four problems with the state of benchmarking evolutionary algorithms; 1) test instances are chosen ad hoc from the literature, 2) results are provided without regard to research objectives, 3) scope of generalized performance is generally too broad, and 4) results are hard to reproduce. Gent and Walsh provide a summary of simple dos and don'ts for experimentally analyzing algorithms [20]. For an excellent introduction to empirical research and experimental design in artificial intelligence see Cohen's book *"Empirical Methods for Artificial Intelligence"* [10].

The theme of the classical works on algorithm testing methodology is that there is a lack of rigor in the field. The following sections will discuss three main problem areas to consider before benchmarking, namely 1) treating algorithms as complex systems that need to be tuned before applied, 2) considerations when selecting problem instances for benchmarking, and 3) the selection of measures of performance and statistical procedures for testing experimental hypotheses. A final section 4) covers additional best practices to consider.

9.6.2   Selecting Algorithm Parameters

Optimization algorithms are parameterized, although in the majority of cases the effect of adjusting algorithm parameters is not fully understood. This is because unknown non-linear dependencies commonly exist between the variables resulting in the algorithm being considered a complex system. Further, one must be careful when generalizing the performance of parameters across problem instances, problem classes, and domains. Finally, given that algorithm parameters are typically a mixture of real and integer numbers, exhaustively enumerating the parameter space of an algorithm is commonly intractable.

There are many solutions to this problem such as self-adaptive parameters, meta-algorithms (for searching for good parameter values), and methods of performing sensitivity analysis over parameter ranges. A good introduction to the parameterization of genetic algorithms is Lobo, Lima et al. [27]. The best and self-evident place to start (although often ignored [14]) is to investigate the literature and see what parameters been used historically. Although not a robust solution, it may prove to be a useful starting point for further investigation. The traditional approach is to run an algorithm on a large number of test instances and generalize the results [37]. We, as a field, haven't really come much further than this historical methodology other than perhaps the application of more and differing statistical methods to decrease effort and better support findings.

A promising area of study involves treating the algorithm as a complex systems, where problem instances may become yet another parameter of the model [7, 36]. From here, sensitivity analysis can be performed in conjunction with statistical methods to discover parameters that have the greatest effect [8] and perhaps generalize model behaviors.

Francois and Lavergne [18] mention the deficiencies of the traditional trial-and-error and experienced-practitioner approaches to parameter tuning, further suggesting that seeking general rules for parameterization will lead to optimization algorithms that offer neither convergent or efficient behaviors. They offer a statistical model for evolutionary algorithms that describes a functional relationship between algorithm parameters and performance. Nannen and Eiben [29, 30] propose a statistical approach called REVAC (previously Calibration and Relevance Estimation) to estimating the relevance of parameters in a genetic algorithm. Coy, Golden et al. [12] use a statistical steepest decent method procedure for locating good parameters for metaheuristics on many different combinatorial problem instances.

Bartz-Beielstein [3] used a statistical experimental design methodology to investigate the parameterization of the Evolutionary Strategy (ES) algorithm. A sequential statistical methodology is proposed by Bartz-Beielstein, Parsopoulos et al. [4] for investigating the parameterization and comparisons between the Particle Swarm Optimization (PSO) algorithm, the Nelder-Mead Simplex Algorithm (direct search), and the Quasi-Newton algorithm (derivative-based). Finally, an approach that is popular within the metaheuristic and Ant Colony Optimization (ACO) community is to use automated Monte Carlo and statistical procedures for sampling discretized parameter space of algorithms on benchmark problem instances [6]. Similar racing procedures have also been applied to evolutionary algorithms [41].

9.6.3   Problem Instances

This section focuses on issues related to the selection of function optimization test instances, but the general theme of cautiously selecting problem instances is generally applicable.

Common lists of test instances include; De Jong [25], Fogel [17], and Schwefel [38]. Yao, Lui et al. [40] list many canonical test instances as does Schaffer, Caruana et al. [37]. Gallagher and Yuan [19] review test function generators and propose a tunable mixture of Gaussians test problem generators. Finally, McNish [28] proposes using fractal-based test problem generators via a web interface.

The division of test problems into classes is another axiom of modern optimization algorithm research, although the issues with this methodology are the taxonomic criterion for problem classes and on the selection of problem instances for classes.

Eiben and Jelasity [14] strongly support the division of problem instances into categories and encourage the evaluation of optimization algorithms over a large number of test instances. They suggest classes could be natural (taken from the real world), or artificial (simplified or generated). In their paper on understanding the interactions of GA parameters, Deb and Agrawal [13] propose four structural properties of problems for testing genetic algorithms; multi-modality, deception, isolation, and collateral noise. Yao, Lui et al. [40] divide their large test dataset into the categories of unimodal, 'multimodal-many local optima', and 'multimodal-few local optima'. Whitley, Rana et al. [39] provide a detailed study on the problems of selecting test instances for genetic algorithms. They suggest that difficult problem instances should be non-linear, non-separable, and non-symmetric.

English [15] suggests that many functions in the field of EC are selected based on structures in the response surface (as demonstrated in the above examples), and that they inherently contain a strong Euclidean bias. The implication is that the algorithms already have some a priori knowledge about the domain built into them and that results are always reported on a restricted problem set. This is a reminder that instances are selected to demonstrate algorithmic behavior, rather than performance.

9.6.4   Measures and Statistical Methods

There are many ways to measure the performance of an optimization algorithm for a problem instance, although the most common involves a quality (efficacy) measure of solution(s) found (see the following for lists and discussion of common performance measures [1, 4, 5, 14, 23]). Most biologically inspired optimization algorithms have a stochastic element, typically in their starting position(s) and in the probabilistic decisions made during sampling of the domain. Thus, the performance measurements must be repeated a number of times to account for the stochastic variance, which could also be a measure of comparison between algorithms.

Irrespective of the measures used, sound statistical experimental design requires the specification of 1) a null hypothesis (no change), 2) alternative hypotheses (difference, directional difference), and 3) acceptance or rejection criteria for the hypothesis. The null hypothesis is commonly stated as the equality between two or more central tendencies (mean or medians) of a quality measure in a typical case of comparing stochastic-based optimization algorithms on a problem instance.

Peer, Engelbrech et al. [32] and Birattari and Dorigo [5] provide a basic introduction (suitable for an algorithm-practitioner) into the appropriateness of various statistical tests for algorithm comparisons. For a good introduction to statistics and data analysis see Peck et al. [31], for an introduction to non-parametric methods see Holander and Wolfe [21], and for a detailed presentation of parametric and nonparametric methods and their suitability of application see Sheskin [23]. For an excellent open source software package for performing statistical analysis on data see the R Project.[5]

To summarize, parametric statistical methods are used for interval and ratio data (like a real-valued performance measure), and nonparametric methods are used for ordinal, categorical and rank-based data. Interval data is typically converted to ordinal data when salient constraints of desired parametric tests (such as assumed normality of distribution) are broken such that the less powerful nonparametric tests can be used. The use of nonparametric statistical tests may be preferred as some authors [9, 32] claim the distribution of cost values are very asymmetric and/or not Gaussian. It is important to remember that most parametric tests degrade gracefully.

Chiarandini, Basso et al. [9] provide an excellent case study for using the permutation test (a nonparametric statistical method) to compare stochastic optimizers by running each algorithm once per problem instance, and multiple times per problem instance. While rigorous, their method appears quite complex and their results are difficult to interpret.

Barrett, Marathe et al. [2] provide a rigorous example of applying the parametric test Analysis of Variance (ANOVA) of three different heuristic methods on a small sample of scenarios. Reeves and Write [34, 35] also provide an example of using ANOVA in their investigation into epistasis on genetic algorithms. In their tutorial on the experimental investigation of heuristic methods, Rardin and Uzsoy [33] warn against the use of statistical methods, claiming their rigidity as a problem, and the importance of practical significance over that of statistical significance. They go on in the face of their own objections to provide an example of using ANOVA to analyze the results of an illustrative case study.

Finally, Peer, Engelbrech et al. [32] highlight a number of case study example papers that use statistical methods inappropriately. In their OptiBench system and method, algorithm results are standardized, ranked according to three criteria and compared using the Wilcoxon Rank-Sum test, a non-parametric alternative to the Student-T test that is commonly used.

9.6.5   Other

Another pervasive problem in the field of optimization is the reproducibility (implementation) of an algorithm. An excellent solution to this problem is making source code available by creating or collaborating with open-source software projects. This behavior may result in implementation standardization, a reduction in the duplication of effort for experimentation and repeatability, and perhaps more experimental accountability [14, 32].

---

[5]R Project is online at http://www.r-project.org

Peer, Engelbrech et al. [32] stress the need to compare to the state-of-the-art implementations rather than the historic canonical implementations to give a fair and meaningful evaluation of performance.

Another area that is often neglected is that of algorithm descriptions, particularly in regard to reproducibility. Pseudocode is often used, although (in most cases) in an inconsistent manner and almost always without reference to a recognized pseudocode standard or mathematical notation. Many examples are a mix of programming languages, English descriptions and mathematical notation, making them difficult to follow, and commonly impossible to implement in software due to incompleteness and ambiguity.

An excellent tool for comparing optimization algorithms in terms of their asymptotic behavior from the field of computation complexity is the Big-O notation [11]. In addition to clarifying aspects of the algorithm, it provides a problem independent way of characterizing an algorithms space and or time complexity.

9.6.6 Summary

It is clear that there is no silver bullet to experimental design for empirically evaluating and comparing optimization algorithms, although there are as many methods and options as there are publications on the topic. The field of stochastic optimization has not yet agreed upon general methods of application like the field of data mining (processes such as Knowledge Discovery in Databases (KDD) [16]). Although these processes are not experimental methods for comparing machine learning algorithms, they do provide a general model to encourage the practitioner to consider important issues before application of an approach.

Finally, it is worth pointing out a somewhat controversially titled paper by De Jong [26] that provides a reminder that although the genetic algorithm has been shown to solve function optimization, it is not innately a function optimizer, and function optimization is only a demonstration of this complex adaptive system's ability to learn. It is a reminder to be careful not to link an approach too tightly with a domain, particularly if the domain was chosen for demonstration purposes.

9.6.7 Bibliography

[1] R. Barr, B. Golden, J. Kelly, M. Rescende, and W. Stewart. Designing and reporting on computational experiments with heuristic methods. *Journal of Heuristics*, 1:9–32, 1995.

[2] C. L. Barrett, A. Marathe, M. V. Marathe, D. Cook, G. Hicks, V. Faber, A. Srinivasan, Y. J. Sussmann, and H. Thornquist. Statistical analysis of algorithms: A case study of market-clearing mechanisms in the power

industry. *Journal of Graph Algorithms and Applications*, 7(1):3–31, 2003.

[3] T. Bartz-Beielstein. Experimental analysis of evolution strategies – overview and comprehensive introduction. Technical report, Computational Intelligence, University of Dortmund, 2003.

[4] T. Bartz-Beielstein, K. E. Parsopoulos, and M. N. Vrahatis. Design and analysis of optimization algorithms using computational statistics. *Applied Numerical Analysis & Computational Mathematics*, 1(2):413–433, 2004.

[5] M. Birattari and M. Dorigo. How to assess and report the performance of a stochastic algorithm on a benchmark problem: Mean or best result on a number of runs? Technical report, IRIDIA, Universite Libre de Bruxelles, Brussels, Belgium, 2005.

[6] M. Birattari, T. Stützle, L. Paquete, and K. Varrentrapp. A racing algorithm for configuring metaheuristics. In *Proceedings of the Genetic and Evolutionary Computation Conference*, pages 11–18. Morgan Kaufmann Publishers Inc., San Francisco, CA, USA, 2002.

[7] F. Campolongo, A. Saltelli, and S. Tarantola. Sensitivity anaysis as an ingredient of modeling. *A Review Journal of The Institute of Mathematical Statistics.*, 15(4):377–395, 2000.

[8] K. Chan, A. Saltelli, and S. Tarantola. Sensitivity analysis of model output: variance-based methods make the difference. In *Proceedings of the 29th conference on Winter simulation (Winter Simulation Conference)*, pages 261–268. ACM Press, New York, NY, USA, 1997.

[9] M. Chiarandini, D. Basso, and T. Stützle. Statistical methods for the comparison of stochastic optimizers. In M. Gendreau, P. Greistorfer, W. J. Gutjahr, R. F. Hartl, and M. Reimann, editors, *MIC2005: Proceedings of the 6th Metaheuristics International Conference*, pages 189–196, 2005.

[10] P. R. Cohen. *Empirical Methods for Artificial Intelligence*. The MIT Press, Cambridge, Massachusetts, USA; London, England, 1995.

[11] T. H. Cormen, C. E. Leiserson, R. L. Rivest, and C. Stein. *Introduction to Algorithms*. MIT Press and McGraw-Hill, 2001.

[12] S. P. Coy, B. L. Golden, G. C. Runger, and E. A. Wasil. Using experimental design to find effective parameter settings for heuristics. *Journal of Heuristics*, 7(1):77–97, 2001.

[13] K. Deb and S. Agrawal. Understanding interactions among genetic algorithm parameters. In Colin R. Reeves, editor, *Proceedings of the Fifth Workshop on Foundations of Genetic Algorithms (FOGA)*, pages 265–286. Morgan Kaufmann, 1999.

[14] A. E. Eiben and M. Jelasity. A critical note on experimental research methodology in ec. In *Proceedings of the 2002 Congress on Evolutionary Computation (CEC '02)*, volume 1, pages 582–587. IEEE Press, USA, 2002.

[15] T. M. English. Evaluation of evolutionary and genetic optimizers: No free lunch. In *Evolutionary Programming V: Proceedings of the Fifth Annual Conference on Evolutionary Programming*, pages 163–169. MIT Press, USA, 1996.

[16] U. Fayyad, G. Piatetsky-Shapiro, and P. Smyth. The KDD process for extracting useful knowledge from volumes of data. *Communications of the ACM*, 39(11):27–34, 1996.

[17] D. B. Fogel. *Evolutionary computation: Toward a new philosophy of machine intelligence*. IEEE Press, 1995.

[18] O. François and C. Lavergne. Design of evolutionary algorithms – a statistical perspective. *IEEE Transactions on Evolutionary Computation*, 5(2):129–148, April 2001.

[19] M. Gallagher and B. Yuan. A general-purpose tunable landscape generator. *IEEE Transactions on Evolutionary Computation*, 10(5):590–603, October 2006.

[20] I. Gent and T. Walsh. How not to do it. In *Presented at the AAAI Workshop on Experimental Evaluation of Reasoning and Search Methods*. 1994.

[21] M. Hollander and D. A. Wolfe. *Nonparametric Statistical Methods*. John Wiley & Sons, Inc., Canada, 1999.

[22] J. N. Hooker. Testing heuristics: We have it all wrong. *Journal of Heuristics*, 1(1):33–42, September 1995.

[23] E. J. Hughes. Assessing robustness of optimisation performance for problems with expensive evaluation functions. In *IEEE Congress on Evolutionary Computation (CEC 2006)*, pages 2920–2927. IEEE Press, USA, 2006.

[24] D. S. Johnson. A theoreticians guide for experimental analysis of algorithms. In D. S. Johnson and C. C. McGeoch, editors, *Proceedings of the 5th and 6th DIMACS Implementation Challenges*, pages 215–250. American Mathematical Society, 2002.

[25] K. A. De Jong. *An analysis of the behavior of a class of genetic adaptive systems.* PhD thesis, University of Michigan Ann Arbor, MI, USA, 1975.

[26] K. A. De Jong. Genetic algorithms are NOT function optimizers. In *Proceedings of the Second Workshop on Foundations of Genetic Algorithms*, pages 5–17. Morgan Kaufmann, 1992.

[27] F. G. Lobo, C. F. Lima, and Z. Michalewicz. *Parameter Setting in Evolutionary Algorithms.* Springer, 2007.

[28] C. MacNish. Benchmarking evolutionary algorithms: The Huygens suite. In F. Rothlauf, editor, *Late breaking paper at Genetic and Evolutionary Computation Conference*, Washington, D.C., USA, 25-29 June 2005.

[29] V. Nannen and A. E. Eiben. A method for parameter calibration and relevance estimation in evolutionary algorithms. In *Proceedings of the 8th annual conference on Genetic and evolutionary computation*, pages 183–190. ACM Press, New York, NY, USA, 2006.

[30] V. Nannen and A. E. Eiben. Relevance estimation and value calibration of evolutionary algorithm parameters. In *Joint International Conference for Artificial Intelligence (IJCAI)*, pages 975–980. Morgan Kaufmann Publishers Inc., 2007.

[31] R. Peck, C. Olsen, and J. Devore. *Introduction to Statistics and Data Analysis.* Duxbury Publishing, USA, 2005.

[32] E. S. Peer, A. P. Engelbrecht, and F. van den Bergh. CIRGUP OptiBench: A statistically sound framework for benchmarking optimisation algorithms. In *The 2003 Congress on Evolutionary Computation*, volume 4, pages 2386–2392. IEEE Press, USA, 2003.

[33] R. L. Rardin and R. Uzsoy. Experimental evaluation of heuristic optimization algorithms: A tutorial. *Journal of Heuristics*, 7(3):261–304, May 2001.

[34] C. Reeves and C. Wright. An experimental design perspective on genetic algorithms. In M. D. Vose, editor, *Foundations of Genetic Algorithms 3*, pages 7–22. Morgan Kaufmann, San Francisco, CA, USA, 1995.

[35] C. R. Reeves and C. C. Wright. Epistasis in genetic algorithms: An experimental design perspective. In *Proceedings of the 6th International Conference on Genetic Algorithms*, pages 217–224. Morgan Kaufmann Publishers Inc., San Francisco, CA, USA, 1995.

[36] A. Saltelli. Making best use of model evaluations to compute sensitivity indices. *Computer Physics Communications*, 145(2):280–297, 2002.

[37] J. D. Schaffer, R. A. Caruana, L. J. Eshelman, and Rajarshi Das. A study of control parameters affecting online performance of genetic algorithms for function optimization. In *Proceedings of the third international conference on Genetic algorithms*, pages 51–60. Morgan Kaufmann Publishers Inc., San Francisco, CA, USA, 1989.

[38] H-P. Schwefel. *Evolution and optimum seeking*. Wiley, New York, USA, 1995.

[39] D. Whitley, S. Rana, J. Dzubera, and K E. Mathias. Evaluating evolutionary algorithms. *Artificial Intelligence - Special volume on empirical methods*, 85(1-2):245–276, 1996.

[40] X. Yao, Y. Liu, and G. Lin. Evolutionary programming made faster. *IEEE Transactions on Evolutionary Computation*, 3(2):82–102, 1999.

[41] B. Yuan and M. Gallagher. Statistical racing techniques for improved empirical evaluation of evolutionary algorithms. In *Problem Solving From Nature*, volume 3242, pages 171–181. Springer, 2004.

Part IV

Appendix

Appendix A

Ruby: Quick-Start Guide

A.1 Overview

All code examples in this book are provided in the Ruby programming language. This appendix provides a high-level introduction to the Ruby programming language. This guide is intended for programmers of an existing imperative or programming language (such as Python, Java, C, C++, C#) to learn enough Ruby to be able to interpret and modify the code examples provided in the Clever Algorithms project.

A.2 Language Basics

This section summarizes the basics of the language, including variables, flow control, data structures, and functions.

A.2.1 Ruby Files

Ruby is an interpreted language, meaning that programs are typed as text into a .rb file which is parsed and executed at the time the script is run. For example, the following snippet shows how to invoke the Ruby interpreter on a script in the file genetic_algorithm.rb from the command line: `ruby genetic_algorithm.rb`

Ruby scripts are written in ASCII text and are parsed and executed in a linear manner (top to bottom). A script can define functionality (as modules, functions, and classes) and invoke functionality (such as calling a function).

Comments in Ruby are defined by a # character, after which the remainder of the line is ignored. The only exception is in strings, where the character can have a special meaning.

413

The ruby interpreter can be used in an interactive manner by typing out a ruby script directly. This can be useful for testing specific behavior. For example, it is encouraged that you open the ruby interpreter and follow along this guide by typing out the examples. The ruby interpreter can be opened from the command line by typing `irb` and exited again by typing `exit` from within the interpreter.

A.2.2 Variables

A variable holds a piece of information such as an integer, a scalar, boolean or a string.

```ruby
a = 1 # a holds the integer value '1'
b = 2.2 # b holds the floating point value '2.2'
c = false # c holds the boolean value false
d = "hello, world" # d holds the string value 'hello, world'
```

Ruby has a number of different data types (such as numbers and strings) although it does not enforce the type safety of variables. Instead it uses 'duck typing', where as long as the value of a variable responds appropriately to messages it receives, the interpreter is happy.

Strings can be constructed from static text as well as the values of variables. The following example defines a variable and then defines a string that contains the variable. The #{} is a special sequence that informs the interrupter to evaluate the contents of inside the brackets, in this case to evaluate the variable n, which happens to be assigned the value 55.

```ruby
n = 55 # an integer
s = "The number is: #{n}" # => The number is: 55
```

The values of variables can be compared using the $==$ for equality and $!=$ for inequality. The following provides an example of testing the equality of two variables and assigning the boolean (true or false) result to a third variable.

```ruby
a = 1
b = 2
c = (a == b) # false
```

Ruby supports the classical && and || for AND and or OR, but it also support the **and** and **or** keywords themselves.

```ruby
a = 1
b = 2
c = a==1 and b==2 # true
```

A.2.3 Flow Control

A script is a sequence of statements that invoke pre-defined functionality. There are structures for manipulating the flow of control within the script such as conditional statements and loops.

Conditional statements can take the traditional forms of `if` *condition then action*, with the standard variants of *if-then-else* and *if-then-elseif*. For example:

```
1   a == 1
2   b == 2
3   if(a == b)
4       a += 1 # equivalent to a = a + a
5   elsif a == 1 # brackets around conditions are optional
6       a = 1 # this line is executed
7   else
8       a = 0
9   end
```

Conditional statements can also be added to the end of statements. For example a variable can be assigned a value only if a condition holds, defined all on one line.

```
1   a = 2
2   b = 99 if a == 2 # b => 99
```

Loops allow a set of statements to be repeatedly executed `until` a condition is met or `while` a condition is not met

```
1   a = 0
2   while a < 10 # condition before the statements
3       puts a += 1
4   end
```

```
1   b = 10
2   begin
3       puts b -= 1
4   end until b==0 # condition after the statements
```

As with the if conditions, the loops can be added to the end of statements allowing a loop on a single line.

```
1   a = 0
2   puts a += 1 while a<10
```

A.2.4 Arrays and Hashs

An array is a linear collection of variables and can be defined by creating a new **Array** object.

```
1   a = [] # define a new array implicitly
2   a = Array.new # explicilty create a new array
3   a = Array.new(10) # create a new array with space for 10 items
```

The contents of an array can be accessed by the index of the element.

```
1  a = [1, 2, 3] # inline declaration and definition of an array
2  b = a[0] # first element, equivilient to a.first
```

Arrays are also not fixed sized and elements can be added and deleted dynamically.

```
1  a = [1, 2, 3] # inline declaration and definition of an array
2  a << 4 # => [1, 2, 3, 4]
3  a.delete_at(0) # => returns 1, a is now [2, 3, 4]
```

A hash is an associative array, where values can be stored and accessed using a key. A key can be an object (such as a string) or a symbol.

```
1  h = {} # empty hash
2  h = Hash.new
3
4  h = {"A"=>1, "B"=>2} # string keys
5  a = h["A"] # => 1
```

```
1  h = {:a=>1, :b=>2} # label keys
2  a = h[:a] # => 1
3  h[:c] = 3 # add new key-value combination
4  h[:d] # => nil as there is no value
```

A.2.5   Functions and Blocks

The puts function can be used to write a line to the console.

```
1  puts("Testing 1, 2, 3") # => Testing 1, 2, 3
2  puts "Testing 4, 5, 6" # note brackets are not required for the function call
```

Functions allow a program to be partitioned into discrete actions and pre-defined and reusable. The following is an example of a simple function.

```
1  def test_function()
2    puts "Test!"
3  end
4
5  puts test_function # => Test!
```

A function can take a list of variables called function arguments.

```
1  def test_function(a)
2    puts "Test: #{a}"
3  end
4
5  puts test_function("me") # => Test: me
```

Function arguments can have default values, meaning that if the argument is not provided in a call to the function, that the default is used.

```
1  def test_function(a="me")
2    puts "Test: #{a}"
3  end
4
5  puts test_function() # => Test: me
6  puts test_function("you") # => Test: you
```

A function can return a variable, called a return value.

```
1  def square(x)
2    return x**2 # note the ** is a power-of operator in Ruby
3  end
4
5  puts square(3) # => 9
```

A block is a collection of statements that can be treated as a single unit. A block can be provided to a function and it can be provided with parameters. A block can be defined using curly brackets {} or the do and end keywords. Parameters to a block are signified by |var|.

The following examples shows an array with a block passed to the constructor of the Array object that accepts a parameter of the current array index being initialized and return's the value with which to initialize the array.

```
1  b = Array.new(10) {|i| i} # define a new array initialized 0..9
2
3  # do...end block
4  b = Array.new(10) do |i| # => [0, 1, 4, 9, 16, 25, 36, 49, 64, 81]
5    i * i
6  end
```

Everything is an object in ruby, even numbers, and as such everything has some behaviors defined. For example, an integer has a .times function that can be called that takes a block as a parameter, executing the block the integer number of times.

```
1  10.times {|i| puts i} # prints 0..9 each on a new line
```

A.3 Ruby Idioms

There are standard patterns for performing certain tasks in Ruby, such as assignment and enumerating. This section presents the common Ruby idioms used throughout the code examples in this book.

A.3.1 Assignment

Assignment is the definition of variables (setting a variable to a value). Ruby allows mass assignment, for example, multiple variables can be assigned to respective values on a single line.

```
1  a,b,c = 1,2,3
```

Ruby also has special support for arrays, where variables can be mass-assigned from the values in an array. This can be useful if a function returns an array of values which are mass assigned to a collection of variables.

```
1  a, b, c = [1, 2, 3]
2
3  def get_min_max(vector)
4    return [vector.min, vector.max]
5  end
6
7  v = [1,2,3,4,5]
8  min, max = get_min_max(v) # => 1, 5
```

A.3.2   Enumerating

Those collections that are enumerable, such as arrays, provide convenient functions for visiting each value in the collection. A very common idiom is the use of the .each and .each_with_index functions on a collection which accepts a block. These functions are typically used with an in-line block {} so that they fit onto one line.

```
1  [1,2,3,4,5].each {|v| puts v} # in-line block
2
3  # a do...end block
4  [1,2,3,4,5].each_with_index do |v,i|
5    puts "#{i} = #{v}"
6  end
```

The sort function is a very heavily used enumeration function. It returns a copy of the collection that is sorted.

```
1  a = [3, 2, 4, 1]
2  a = a.sort # => [1, 2, 3, 4]
```

There are a few versions of the sort function including a version that takes a block. This version of the sort function can be used to sort the variables in the collection using something other than the actual direct values in the array. This is heavily used in code examples to sort arrays of hash maps by a particular key-value pair. The <=> operator is used to compare two values together, returning a -1, 0, or 1 if the first value is smaller, the same, or larger than the second.

```
1  a = {:quality=>2, :quality=>3, :quality=>1}
2  a = a.sort {|x,y| x[:quality]<=>y[:quality] } # => ordered by quality
```

A.3.3 Function Names

Given that everything is an object, executing a function on a object (a behavior) can be thought of as sending a message to that object. For some messages sent to objects, there is a convention to adjust the function name accordingly. For example, functions that ask a question of an object (return a boolean) have a question mark (?) on the end of the function name. Those functions that change the internal state of an object (its data) have an exclamation mark on the end (!). When working with an imperative script (a script without objects) this convention applies to the data provided as function arguments.

```ruby
def is_rich?(amount)
  return amount >= 1000
end
puts is_rich?(99) # => false

def square_vector!(vector)
  vector.each_with_index {|v,i| vector[i] = v**2}
end
v = [2,2]
square_vector!(v)
puts v.inspect # => [4,4]
```

A.3.4 Conclusions

This quick-start guide has only scratched the surface of the Ruby Programming Language. Please refer to one of the referenced text books on the language for a more detailed introduction into this powerful and fun programming language [1, 2].

A.4 Bibliography

[1] D. Flanagan and Y. Matsumoto. *The Ruby Programming Language*. O'Reilly Media, 2008.

[2] D. Thomas, C. Fowler, and A. Hunt. *Programming Ruby: The Pragmatic Programmers' Guide*. Pragmatic Bookshelf, second edition, 2004.

.

Index

Breinigsville, PA USA
11 April 2011
259563BV00001BA/1/P